FOURTH EDITION

The Enjoyment of
MUSIC

ESSENTIAL LISTENING

FOURTH EDITION

The Enjoyment of
MUSIC

ESSENTIAL LISTENING

Kristine Forney

Professor of Music
California State University, Long Beach

Andrew Dell'Antonio

Distinguished Teaching Professor of Music
The University of Texas at Austin

W.W. NORTON & COMPANY
NEW YORK   LONDON

W. W. Norton & Company has been independent since its founding in 1923, when William Warder Norton and Mary D. Herter Norton first began publishing lectures delivered at the People's Institute, the adult education division of New York City's Cooper Union. The firm soon expanded its program beyond the Institute, publishing books by celebrated academics from America and abroad. By midcentury, the two major pillars of Norton's publishing program—trade books and college texts—were firmly established. In the 1950s, the Norton family transferred control of the company to its employees, and today—with a staff of five hundred and hundreds of trade, college, and professional titles published each year—W. W. Norton & Company stands as the largest and oldest publishing house owned wholly by its employees.

Editor: Chris Freitag
Developmental editor: Susan Gaustad
Media editor: Steve Hoge
Production manager: Elizabeth Marotta
Managing editor, college: Marian Johnson
Managing editor, college digital media: Kim Yi
Assistant editor, music: Julie Kocsis
Media assistant editor: Eleanor Shirocky
Media senior project editor: Meg Wilhoite
Marketing manager, music: Trevor Penland
Designer: Lissi Sigillo
Photo editors: Aga Millhouse, Mike Cullen, Travis Carr
Permissions manager: Bethany Salminen
Indexer: Marilyn Bliss
Composition: Six Red Marbles
Manufacturing: TC-Transcontinental Printing

The text of this book is composed in Dante with the display set in Gill Sans.

Library of Congress Cataloging-in-Publication Data
Names: Forney, Kristine, author. | Dell'Antonio, Andrew, author.
Title: The enjoyment of music / Kristine Forney, Andrew Dell'Antonio.
Description: Essential listening edition. | New York : W. W. Norton & Company, 2020. | Includes index.
Identifiers: LCCN 2019041397 | ISBN 9780393417272 (paperback) | ISBN 9780393421569 (epub)
Subjects: LCSH: Music appreciation.
Classification: LCC MT90 .M23 2020 | DDC 780—dc23 LC record available
    at https://lccn.loc.gov/2019041397

W. W. Norton & Company, Inc., 500 Fifth Avenue, New York, NY 10110
www.wwnorton.com

W. W. Norton & Company Ltd., 15 Carlisle Street, London W1D 3BS

2 3 4 5 6 7 8 9 0

ABOUT *THE ENJOYMENT OF MUSIC*

"BECAUSE OF YOU, MILLIONS OF AMERICAN STUDENTS HAVE COME TO UNDERSTAND AND LOVE THE GREAT LEGACY OF WESTERN CLASSICAL MUSIC." – Allen Lee Sessoms to Joseph Machlis on awarding him the honorary degree of Doctor of Humane Letters from Queens College

With the publication of the first edition of *The Enjoyment of Music* in 1955, Joseph Machlis essentially invented the modern music appreciation course. Previous books had set out to popularize or explain classical music for a general audience, but *The Enjoyment of Music* was the first to do so with the college classroom in mind. It was an immediate success, and over succeeding editions it has been transformed by a score of innovations, from the groundbreaking—and now ubiquitous—Listening Guides to the use of multimedia and technology for music teaching and learning. Those innovations have allowed the book to keep pace with broader changes in the course and the world.

The successful evolution of *The Enjoyment of Music* is a testament to the clarity of the original vision of Joseph Machlis, and to the talents and insights of subsequent authors. Kristine Forney teamed with Machlis for the Sixth and Seventh editions, starting in 1990, and became the sole author after his death in 1998. She broadened the repertory to include works by women, popular music, and music from outside the Western tradition. She was later joined by Andrew Dell'Antonio, whose pedagogical ideas informed the Second Essentials Edition of the text, published in 2013. Together, the authors have worked to keep this venerable franchise fresh and relevant for today's students and instructors. *The Enjoyment of Music* in its current versions is largely in their words and reflects their choices. But the spirit of Joseph Machlis, and his passion for bringing great music to new audiences, lives on in the work.

CONTENTS

PART 2

The Middle Ages and
Renaissance 60

PART 3

The Baroque Era 96

PART 4

Eighteenth-Century Classicism

PRELUDE 4 Music as Order and Logic

Classicism and Enlightenment Culture / Elements of Classical Style / The Patronage System

PART 5

The Nineteenth Century 186

PART 6

Twentieth-Century Modernism...... 258

PREFACE

The Enjoyment of Music is a classic—it's been around for more than half a century. Its contents and pedagogical mastery have been constantly updated to offer an exceptionally appealing repertory and the latest scholarship, integrated with unparalleled media resources every step of the way.

This fourth *Essential Listening* edition takes a listening-focused approach to learning about music in Western (and notably American) culture. Each part of the book begins with **Listening Objectives** for that part, along with a **First, listen . . .** prompt; in Parts 2–7, this feature gives you an opportunity to apply principles you learned in Part 1 ("Materials of Music") to a work from the era you will be studying. Each chapter also begins with **First, listen . . .**—here, you listen for a specific element in the musical work discussed in that chapter. As you progress through the book, knowledge of these elements will help you break down increasingly complex features of the music.

After you read the chapter and work through its **Listening Guide**, designed to solidify your understanding of key "What to Listen For" points, open-ended questions will help you **Reflect** on your personal reaction to the expressive qualities in the music. Finally, at the end of each part, you'll be given a **Listening Challenge**, where you'll listen to a "mystery selection" from that era and answer questions about its various elements. The accompanying brief summary of the era's style traits may help you, but by this point you'll likely feel confident in your responses. These features, described below along with others in the text and online, will greatly enhance your listening, help with study skills, and improve your performance in class.

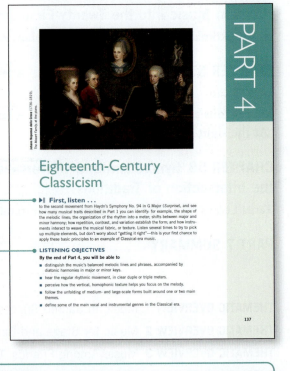

PART 4

Johann Nepomuk della Croce (1736–1819),
The Mozart Family at the piano.

Eighteenth-Century Classicism

▶❙ **First, listen . . .**
to the second movement from Haydn's Symphony No. 94 in G Major (*Surprise*), and see how many musical traits described in Part 1 you can identify: for example, the shape of the melodic lines; the organization of the rhythm into a meter; shifts between major and minor harmony; how repetition, contrast, and variation establish the form; and how instruments interact to weave the musical fabric, or texture. Listen several times to try to pick up multiple elements, but don't worry about "getting it right"—this is your first chance to apply these basic principles to an example of Classical-era music.

LISTENING OBJECTIVES
By the end of Part 4, you will be able to
- distinguish the music's balanced melodic lines and phrases, accompanied by diatonic harmonies in major or minor keys.
- hear the regular rhythmic movement, in clear duple or triple meters.
- perceive how the vertical, homophonic texture helps you focus on the melody.
- follow the unfolding of medium- and large-scale forms built around one or two main themes.
- define some of the main vocal and instrumental genres in the Classical era.

137

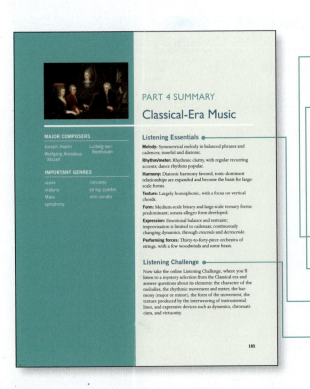

PART 4 SUMMARY
Classical-Era Music

MAJOR COMPOSERS
Joseph Haydn
Wolfgang Amadeus Mozart
Ludwig van Beethoven

IMPORTANT GENRES
opera
oratorio
Mass
symphony
concerto
string quartet
solo sonata

Listening Essentials
Melody: Symmetrical melody in balanced phrases and cadences; tuneful and diatonic.
Rhythm/meter: Rhythmic clarity, with regular recurring accents; dance rhythms popular.
Harmony: Diatonic harmony favored; tonic-dominant relationships are expanded and become the basis for large-scale forms.
Texture: Largely homophonic, with a focus on vertical chords.
Form: Medium-scale binary and large-scale ternary forms predominant; sonata-allegro form developed.
Expression: Emotional balance and restraint; improvisation is limited to cadenzas; continuously changing dynamics, through *crescendo* and *decrescendo*.
Performing forces: Thirty-to-forty-piece orchestra of strings, with a few woodwinds and some brass.

Listening Challenge
Now take the online Listening Challenge, where you'll listen to a mystery selection from the Classical era and answer questions about its elements: the character of the melodies, the rhythmic movement and meter, the harmony (major or minor), the form of the movement, the texture produced by the interweaving of instrumental lines, and expressive devices such as dynamics, chromaticism, and virtuosity.

185

- **First, listen . . .** at the beginning of each part introduces you to a piece of music from the upcoming era.
- **Listening Objectives** inform you of what you will learn in that part.
- **Listening Essentials** at the end of each part summarize that era's style traits.
- The online **Listening Challenge** poses questions about a mystery work for you to answer.

- A **varied repertory** broadly represents classical masters, including women composers and living composers, as well as jazz, musical theater, and film music.

- **First, listen . . .** , at the beginning of each chapter, asks you to listen for one particular element in the chapter's featured work.

- **Marginal sideheads** and **boldface type** identify key terms defined in the text and focus attention on important concepts.

- **Key Points** briefly summarize the terms and main ideas in that chapter.

CHAPTER

51

New Sound Palettes: A Mid-Twentieth-Century American Experimentalist

66 I thought I could never compose socially important music. Only if I could invent something new, then would I be useful to society."

—John Cage

▶❙❙ First, listen...

to the movement from Cage's *Sonatas and Interludes.* How might you describe the timbre of the piano? What do you notice is different from the works for solo piano we have studied so far?

Since the beginning of recorded history, musicians have been expanding their sound-production resources—by inventing new scales and harmonies, developing increasingly complex and versatile instruments, and training their bodies to sing and play in experimental ways. In order to do so, they have reached out to other cultures for inspiration, but also taken advantage of the inventiveness of their fellow musicians. The mid-twentieth century was an especially fertile time for musical expansion in North America, and we will consider one example by a composer who shaped such expansion: John Cage.

EARLY EXPERIMENTS

Henry Cowell

Tone clusters

Two earlier composers in particular helped shape Cage's pioneering genius. One, Henry Cowell (1897–1965), was drawn toward a variety of non-Western sources. His studies of the musics of Japan, India, and Iran led him to combine Asian instruments with traditional Western ensembles. Cowell also experimented with foreign scales, which he harmonized with Western chords. Several of his innovations involved the piano; these include **tone clusters** (groups of adjacent notes played with the fist, palm, or forearm) and the plucking of the piano strings directly with the fingers. This novel approach to the piano helped to inspire Cage's idea of the "prepared piano," which we will encounter below.

KEY POINTS

- Contemporary music often calls for innovative and highly virtuosic effects that challenge performers to new technical levels.

- Composer John Cage used a specially modified **"prepared" piano** to simulate the sound of the **Javanese gamelan,** an ensemble of metallic percussion instruments played in Indonesia (on the islands of Java and Bali, in particular).

302

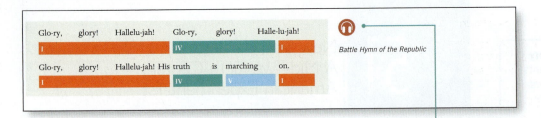

Glo-ry,	glory!	Hallelu-jah!	Glo-ry,	glory!	Halle-lu-jah!
I			IV		I

Glo-ry,	glory!	Hallelu-jah! His truth	is marching	on.
I		IV	V	I

Battle Hymn of the Republic

> ■ **Icons** direct you to the relevant online resources:
> **Listening Examples** (short clips from traditional, world, and classical selections) and recordings are represented by a headphone icon.
> **Videos** (operas and instrumental works streamed online) are designated by a video icon.

LISTENING GUIDE 1   🎧 ▶ 16:36

Britten: *The Young Person's Guide to the Orchestra* (*Variations and Fugue on a Theme of Purcell*)

DATE: 1946

BASIS: Dance from Purcell's incidental music to the play *Abdelazar* (*The Moor's Revenge*)

PERFORMED BY: English Chamber Orchestra; Steuart Bedford, conductor

> ■ **Composer biographies** are set off from the text's narrative for quick reference, along with a list of each composer's major works by genre.
> ■ **In His/Her Own Words** offer relevant quotes throughout from composers and important historical figures.

Antonín Dvořák (1841–1904)

Dvořák was born in Bohemia (now part of the Czech Republic). At sixteen, he moved to Prague, where he secured a position playing viola in the Czech National Theater under the baton of Bedřich Smetana, a notable Czech nationalist composer. In 1874, he resigned his orchestra post to devote himself to composing, in which he was much encouraged by Johannes Brahms. Later, he took up a position as professor of composition at the Conservatory of Prague, where he was able to exert an important influence on the musical life of his country.

In 1891, Jeannette Thurber, who ran the National Conservatory of Music in New York City, invited Dvořák to become its director. His stay in the United States was highly productive, resulting in, among other works, his *New World* Symphony (No. 9), which drew inspiration from African American spirituals. During his time in the United States, Dvořák challenged American composers to embrace "the beautiful and varied themes" that are "the folk songs of America." Several of his students did just so, including Harry T. Burleigh, who published a land-

mark collection of spirituals arranged as art music. After three years in New York, Dvořák returned to his beloved Bohemia and spent his remaining years in Prague. He died at sixty-three, revered throughout his native land as a national artist.

Dvořák's great gift for melody, love of native folk tunes, and solid craftsmanship enabled him to shape musical ideas into large forms notable for their clarity. His operas, many based on Czech themes, are the most strongly national of his country. His symphonies reflect a mastery of Classical procedures, and the Cello Concerto is a crowning achievement in that instrument's repertory.

MAJOR WORKS: Orchestral music, including nine symphonies (No. 9, *From the New World*, 1893), symphonic poems, other symphonic works (*Slavonic Dances*, 1878/87) • Concertos, including one for cello • Vocal music, including 14 operas • Choral music (including a *Requiem*, 1890) • Chamber music (*American* String Quartet) • Songs • Keyboard music, including dances and character pieces.

In His Own Words

❝ Can you see the notes behave like waves? Up and down they go! Look, you can also see the mountains. You have to amuse yourself sometimes after being serious so long."

—Joseph Haydn

At the end of each chapter:

- **Reflect** prompts allow you to focus on your personal responses to the music you've just heard.
- **Your Turn to Explore** boxes offer suggestions for independent investigation of the issues raised in the chapter, whether within or beyond the confines of the course.

▶|◀ **Reflect**

How does the change in instrumentation for the two themes affect you as a listener? Do the separate instrumentations continue throughout the movement? What happens at the end? What do you think Berlioz is trying to convey through the contrasts in theme and timbre?

YOUR TURN TO EXPLORE

What excerpts from your favorite music might you use to tell a story about yourself and your emotional life? List the songs or pieces. How might you want to modify the music (its tempo, instrumentation, texture, etc.) to convey your emotions more precisely? How would you try to make sure a listener would understand your story accurately?

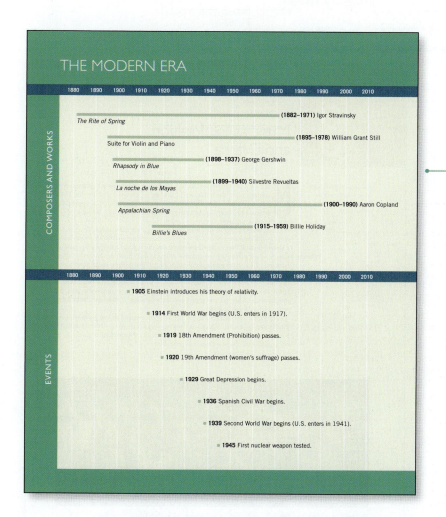

- **Timelines,** placed at the beginning of each part, provide a chronological orientation for composers as well as world events and important historical figures.

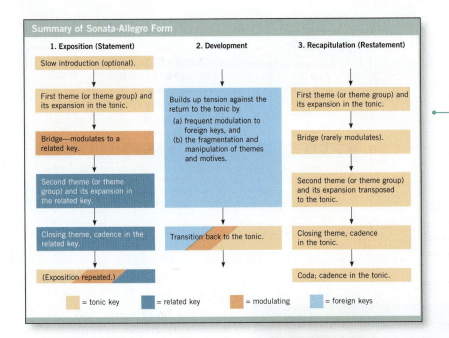

Summary of Sonata-Allegro Form

1. Exposition (Statement)	2. Development	3. Recapitulation (Restatement)
Slow introduction (optional).		
First theme (or theme group) and its expansion in the tonic.	Builds up tension against the return to the tonic by (a) frequent modulation to foreign keys, and (b) the fragmentation and manipulation of themes and motives.	First theme (or theme group) and its expansion in the tonic.
Bridge—modulates to a related key.		Bridge (rarely modulates).
Second theme (or theme group) and its expansion in the related key.		Second theme (or theme group) and its expansion transposed to the tonic.
Closing theme, cadence in the related key.	Transition back to the tonic.	Closing theme, cadence in the tonic.
(Exposition repeated.)		Coda; cadence in the tonic.

= tonic key   = related key   = modulating   = foreign keys

■ Colorful **charts** visually reinforce concepts presented in the text.

■ Comprehensive **Preludes** in each part introduce historical eras in their cultural context—through political events as well as literary, artistic, and technological trends—and provide a window onto musicians' social and economic circumstances.

PRELUDE

3

Music as Exploration and Drama

> 66 These harmonic notes are the language of the soul and the instruments of the heart."
>
> —Barbara Strozzi (1619–1677)

Virtuosity

Music intensifies emotion. This may seem self-evident to us in the twenty-first century, but it was in the period that we are about to explore—the 1600s and early 1700s—that Europeans set out to develop musical approaches designed to "ramp up" various emotional states and help listeners experience their diversity more deeply.

Composers and performers became increasingly interested in how music could enhance the expression of words—most prominently through the development of a kind of musical theater called opera, but also through the training of specialized singers whose **virtuosity** (remarkable technical skill) made the amateur singing tradition of the Renaissance seem outdated and bland. Even more novel was a significant focus on the expressive power of musical instruments—not only in conjunction with voices, but on their own. While purely instrumental music existed before the 1600s, in the Baroque era it became much more prominent with the development of several new genres and the refinement of instrumental building and performance techniques.

During the early part of this period, musicians seemed almost giddy with the possibilities for intense expression, creating works that appear designed to swing between musical extremes. As time passed, such experimentation gave way to more predictable musical forms and procedures.

The Flemish painter **Peter Paul Rubens** (1577–1640) instills his paintings with high energy and drama. His voluptuous nudes, as in *Diana and Her Nymphs*, established the seventeenth-century ideal of feminine beauty.

98

66 I have always believed that opera is a planet where the muses work together, join hands and celebrate all the arts."

—Franco Zeffirelli
(1923–2019)

Like his royal father, King Louis XIV of France (r. 1643–1715) loved to dance in the court ballet. He's shown here in one of his first roles, as "the Sun," at age fourteen.

Music has been integrated into multimedia productions—involving speech, staging, and other visual or choreographed effects—since the earliest documented history of the West. The theatrical traditions of ancient Greece incorporated musical instruments, and actors intoned their lines in a style that was somewhere between speech and song. Dramatized scenes from biblical scripture were featured in Christian celebrations in the Middle Ages, building on the tradition of collective sung prayer.

As European traditions of stage performance developed in the Middle Ages and Renaissance, music often punctuated the action, as part of the plot (for example, a lover's serenade) or as sonic interludes between scenes. The plays of renowned authors such as Shakespeare are peppered with musical references, and there's evidence that characters would break into song in the

TO-5

■ **Thematic Overviews** give a historical survey of each theme in the alternate contents. However you use this book, chronologically or thematically, these Overviews provide a fresh way of looking at the book's repertory and make essential connections between the works discussed.

Appendixes:

■ **Musical Notation** (Appendix I) gives explanations of musical symbols used for pitch and rhythm to help you understand musical examples.

■ **Glossary** (Appendix II) offers concise definitions of all musical terms covered in the book.

■ **Maps** located throughout the book reinforce the location and names of composers associated with major musical centers. A **world map** is found at the back of the book, with detail on Europe, the United States, and Canada.

About the Listening Guides

Listening is at the heart of *The Enjoyment of Music*, and the **Listening Guides** (LGs) are the book's essential feature; follow along with them as you listen to the recordings. These guides will enhance your knowledge and appreciation of each piece.

1. The composer's name, title of work, duration, date, genre, and featured performers appear at the top of each guide.

2. The "What to Listen For" box focuses your listening by drawing your attention to selected musical elements.

3. The body of the guide includes timed moment-by-moment descriptions that lead you through the selection. Texts and translations (if necessary) are given for all vocal works.

4. Short examples of the important musical theme(s) are sometimes provided as visual cues.

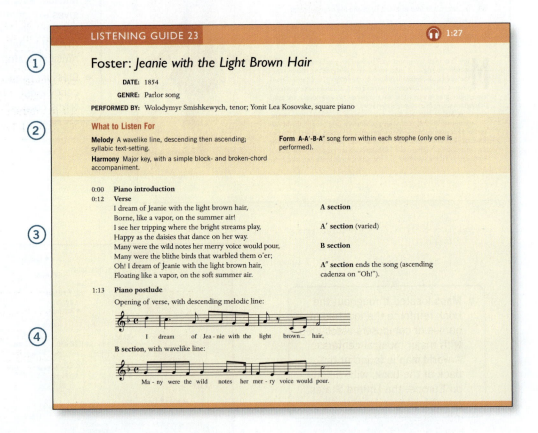

Online listening tools take advantage of the power of technology to blend word and sound together in a rich listening experience. For example:

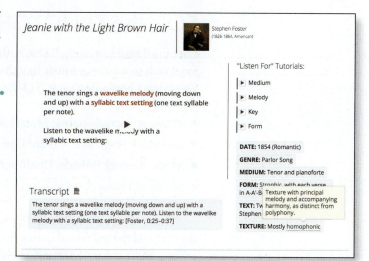

■ The "What to Listen For" section becomes a "Listen For" tutorial that provides a video walk-through, highlighting the use of musical materials in the selection.

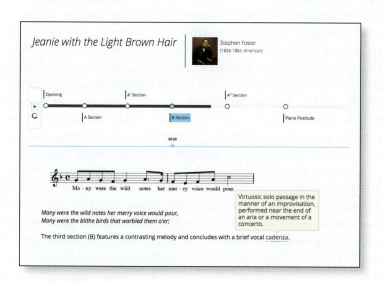

■ The Interactive Listening Guide (iLG) combines an easy-to-navigate diagram of the form with descriptions and examples that appear in real time as the music plays. The design allows you to interact with the music on computer, phone, or tablet.

■ Listening activities powered by Norton's adaptive InQuizitive engine develop listening skills with proven results. Each activity begins with a few simple questions that introduce musical concepts. Feedback often includes audio examples that help you improve your listening acuity and comprehension.

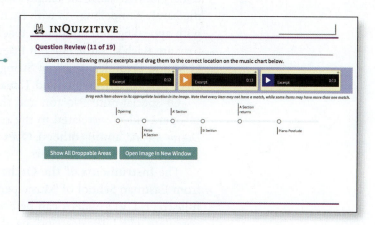

FOR INSTRUCTORS: WHAT'S NEW

Like the Third Listening Edition, this edition makes possible an alternate thematic approach to teaching music in culture, as well as the chronological. The Thematic Overviews beginning on p. TO-1 organize the chapters into four groups:

- Music in Sacred Spaces: Mass, motet, cantata, and oratorio
- Music for Stage and Screen: Opera, ballet, film
- Music Among Friends: Chamber music and small-scale works
- Music in Public Spaces: Works for the orchestra and concert hall

These Overviews sum up the history of the genres associated with each theme, and the ever-vital issues they raise. As the Preludes introduce each historical era, the Thematic Overviews introduce each topic.

New to this edition is an expansion of the previous edition's groundbreaking pedagogical structure, designed to foster "essential listening" strategies. At the beginning of each historical part (Parts 2–7), students **First, listen . . .** to a work from that particular era and try to describe as many elements discussed in Part 1 ("Materials of Music") as they can. Then each chapter opens with an instruction to **First, listen . . .** to part of the musical work featured in that chapter, focusing on a specific element (melody, rhythm, texture, word-painting, and so on). We have planned the sequence of these elements to point the student toward increasingly complex aspects of a work; the prompts are designed to build discrete listening and ear-training skills, which can be reliably tested through our robust online materials.

Further, each Listening Guide is followed by a set of questions that encourage students to **Reflect** on their less quantifiable but equally crucial emotional and aesthetic responses to the piece they have heard. These could be tied to class discussion, writing exercises, or any other formal or informal assignment you choose. **Your Turn to Explore** boxes invite students to investigate similar genres in twenty-first-century music, observe performance behaviors across all styles, discover connections with music they listen to every day, and much more.

More than ever, the clear writing in this edition engages directly with today's undergraduates, and the chapter structure aims to provide arguments that are immediately compelling. As with each new edition, the repertory has been refreshed with appealing and eminently teachable new works. Notable among new repertory are Bach's "Little" Organ Fugue in G Minor, Mozart's Symphony No. 40 in G Minor, Dvořák's *American* String Quartet, Gershwin's *Rhapsody in Blue,* Philip Glass's *Heroes* Symphony, and Tania León's *Inura.*

Of special note: Norton and the **Metropolitan Opera** have released a DVD of opera video correlated to the repertory in this edition (*Rigoletto, Die Walküre, Doctor Atomic,* among others). Over two hours of top-quality live performances are available to all *Enjoyment* users.

The **Instruments of the Orchestra DVD** combines all the instrument videos from Eastman School of Music performers into an easily navigable, high-quality, full-screen DVD. Videos can be accessed alphabetically or by instrument family, complete with basic descriptions of each one. They are also available online.

MEDIA RESOURCES: TOTAL ACCESS

Thanks to **Total Access**, students and teachers can take full advantage of all the book's superb online offerings—audio, video, and assessment content—in a flexible format that's easily integrated with campus learning systems. Look for the unique registration code printed on a card in the book, and register at digital.wwnorton.com/enjmusic4ess.

- Adaptive **listening** and **chapter review activities**, powered by **InQuizitive**, offer students a popular and proven approach to learning the music and its history with game-like questions and helpful feedback.
- **Listening Challenges** expand the coverage of musical concepts and styles in a capstone activity for six of the book's seven parts. Students encounter an unfamiliar musical selection and work through a set of puzzles to hone their understanding of musical traits related to the specific era.
- Assignments are easy to set up, and reporting to the campus LMS is easily enabled.
- Other digital resources include **streaming audio**; **interactive Listening Guides**; **"Materials of Music"** and **"What to Listen For"** tutorials; Metropolitan Opera and instrument videos; and
- a media-integrated **ebook**.

INSTRUCTOR RESOURCES

See the Instructor Resources tile from digital.wwnorton.com/enjmusic4ess to access the following.

Coursepacks

High-quality digital media is available for your online, hybrid, or lecture course at no cost. Norton Coursepacks work within your existing learning-management system; there's no new system to learn, and access is free and easy. The customizable content includes

- chapter quizzes (multiple-choice and true/false questions);
- listening quizzes for each featured work;
- quiz results reported to your LMS via LTI integration;
- chapter outlines;
- flash cards of major terms, arranged by chapter.

Interactive Instructor's Guide (IIG)

The IIG is an easy-to-use, searchable resource for instructors to prepare course materials. In addition to chapter outlines and suggested lecture and discussion topics, the IIG includes

- graphic content (art, images, charts) from the text;
- model responses to the "Your Turn to Explore" research prompts at the end of each chapter.

Test Bank

The Test Bank includes over 2,000 multiple-choice, true/false, and essay questions written in accordance with the Norton Assessment Guidelines. Each question is identified with a topic, question type, and difficulty level, enabling instructors to customize exams for their students.

ACKNOWLEDGMENTS

Any project of this size is dependent on the expertise and assistance of many individuals to make it a success. First, we wish to acknowledge the many loyal users of *The Enjoyment of Music* who have taken the time to comment on the text and ancillary package. As always, their suggestions help us shape each new edition. We also wish to thank those instructors who reviewed the text or media for this edition and provided invaluable feedback: Erin Brooks (University of Wisconsin, Madison), Debra Brown (Johnson Country Community College), Kevin R. Burke (Franklin College), Ellen J. Burns (University of Albany), Lisa Butts (San Joaquin Delta College), Carey Campbell (Weber State University), Richard C. Cole (Virginia Tech), Edward Eanes (Kennesaw State University), Donald Foster (Moreno Valley College), Kurt Fowler (Indiana State University), Richard Freedman (Haverford College), Russell Gartner (Rowan College), Robin Gehl (Concordia University), Judith Hand (McNeese State University), J. T. Harrell (Gadsden State Community College), Keith Heamsberger (Arkansas Northeastern College), Julie Hubbert (University of South Carolina), William J. Ikner (Auburn University), Miles M. Ishigaki (California State University, Fresno), Ellie Jenkins (Dalton State College), Heather Killmeyer (East Tennessee State University), Jonathan Kulp (University of Louisiana, Lafayette), Melissa Lesbines (Appalachian State University), David Lopez (Cerritos College), Natalie Mann (Moreno Valley College), Andrew Maz (Cerritos College), Barry McVinney (Pulaski Technical College), Nancy Newman (State University of New York, Albany), Carolyn L. Quin (Moreno Valley College), Gerald Ringe (Tarrant County College), Donald C. Sanders (Samford University), Andrew Santander (University of North Georgia), Sarah Satterfield (College of Central Florida), Peter Schimpf (Metropolitan State University of Denver), Brian Short (Madison Area Technical College), Joanna Smolko (Athens Technical

College), Randall Sorensen (Louisiana Tech University), Nancy Stewart (Greenville Technical College), Michael Sundblad (Thomas Nelson Community College), Jonas Thoms (Wright State University), Matthew Tresler (Irvine Valley College), I-Ching Tsai (Riverside City College), James White (Penn State, Altoona), Mary Wolinski (Western Kentucky University), Tom Zlabinger (York College / CUNY), and Inaki Zubizarreta (Norco College).

The Fourth Edition's team of media authors is unparalleled. Many thanks to Sherri Bishop (Indiana University), Joshua Kalin Busman (University of North Carolina, Pembroke), Alicia Doyle (California State University, Long Beach), Elizabeth Hoover (Miami University of Ohio), Melissa Lesbines (Appalachian State University), and Alisha Nypaver (Temple University). Nick D'Angiolillo of the Concord Music Group assembled, licensed, and mastered the recording package. And our spouses, William Prizer (professor emeritus, University of California, Santa Barbara) and Felicia Miyakawa, assisted in more ways than can possibly be named.

This Fourth Edition could not have been realized without the very capable assistance of the exceptional Norton team. We owe profound thanks to Chris Freitag, for his invaluable advice and guidance throughout the project; to Susan Gaustad, for her outstanding editing of the book and overseeing of all aspects of its production; to Steve Hoge, for creating and coordinating our stellar media package; to Lissi Sigillo, for her stunning design; to Elizabeth Marotta, for superbly managing the complex production process of the entire *Enjoyment of Music* package; to Julie Kocsis, for her capable editorial assistance; to Aga Millhouse, Mike Cullen, and Travis Carr for their invaluable help with selecting and licensing the illustrations; to Eleanor Shirocky, for handling numerous details of the media package; to Marilyn Bliss, for her meticulous index; to Bethany Salminen, for clearing permissions.

We finally wish to express our deep appreciation to four former music editors at Norton—Maribeth Payne, Michael Ochs, Claire Brook, and David Hamilton—who over the years have guided and inspired *The Enjoyment of Music* to its continued success.

Kristine Forney
Andrew Dell'Antonio

FOURTH EDITION

The Enjoyment of
MUSIC

ESSENTIAL LISTENING

OVERVIEW

MATERIALS OF MUSIC

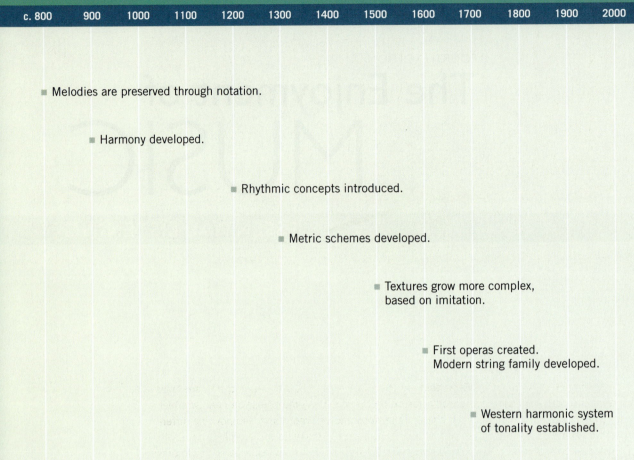

■ Melodies are preserved through notation.

■ Harmony developed.

■ Rhythmic concepts introduced.

■ Metric schemes developed.

■ Textures grow more complex,
based on imitation.

■ First operas created.
Modern string family developed.

■ Western harmonic system
of tonality established.

Symphony orchestra flourishes. ■
Large-scale compositions written for orchestra and small ensemble.

Revolutionary concepts in harmony and rhythm introduced. ■

Electronic and computer music flourish. ■
Global music concepts explored.

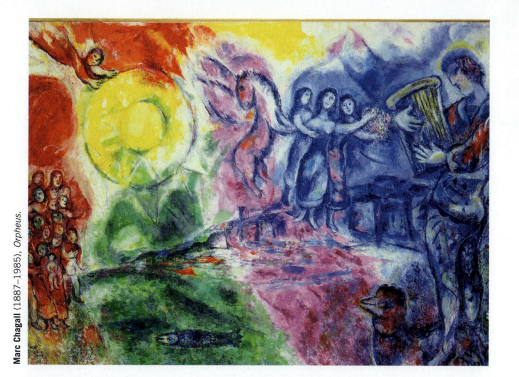

PART I

Materials of Music

▶‖ **First, listen . . .**

to an orchestral work titled *Farandole,* by French composer Georges Bizet, and see how many musical traits you can identify (for example, how many melodies you hear, whether any are repeated, what effect the changing tempos and volumes have, and how the different instruments interact with each other). Listen several times to try to pick up multiple features. But don't worry about "getting it right"— in this part, you will learn how to distinguish and describe the basic elements that make up musical works.

LISTENING OBJECTIVES

By the end of Part 1, you will be able to

■ hear how melodies have varied shapes and how they move in time through rhythm and meter.

■ grasp some of the basic precepts of Western harmony and hear how harmony adds depth to the music.

■ perceive how different lines can interact to form varied musical textures.

■ recognize how simple shapes, or forms, in a piece are created through repetition and contrasting ideas.

■ appreciate how changing the tempo and the dynamics (loudness and softness) in music lends expression to a work.

■ distinguish the unique sound, or timbre, of each instrument or voice, and learn how voices and instruments are combined in various music ensembles.

■ understand how musicians combine the elements above in different ways to make one musical work sound different from another.

Listening to Music Today

As with any new endeavor, it takes practice to become an experienced listener. We often "listen" to music as a background to another activity—perhaps studying or just relaxing. In either case, we are probably not concentrating on the music. This type of "partial listening" is normal and appealing, but this book aims to develop listening skills that expand your musical memory.

You probably have favorite books, movies, or songs that you like to revisit again and again, and each time you may notice something new, or appreciate even more a moment you have grown to cherish. It's precisely through repeated encounters that we gain both familiarity with and understanding of the touchstones of our culture. And one of the wonders of the present-day world is that we have the opportunity to listen to recorded music almost any time we want. We encourage you to listen repeatedly to the examples this book provides: with this kind of repeated, attentive listening, you will gain skills you can then transfer to new repertories as well as to your favorite songs.

At the same time, while recordings facilitate repeated listening, it's important to hear music in performance, for nothing can equal the excitement of a live concert. The crowded hall, the visual and aural stimulation of a performance, and even the element of unpredictability—of what might happen on a particular night—all contribute to the unique communicative powers of people making music.

There are certain traditions surrounding concerts and concertgoing: these include the way performers dress, the appropriate moments to applaud, and even the choice of seats. These aspects of performance differ between art-music and popular-music concerts. Understanding the differing traditions, and knowing what to expect, will contribute to your enjoyment of the event.

Attending Concerts

Regardless of where you live, it's likely that you have a rich choice of musical events available. To explore concerts in your area, check with the Music Department for on-campus concerts, read local and college newspapers for a calendar of upcoming events, or consult websites for nearby concert venues and calendars.

Ticket prices vary, depending on the concert. For university events, tickets are usually reasonable (under $20). For a performance in a major concert hall, you will probably pay more, generally $35 to over $100, depending on the location of your seat. Today, most new concert halls are constructed so that virtually all the seats are satisfactory. For small chamber groups, try to get front orchestra seats, close to the performers. For large ensembles—orchestras and operas, or even popular concerts—the best places are probably near the middle of the hall or in the balcony, where you also have a good view. For some concerts, you may need to

No matter where or when it happens, all that live music requires is a performer—and perhaps an audience.

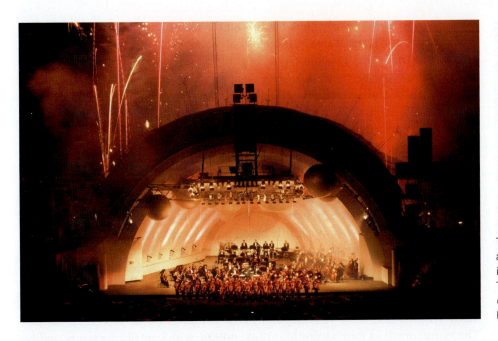

The audience delights in a fireworks display during a performance of Tchaikovsky's *1812 Overture* at the Hollywood Bowl, in Los Angeles.

purchase tickets in advance, either by phone or online, paying with a credit card. Be sure to ask for student discounts when appropriate.

Before you attend a concert, you may want to prepare by doing some reading. First, find out what works will be performed. Then check your textbook and its online materials as well as the Internet for information about the composers and works. It's especially important to read about an opera before the performance because it may be sung in the original language (e.g., Italian), though many venues provide supertitle translations.

What you choose to wear should depend on the degree of formality and the location of the event. Whatever the occasion, you should be neatly attired out of respect for the performers.

Plan to arrive at least twenty minutes before a concert starts, and even earlier if it is open seating or you must pick up your ticket at the box office. Be sure to

In His Own Words

❝ The life of the arts is close to the center of a nation's purpose, and is a test of the quality of a nation's civilization."

—John F. Kennedy (1917–1963)

Summary: Attending Concerts

- Consult websites, your local and college newspapers, the Music Department, and bulletin boards on campus to learn about upcoming concerts in your area.

- Determine if you must purchase your tickets in advance or at the door.

- Read about the works in advance in your textbook or on the Internet.

- Consider what to wear; your attire should suit the occasion.

- Arrive early to purchase or pick up your ticket and to get a good seat.

- Review the program before the concert starts to learn about the music.

- Be respectful to the performers and those sitting near you by not making noise.

- Follow the program carefully to know when to applaud.

- Be aware of and respectful of concert hall traditions.

- Above all, enjoy the event!

Wynton Marsalis (b. 1961), one of the most successful jazz and classical trumpet players today.

get a program from the usher and read about the music and the performers before the event begins. Translations into English of vocal texts are generally provided as well. If you arrive after the concert has begun, you will not be able to enter the hall until after the first piece is finished or an appropriate break in the music occurs. Be respectful of the performers and those around you by not talking and not leaving your seat except at intermission (the break that usually occurs about halfway through the performance).

The Concert Program

One key aspect of attending a concert is understanding the program. A sample program for a university orchestra concert appears below. The concert opens with an overture, with a familiar title based on Shakespeare's *A Midsummer Night's Dream*. We will see later that some works have a literary basis for the composer's ideas. Felix Mendelssohn's dates establish him as an early Romantic master.

The concert continues with a symphony by Wolfgang Amadeus Mozart, of whom you have undoubtedly heard. You can deduce by the title that Mozart wrote many symphonies; what you may not know is that this one (No. 41) is his last. The symphony is in four sections, or **movements**, with contrasting tempo indications for each movement, in Italian. (You can read more about the tempo terms in Chapter 7 and the forms of individual movements in Chapters 25–31.)

After the intermission, the second half is devoted to a single work: a piano concerto by the late nineteenth-century Russian composer Peter Ilyich Tchaikovsky. This concerto is in three movements, again a standard format (fast-slow-fast). The tempo markings are, however, much more descriptive than those for the Mozart

In Her Own Words

66 Applause is the fulfillment. . . . Once you get on the stage, everything is right. I feel the most beautiful, complete, fulfilled."

—Singer Leontyne Price (b. 1927)

Program

Overture to *A Midsummer Night's Dream*	Felix Mendelssohn (1809–1847)

Symphony No. 41 in C Major, K. 551 (*Jupiter*)
  I. Allegro vivace
  II. Andante cantabile
  III. Menuetto (Allegretto) & Trio
  IV. Finale: Molto allegro
	W. A. Mozart (1756–1791)

Intermission

Concerto No. 1 for Piano and Orchestra in B-flat Minor, Op. 23
  I. Allegro non troppo e molto maestoso;
     Allegro con spirito
  II. Andantino semplice; Prestissimo; Tempo I
  III. Allegro con fuoco
	P. I. Tchaikovsky (1840–1893)

Barbara Allen, piano

The University Symphony Orchestra
Eugene Castillo, conductor

symphony, using words like *maestoso* (majestic), *con spirito* (with spirit), and *con fuoco* (with fire). This is typical of the Romantic era, as is the work's expressive minor key. In the concerto, your interest will be drawn sometimes to the soloist, performing virtuoso passages, and at other times to the orchestra.

In addition to the works being performed, the program may include short notes about each composition and biographical sketches about the soloist and conductor.

During the Performance

At a typical concert, the house lights are usually dimmed just before it begins. Make sure your cell phone is turned off and that you don't make noise with candy wrappers or shuffling papers if you are taking notes. As you will see, it is customary to applaud at the entrance of performers, soloists, and conductors. In an orchestra concert, the **concertmaster** (the first-chair violinist) will make a separate entrance and then tune the orchestra by asking the oboe player to play a pitch, to which all the instruments tune in turn. When the orchestra falls silent, the conductor enters, and the performance begins.

Knowing when to applaud during a concert is part of the necessary etiquette. Generally, the audience claps after complete works such as a symphony, a concerto, a sonata, or a song cycle, rather than between movements or songs. Sometimes short works are grouped together on the program, suggesting that they are a set. In this case, applause is suitable at the close of the group. If you are unsure, follow the lead of others in the audience. At the opera, the conventions are a little different; the audience might interrupt with applause and "Bravo!" after a particularly fine delivery of an aria.

You might be surprised at the formality of the performers' dress. It is traditional for ensemble players to wear black—long dresses or black pants and tops for the women, tuxedos or tails for the men—to minimize visual distraction. Soloists, however, might dress more colorfully.

Pianist Beatrice Rana (b. 1993) performs with the Fort Worth Symphony, conducted by Leonard Slatkin, as part of the Van Cliburn Piano Competition.

The entire orchestra usually stands at the entrance of the conductor, and a small group, such as a string quartet, will bow to the audience in unison. The performers often do not speak to the audience until the close of the program—although this tradition is changing—and then only if an additional piece is demanded by extended applause. In this case, the **encore** (French for "again") is generally announced. Some musicians, like pianists, perform long, complex works from memory. To do so requires intense concentration and many arduous hours of study and practice.

You will undoubtedly sense an aura of suspense surrounding concerts. Try to take full advantage of the opportunities available—try something completely unfamiliar, perhaps an opera or a symphony, as you continue to enjoy performances of whatever music you already like.

Melody: Musical Line

We tend to characterize any musical sound as one that has a perceivable and measurable **pitch**, determined by its **frequency** (number of vibrations per second). This pitch depends on the length or size of a vibrating object. For example, a short string vibrates faster (has a higher frequency) than a long string (which has a lower frequency). This is why a violin sounds higher than a cello: its strings are shorter overall. When a musician places a finger on the string of a violin or cello, the vibrating length of the string is shortened, and the pitch/frequency changes accordingly.

In the Western tradition, we represent each pitch with a symbol called a **note**, which is placed on a **staff** (five parallel lines; see Appendix 1 for more on notation). This symbol designates the frequency and the **duration**, or length of time, of the pitch. A pitch also has a certain **volume** (loudness or softness) and a distinct quality known as **tone color**, or **timbre**; this last quality distinguishes voices from instruments, a trumpet from a clarinet.

A **melody** is a succession of single pitches that we hear as a recognizable whole. We relate to the pitches of a melody in the same way we hear the words of a sentence—not singly but as an entire cohesive thought. We know a good melody when we hear one, and we recognize its power to move us, as do most musical cultures of the world.

This modern apartment building in Vejle, Denmark, designed by **Hanning Larsen**—called The Wave—resembles the wave-like shape heard in many melodies.

Each melody goes up and down in its own distinct way, with one pitch being higher or lower than another; its **range** is the distance between the lowest and highest notes. This span can be very narrow, as in an easy children's song, or very wide, as in some melodies played on an instrument. Although this distance can be measured in the number of notes, we will describe range in approximate

KEY POINTS

- A **melody** is the tune in music.
- Each melody is unique in **contour** (how it moves up and down) and in **range**, or span of pitches.
- An **interval** is the distance between any two pitches. A melody that moves in small, connected intervals is **conjunct**, while one that moves by leaps is **disjunct**.

- The units that make up a melody are **phrases**; phrases end in resting places called **cadences**.
- A melody may be accompanied by a secondary melody, or a **countermelody**.

terms—narrow, medium, or wide. The **contour** of a melody is its overall shape as it turns upward or downward or remains static. You can visualize a melody as a line graph, resulting in an ascending or descending line, an arch, or a wave (see "Melodic Examples" below).

The distance between any two pitches is called an **interval**. Melodies that move principally by small intervals in a joined, connected manner (like *Joy to the World*) are called **conjunct**, while those that move in larger, disconnected intervals (like *The Star-Spangled Banner*) are described as **disjunct**. A tune's movement need not necessarily remain the same throughout: it may, for example, begin with a small range and conjunct motion and, as it develops, expand its range and become more disjunct.

Contour

Interval

THE STRUCTURE OF MELODY

The component units of a melody are like parts of a sentence. A **phrase** in music, as in language, is a unit of meaning within a larger structure. The phrase ends in a resting place, or **cadence**, which punctuates the music in the same way that a comma or period punctuates a sentence. The cadence may be inconclusive, leaving the impression that more is to come, or it may sound final, giving you the sense that the melody has reached the end. The cadence is where a singer or instrumentalist pauses to draw a breath.

Phrase

Cadence

If the melody has words, the text lines and the musical phrases will usually coincide. Consider the well-known hymn *Amazing Grace* (p. 10). Its four phrases, both the text and the music, are of equal length, and the **rhyme scheme** of the text

Rhyme scheme

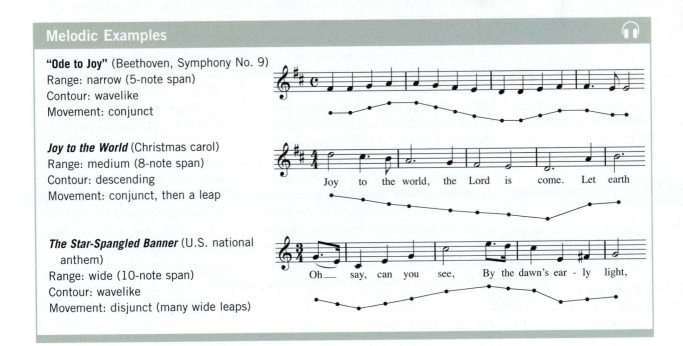

Melodic Examples

"Ode to Joy" (Beethoven, Symphony No. 9)
Range: narrow (5-note span)
Contour: wavelike
Movement: conjunct

Joy to the World (Christmas carol)
Range: medium (8-note span)
Contour: descending
Movement: conjunct, then a leap

Joy to the world, the Lord is come. Let earth

The Star-Spangled Banner (U.S. national anthem)
Range: wide (10-note span)
Contour: wavelike
Movement: disjunct (many wide leaps)

Oh— say, can you see, By the dawn's ear - ly light,

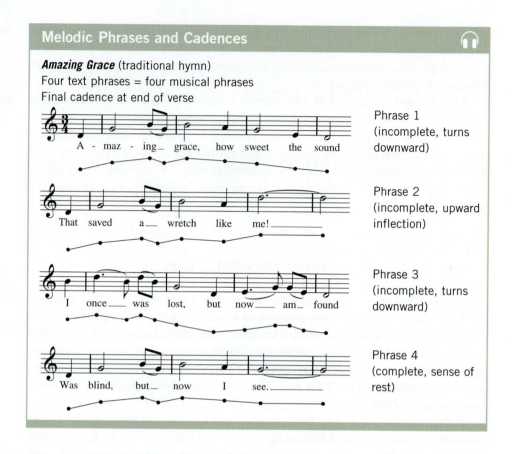

Melodic Phrases and Cadences

Amazing Grace (traditional hymn)
Four text phrases = four musical phrases
Final cadence at end of verse

A - maz - ing_ grace, how sweet the sound — **Phrase 1** (incomplete, turns downward)

That saved a_ wretch like me!_ — **Phrase 2** (incomplete, upward inflection)

I once_ was lost, but now_ am_ found — **Phrase 3** (incomplete, turns downward)

Was blind, but_ now I see._ — **Phrase 4** (complete, sense of rest)

(the way the last syllables in each line rhyme) is a-b-a-b. The first three cadences (at the end of each of the first three phrases) are inconclusive, or incomplete; notice the upward inflection like a question at the end of phrase 2. Phrase 4, with its final downward motion, provides the answer; it gives you a sense of closure.

In order to maintain the listener's interest, a melody must be shaped carefully, either by the composer or by the performer who invents it on the spot. What makes a striking effect is the **climax**, the high point in a melodic line, which usually represents a peak in intensity as well as in range. Sing through, or listen to, *The Star-Spangled Banner* and note its climax in the last stirring phrase, when the line rises to the words "O'er the land of the free."

The Star-Spangled Banner
The Stars and Stripes Forever

More complex music can feature several simultaneous melodies. Sometimes the relative importance of one over the other is clear, and the added tune is called a **countermelody** (literally, "against a melody"). You may have heard the high-range countermelody played by the piccolos in the famous *Stars and Stripes Forever* march by John Philip Sousa. In other styles, each melodic line is of seemingly equal importance. For much of the music we will study, melody is the most basic element of communication between the composer or performer and the listener. It's what we remember, what we whistle and hum.

Countermelody

Rhythm and Meter: Musical Time

Music is propelled forward by **rhythm**, the movement of music in time. Each individual note has a length, or duration—some long and some short. The basic unit of rhythm is the **beat**, a regular pulse that divides time into equal segments. Some beats are stronger than others; we perceive these as **accented** beats. In much of Western music, these strong beats occur at regular intervals—every other beat, every third beat, every fourth, and so on—and thus we hear groupings of two, three, or four. These organizing patterns are called **meters** and, in notation, are marked off in **measures** (or **bars**). Each measure contains a fixed number of beats, and the first beat in a measure usually receives the strongest accent. Measures are designated with **measure (bar) lines**, regular vertical lines through the staff (on which the music is notated; see Appendix I).

Meter and measure

Meter organizes the flow of rhythm in music. In Western music, its patterns are simple, paralleling the alternating accents heard in poetry. Consider, for example, this well-known stanza by the American poet Robert Frost. Its meter alternates a strong beat with a weak one (this is iambic meter, da DUM, da DUM, da DUM, da DUM). A metrical reading of the poem will bring out the regular pattern of accented (′) and unaccented (−) syllables:

The woods are love-ly, dark and deep,

But I have prom-is-es to keep,

And miles to go be-fore I sleep,

And miles to go be-fore I sleep.

METRICAL PATTERNS

You will hear the regularly recurring patterns of two, three, or four beats in much of the music we will study. As in poetry, these patterns, or meters, depend on regular accents. The first accented beat of each pattern is known as a **downbeat**,

KEY POINTS

- Rhythm is what moves music forward in time.
- **Meter,** marked off in **measures** (or **bars**), organizes the **beats** (the basic units) in music.
- Measures often begin with a strong **downbeat**.
- **Simple meters**—duple, triple, and quadruple—are the most common; each beat is divided into two.
- **Compound meters** divide each beat into three rather than two.
- Rhythmic complexities occur with **offbeats**, **syncopation**, and **polyrhythm**.
- Some music is **nonmetric**, without an identifiable meter or clear beat.

11

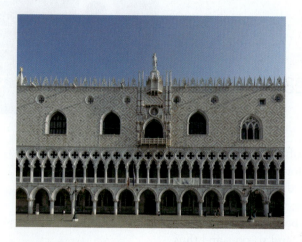

The Gothic arches of the Doge's Palace in Venice clearly show duple subdivisions, much like simple meters in music.

referring to the downward stroke of a conductor's hand (see conducting patterns, p. 51). The most basic pattern, known as **duple meter**, alternates a strong downbeat with a weak beat: ONE two, ONE two; or, if you marched it, LEFT right, LEFT right.

Triple meter, another basic pattern, has three beats to a measure—one strong beat and two weak ones (ONE two three). This meter is traditionally associated with dances such as the waltz and the minuet.

Quadruple meter contains four beats to the measure, with a primary accent on the first beat and a secondary accent on the third. Although it is sometimes difficult to distinguish duple and quadruple meter, quadruple meter usually has a broader feeling.

In **simple meters** (simple duple, simple triple, and simple quadruple), the beat is divided into two (ONE-and, two-and; or ONE-and, two-and, three-and). However, in some patterns, the beat is divided into three; these are known as **compound meters**. The most common compound meter is **sextuple meter** (compound duple), which has six beats to the measure, or two main beats that each divides into three (ONE-and-a, TWO-and-a). Marked by a gently flowing effect, this pattern is often found in lullabies and nursery rhymes:

Lit-tle Boy Blue, come blow your horn, the

sheep's in the mea-dow, the cow's in the corn.

The examples on page 13 illustrate the four basic patterns. Not all pieces begin on a downbeat (beat 1). For example, *Greensleeves,* in sextuple meter, begins with an **upbeat** (beat 6). (Notice that the Frost poem given earlier is in duple meter and begins with an upbeat on "the.")

RHYTHMIC COMPLEXITIES

Composers have devised a number of ways to keep the recurrent accent from becoming monotonous. The most common technique is **syncopation**, a deliberate upsetting of the normal pattern of accents. Instead of falling on the strong beat of the measure, the accent is shifted to a weak beat, or **offbeat** (in between the stronger beats). Syncopation is heard in many kinds of music, and is particularly characteristic of the African American dance rhythms out of which jazz developed. The example opposite illustrates the technique.

Like meter in music, basic repeated patterns can be found in nature, such as in this close-up of a spiral leaf pattern.

Polyrhythm

Syncopation is only one technique that throws off the regular patterns. A composition may change meters during its course; certain twentieth-century pieces shift meters nearly every measure. Another technique is the simultaneous use of rhythmic patterns that conflict with the underlying beat, such as "two against three" or "three against four"—in a piano piece, for example, the left hand might play two notes to a beat, while the right hand plays three notes to the same beat. This is called **polyrhythm** ("many rhythms") and characterizes some early twentieth-century compositions as well as the music of several world cultures.

Examples of Meters

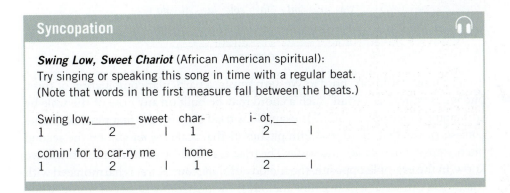

´ = primary accent   ˘ = secondary accent   ‾ = unaccented beat

Duple meter: *Ah, vous dirai-je Maman* (Mozart), same tune as *Twinkle, Twinkle, Little Star*

Accents: Twin- kle, twin- kle, lit- tle star
Meter: 1   2 | 1   2 | 1   2 | 1   2

Triple meter: *America* (patriotic song)

My coun- try 'tis   of thee,
1   2   3 | 1   2   3

Sweet land of li- - ber-ty.
1   2   3 | 1   2   3

Quadruple meter: *Battle Hymn of the Republic* (Civil War song)

Glo- ry, glo-ry hal-le-lu- - jah!   Glo-   ry, glo-ry hal-le-lu - jah!
1 2   3   4 | 1   2   3   4 | 1   2   3   4 | 1   2   3   4

Sextuple meter: *Greensleeves* (English folk song)

A- las   my love,   you do   me wrong,   to cast   me off   dis- cour- teous- ly,
6 | 1 2   3   4   5   6 | 1   2   3   4   5   6 | 1 2   3   4   5   6 | 1 2   3   4   5

Syncopation

Swing Low, Sweet Chariot (African American spiritual):
Try singing or speaking this song in time with a regular beat.
(Note that words in the first measure fall between the beats.)

Swing low,_____ sweet char-   i- ot,____
1   2 | 1   2 |

comin' for to car-ry me   home   _____
1   2 | 1   2 |

Some music moves without any strong sense of beat or meter. We might say that such a work is **nonmetric** (this is the case in the chants of the early Christian church): the pulse is veiled or weak, with the music moving in a floating rhythm that typifies certain non-Western styles.   **Nonmetric**

Time is a crucial dimension in music. This is the element that binds together the parts within the whole: the notes within the measure and the measure within the phrase. It is therefore the most fundamental element of music.

Harmony: Musical Depth

Chord

Scale
Octave

To the linear movement of the melody, harmony adds another dimension: depth. **Harmony** is the simultaneous combination of sounds. It can be compared to the concept of perspective in artworks (see p. 15). Not all musics of the world rely on harmony, but it is central to most Western styles.

Harmony determines the relationships of intervals and chords. Intervals, the distance between any two notes, can occur successively or simultaneously. When three or more notes are sounded together, a **chord** is produced. Harmony describes a piece's chords and the progression from one chord to the next. It is the progression of harmony in a musical work that creates a feeling of order and unity.

The intervals from which chords and melodies are built are chosen from a particular collection of pitches arranged in ascending or descending order known as a **scale**. To the notes of the scale we assign syllables, *do–re–mi–fa–sol–la–ti–do,* or numbers, 1–2–3–4–5–6–7–8. An interval spanning eight notes is called an **octave**.

do	*re*	*mi*	*fa*	*sol*	*la*	*ti*	*do*
1	2	3	4	5	6	7	8

octave

Triad

The most common chord in Western music, a particular combination of three pitches, is known as a **triad**. Such a chord may be built on any note of the scale by combining every other note. For example, a triad built on the first pitch of a scale consists of the first, third, and fifth pitches of that scale *(do-mi-sol);* on the second pitch, steps 2-4-6 *(re-fa-la)*; and so on. The triad is a basic formation in most music we know. In the example opposite, the melody of *Camptown Races* is harmonized with triads. You can see at a glance how melody is the horizontal aspect of music, while

KEY POINTS

- **Harmony** describes the vertical aspects of music: how notes (pitches) sound together.

- A **chord** is the simultaneous sounding of three or more pitches; chords are built from a particular **scale**, or sequence of pitches.

- The most common chord in Western music is a **triad**, three alternate pitches of a scale.

- Most Western music is based on **major** or **minor scales**, from which melody and harmony are derived.

- The **tonic** is the central pitch around which a melody and its harmonies are built; this principle of organization is called **tonality**.

- **Dissonance** is created by an unstable, or discordant, combination of pitches. **Consonance** occurs with a resolution of dissonance, producing a stable or restful sound.

harmony, comprising blocks of notes (the chords), constitutes the vertical. Melody and harmony do not function independently of one another. On the contrary, the melody suggests the harmony that goes with it, and each constantly influences the other.

THE ORGANIZATION OF HARMONY

In all music, regardless of the style, certain notes assume greater importance than others. In most Western music, the first note of the scale, *do*, is considered the **tonic** and serves as a home base around which the others revolve and to which they ultimately gravitate. We observed this principle at work earlier with *Amazing Grace* (p. 10): the tune does not reach a final cadence, or stopping point, on the tonic note until its last phrase. It is this sense of a home base that helps us recognize when a piece of music ends.

Harmony lends a sense of depth to music, as perspective does in this photograph, by **Fernand Ivaldi**, of a view down a tree-lined canal in France.

The principle of organization around a central note, the tonic, is called **tonality**. The scale chosen as the basis of a piece determines the identity of the tonic and the key of the piece. Two different types of scales predominate in Western music written between about 1650 and 1900: major and minor. Each scale has a distinct sound because of its unique combination of intervals, as we will see in Chapter 4.

CONSONANCE AND DISSONANCE

The movement of harmony toward resolution is the dynamic force in Western music. As music moves in time, we feel moments of tension and release. The tension results from **dissonance**, a combination of notes that sounds unstable, sometimes harsh, and in need of resolution. Dissonance introduces conflict into music in the same way that suspense creates tension in drama. Dissonance resolves in

Examples of Harmony

Camptown Races (Stephen Foster)

Just as dissonance provides tension in music, this image of global researchers sunbathing on the edge of a frozen fjord in the Arctic to emphasize the dramatic rate of global warming is discordant to the eye.

consonance, an agreeable-sounding combination of notes that provides a sense of relaxation and fulfillment. Each complements the other, and each is a necessary part of the artistic whole.

Harmony appeared much later historically (around 900) than melody, and its development took place largely in Western music. In many Asian cultures, harmony is relatively simple, consisting of a single sustained pitch, called a **drone**, against which melodic and rhythmic complexities unfold. This harmonic principle also occurs in some European folk music, where, for example, a bagpipe might play one or more accompanying drones to a lively dance tune.

Drone

Our system of harmony has advanced steadily over the past millennium, continually responding to new needs. Composers have tested the rules, changing our notion of what sounds consonant, as they have experimented with innovative sounds and procedures. Yet their goal remains the same: to impose order on sound, organizing the pitches so that we perceive a unified idea.

The Organization of Musical Sounds

Here we consider how melody and harmony, two of the essential building blocks of musical compositions, function together to construct a musical system, both in the West and elsewhere.

Pitches are named using the first seven letters of the alphabet (A through G), which just start over again when you reach an octave. As noted earlier, an octave is an interval spanning eight notes of the scale. When we hear any two notes an octave apart, we recognize that they sound "the same." (These two notes take the same pitch name: for example, a C and the C an octave higher.)

One important variable in the different languages of music around the world is the way the octave is divided. In Western music, it is divided into twelve equal semitones, or **half steps**; from these are built different kinds of scales, which have constituted the basis of this musical language for nearly four hundred years.

> 66 If only the world could feel the power of harmony."
>
> —W. A. Mozart

Octave

Half step

THE CHROMATIC SCALE

The twelve half steps that make up the octave constitute what is known as the **chromatic scale**. You can see these twelve half steps on the keyboard (p. 18), counting all the white and black keys from C to the C above it. Virtually all Western music, no matter how intricate, is made up of the same twelve pitches and their duplications in higher and lower octaves.

You will notice that the black keys on the piano are named in relation to their white-key neighbors. The black key between C and D can be called C-sharp (♯) or D-flat (♭), depending on the context of the music. This plan applies to all the black

KEY POINTS

- An **octave** is the interval spanning eight notes of the scale. In Western music, the octave is divided into twelve **half steps**, the smallest interval; two half steps make a **whole step**.

- The **chromatic scale** is made up of all twelve half steps, while a **diatonic scale** consists of seven whole and half steps whose patterns form **major** and **minor** scales.

- A **sharp** (♯) is a symbol that raises a pitch by a half step; a **flat** (♭) lowers a pitch by a half step.

- The **tonic chord**, built on the first scale note, is the home base to which **active chords** (**dominant** and **subdominant**) need to resolve.

- Composers can shift the pitch level (**key**) of an entire work (**transposition**), or change the key during a work (**modulation**).

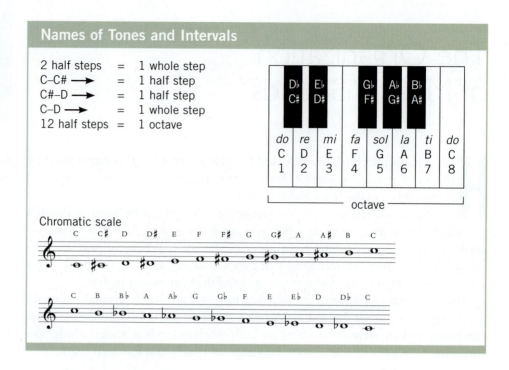

Names of Tones and Intervals

2 half steps	=	1 whole step
C–C# →	=	1 half step
C#–D →	=	1 half step
C–D →	=	1 whole step
12 half steps	=	1 octave

Chromatic scale

Sharp and flat   keys. Thus, a **sharp** raises a note by a half step, and a **flat** lowers a note a half step. The distance between C and D is two half steps, or one **whole step**.

THE MAJOR SCALE

Chapter 3 introduced the notion that certain notes in music assume greater importance than others; in Western music, the first pitch of the scale, the tonic, is the home base to which the music gravitates. Two main scale types—major and minor—function within this organizational system known as tonality. When you **Key** listen to a composition in the **key** of C major, you hear a piece built around the central tone C, using the harmonies formed from the C major scale. Tonality is the basic harmonic principle at work in most Western music written from around 1600 to 1900 and in most popular music still today.

The **major scale** is the most familiar sequence of pitches. You can produce a C major scale (*do–re–mi–fa–sol–la–ti–do*) by playing only the white keys on the piano from one C to the next C. Looking at the keyboard above, you will see that there is no black key between E and F (*mi–fa*) or between B and C (*ti–do*). These notes are a half step apart, while the other white keys are a whole step apart. Consequently, a major scale is created by a specific pattern of whole (W) and half (H) steps—(W–W–H–W–W–W–H)—and can be built with this pattern starting on any pitch, even a black key.

Within each major scale are certain relationships based on tension and resolution. One of the most important is the thrust of the seventh pitch to the eighth (*ti* resolving to *do*). Similarly, we feel resolution when *re* moves to *do*; *fa* gravitates

In His Own Words

❝ There are only twelve tones. You must treat them carefully."

—Paul Hindemith
(1895–1963)

to *mi;* and *la* descends to *sol.* You can hear some of these relationships at work in the beginning of the well-known carol *Joy to the World.* It starts on the tonic note (*do*) ("Joy"), then descends and pauses on the **dominant** note (*sol*) ("world"), after which it continues downward, feeling a strong pull to the final *do* (on "come"; see melody on p. 9 and chart below).

(see melody on p. 9 and chart below)

Dominant

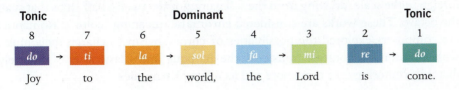

Tonic			Dominant				Tonic
8	7	6	5	4	3	2	1
do →	*ti*	*la* →	*sol*	*fa* →	*mi*	*re* →	*do*
Joy	to	the	world,	the	Lord	is	come.

Joy to the World

Most important of all, the major scale defines two poles of traditional harmony: the tonic, the point of ultimate rest; and the dominant, which represents the active harmony. Tonic going to dominant and returning to tonic is a basic progression of harmony in Western music. Songs and pieces in a major key, like this carol, generally sound cheerful or triumphant to our ears (more a cultural convention than an absolute trait).

THE MINOR SCALE

The **minor scale** sounds quite different from the major. One reason is that it has a lowered, or flatted, third note. Therefore, in the scale of C minor, there is an E-flat rather than the E-natural (white-key E) of the major scale; the interval C to E-flat is smaller than the interval C to E. Minor-key pieces sound sadder, darker than major-key. In the famous Bach theme to *The Art of Fugue,* you hear the smaller third interval right at the onset, as the melody outlines this interval (a minor third), then descends in a minor scale. The intervals of the minor scale (W–H–W–W–H–W–W) are shown in the table below.

The Art of Fugue

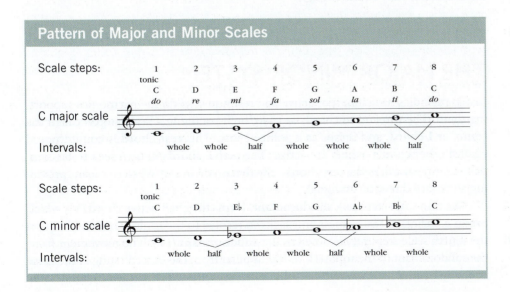

Pattern of Major and Minor Scales

Scale steps:	1 tonic	2	3	4	5	6	7	8
	C *do*	D *re*	E *mi*	F *fa*	G *sol*	A *la*	B *ti*	C *do*
C major scale								
Intervals:	whole	whole	half	whole	whole	whole	half	

Scale steps:	1 tonic	2	3	4	5	6	7	8
	C	D	E♭	F	G	A♭	B♭	C
C minor scale								
Intervals:	whole	half	whole	whole	half	whole	whole	

DIATONIC VS. CHROMATIC

Music in a major or minor key focuses on the seven notes of the respective scale and is considered **diatonic**. In diatonic music, both the melody and the harmony are firmly rooted in the key. But some compositions introduce other notes that are foreign to the scale, drawing from the full gamut of the twelve half steps that span the octave. These works are considered **chromatic** (meaning "color"). Romantic-era composers explored the possibilities of chromaticism to charge their music with emotion. In contrast, music of the Baroque and Classical eras is largely diatonic, centering on a tonic note and its related harmonies.

Other Scale Types

The Western musical system is only one way to structure music. The musical languages of other cultures often divide the octave differently, producing different scale patterns. Among the most common is the **pentatonic**, or five-note, scale, used in some African, Asian, and Native American musics. (*Amazing Grace*, on p. 10, is a pentatonic, folk-like melody.)

Some scales are not easily playable on Western instruments because they employ intervals smaller than the half step. Such intervals, known as **microtones**, may sound "off-key" to Western ears. One way of producing microtonal music is by an **inflection** of a pitch, making a brief microtonal dip or rise from the original pitch; this technique, similar to that of the "blue note" in jazz (see Chapter 46), makes possible a host of subtle pitch changes.

The musical system and the notes chosen in that system determine the sound and character of each work, whether classical, popular, or traditional. They are what make Western music sound familiar to us and why sometimes the music of other cultures may sound foreign.

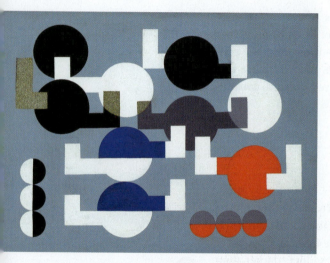

Sophie Taeuber-Arp (1889–1943), *Composition in Circles and Overlapping Angles* (1930). The overlapping and repeated shapes in this artwork can be compared, in music, to new pitch levels or to modulations to another key.

THE MAJOR-MINOR SYSTEM

Just as melodies have inherent active and rest notes, so do the harmonies supporting them. The three-note chord, or triad, built on the first scale step is called the **tonic**, or **I chord**, and serves as a point of rest. This **rest chord** is counterposed against other chords, which are active. The **active chords** in turn seek to be completed, or resolved, in the rest chord—the dynamic force in Western music, providing a forward direction and goal.

Tonic (rest) chord (I)

Dominant (active) chord (V)

Subdominant chord (IV)

The fifth scale step (*sol*), the **dominant**, forms the chief active chord (**V**), which brings a feeling of restlessness and seeks to resolve to the tonic. The triad built on the fourth scale step (*fa*) is known as the **subdominant** (**IV**). The movement from the subdominant to the tonic (IV to I) is familiar from the "Amen" sung at the close of many hymns.

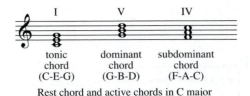

Rest chord and active chords in C major

These three basic triads are enough to harmonize many simple tunes. The Civil War song *Battle Hymn of the Republic* is a good example:

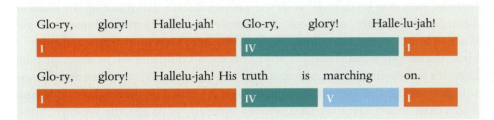

Battle Hymn of the Republic

The Key as a Form-Building Element

The three main chords of a musical work—tonic (I), dominant (V), and subdominant (IV)—are the foundations over which melodies and harmonic progressions unfold. Thus, a piece's key becomes a prime factor for musical unity.

At the same time, contrast between keys adds welcome variety. Composers begin by establishing the home key (for example, C major), then change to a related key, perhaps the dominant (G major), through a process known as **modulation**. In so doing, they create tension, because the dominant key is unstable compared with the tonic. This tension requires resolution, which is provided by the return to the home key.

Modulation

The progression, or movement, from home key to contrasting key and back outlines the basic musical pattern of statement-departure-return. The home key provides unity; the foreign key ensures variety and contrast.

The twelve major and twelve minor keys may be compared to rooms in a house, with the modulations equivalent to corridors leading from one to the other. A composer establishes the home key, then shapes the passage of modulation (the "corridor") into a key area that is not far away from the starting point. Alternately, composers may take an entire work and **transpose** it to a new key (making a transposition). This is convenient when a song's original key is too high or low to sing or play easily. You could begin on a different pitch and shift all the other pitches a uniform distance. In this way, the same song can be sung in various keys by differing voice ranges (soprano, alto, tenor, or bass).

Transposition

Although we are not always conscious of key centers and chord progressions while listening to music, these basic principles are deeply ingrained in our responses. We perceive and react to the tension and resolution provided by the movement of harmony, and we can sense how composers have used the harmonic system to give a coherent shape and meaning to their works.

Musical Texture

TYPES OF TEXTURE

Melodic lines may be thought of as the various threads that make up the musical fabric, or the **texture**, of a piece. The simplest texture is **monophony**: a single voice. ("Voice" refers to an individual part or line, even in instrumental music.)

Monophony Here, the melody is heard without any harmonic accompaniment or other melodic lines; it's you singing in the shower. It may be accompanied by rhythm and percussion instruments that embellish it, but interest is focused on the single melodic line rather than on any harmony. Until about a thousand years ago, the Western music we know about was monophonic.

Polyphony **Polyphony** ("many-voiced") describes a texture in which two or more different melodic lines are combined, thus distributing melodic interest among all the parts. Polyphonic texture is based on **counterpoint**; that is, one musical line set against another.

Homophony In perhaps the most commonly heard texture, **homophony**, a single voice takes over the melodic interest, while the accompanying lines are subordinate. Normally, the accompanying lines become blocks of harmony, the chords that support, color, and enhance the principal line. Homophonic texture is heard when a pianist plays a melody in the right hand while the left sounds the chords, or when a singer or violinist carries the tune against a harmonic accompaniment on the piano. Homophonic texture, then, is based on harmony, just as polyphonic texture is based on counterpoint. The differences between the two can be subtle, depending on whether a listener perceives additional musical lines as equal or subordinate to a primary melody.

KEY POINTS

- **Texture** refers to the interweaving of the melodic lines with harmony.

- The simplest texture is **monophony**, a single voice or line without accompaniment.

- **Polyphony** describes a many-voiced texture with different melodic lines, based on **counterpoint**—one line set against another.

- **Homophony** occurs when one melodic voice is prominent over the accompanying lines or voices.

- **Imitation**—when a melodic idea is presented in one voice, then restated in another—is a common unifying technique in polyphony; **canons** and **rounds** are two types of strictly imitative works.

Examples of Musical Texture

Monophonic: One melodic line, no accompaniment.
Hildegard of Bingen: *Kyrie* (chant):

Ky - ri - e ————— *e - lei - son

Polyphonic: Two independent melodic lines combined.
Bach: Organ chorale prelude *Jesu, Joy of Man's Desiring* (example begins 20 seconds into the recording):

Homophonic: One melody with subordinate accompaniment.
Haydn: **Symphony No. 94 (*Surprise*), II**:

Homorhythmic: A type of homophonic texture in which all voices move together, with the same words.
Handel: **"Hallelujah Chorus,"** from *Messiah*:

Rhythm			
Soprano	Hal - le - lu - jah,	Hal - le - lu - jah,	Hal - le - lu - jah,
Alto	Hal - le - lu - jah,	Hal - le - lu - jah,	Hal - le - lu - jah,
Tenor	Hal - le - lu - jah,	Hal - le - lu - jah,	Hal - le - lu - jah,
Bass	Hal - le - lu - jah,	Hal - le - lu - jah,	Hal - le - lu - jah,

Finally, there is **homorhythm**, a kind of homophony where all the voices or lines move together in the same rhythm. When there is text, all words are clearly sounded together. Like homophony, it is based on harmony moving in synchronization with a melody.

Homorhythm

As in music, line and texture are the focus of this Kente cloth from Ghana, in Africa.

A composition need not use one texture exclusively throughout. For example, a large-scale work may begin by presenting a melody with accompanying chords (homophony), after which the interaction of the parts becomes increasingly complex as more independent melodies enter (creating polyphony).

We have noted that melody is the horizontal aspect of music, while harmony is the vertical. Comparing musical texture to the cross weave of a fabric makes the interplay of the parts clear. The horizontal threads, the melodies, are held together by the vertical threads, the harmonies. Out of their interaction comes a texture that may be light or heavy, coarse or fine.

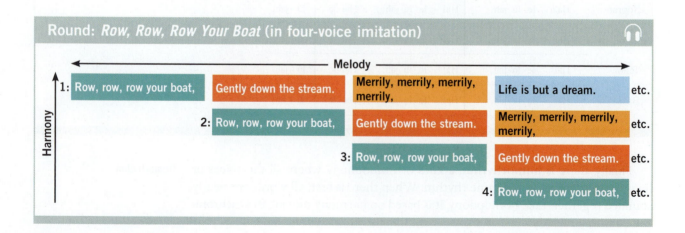

Round: *Row, Row, Row Your Boat* (in four-voice imitation)

Melody →

Harmony ↑

1: Row, row, row your boat,   Gently down the stream.   Merrily, merrily, merrily, merrily,   Life is but a dream.   etc.

2: Row, row, row your boat,   Gently down the stream.   Merrily, merrily, merrily, merrily,   etc.

3: Row, row, row your boat,   Gently down the stream.   etc.

4: Row, row, row your boat,   etc.

CONTRAPUNTAL DEVICES

When several independent lines are combined (in polyphony), one method that composers use to give unity and shape to the texture is **imitation**, in which a melodic idea is presented in one voice and then restated in another. While the imitating voice restates the melody, the first voice continues with new material. Thus, in addition to the vertical and horizontal threads in musical texture, a third, diagonal line results from imitation (see example opposite).

Imitation

The duration of the imitation may be brief or it may last the entire work. A strictly imitative work is known as a **canon**; and the simplest and most familiar form of canon is a **round**, in which each voice enters in succession with the same melody that can be repeated endlessly. Well-known examples include *Row, Row, Row Your Boat* and *Frère Jacques* (*Are You Sleeping?*). In the example opposite, the round begins with one voice singing "Row, row, row your boat," then another voice joins it in imitation, followed by a third voice and finally a fourth, creating a four-part polyphonic texture.

Canon and round

Musical Texture and the Listener

Different textures require different kinds of listening. Monophonic music has only one focus—the single line of melody unfolding in real time. In homophonic music, the primary focus is on the main melody with subordinate harmonies as accompaniment. Indeed, much of the music we have heard since childhood—including traditional and popular styles—consists of melody and accompanying chords. Homorhythmic texture is easily recognizable as well, in its simple, vertical conception and hymnlike movement; the melody is still the most obvious line. Polyphonic music, with several independent melodies woven together, requires more experienced listening, but a good place to start is the round, the simplest polyphonic texture. With practice, you can hear the roles of individual voices and determine how they relate to each other, providing texture throughout a musical work.

Musical Form

Form refers to a work's structure or shape, the way the elements of a composition have been combined by the composer to make it understandable to the listener. In all the arts, a balance is required between unity and variety, symmetry and asymmetry, activity and rest. Nature too has embodied this balance in the forms of plant and animal life and in what is perhaps the supreme achievement—the human form.

STRUCTURE AND DESIGN IN MUSIC

Music of all cultures mirrors life in its basic elements of **repetition** and **contrast**, the familiar and the new. Repetition fixes the material in our minds and satisfies our need for the familiar, while contrast stimulates our interest and feeds our desire for change. Every kind of musical work, from a nursery rhyme to a symphony, has a conscious structure. One of the most common in vocal **Strophic form** music, both popular and classical, is **strophic form**, in which the same melody is repeated with each stanza of the text, as for a folk song or carol (*Silent Night*). In this structure, while the music within a stanza offers some contrast, its repetition binds the song together. The direct opposite of strophic form in a song **Through-composed form** would be **through-composed form**, where no main section of the music or text is repeated.

Variation One kind of form that falls *between* repetition and contrast is **variation**, where some aspects of the music are altered but the original is still recognizable.

KEY POINTS

- **Form** is the organizing principle in music; its basic elements are repetition, contrast, and variation.

- **Strophic form**, common in songs, features repeated music for each stanza of text. In **through-composed form**, there are no large repeated sections.

- **Binary form (A-B)** and **ternary form (A-B-A)** are basic structures in music.

- A **theme**, a melodic idea in a large-scale work, can be broken into small, component fragments (**motives**). A **sequence** results when a motive is repeated at a different pitch.

- Many cultures use **call-and-response** (or **responsorial**) music, a repetitive style involving a soloist and a group. Some music is created spontaneously in performance, through **improvisation**.

- An **ostinato** is the repetition of a short melodic, rhythmic, or harmonic pattern.

- Large-scale compositions, such as symphonies and sonatas, are divided into sections, or **movements**.

You hear this formal technique when you listen to a new arrangement of a well-known popular song: the tune is recognizable, but many features of the known version are changed.

While all musical structures are based in one way or another on repetition and contrast, the forms are not fixed molds into which composers pour their material. What makes each piece of music unique is the way the composer adapts a general plan to create a wholly individual combination. And performers sometimes participate in shaping a composition. In works based mostly on **improvisation** (pieces created spontaneously in performance—typical of jazz, rock, and certain non-Western styles), repetition, contrast, and variation all play a role. We will see that in jazz, musicians organize their improvised melodies within a pre-established harmonic pattern, time frame, and melodic outline that is understood by all the performers.

This famous painting by **Andy Warhol** (1928–1987), *32 Campbell's Soup Cans*, illustrates the reliance of artists on the basic elements of repetition and variation.

Binary and Ternary Form

Two basic structures are widespread in art and in music. **Binary** (two-part) **form** is based on a statement and a departure, without a return to the opening section. **Ternary** (three-part) **form** extends the idea of statement and departure by bringing back the first section. Formal patterns are generally outlined with letters: binary form as **A-B** and ternary form as **A-B-A** (illustrated in the chart on p. 28).

Both two-part and three-part forms are found in short pieces such as songs and dances. The longer ternary form, with its logical symmetry and its balance of the outer sections against the contrasting middle one, constitutes a clear-cut formation that is favored by architects and painters as well as composers.

In His Own Words

" Improvisation is not the expression of accident but rather of the accumulated yearnings, dreams, and wisdom of our very soul."

—Yehudi Menuhin
(1916–1999)

THE BUILDING BLOCKS OF FORM

When a melodic idea is used as a building block in the construction of a larger work, we call it a **theme**. The introduction of a theme and its elaboration are the essence of musical thinking. This process of growth has its parallel in writing, when an idea, a topic sentence, is stated at the beginning of a paragraph and enlarged upon and developed by the author. Just as each sentence leads logically from one to the next, every musical idea takes up where the one before left off and continues convincingly to the next. The expansion of a theme, achieved by varying its melody, rhythm, or harmony, is considered **thematic development**. This is one of the most important techniques in music and requires both imagination and craft on the part of the creator.

Theme

Thematic development

Binary and Ternary Form

Binary form = A-A-B-B: *Greensleeves* (English folk song)
Statement **A** (repeated with varied final cadences):

Departure **B** (with different cadences):

Ternary form = A-B-A: *Simple Gifts* (Shaker hymn)
Statement **A** (repeated):

'Tis the gift to be sim - ple, 'tis the gift to be free, 'Tis the

gift to come down where we ought to be, And when we find our-selves—

Departure **B** (the ending resembles **A** with new text):

When true sim - pli - ci - ty is gained, To bow and to bend we will

not be a-shamed. To turn,— to— turn,— will— be our de-light,

Repeated statement **A**:

'Tis the gift to be sim - ple, 'tis the gift to be free,

Thematic development is generally too complex a process for short pieces, where a simple contrast between sections and modest expansion of material usually supply the necessary continuity. But it's necessary in larger forms of music, where it provides clarity, coherence, and logic.

Certain procedures help the music flow logically. The simplest is repetition, which may be either exact or varied. Or the idea may be restated at a higher or **Sequence** lower pitch level; this restatement is known as a **sequence**. Within a theme, a small **Motive** fragment that forms a melodic-rhythmic unit is called a **motive**. Motives are the cells of musical growth, which, when repeated, varied, and combined into new

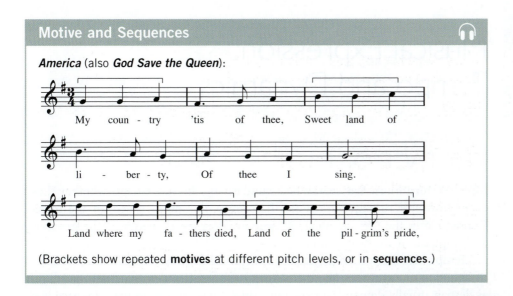

Motive and Sequences

America (also *God Save the Queen*):

My coun - try 'tis of thee, Sweet land of

li - ber - ty, Of thee I sing.

Land where my fa - thers died, Land of the pil - grim's pride,

(Brackets show repeated **motives** at different pitch levels, or in **sequences**.)

patterns, impart the qualities of evolution and expansion. These musical building blocks can be seen even in simple songs, like the national tune *America* (above). The opening three-note motive ("My country") is repeated in sequence (at a different pitch level) on the words "Sweet land of." A longer melodic idea is treated sequentially in the third line, where the musical phrase "Land where my fathers died" is repeated one note lower on the words "Land of the pilgrim's pride."

Whatever the length or style of a composition, it will show the principles of repetition and contrast, of unity and variety. One formal practice based on repetition and heard throughout the world is **call and response**, or **responsorial** music. In this style of performance, predominant in early Western church music and also in the music of African, Native American, and African American cultures, a singing leader is imitated or answered by a chorus of followers. This is a typical singing style for spirituals and gospel music.

Another widely used procedure linked to the principle of repetition is **ostinato**, a short musical pattern—melodic, rhythmic, or harmonic—that is repeated throughout a work or a major section of a piece. This unifying technique is especially prevalent in popular styles such as blues, jazz, rock, and rap, which rely on repeated harmonies that provide a scaffolding for musical development.

Music composition is an organic form in which the individual notes are bound together within a phrase, the phrases within a theme, the themes within a section, the sections within a **movement** (a complete, comparatively independent division of a large-scale work), and the movements within the work as a whole (like a symphony)—just as a novel binds together the individual words, phrases, sentences, paragraphs, and chapters into a cohesive whole.

The Gare de Saint-Exupéry, a modern train station in Lyon, France, designed by the Spanish architect **Santiago Calatrava** (b. 1951), shows the importance of symmetrical patterns in architecture.

Movement

Musical Expression: Tempo and Dynamics

THE PACE OF MUSIC

Most Western music has steady beats underlying the movement; whether these occur slowly or rapidly determines the **tempo**, or rate of speed, of the music. Consequently, the flow of music in time involves metric patterns (the grouping and emphasis of the beats) and tempo.

Tempo also carries emotional implications. We hurry our speech in moments of agitation or eagerness. Vigor and gaiety are associated with a brisk speed, just as despair usually demands a slow one. Since music moves in time, its pace is of prime importance, drawing from listeners responses that are both physical and psychological.

Because of the close connection between tempo and mood, tempo markings indicate the character of the music as well as the pace. The markings, along with other indications of expression, are traditionally given in Italian. This practice reflects the domination of Italian music in Europe from around 1600 to 1750, when performance directions were established. Here are some of the most common tempo markings:

In His Own Words

❝ Any composition must necessarily possess its unique tempo. . . . A piece of mine can survive almost anything but a wrong or uncertain tempo."

—Igor Stravinsky

grave: solemn (very, very slow)	*moderato*: moderate
largo: broad (very slow)	*allegro*: fast (cheerful)
adagio: quite slow	*vivace*: lively
andante: a walking pace	*presto*: very fast

You frequently encounter modifiers such as *molto* (very), *meno* (less), *poco* (a little), and *non troppo* (not too much). Also important are terms indicating a change of tempo, among them *accelerando* (getting faster), *ritardando* (holding back, getting slower), and *a tempo* (in time, or returning to the original pace).

KEY POINTS

- **Tempo** is the rate of speed, or pace, of the music.
- We use Italian terms to designate musical tempo: some of the most familiar are *allegro* (fast), *moderato* (moderate), *adagio* (quite slow), *accelerando* (speeding up), and *ritardando* (slowing down).
- **Dynamics** describe the volume, or how loud or soft the music is played; Italian terms for dynamics include *forte* (loud) and *piano* (soft).
- Composers indicate tempo and dynamics as a means of expression.

Speed and movement are easily perceived in this photograph of the 2002 Tour de France. Here, the cyclists are racing toward the finish on Paris's famous Avenue des Champs-Élysées.

LOUDNESS AND SOFTNESS

Dynamics denote the volume (degree of loudness or softness) at which music is played. Like tempo, dynamics can affect our emotional response. The main dynamic indications, listed below, are based on the Italian words for soft *(piano)* and loud *(forte)*.

pianissimo (***pp***): very soft
piano (***p***): soft
mezzo piano (***mp***): moderately soft

mezzo forte (***mf***): moderately loud
forte (***f***): loud
fortissimo (***ff***): very loud

Directions to change the dynamics, either suddenly or gradually, are also indicated by words or signs:

crescendo (<): growing louder
decrescendo or *diminuendo* (>): growing softer

TEMPO AND DYNAMICS AS ELEMENTS OF EXPRESSION

The composer adds markings for tempo and dynamics to help shape the expressive content of a work. These expression marks increased in number during the late eighteenth and nineteenth centuries, when composers tried to make their intentions known ever more precisely; by the early twentieth century, few decisions were left to the performer at all.

In His Own Words

❝ Voices, instruments, and all possible sounds—even silence itself—must tend toward one goal, which is expression."

—C. W. Gluck
(1714–1787)

Dynamics in music may be compared to the light and shade in this photograph of the sun shining through a forest of trees.

Tempo and Dynamics in a Music Score

Beethoven: **Symphony No. 5**, opening:

Tempo: Fast (*Allegro*), with vigor (*con brio*)
Dynamics: Very loud (*fortissimo*), then soft (*piano*)

If tempo and dynamics are the domain of the composer, what is the role of performers and conductors in interpreting a musical work? Performance directions can be somewhat imprecise—what is loud or fast to one performer may be moderate in volume and tempo to another. Even when composers give precise tempo markings in their scores (the exact number of beats per minute), performers have the final say in choosing a tempo that best delivers the message of the music.

Music and Words

Today, thanks largely to iTunes, many people consider "song" synonymous with any musical selection, with or without words. Though the term correctly refers to a union of music and words—something that is sung—the original Greek word for "music," *mousikas,* implied a union of melody, language, *and* movement.

There are many facets of text and music we can consider here. For starters, does the text communicate something that can be understood, or are the syllables **nonlexical** (nonsensical)? Examples of nonlexical syllables are "Na na na na, na na na na, na na na na, hey Jude"(from the Beatles' *Hey Jude*) and "Zip-a-dee-doo-dah, zip-a-dee-ay" (from Disney's *Song of the South*). Jazz singers often launch into **scat-singing**, a vocal improvisation using wordless vocables, like "Shoo-be-doo-be doo-wop" (Louis Armstrong famously invented this technique), and in English madrigals and Christmas carols you'll sometimes hear syllables like "fa la la la la" as a refrain. In all these cases, the sounds and rhythms of the "text" contribute to the music and its broad meaning. The voice can even be used for its timbral characteristics, like any other instrument—as in the technique called **vocalise**, or wordless melody (singing on a neutral vowel like "ah").

Throughout this book, you will encounter music with texts in a variety of languages other than English. Music for worship has been set for centuries in Hebrew, Greek, and Latin. Not only was **Latin** the language of the Roman Empire, it was also the language of learning at medieval and Renaissance universities and of the Roman Catholic Church until the Second Vatican Council of 1962, when the church approved the use of the **vernacular** (the language of the people) for the Mass. **Secular** (nonreligious) music has traditionally been in vernacular languages. You will hear most selections sung in their original language (although we provide

> " Let the words be the mistress of the melody, not its slave."
>
> —Claudio Monteverdi

Singing without words

Languages

KEY POINTS

- A song's text can convey the meaning of the words or simply sounds. Some composers use the voice as an instrument, as in **vocalise** (melodies sung on a neutral sound like "ah") or **scat-singing** in jazz (to made-up syllables).

- **Secular** (nonreligious) music is generally sung in the language of the people (the **vernacular**). Much Western **sacred** (religious) music is in **Latin**, the language of the Roman Catholic Church.

- Composers may set an already-written text to music, or, as in opera and musical theater, work together with lyricists as a songwriting team.

- Each syllable of a song text may get one note (**syllabic** setting); one syllable may get a few notes (**neumatic** setting); or one syllable may get many notes (**melismatic** setting).

- Composers use **word-painting** to emphasize the text, perhaps with a drawn-out word over many notes (**melisma**) or with a melody that pictorializes a word.

an English translation), since a sung translation will never fit the musical line as well as the original words. In the case of a famous lullaby by Brahms, though, you probably know the English version better than the original German:

Brahms, *Lullaby*

Gu - ten A - bend, gut' Nacht, mit__ Ro - sen be -
Lul - la - by and good night, with__ ro - ses be -

dacht,__ mit__ Näg' - lein be - steckt, schlupf'__ un - ter die Deck',
dight,__ with__ li - lies o'er__ spread, is__ ba - by's wee bed,

As we encounter words in other languages, their translations often have meanings that are slightly different from the original; if you have studied (or grown up with) a language other than English, you know that some terms or concepts really don't translate perfectly from language to language or culture to culture. This is another reason why it's important to consider the texts of songs in their original language even as we also try to grasp the meaning through the translation.

Which comes first in a song, the melody or the words? As we will see, many composers select an already existing poem or prose text to set to music, so clearly those words precede the tune. But great teams of lyricists / composers have worked together to come up with enduring songs, and there is no clear formula for their creations. When George Gershwin composed the tune that became *I Got Rhythm*, his partner / brother Ira set out to write lyrics that fit the syncopated rhythms. It took him several tries, and the famous ones they settled on do not rhyme ("I got rhythm, I got music, I got my girl, who could ask for anything more"). Likewise, the lyrics for the Talking Heads' famous song *Burning Down the House* were added after the band had found a set of rhythmic and melodic ideas that they liked.

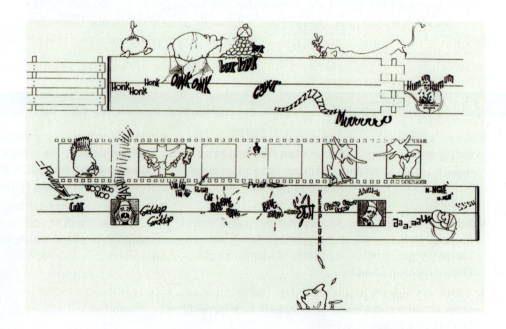

This humorous score of *Stripsody*, by soprano Cathy Berberian, features comic-book images that ask the vocalist to make sounds matching the pictures.

Examples of Text-Setting Styles (from Handel's *Messiah*)

Syllabic: one note set to each syllable of text (from "Hallelujah Chorus")

Hal - le - lu - jah,   Hal - le - lu - jah,   Hal - le - lu - jah,   Hal - le - lu - jah,

Neumatic: a few notes set to one syllable (from "Hallelujah Chorus")

and he shall reign, _____ and he shall reign _____ for - ev - er and ev - er,

Melismatic: many notes set to one syllable (from aria "Rejoice greatly")

O daugh - ter of __ Zi - on, re - joice, _____ re - joice, _____

The text of a song may help organize the tune. Words flow in phrases, just as melodies do, and both are punctuated (by cadences, in the case of music). Poems are often written in rhymed **stanzas**, or **strophes**. As mentioned earlier, the most common type of musical setting, in both popular and art music, is **strophic form**, in which the same music is repeated for each stanza. Or the song might feature a **refrain**, or **chorus**, words and music that recur after each stanza. In sung dramas (like operas), the text may be free (unrhymed, metrical) verse or even prose, as people speak to each other. We will hear a variety of melodic styles in opera: some song-like passages (called arias) are very lyrical, while others are more speech-like.

How the words fit into the flow—both melodic and rhythmic—of a song makes the difference between a memorable song and an easily forgotten one. The simplest way that words and melody can fit together is a one-to-one match called **syllabic**: each syllable gets one note, as in *"Happy Birthday."* The opposite style of syllabic is **melismatic**, in which a single syllable is elongated by many notes, thereby giving a particular word more emphasis. Both styles, and a middle ground called **neumatic** (with a few notes to each syllable), are represented in the examples above from Handel's *Messiah* (Chapter 21). In the last example, you can see how "rejoice" is drawn out in a long **melisma**, not only emphasizing the word, but capturing its joyful meaning through music. This technique is called **word-painting**, and you will hear it frequently in vocal music. Gospel, as well as some pop singers—such as Mariah Carey, Christina Aguilera, and Beyoncé Knowles—use melismas as part of their signature style.

The words of a song offer a way for all of us to understand the music, no matter what our cultural or aesthetic backgrounds. But keep in mind that often, especially when the text is a poem, the words themselves have purposefully vague or multiple implications, or are chosen by the poet (or the musician) for their sound and rhythm as much as for their specific meaning. One thing is sure: when words are sung, their power and effect always go well beyond their literal meaning on the page.

Stanza/strophe

Refrain/chorus

Text-setting styles

Word-painting

Voices and Instrument Families

MUSICAL TIMBRE

A fourth property of sound besides pitch, duration, and volume—**timbre**, or **tone color**—accounts for the striking differences in the sound quality of musical **instruments**, mechanisms that generate vibrations and launch them into the air. It's what makes a trumpet sound altogether different from a guitar or a clarinet. Timbre is influenced by a number of factors, such as the size, shape, and proportions of the instrument, the material from which it is made, and the manner in which the vibration is produced. A string, for example, may be bowed, plucked, or struck.

Each voice type and instrument has a limited melodic range (the distance from the lowest to the highest note) and dynamic range. We describe a specific area in the range of an instrument or voice, such as low, middle, or high, as its **register**.

THE VOICE AS INSTRUMENT

The human voice is the most natural of all musical instruments; it is also one of the most universal—all cultures enjoy some form of vocal music. Each person's voice displays a particular quality (or character) and range. The standard designations for vocal ranges, from highest to lowest, are **soprano**, **mezzo-soprano**, and **alto** (short for "contralto") for female voices; and **tenor**, **baritone**, and **bass** for male voices.

In earlier eras, Western social and religious customs severely restricted women's participation in public musical events. Thus, young boys, and occasionally men with soprano-or alto-range voices, sang female parts in church music and

KEY POINTS

- Properties of sound include pitch, duration, volume, and **timbre**, or **tone color.**

- An **instrument** generates vibrations and transmits them into the air.

- The human voice can be categorized into various ranges, including **soprano** and **alto** for female voices, and **tenor** and **bass** for male voices.

- The world instrument classification system divides into **aerophones** (such as flutes or horns), **chordophones** (violins or guitars), **idiophones** (bells or cymbals), and **membranophones** (drums).

on the stage. In the sixteenth century, women singers came into prominence in secular (nonreligious) music. Tenors were most often featured as soloists in early opera, while baritones and basses became popular soloists later, in the eighteenth century. In other cultures, the sound of women's voices has always been preferred for certain styles of music, such as lullabies.

Throughout the ages, the human voice has served as a model for instrument builders, composers, and players who have sought to duplicate its lyric beauty, expressiveness, and ability to produce **vibrato** (a throbbing effect) on their instruments.

LEFT: Luciano Pavarotti (1935–2007), one of the greatest operatic tenors of all time.

RIGHT: E. J. Jones plays folk songs and dances on Scottish small pipes (aerophone), a quieter version of bagpipe.

THE WORLD OF MUSICAL INSTRUMENTS

The diversity of musical instruments played around the world defies description. Since every conceivable method of sound production is used, and every possible raw material, it would be impossible to list them all here. However, specialists have devised a method of classifying instruments based solely on the way their sound is generated. The system designates four basic categories. **Aerophones** produce sound by using air. Instruments in this category include flutes, whistles, and horns—in short, any wind instrument. One of the most common aerophones around the world is the **bagpipe**, with a somewhat raucous tone and built-in drones for harmony.

A steel drum band playing steel-pans (idiophones) competes in the famous Panorama competition in Trinidad.

A drum (membranophone) ensemble from Burundi in Central Africa.

Chordophones produce sound from a vibrating string stretched between two points. The string may be set in motion by bowing, as on a violin; by plucking, as on a guitar or an Indian sitar (below); or by striking, as on a hammered dulcimer.

Idiophones produce sound from the substance itself. They may be struck, as are steel drums from Trinidad (p. 37); scraped or shaken, as are African rattles; or plucked, as is the mbira, or African "thumb piano." The variety of idiophones around the world is staggering. **Membranophones** are drum-type instruments that are sounded from tightly stretched membranes. They too can be struck, plucked, rubbed, or even sung into, to set the skin in vibration.

In the next chapter, we will review the instruments used most frequently in Western music. Throughout the book, however, you will learn about other instruments associated with popular and art music cultures around the world that have influenced the Western tradition.

Composer and sitar player Ravi Shankar (1920–2012), performing here with his daughter Anoushka, was the most renowned and honored figure in Indian classical music of the twentieth century.

Western Musical Instruments

The instruments of the Western world, and especially those of the orchestra, may be categorized into four groups of their own: strings, woodwinds, brass, and percussion. Not all woodwinds, however, are made of wood, nor do they share a common means of sound production. Furthermore, certain instruments do not fit neatly into any of these convenient categories (the piano, for example, is both a string and a percussion instrument).

> **"** In music, instruments perform the function of the colors employed in painting."
>
> —Honoré de Balzac
> (1799–1850)

STRING INSTRUMENTS

The string family, all chordophones, includes two types of instruments: those that are **bowed** and those that are **plucked**. In the bowed-string family, there are four principal members: violin, viola, violoncello, and double bass, each with four strings (double basses sometimes have five) that are set vibrating by drawing a bow across them. The bow is held in the right hand, while the left hand is used to "stop" the string by pressing a finger down at a particular point, thereby leaving a certain portion of the string free to vibrate. By stopping the string at another point, the performer changes the length of the vibrating portion, and with it the rate of vibration and the pitch.

The **violin** evolved to its present form at the hands of the master instrument makers who flourished in Italy from around 1600 to 1750. It is capable of brilliance and dramatic effect, subtle nuances from soft to loud, and great agility in rapid passages throughout its extremely wide range.

Violin

KEY POINTS

- The four families of Western instruments are **strings, woodwinds, brass,** and **percussion.**

- String instruments (chordophones) are sounded by **bowing** and **plucking.** Bowed strings include the violin, viola, cello, and double bass; plucked strings include the harp and guitar.

- Woodwind instruments (aerophones) include the flute, oboe, clarinet, bassoon, and saxophone.

- Brass instruments (aerophones) include the trumpet, French horn, trombone, and tuba.

- Percussion instruments include idiophones (xylophone, cymbals, triangle) and membranophones (timpani, bass drum); some are pitched (chimes), while others are unpitched (tambourine).

- Keyboard instruments, such as the piano and organ, do not fit neatly into the Western classification system.

LEFT: Grammy-Award-winning violinist Hilary Hahn (b. 1979) enjoys a prominent career as a soloist.

RIGHT: Yo-Yo Ma (b. 1955) is a revered and wide-ranging virtuoso cellist.

The color coding helps this young harpist position her hands as she plucks the strings.

that are bowed and those that are plucked. In the bowed string group, the

The **viola** is somewhat larger than the violin and thus has a lower range. Its strings are longer, thicker, and heavier. The tone is husky in the low register, somber and penetrating in the high. It often fills in the harmony, or it may **double** another part—that is, reinforce another part when it plays the same notes an octave higher or lower.

The **violoncello**, popularly known as the **cello**, is lower in range than the viola and is notable for its singing quality and its dark resonance in the low register. Cellos often play the melody, and they enrich the sound with their full timbre.

The **double bass**, known also as a **contrabass** or **bass viol**, is the lowest of the orchestral string instruments. Accordingly, it plays the bass part—the foundation of the harmony. Its deep tones support the cello part an octave lower. These four string instruments constitute the core or "heart" of the orchestra, a designation that indicates the section's versatility and importance.

String instruments can be played in many styles and can produce striking special effects. They excel at playing **legato** (smoothly, connecting the notes) as well as the opposite, **staccato** (with notes short and detached). A different effect, **pizzicato** (plucked), is created when a performer plucks the string with a finger instead of using the bow. **Vibrato**, a slight throbbing, is achieved by a rapid wrist-and-finger movement on the string that slightly alters the pitch. For a **glissando**, a finger of the left hand slides along the string while the right hand draws the bow, gathering all the pitches under the left-hand finger in

LEFT: American Christian McBride (b. 1972) playing the double bass at a jazz festival in East Sussex, England, 2014.

RIGHT: Bass guitarist Ricardo Winandy (b. 1983) performs in the Brazilian progressive band Mindflow.

one swooping sound. **Tremolo**, the rapid repetition of a tone through a quick up-and-down movement of the bow, is associated with suspense and excitement. No less important is the **trill**, a rapid alternation between a note and one adjacent to it.

String instruments are capable of playing several notes simultaneously, thereby producing harmony: **double-stopping** means playing two strings at once; playing three or four strings together is called **triple-** or **quadruple-stopping**. Another effect is created by the **mute**, a small attachment that fits over the bridge, muffling the sound. **Harmonics** are eerie, crystalline tones in a very high register that are produced by lightly touching the string at certain points while the bow is drawn across it.

Two popular plucked-string instruments are the harp and the guitar. The **harp** is one of the oldest of musical instruments, with a home in many cultures outside Europe. Its plucked strings, whose pitches are changed by means of pedals, produce an ethereal tone. Chords on the harp are frequently played in broken form—that is, the notes are sounded one after another instead of simultaneously. From this technique comes the term **arpeggio**, which means "broken chord" (*arpa* is Italian for "harp"). Arpeggios can be created in a variety of ways on many instruments.

The **guitar**, another old instrument, dating back at least to the Middle Ages, probably originated in the Middle East. A favorite solo instrument, it is associated today with folk and popular music as well as classical styles. The standard acoustic (as opposed to electric) **guitar** is made of wood and has a fretted fingerboard and six nylon strings, which are plucked with the fingers of the right hand or with a pick. The electronically amplified **electric guitar**, capable of many specialized techniques, comes in two main types: the hollow-bodied (or electro-acoustic), favored by jazz and popular musicians; and the solid-bodied, used more by rock musicians. Related to the guitar are such traditional instruments as the **banjo** and **mandolin**.

String effects

Harp

Arpeggio

Guitar

Flutist James Galway (b. 1939), the "man with the golden flute."

WOODWIND INSTRUMENTS

Woodwind instruments (aerophones) produce sound with a column of air vibrating within a pipe that has fingerholes along its length. When one or another of these holes is opened or closed, the length of the vibrating air column is changed. Woodwind players are capable of remarkable agility on their instruments by means of an intricate mechanism of keys arranged to suit the natural position of the fingers.

Nowadays woodwinds are not necessarily made of wood, and they employ several different methods of setting up vibration: blowing across a mouth hole (flute), blowing into a mouthpiece that has a single reed (clarinet and saxophone), or blowing into a mouthpiece fitted with a double reed (oboe and bassoon). They do, however, have one important feature in common: the holes in their pipes. In addition, their timbres are such that composers think of them and write for them as a group.

The **flute** is the soprano voice of the woodwind family. Its tone is cool and velvety in the expressive low register, and often brilliant in the upper part of its range. The present-day flute, made of a metal alloy rather than wood, is a cylindrical tube, closed at one end, that is held horizontally. The player blows across a mouth hole cut in the side of the pipe near the closed end. The flute is used frequently as a melody instrument—its timbre stands out against the orchestra—and offers the performer great versatility in playing rapid repeated notes, scales, and trills. The **piccolo** (from the Italian *flauto piccolo,* "little flute") is the highest pitched instrument in the orchestra. In its upper register, it takes on a shrillness that is easily heard even when the orchestra is playing *fortissimo.*

The **oboe** continues to be made of wood. The player blows directly into a double reed, which consists of two thin strips of cane bound together with a narrow passage for air. The oboe's timbre, generally described as nasal and reedy, is often associated with pastoral effects and nostalgic moods. The oboe traditionally sounds the tuning note (A) for the other instruments of the orchestra. The **English horn** is an alto oboe. Its wooden tube is wider and longer than that of the oboe and ends in a pear-shaped opening called a **bell,** which largely accounts for its soft, expressive timbre.

LEFT: Bassoon players in an orchestra.

RIGHT: Oboe players in an orchestra.

The **clarinet** uses a single reed, a small, thin piece of cane fastened against its chisel-shaped mouthpiece. The instrument's tone is smooth and liquid, and its range remarkably wide in both pitch and volume. It too displays an easy command of rapid scales, trills, and repeated notes. The **bass clarinet**, one octave lower in range than the clarinet, has a rich dark tone and a wide dynamic range.

The **bassoon**, another double-reed instrument, sounds weighty in the low register and reedy and intense in the upper. Capable of a hollow-like staccato and wide leaps that can sound humorous, it is at the same time a highly expressive instrument. The **contrabassoon** produces the lowest tone of the woodwinds. Its function in the woodwind section of supplying a foundation for the harmony may be likened to that of the double bass among the strings.

The **saxophone**, invented by the Belgian Adolphe Sax in 1840, is the most recent of the woodwind instruments. It was created by combining the single reed of the clarinet with a conical bore and the metal body of the brass instruments. There are various sizes of saxophone: the most common are soprano, alto, tenor, and baritone. Used only occasionally in the orchestra, the saxophone had become the characteristic instrument of the jazz band by the 1920s, and it remains a favorite sound in popular music today.

BRASS INSTRUMENTS

Clarinet player in an orchestra.

The main instruments of the brass family (aerophones) are the trumpet, French horn (or horn), trombone, and tuba. All these instruments consist of cup-shaped mouthpieces attached to a length of metal tubing that flares at the end into a bell. The column of air within the tube is set vibrating by the tightly stretched lips of the player, which are buzzed together. Going from one pitch to another involves not only mechanical means, such as a slide or valves, but also muscular control to vary the pressure of the lips and breath. Brass and woodwind instrument players often refer to their **embouchure**, the entire oral mechanism of lips, lower facial muscles, and jaw.

Trumpets and horns were prevalent in the ancient world. At first, they were fashioned from animal horns and tusks and were used chiefly for religious ceremonies and military signals. The **trumpet**, highest in pitch of the brass family, asserts itself with a brilliant, clear timbre. It is often associated with ceremonial display. The trumpet can also be muted, with a pear-shaped, metal or cardboard device that is inserted in the bell to achieve a muffled, buzzy sound.

The **French horn** is descended from the ancient hunting horn. Its mellow resonance can be mysteriously remote in soft passages and sonorous in loud ones; muted, it sounds distant. The horn is played with the right hand, cupped slightly, inserted in the bell and is sometimes "stopped" by plugging the bell tightly with the hand, producing an eerie and rasping quality. The timbre of the horn blends well with woodwinds, brasses, and strings.

The **trombone**—the Italian word means "large trumpet"—offers a full and rich sound in the tenor range. In place of valves, it features a movable U-shaped slide that alters the length of the vibrating air column in the tube. The **tuba,** the bass instrument of the brass family, furnishes the foundation for the harmony, like the

Classical trumpeter Alison Balsom (b. 1978) performs in a Christmas special in London, 2015.

LEFT: Kenny Garrett (b. 1960) plays alto saxophone at a jazz festival in New York City, 2013.

MIDDLE: The French horn section of an orchestra.

RIGHT: This young woman demonstrates the tuba, largest of the brass family.

double bass and contrabassoon. The tuba adds depth to the orchestral tone, and a dark resonance ranging from velvety softness to a rumbling growl.

Other brass instruments are used in concert and marching bands. Among these is the **cornet**, similar to the trumpet and very popular in concert bands in the early twentieth century. The **bugle**, which evolved from the military (or field) trumpet of early times, sends out a powerful tone that carries well in the open air. Since it has no valves, it is able to sound only certain pitches of the scale, which accounts for the familiar pattern of duty calls (and "Taps") in the army. The **fluegelhorn**, often used in jazz bands, is really a valved bugle with a wide bell. The **euphonium** is a tenor-range instrument whose shape resembles the tuba. And the **sousaphone**, an adaptation of the tuba designed by the American bandmaster John Philip Sousa, features a forward bell and is coiled to rest over the shoulder of the marching player.

This father-daughter duo are playing trombone and the larger bass trombone.

PERCUSSION INSTRUMENTS ▶️

The percussion instruments of the orchestra accentuate the rhythm, generate excitement at the climaxes, and inject splashes of color into the orchestral sound. This family (encompassing a vast array of idiophones and membranophones) is divided into two categories: instruments capable of producing definite pitches, and those that produce an indefinite pitch. In the former group are the **timpani**, or **kettledrums**, which are generally played in sets of two or four. The timpani has a hemispheric copper shell across which is stretched a "head" of plastic or calfskin held in place by a metal ring. A pedal mechanism enables the player to change the tension of the head, and with it the pitch. The instrument is played with two padded sticks. Its dynamic range extends from a mysterious rumble to a thunderous roll. The timpani first arrived in Western Europe from the Middle East, where Turks on horseback used them in combination with trumpets.

Also among the pitched percussion instruments is the **xylophone** family; instruments of this general type are used in Africa, Southeast Asia, and throughout the Americas. The xylophone consists of tuned blocks of wood laid out in the shape of a keyboard. Struck with mallets with hard heads, the instrument produces a dry, crisp sound. The **marimba** is a more mellow xylophone of African origin. The **vibraphone**, used in jazz as well as art music, combines the principle of the xylophone with resonators, each containing revolving disks operated by electric motors that produce an exaggerated vibrato.

Pitched percussion

The **glockenspiel** (German for "set of bells") consists of a series of horizontal tuned steel bars of various sizes, which when struck produce a bright, metallic, bell-like sound. The **celesta**, a kind of glockenspiel that is operated by means of a keyboard, resembles a miniature upright piano. Its steel plates are struck by small hammers to produce a sound like a music box. **Chimes**, or **tubular bells**, a set of tuned metal tubes of various lengths suspended from a frame and struck with a hammer, are frequently called on to simulate church bells.

Percussion instruments that do not produce a definite pitch include the **snare drum** (or **side drum**), a small cylindrical drum with two heads (top and bottom) stretched over a shell of wood or metal and played with two drumsticks. This instrument owes its brilliant tone to the vibrations of the lower head against taut snares (strings). The **bass drum** is played with a large, soft-headed stick and produces a low, heavy sound. The **tom-tom** is a colloquial name given to Native American or African drums of indefinite pitch. The **tambourine** is a round, hand-held drum with "jingles"—little metal plates—inserted in its rim. The player can strike the drum with the fingers or knee, shake it, or pass a hand over the jingles. Of Middle Eastern origin, it is particularly associated with music of Spain, as are **castanets**, little wood clappers mounted on wooden boards or, for Spanish dancing, moved by the player's fingers.

Evelyn Glennie (b. 1965) is a virtuoso solo percussionist in spite of being profoundly deaf.

Unpitched percussion

The **triangle** is a slender rod of steel bent into a three-cornered shape; when struck with a steel beater, it gives off a bright, tinkling sound. **Cymbals**, which arrived in the West from central Asia during the Middle Ages, consist of two large circular brass plates of equal size; when struck against each other, they produce a shattering sound. The **gong** and the **tam-tam** are both broad circular disks of metal, suspended to a frame so as to hang freely. The tam-tam is a flat gong of indefinite pitch; the gong, however, with a raised metal center, has a definite pitch and when struck with a heavy drumstick produces a deep roar.

Pianist Lang Lang (b. 1982) is one of the most sought-after soloists today.

KEYBOARD INSTRUMENTS

Piano The **piano** was originally known as the *fortepiano*, Italian for "loud-soft," which suggests its wide dynamic range and capacity for nuance. Its strings are struck with hammers controlled by a keyboard mechanism. The piano cannot sustain a tone as well as the string and wind instruments, but in the hands of a fine performer, it is capable of producing a singing melody.

The piano boasts a notable capacity for brilliant scales, arpeggios, trills, rapid passages, and octaves, as well as chords. Its range from lowest to highest pitch spans more than seven octaves, or eighty-eight semitones. Its several foot pedals govern the length of time a string vibrates as well as its volume.

Organ The **organ**, one of the earliest keyboard instruments, is also a type of wind instrument. The air flow to each of its many pipes is controlled by the organist from a console containing two or more keyboards and a pedal keyboard played by the feet. The organ's multicolored sonority can easily fill a huge space. Electronic keyboards, or synthesizers, capable of imitating pipe organs and other timbres have become commonplace. Another early keyboard instrument, much used in **Harpsichord** the Baroque era, is the **harpsichord**. Its sound is produced by quills that pluck its metal strings.

The instruments described in this and the previous chapter form a vivid and diversified group, which can be heard and viewed with your book's online materials. To composers, performers, and listeners alike, they offer an endless variety of colors and shades of expression.

Musical Ensembles

The great variety in musical instruments is matched by a wide assortment of ensembles, or performance groups. Some are homogeneous—for example, choral groups using only voices or perhaps only men's voices. Others are more heterogeneous—for example, the orchestra, which features instruments from the different families. Across the world, any combination is possible.

> 66 Conductors must give unmistakable and suggestive signals to the orchestra—not choreography to the audience."
>
> —George Szell (1897–1970)

CHORAL GROUPS

Choral music is sung around the world, both for religious purposes (sacred music) and for nonspiritual (secular) occasions. Loosely defined, a **chorus** is a fairly large body of singers who perform together; their music is usually sung in several voice parts. Many groups include both men and women, but choruses can also be restricted to women's or men's voices only. A **choir,** traditionally a smaller group, is often connected with a church or with the performance of sacred music. The standard voice parts in both chorus and choir correspond to the voice ranges described earlier: soprano, alto, tenor, and bass (abbreviated **SATB**). In early times, choral music was often performed without accompaniment, a style of singing known as *a cappella* (meaning "in the chapel"). Smaller, specialized vocal ensembles include the madrigal choir and chamber choir.

The Washington National Cathedral Girls Choir sings an evening church service.

KEY POINTS

- Choral groups often feature *a cappella* singing, with no accompaniment.
- **Chamber music** is ensemble music for small groups, with one player per part.
- Standard chamber ensembles include **string quartets, piano trios,** and **brass quintets.**
- The modern **orchestra** can feature over one hundred players.

- Most **bands—wind, marching, jazz, rock**—feature a core of winds and percussion.
- Large ensembles are generally led by a **conductor** who beats patterns with a baton to help performers keep the same tempo.

Standard Chamber Ensembles			
Duos	**Quartets**	**Quintets**	
Solo instrument (e.g., violin or clarinet)	String quartet	String quintet	Woodwind quintet
Piano	Violin 1	Violin 1	Flute
	Violin 2	Violin 2	Oboe
Trios	Viola	Viola 1	Clarinet
	Cello	Viola 2	Bassoon
String trio	Piano quartet	Cello	French horn (a brass instrument)
Violin 1	Piano	Piano quintet	Brass quintet
Viola or violin 2	Violin	Piano	Trumpet 1
Cello	Viola	String quartet	Trumpet 2
Piano trio	Cello	(violin 1, violin 2, viola, cello)	French horn
Piano			Trombone
Violin			Tuba
Cello			

The Ying String Quartet, founded in 1988 by four siblings.

CHAMBER ENSEMBLES

Chamber music is ensemble music for a group of two to about a dozen players, with only one player to a part—as distinct from orchestral music, in which a single instrumental part may be performed by as many as eighteen players or more. The essential trait of chamber music is its intimacy.

Several of the standard chamber music ensembles consist of string players. The most well-known combination is probably the **string quartet**, made up of two violins, viola, and cello. Other popular combinations are the **duo sonata** (soloist with piano); the **piano trio**, **piano quartet**, and **piano quintet**, each made up of a piano and string instruments; the string quintet; as well as larger groups— the **sextet**, **septet**, and **octet**. Winds too form standard combinations, especially **woodwind** and **brass quintets**. Some of these ensembles are listed above.

Contemporary composers have experimented with new groupings that combine the voice with small groups of instruments and electronic elements with live performers. In some cultures, chamber groups mix what might seem to be unlikely timbres to the Western listener—in India, for example, plucked strings and percussion are standard.

THE ORCHESTRA

In its most general sense, the term "orchestra" may be applied to any performing body of diverse instruments—this would include the **gamelan** orchestras of Bali and Java, made up largely of gongs, xylophone-like instruments, and drums. In the West,

Typical Distribution of Orchestral Instruments			
Strings	16–18	first violins	10–12 cellos
	16–18	second violins	8–10 double basses
	12	violas	1–2 harps, when needed
Woodwinds	2–3	flutes, 1 piccolo	3 clarinets, 1 bass clarinet
	2–3	oboes, 1 English horn	3 bassoons, 1 contrabassoon
Brass	4–6	French horns	3 trombones (1 is a bass)
	4	trumpets	1 tuba
Percussion	3–5	players	1 timpani player (2–5 timpani)

the term is now synonymous with **symphony orchestra**, an ensemble of strings coupled with an assortment of woodwinds, brass, and percussion instruments.

The symphony orchestra has varied in size and makeup throughout its history but has always featured string instruments at its core. From its origins as a small group, the orchestra has grown into an ensemble of more than a hundred musicians, approximately two-thirds of whom are string players. The chart above shows the distribution of instruments typical of a large orchestra today.

The instruments are arranged to achieve the best balance of tone: most of the strings are near the front, as are the gentle woodwinds, with the louder brass and percussion at the back. A characteristic seating plan is shown on page 51.

WIND, JAZZ, AND ROCK BANDS

Band is a generic name applied to a variety of ensembles, most of which rely on winds and percussion. The band is a much-loved American institution. One American bandmaster, John Philip Sousa, achieved worldwide fame with his **wind**, or **concert**, **band** and the repertory of marches he wrote for it.

In the United States today, the wind band, ranging in size from forty to eighty or so players, is an established institution in most secondary schools, colleges, and universities and in many communities as well. Modern composers like to write for this ensemble, since it is usually willing to play new compositions. The familiar marching band usually entertains at sports events and parades. Besides its core of winds and percussion, this group often features remnants from its military origins, including a display of drum majors (or majorettes), flags, and rifles. The repertory of marching bands is extensive, but almost always includes Sousa marches, such as the well-known *Stars and Stripes Forever*.

The University of Texas Longhorn Marching Band in the 2006 Rose Parade in Pasadena, California.

The precise instrumentation of **jazz bands** depends on the particular music being played but usually includes a reed section made up of saxophones and an occasional clarinet, a brass section of trumpets and trombones, and a rhythm

The Vancouver Symphony Orchestra rehearsing in the city's Orpheum Theatre, 2008.

section of percussion, piano, double bass, and electric guitar. **Rock bands** often supplement amplified guitars and percussion with synthesizers, and may also feature other winds and brass.

THE CONDUCTOR

Large ensembles, such as an orchestra, concert band, or chorus, generally need a conductor, who serves as the group's leader. Conductors beat time in standard metric patterns to help the performers keep the same tempo; many conductors use a thin stick known as a **baton**, which is easy to see. These conducting patterns, shown in the diagrams on page 51, further emphasize the strong and weak beats of the measure. Beat 1, the strongest in any meter, is always given a downbeat, or a downward motion of the hand; a secondary accent is shown by a change of direction; and the last beat of each measure, a weak beat, is always an upbeat or upward motion, thereby leaving the hand ready for the downbeat of the next measure.

Baton

Equally important is the conductor's role in interpreting the music for the group. He or she decides the precise tempo (how fast or slow) and the dynamics (how soft or loud) all the way through the piece. In most cases, the composer's markings are relative (how loud is *forte*?) and thus open to interpretive differences. Conductors also rehearse ensembles in practice sessions, helping the musicians to learn their individual parts. String players depend on the conductor, or sometimes the **concertmaster** (the first-chair violinist), to standardize their bowing strokes so that the musical emphasis, and therefore the interpretation, is uniform.

Concertmaster

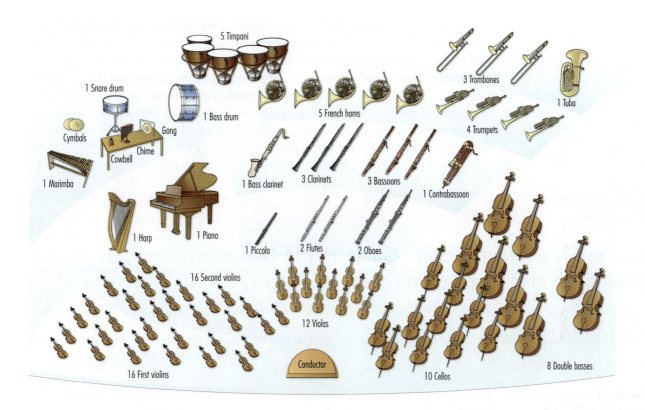

A typical seating plan for an orchestra.

THE ORCHESTRA IN ACTION

A thrilling introduction to the infinite range of the modern orchestra is Benjamin Britten's *Young Person's Guide to the Orchestra,* written expressly to illustrate the timbre of each instrument. The work, composed in 1946 and subtitled *Variations and Fugue on a Theme of Purcell,* is based on a dance tune by the great seventeenth-century English composer Henry Purcell. You can hear Purcell's original tune—in a broad triple meter and a minor key—in the online Listening Examples.

In *The Young Person's Guide,* Britten introduces the sound of the entire orchestra playing together, then the sonorities of each instrument family as a

Purcell, *Rondeau*

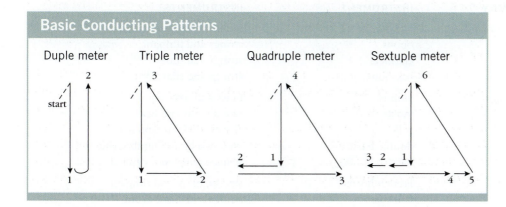

group—woodwinds, strings, brass, percussion—and finally repeats the statement by the full orchestra. With the theme, or principal melody, well in mind, we hear every instrument in order from highest to lowest within each family. Next we encounter variations of the theme, each played by a new instrument (see Listening Guide 1). The work closes with a grand **fugue**, a polyphonic form popular in the Baroque era (1600–1750), which is also based on Purcell's theme. The fugue, like the variations, presents its subject, or theme, in rapid order in each instrument. (For a general discussion of the fugue, see Chapter 24.)

LISTENING GUIDE 1  16:36

Britten: *The Young Person's Guide to the Orchestra (Variations and Fugue on a Theme of Purcell)*

DATE: 1946

BASIS: Dance from Purcell's incidental music to the play *Abdelazar* (*The Moor's Revenge*)

PERFORMED BY: English Chamber Orchestra; Steuart Bedford, conductor

What to Listen For:

Texture Homophonic, focused on the melody (the theme) with accompaniment; polyphonic closing fugue, built on imitation.

Form The main theme is heard throughout a series of variations.

Performing forces Full orchestra, then each of the four instrument families—woodwinds, strings, brass, percussion—with individual instruments within each family taking a turn.

0:00   **I. Theme:** Eight measures in D minor, stated six times to illustrate the orchestral families.

1. Entire orchestra	4. Strings
2. Woodwinds	5. Percussion
3. Brass	6. Entire orchestra

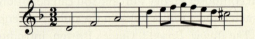

II. Variations: 13 short variations, each illustrating a different instrument.

	VARIATION	FAMILY	SOLO INSTRUMENT	ACCOMPANYING INSTRUMENTS
1:57	1	woodwinds	piccolo, flutes	violins, harp, and triangle
	2		oboes	strings and timpani
	3		clarinets	strings and tuba
	4		bassoons	strings and snare drum
5:00	5	strings	violins	brass and bass drum
	6		violas	woodwinds and brass
	7		cellos	clarinets, violas, and harp
	8		double basses	woodwinds and tambourine
	9		harp	strings, gong, and cymbal
9:34	10	brass	French horns	strings, harp, and timpani
	11		trumpets	strings and snare drum
	12		trombones, tuba	woodwinds and high brass

| 11:53 | 13 | percussion | various | strings |

(Order in which percussion instruments are introduced: timpani, bass drum, and cymbals; timpani, tambourine, and triangle; timpani, snare drum, and wood block; timpani and xylophone; timpani, castanets, and gong; timpani and whip; whole percussion section; xylophone.)

13:47 **III. Fugue:** Subject is based on a fragment of the Purcell theme, played in imitation by each instrument in the same order as the variations.

| Woodwinds:
(highest to lowest) | piccolo
flutes
oboes
clarinets
bassoons |

| Strings:
(highest to lowest) | first violins
second violins
violas
cellos
double basses
harp |

| Brass:
(highest to lowest) | French horns
trumpets
trombones, tuba |

| Percussion: | various |

15:39   Full orchestra at the end with Purcell's theme heard over the fugue.

Gustavo Dudamel (b. 1981), a graduate of the Venezuelan music education system called El Sistema, was appointed conductor of the Los Angeles Philharmonic in 2009 at the age of twenty-seven.

Style and Function of Music in Society

Genre vs. form

Opus number

I n every culture, music is intricately interwoven with the lives and beliefs of its people. Music serves different functions in different societies, though some basic roles are universal. In some cultures, such as in the Western classical tradition, only a few people are involved with the actual performance of music; in others, cooperative work is so much a part of society that the people sing as a group, with each person contributing a separate part to build a complex whole.

There is music for every conceivable occasion, but the specific occasions vary from one culture to another. Thus, musical genres, or categories of repertory, do not necessarily transfer from one society to another, though they may be similar. For example, Japanese *Noh* drama (see opposite) serves essentially the same role as Western opera does. And we can distinguish in most cultures between **sacred music**, for religious purposes, and **secular music**, for entertainment.

It's important to differentiate between genre and form. A **genre** is a more general term that suggests something of the overall character of the work as well as its function. For example, song is a genre, as is **symphony**—usually designating a four-movement orchestral work. As we will see later, each movement of a symphony has a specific internal **form**, or structure. "Symphony" also implies the **medium**, or the specific group that performs the piece—in this case, an orchestra.

Titles for musical compositions occasionally indicate the genre and key: Symphony No. 94 in G Major, by Joseph Haydn, for example. Another way works are identified is through a cataloguing system, often described by **opus number** (*opus* is Latin for "work"; an example is Nocturne in C Minor, Op. 48, No. 1, a piano work by Frédéric Chopin). Other titles are more descriptive, such as *The Nutcracker* (a ballet by the Russian composer Peter Ilyich Tchaikovsky) and *The Trout* (a song by Franz Schubert, an Austrian composer).

KEY POINTS

- Most cultures around the world employ **sacred music** for religious functions, and **secular music** for entertainment and other nonreligious activities.

- There are many **genres,** or categories, of music; some works **cross over** categories, borrowing elements of one genre for use in another.

- The **medium** is the specific group (e.g., orchestra, chorus) that performs a piece.

- Some music is not written down, but is known through **oral transmission.**

- The distinctive features of any artwork make up its **style.** A musical style is created through individual treatment of the basic musical elements.

- We organize styles of artworks into historical periods, each with its own characteristics.

Just as the context for music—when, why, and by whom a piece is performed—varies from culture to culture, so do aesthetic judgments. For example, the Chinese consider a thin, tense vocal tone desirable in their operas, while the Italians prefer a full-throated, robust sound in theirs.

Not all music is written down. Music of most cultures of the world, including some styles of Western music, is transmitted by example or by imitation and is performed from memory. The preservation of music without the aid of written notation is referred to as **oral transmission**. In modern times, music scholars known as ethnomusicologists, who study music in its cultural context, have attempted to "capture" music that had never previously been written down through field recordings.

While we will consider how music operates in several different traditions, our Listening Guides focus primarily on Western art music—that is the notated and **cultivated** music of European and Euro-American society. We often label art music as "classical" or "serious," for lack of better terms. However, the lines that distinguish art music from other kinds can be blurred. **Vernacular** musics (often called "popular" or "traditional," wrongly understood as spontaneously generated by untrained musicians) are essential traditions in their own right, and both rock and especially jazz are believed by many to be new art forms, having already stood the test of time.

In Japanese *Noh* drama, performers often wear symbolic masks.

Note the stylistic differences between paintings of similar subject matter. LEFT: *The Guitar Player*, by **Jan Vermeer** (1632–1675). RIGHT: *The Old Guitar Player*, by **Pablo Picasso** (1881–1973).

An oral music lesson with famed cellist Pablo Casals (1876–1973).

THE CONCEPT OF STYLE

Style may be defined as the characteristic way an artwork is presented. The word may also indicate the creator's personal manner of expression—the distinctive flavor that sets one artist apart from all others. Thus, we speak of the literary style of Dickens or Hemingway, the painting style of Picasso or Rembrandt, or the musical style of Bach or Mozart (compare the paintings on p. 55).

What makes one musical work sound similar to or different from another? It's the style, or individualized treatment of the elements of music. We have seen that Western music is largely a melody-oriented art based on a particular musical system from which the underlying harmonies are also built. Musics of other cultures may sound foreign to our ears, because they are based on entirely different systems, and many do not involve harmony to any great extent. Complex rhythmic procedures and textures set some world musics apart from Western styles, while basic formal considerations—such as repetition, contrast, and variation—bring musics of disparate cultures closer. In short, a style is made up of pitch, time, timbre, and expression, creating a sound that each culture recognizes as its own.

Musical Styles in History

Each historical period has its own stylistic characteristics; although the artists, writers, and composers of a particular era may vary in outlook, they all share certain qualities. Because of this, we can tell at once that a work of art—whether music, poetry, painting, sculpture, or architecture—dates from the Middle Ages or the eighteenth century. The style of a period, then, is the total language of all its artists as they react to the political, economic, religious, and philosophical forces that shape their environment. A knowledge of historical styles will help you place a musical work within the context (time and place) in which it was created.

The timeline opposite shows the generally accepted style periods in the history of Western music. Each represents a conception of form and technique, an ideal of beauty, a manner of expression and performance attuned to the cultural climate of the period—in a word, a style!

WHAT TO LISTEN FOR

Throughout the book, each Listening Guide focuses your attention, and ear, on the most prominent and relevant features of that particular work—in the box labeled "What to Listen For." You may have already tried out Listening Guide 1, for Britten's *Young Person's Guide to the Orchestra* (in Chapter 11). Now, to help you make the most of these guides, let's listen several times to a short dance coming up in Part 5, focusing on specific musical elements each time. The nine relevant elements are listed below; you may want to review them first, either in their respective chapter or chapters (given in parentheses) or in the Glossary (Appendix II).

Melody (Chapter 1)
Rhythm/meter (2)
Harmony (3-4)
Texture (5)
Form (6)
Expression: tempo and dynamics (7)
Text (8)
Timbre (9-10)
Performing forces (9-11)

The *Trepak* is a Russian Cossack dance from the famous ballet *The Nutcracker,* by Peter Ilyich Tchaikovsky. If you recognize the music, you may have heard it in the classic 1940 Disney film *Fantasia* (danced by flowers rather than Russian men), or in the "Victory Fanfare" of the Game Boy version of *Tetris*. This is a late Romantic-era work (composed in 1892), and its musical traits are characteristic of the style of that era. With each listening, we suggest focusing on two or three traits at a time.

1. On your first listening, focus on the **melody** and **rhythm/meter**. Listen for the short melodic phrases, which are treated in descending sequences. Note too that the melody features staccato (short) notes. As for the rhythm and meter, listen for the regularly accented notes that help delineate the dancelike duple meter (the accents come every other measure).

2. On a second listening, consider how **tempo** and **dynamics** as well as **timbre** (tone color) are central to Tchaikovsky's approach to musical expression. The dance begins very fast (*molto vivace*) and, at the end, speeds up with an *accelerando*. These tempos tell us something about the frenetic nature of the dance itself. Sudden dynamic changes (*forte* to *piano,* and *sforzandos*) are also part of the composer's expressive techniques.

A performance of the *Trepak* from *The Nutcracker*, by the Royal Ballet at Covent Garden, London, in 2008.

In the opening and again near the end of the dance, our ear is drawn toward the violins playing the melody; but in the middle, lower-range instruments (strings and woodwinds) take over. Listen also for the unique jingling sound of the tambourine throughout, and the prominent trumpet fanfare in the fast closing.

3. With a third listening, we can now tackle some of the more complex elements in the music: its **form**, **harmony,** and **texture**. Having recognized the change in instruments that play the melody in the middle of the dance, we can identify a basic three-part (ternary), or **A-B-A**, form. Focus on how the harmony changes in these **A** and **B** sections. Both are in a major key, but the middle section (**B**) travels away from the tonic, the home base, to the dominant; the music then returns to the tonic for the last section (**A**), by means of a modulation, a vague shifting of harmony.

    Finally, the texture—how the various lines in the music interact—changes somewhat in this three-part structure as well. In the opening section, the violin melody dominates over a sparse accompaniment in a homophonic texture; but in the middle section, featuring the lower-pitched instruments, there is more activity between the parts (making it contrapuntal) and a swirling accompaniment.

It is these specific characteristics that define the unique style of Tchaikovsky's *Trepak* and set it off from other compositions. The rhythmic treatment and three-part form suggest this work is a dance; and the wide-ranging dynamics and tempos, as well as the performing forces—a large orchestra, with specialized percussion (tambourine) and newer instruments (such as tuba, bass clarinet, and English horn)—help identify the music as late Romantic. Don't worry if you didn't hear these particular new instruments, as their timbres are blended into the overall sound of the rich orchestra.

Although each Listening Guide's composition will feature a unique combination of musical elements, the "What to Listen For" characteristics can help you identify its historical era, genre, or even composer, and allow you to explore similar works that share some of the same traits. These are, in fact, the kinds of music-discovery tools that streaming services such as Pandora, Spotify, and Apple Music employ to provide personalized music recommendations and playlists, based on your listening history.

As you listen to the works featured throughout this book, try to direct your attention to the individual "What to Listen For" elements through multiple listenings, as we did above. In this way, you will enhance your listening experience as well as your understanding of musical styles. We believe this process will contribute greatly to your enjoyment of music—which is the ultimate goal.

Musical Styles in History

Period	Description	Featured Composers
Middle Ages **400–1450**	The earliest notated music; church music prevails; harmony and rhythmic concepts introduced.	Notre Dame school Hildegard of Bingen Raimbaut de Vaqueiras Guillaume de Machaut
Renaissance **1450–1600**	Printing and distribution of music; musical focus moves from church to palace; development of national styles.	Josquin des Prez Giovanni Pierluigi da Palestrina John Farmer Thomas Weelkes
Baroque **1600–1750**	Invention of opera; development of instrumental music and genres; tonal harmony developed.	Claudio Monteverdi Henry Purcell Antonio Vivaldi Johann Sebastian Bach George Frideric Handel
Classical **1750–1825**	Public concerts featured; symphony orchestra flourishes; large-scale compositions developed.	Joseph Haydn Wolfgang Amadeus Mozart Ludwig van Beethoven
Romantic **1820–1900**	Composer as independent artist; rise of virtuoso performer; chromatic harmony and more dissonance featured; programmatic music; nationalism in composition.	Franz Schubert Frédéric Chopin Franz Liszt Fanny Mendelssohn Hensel Hector Berlioz Edvard Grieg Giuseppe Verdi Richard Wagner Johannes Brahms Antonín Dvořák P. I. Tchaikovsky
Post-Romantic and Impressionist (1890–1915)	Modal and exotic scales; music influenced by art and literary movements.	Claude Debussy Maurice Ravel
Early 20th century modernist	Revolutionary concepts in harmony and rhythm; influence of jazz, traditional, and popular music; unusual instrumental combinations; development of recording.	Igor Stravinsky Arnold Schoenberg William Grant Still George Gershwin Aaron Copland Silvestre Revueltas
Later 20th–early 21st century postmodernist	Influence of technology; idiosyncratic approaches to music; expanded instrumental techniques and ranges; global music influences.	John Cage George Crumb Leonard Bernstein John Williams Philip Glass Jennifer Higdon John Adams Tania León

MEDIEVAL / RENAISSANCE

	500	600	700	800	900	1000	1100	1200	1300	1400	1420	1440	1460	1480	1500	1520	1540	1560	1580	1600

COMPOSERS AND WORKS

(**10ᵗʰ century**) *Kyrie*

(**1098–1179**) Hildegard of Bingen
Alleluia, O virga mediatrix

(**1100–1300**) Notre Dame School
Organum

(**1155–1207**) Raimbaut de Vaqueiras
Kalenda maya

(**1300–1377**) Guillaume de Machaut
Ma fin est mon commencement

Josquin des Prez (**c.1450–1521**)
Ave Maria . . . virgo serena

Giovanni Pierluigi da Palestrina (**c. 1525–1594**)
Pope Marcellus Mass

Claudio Monteverdi (**1567–1643**)
Madrigals

John Farmer (**c. 1570–1601**)
Fair Phyllis

	500	600	700	800	900	1000	1100	1200	1300	1400	1420	1440	1460	1480	1500	1520	1540	1560	1580	1600

EVENTS

476 Fall of the Roman Empire

800 Charlemagne crowned first Holy Roman Emperor.

1271 Marco Polo travels to China.

1291 Last Crusade to the Holy Land.

1308 Dante Alighieri begins writing *The Divine Comedy*.

1348 Black Death strikes in Europe.

Gutenberg Bible printed. **1456**

Columbus discovers the New World. **1492**

First music book printed in Italy. **1501**

Michelangelo completes the sculpture *David*. **1504**

Council of Trent begins. **1545**

Elizabeth I crowned in England. **1559**

Shakespeare's *Hamlet* produced. **1602**

Detail from *Adimari Wedding Chest* (c. 1440), by **Giovanni di ser Giovanni Guidi.**

PART 2

The Middle Ages and Renaissance

▶‖ First, listen ...

to the medieval Christmas carol *There Is No Rose of Such Virtue,* and see how many musical traits described in Part 1 you can indentify: for example, the shape of the melodic lines, how the rhythmic patterns are organized into a meter, the quality of the harmony made by the voices, how the form relies on the principles of repetition and contrast, and the texture that arises from the interaction of the voices. Listen several times to try to pick up multiple elements, but don't worry about "getting it right"; this is your first chance to apply these basic principles to an example of medieval/Renaissance music.

LISTENING OBJECTIVES

By the end of Part 2, you will be able to

- distinguish the free-flowing melodic lines in less familiar scales (modes); the hollow-sounding, modal harmonies and cadences in medieval and early Renaissance music; and the fuller sounds resembling major and minor tonality in later Renaissance music.

- recognize how the music of this era follows the words and how the text (whether in English, French, Latin, or other language) helps determine repeated sections of music.

- hear how some of the earliest music (chant) moves with no perceptible pulse (it's nonmetric), while other music moves in a metered pattern (whether triple or duple).

- perceive how the texture becomes more complex as more lines/voices are added, and be able to describe how they interact with each other.

- define some of the main sacred and secular genres (categories of music) in the Middle Ages and Renaissance.

Music as Commodity and Social Activity

> "Nothing exists without music, for the universe is said to have been framed by a kind of harmony of sounds, and heaven itself revolves under the tones of that harmony."
>
> —Isidore of Seville (c. 560–636)

Angel musicians abound in the famous Linaiuoli Altarpiece, an early masterpiece by **Fra Angelico** (c. 1395–1455).

Humans have been using sound to enhance their communication for thousands of years—in fact, some scholars argue that what we call "song" may have been the earliest form of speech. But our story begins when Europeans came up with the idea of putting sound to paper—the concept of musical **notation**, which is not unique to Western culture (musical notation from China dates back at least 2,500 years) but has defined the development of Western music and allowed for its astonishing variety, diffusion, and staying power.

Musical styles that stem from the European tradition are at the core of music-making throughout the world today, a level of influence that surpasses any language or religion. And this is because of notation, which allows us to think of a song or other musical work as a product or commodity to be preserved, taught and learned, bought and sold. Still, in Western culture as in all world cultures, making music is also a social activity that allows individuals to feel closely connected to a group, and to express their feelings both recreationally and spiritually.

Music notation was invented to further the goals of Christian worship, and social music-making was essential to the early Christian church. Therefore, much of the music we still have from the Middle Ages and Renaissance was intended for **sacred** purposes: sounds designed to inspire the faithful to worship. We will be exploring various ways in which these early worship-music traditions expanded and shifted to meet the needs of a changing society.

Despite the predominance of sacred music, more and more through this period we have evidence of **secular** music, social music-making for entertainment and personal expression. It's especially in the secular context that music becomes both a social activity and a commodity item—already in these early centuries of the Western tradition.

FROM ANTIQUITY TO THE MIDDLE OF THINGS

While we believe that many ancient civilizations enjoyed flourishing musical cultures, only a few fragments of their music survive today. We do know that ancient Mediterranean cultures provided the foundation of the Western musical heritage, as well as the traditions that it shares with the Middle East.

The fall of the Roman Empire, commonly set in the year 476 CE, marked the beginning of a thousand-year period usually described as the Middle Ages. The first half of this millennium, from around 500 to 1000, was a period of political and cultural consolidation. During this era, all power flowed from kings, with the approval of the Roman Catholic Church. The struggle between these two centers of power, church and state, is at the core of European history and has resonances to this day. The modern concept of a strong, centralized government as the guardian of law and order is generally credited to Charlemagne (742–814), the celebrated emperor of the Franks. A progressive monarch, Charlemagne encouraged education and left behind him an extensive system of social justice. It was during his reign that Europeans started to make systematic use of music notation.

During the later Middle Ages, from around 1000 to 1450, universities were founded throughout Europe, and cities emerged as centers of art and culture. Literary landmarks such as the *Chanson de Roland* (c. 1100) in France, Dante's *Divine Comedy* (1307) in Italy, and Chaucer's *Canterbury Tales* (1386) in England helped shape their respective languages. This time also witnessed the construction of the great cathedrals, including Notre Dame in Paris, one of the first centers in which **polyphony** (multivoiced music) was notated and integrated into musical worship—an awe-inspiring tribute to divine power.

Reliquary of the emperor Charlemagne in the form of a portrait bust, c. 1350.

MARKETS AND COURTS

In the later Middle Ages, a merchant class that drew its wealth from trade and commerce arose outside of feudal society. Although travel was perilous—the roads were plagued by robbers and the seas by pirates—each region of Europe exchanged its natural resources for those it lacked: the plentiful timber and furs of Scandinavia were traded for English wool and cloth manufactured in Flanders; England wanted German silver and, above all, French and Italian wine; and European goods of all kinds flowed through the seaport of Venice to Constantinople in exchange for Eastern luxuries. Musicians and their works also moved along the trade routes: music became both a necessity (for worship activities) and a desirable recreational ornament, a crucial commodity in the economies of Europe.

In an era of violence brought on by deep-set religious beliefs, knights embarked on holy—and bloody—Crusades to capture the Holy Land from the Muslims. Although feudal society was male-dominated and idealized the figure of the fearless warrior, the status of women was raised by the universal cult of Mary, mother of Christ (see illustrations on p. 86), and by the concepts of chivalry that arose among the knights. In the songs of the court minstrels, women were adored with a fervor that laid the foundation for our concept of romantic love. This poetic attitude found its perfect symbol in the faithful knight who worshiped his lady from afar and was inspired by her to deeds of great daring and self-sacrifice, and led to the first great flowering of secular music written in the **vernacular** (the language of the people, as opposed to **Latin**, the formal language of the church and the sacred tradition).

Most prominent in this secular tradition were the **troubadours** of Languedoc (what is now southern France) and the **trouvères** of northern France, who not only left us the first extensive notated tradition of love song, but also helped to introduce increasingly complex instruments into the Western tradition. Many instruments and song styles were adapted from the highly sophisticated Middle

In His Own Words

66 We may compare the best form of government to the most harmonious piece of music; the oligarchic and despotic to the most violent tunes; and the democratic to the soft and gentle airs."

—Aristotle (384–322 BCE)

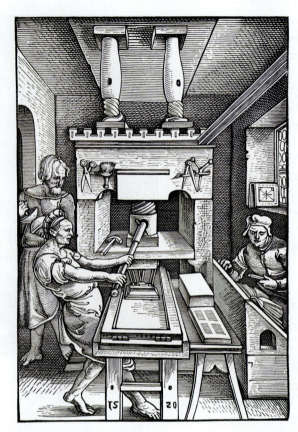

The printing press, developed by Johannes Gutenberg (c. 1400-1468), brought books to a wide readership throughout Europe.

Eastern traditions of the time (see illustration below): a number of European courts (notably the court of Alfonso the Wise in what is now Spain) maintained good private relations with Muslim princes, despite their public rejection of Islam.

LOOKING OUT AND LOOKING IN

Though there was significant cultural continuity from the 1400s into the 1500s, a number of important new concerns arose in the early part (1450–1520) of the time frame we now call the Renaissance. Europeans embarked (with the help of the newly developed compass) on voyages of discovery that opened up new horizons, both external and internal. Explorers of this age, in search of a new trade route to the riches of China and the Indies, stumbled on North and South America. During the course of the sixteenth and seventeenth centuries, these new lands became increasingly important to European treasuries and society.

After the fall of Constantinople to the Turks (1453), ancient Greek and Roman writings, many of which had been tightly guarded by the church during the Middle Ages, were brought to Europe in increasing numbers. They were distributed ever more widely through the medium of print, the European introduction of which (c. 1455) is generally credited to the German goldsmith and inventor Johannes Gutenberg. These writings from classical antiquity encouraged a tendency for individuals to look within, at their personal thoughts, beliefs, and reactions. While this led to increasing interest in human (secular) rather than divine (sacred)

In this miniature from the *Prayer Book* of Alfonso the Wise, King David is playing a rebec, in the manner of the Middle Eastern rabab.

concerns, far-reaching religious reformations of the 1500s, both Protestant and Catholic, also gave this inward exploration a religious grounding.

The ideals that the ancient writings exemplified began to have a great influence in architecture, painting, and sculpture. Instead of the Gothic cathedrals and fortified castles of the medieval world, lavish Renaissance palaces and spacious villas were built according to the harmonious proportions of the classical style, which strove for order and balance. This phenomenon first came to flower in Italy, the nation that stood closest to the classical Roman culture. As a result, the great names we associate with its painting and sculpture are predominantly Italian: Botticelli, Leonardo da Vinci, Michelangelo, and Titian. The nude human form, denied or covered for centuries, was revealed as a thing of beauty and used for anatomical study. Painters also began exploring the beauties of nature and conforming to the laws of perspective and composition.

In *The Concert* (c. 1530–40), three ladies perform a French secular song with voice, flute, and lute. The Flemish artist is known only as the Master of the Female Half-Lengths.

MUSICIANS IN MEDIEVAL AND RENAISSANCE SOCIETY

Musicians were supported by the chief institutions of their society—the church, city, and state, as well as royal and aristocratic courts. They found employment as choirmasters, singers, organists, instrumentalists, copyists, composers, teachers, instrument builders, and, by the sixteenth century, music printers. There was a corresponding growth in a number of supporting musical institutions: church choirs and schools, music-publishing houses, civic wind bands. And there were increased opportunities for apprentices to study with master singers, players, and instrument builders. A few women can be identified as professional musicians in the Renaissance era, earning their living as court singers.

The rise of the merchant class in the later Middle Ages brought with it a new group of music patrons. This development was paralleled by the emergence, among the cultivated middle and upper classes, of amateur musicians—men and women alike—who sang secular songs (chansons and madrigals) and played simple dances on instruments. When the system for printing from movable type was successfully adapted to music in the early sixteenth century, printed music books became available and affordable. As a result, music literacy spread dramatically.

The concerns of musicians surrounding worship and play, individuality and community, and music both as commodity and as social activity were grounded in the historical circumstances in which they lived. But such issues also resonate with ways in which music is still enmeshed in culture to this day. In the next few chapters, we will examine how these long-standing concerns became rooted in Western society.

Voice and Worship: Tradition and Individuality in Medieval Chant

Monasteries

▶‖ **First, listen …**

to Hildegard's *Alleluia, O virga mediatrix*, focusing solely on the movement of the music. How would you describe the way the melody moves?

Voices raised in song as people connect to a spiritual power: wherever you are from, you may have encountered this in your own community, whether it's a church choir, an Islamic call to prayer, or a cantor addressing a synagogue. This is one of the most widespread purposes of music throughout world cultures—and in medieval Europe, communities of men and women dedicated themselves fully to sung prayer, seeking the salvation of humanity through music.

The culture of this period was shaped in large part by the rise of **monasteries**. It was the members of these religious communities who preserved the learning of the ancient world and transmitted it, through their manuscripts, to later European scholars. Because music was at the core of Christian prayer and could effectively enhance the church service, the religious communities supported it extensively. Women as well as men played a role in preserving knowledge and cultivating music for the church, since nuns figured prominently in church society.

LIFE IN THE MEDIEVAL MONASTERY

Both men and women in the Middle Ages withdrew from secular society into the shelter of monasteries, where they devoted themselves to prayer, scholarship, preaching, charity, or healing the sick, depending on the religious order they

KEY POINTS

- Sung worship is a shared feature among many world cultures, allowing for a more intense personal and collective connection with the divine.

- Religious communities (monasteries) fostered the extensive development of worship music, starting in the Middle Ages.

- The music of the early Christian church, called **plainchant** (or just **chant**), features monophonic,

nonmetric melodies set in one of the church **modes**, or scales.

- Chant melodies fall into three categories (**syllabic, neumatic, melismatic**), based on how many notes are set to each syllable of text.

- The expressive music of Hildegard of Bingen exemplifies the tension between an individual, creative response to divine inspiration and community expectations of worship.

joined. Parents might choose a religious life for a child if they had no land holdings to give a son or no dowry for a daughter's wedding. Others might take this spiritual path as an adult—a widow who did not wish to remarry or a young woman who longed for the education that cloistered life provided.

A life devoted to the church was not an easy one; the discipline was arduous. A typical day began at 2:00 or 3:00 A.M. with the celebration of the first of the daily services, the reading of lessons, and the singing of psalms. Each day in the church calendar had its own ritual and its own order of prayers. The members of the community interspersed their religious duties with work in the fields or the library, or producing items that could be sold—wine, beer, or cheese—thus bringing in revenue to the order. Many in religious life dedicated themselves to writing and preserving knowledge from earlier times. Such a person was Hildegard of Bingen, one of the most remarkable women of the Middle Ages, who was renowned in her day as a poet and prophet and whose serenely beautiful music has regained popularity in recent years.

In this fourteenth-century manuscript illumination, clerics celebrate a Mass dedicated to the Virgin Mary.

PLAINCHANT: MUSIC OF THE CHURCH

The early music of the Christian church is testimony to the highly spiritual nature of the Middle Ages. **Plainchant** consists of a single-line melody; it is thus monophonic in texture, lacking either harmony or counterpoint. Its freely flowing vocal line subtly follows the inflections of the Latin text and is generally free from regular accent. These beautiful melodies, shaped in part by Greek, Hebrew, and Syrian influences, represent the starting point of artistic creativity in Western music. In time, it became necessary to assemble the ever-growing body of music into an organized **liturgy**, a term that refers to the set order of church services and the structure of each service. The task extended over several generations, though tradition often credits Pope Gregory the Great (r. 590–604) with codifying these melodies, known today as **Gregorian chant**.

Liturgy

The Gregorian melodies, numbering more than three thousand, form an immense body of music, nearly all of it anonymous. In fact, tradition held that Pope Gregory had received the melodies of "true prayer" directly from the Holy Spirit in the form of a dove whispering into his ear (see p. 68)—therefore, in a very real sense, those who sang Gregorian plainchant in the Middle Ages believed it to have been composed by a divine and not human mind.

Gregorian chant avoids wide leaps, allowing its gentle contours to create a kind of musical speech. Chant melodies fall into three main classes, according to the way they are set to the text: **syllabic**, with one note sung to each syllable of text; **neumatic**, generally with small groups of three to five notes sung to a syllable; and **melismatic**, with many notes set to a single syllable (see chart on p. 35). The melismatic style, which descended from the elaborate improvisations heard in Middle Eastern music, became an expressive feature of Gregorian chant and exerted a strong influence on subsequent Western music.

Melodic contours

From Gregorian chant through music of the Renaissance, Western music used a variety of scale patterns, or **modes**. These preceded major and minor scales (scales are also types of modes), which are characterized by a strong pull toward a

Modes

tonic note; the earlier modes lacked this sense of attraction. You may find that the melodic shapes of medieval modal music (and the examples we will consider) seem unfamilar. This is because for those of us in Western culture, **tonal** melody and harmony are deeply ingrained in our musical experience.

THE MASS

Ever since the Middle Ages, chanted prayers have been central to two types of services: the daily **Offices**—a series of services celebrated in religious communities at various hours of the day—and the **Mass**, a reenactment of Christ's Last Supper with his disciples. The Mass is the primary (and most solemn) ritual of the Roman Catholic Church, and the one generally attended by public worshippers.

The prayers that make up the Mass (its liturgy) fall into two categories: the **Proper**, texts that vary from day to day throughout the church year, depending on the feast being celebrated; and the **Ordinary**, texts that remain the same in every Mass. (See the chart on p. 91.) Gregorian melodies remain central to the celebration of the Mass. Until the middle of the twentieth century, most of the Mass text was in Latin, the language of the ancient Romans, which continued to be a shared language of learning for Europeans through the Middle Ages and Renaissance and beyond.

A Gregorian Melody: *Kyrie*

We will consider one of many settings of the **Kyrie**, the first item in the Ordinary (fixed portion) of the Mass, as an excellent example of the flowing melodic structure of Gregorian chant (LG 2). The text of the Kyrie is a Greek prayer for mercy taken from the central-Mediterranean Christian tradition. Its three-part form

Manuscript illumination of Pope Gregory the Great dictating to his scribe Peter. A dove, representing the Holy Spirit, sits on his shoulder.

A Kyrie chant in Gregorian notation, from the *Liber usualis*.

consists of nine invocations to God: three of "Kyrie eleison" ("Lord, have mercy upon us"), three of "Christe eleison" ("Christ, have mercy upon us"), and again three of "Kyrie eleison." The structure is symbolic: the number three evokes the Trinity—Father, Son, and Holy Spirit—and thus represents perfect unity.

The melody of this *Kyrie* moves freely in waves; its range is narrow at first, but grows slightly wider and higher in the second and third sections. You will hear that it's sung *a cappella* (voices alone) and in an **antiphonal** manner, alternating between two groups of singers. At first, they sing only a few notes per syllable (a neumatic text setting); as the second and third phrases grow longer, however, some syllables are stretched over many notes, producing a melismatic setting.

A cappella, **antiphonal**

A Song for Worship by Hildegard

Hildegard set many of her own texts to music; her poetry is characterized by brilliant imagery and creative language. Some of her songs celebrate the lives of local saints such as Saint Rupert, the patron of her monastery, while others praise the Virgin Mary, comparing her to a blossoming flower or branch and celebrating her purity. Our example is an *Alleluia* (LG 2), derived from the Hebrew words for "Praise [be] to God"; to this day, some version of the "Alleluia" is used in most Christian communities to express joyful celebration. Hildegard wrote this chant for a specific occasion—a feast day for the Virgin Mary. Might Hildegard have found particular inspiration as a woman writing in honor of a woman?

The chant is in three parts, beginning and ending with the word "Alleluia" (generally sung with a solo opening phrase and choral response) and featuring a **verse** in the middle, sung by a single leader. Hildegard elaborates some words with melismas, especially in the last line of the verse, describing the Virgin's purity. Other elaborations include distinctive upward leaps at the beginning of phrases and soaring lines in a high range.

In Her Own Words

❝ The words I speak come from no human mouth; I saw and heard them in visions sent to me. . . . I have no confidence in my own capacities—I reach out my hand to God that He may carry me along as a feather borne weightlessly by the wind."

—Hildegard of Bingen

Hildegard of Bingen (1098–1179)

Hildegard of Bingen was the daughter of a noble German couple who promised her, as their tenth child, to the service of the church as a tithe (the practice of giving one-tenth of what one owns). Raised by a religious recluse from age eight, she lived in a stone cell with one window and took her vows at the age of fourteen. From childhood, Hildegard experienced visions, which intensified in later life. She was reportedly able to foretell the future.

Around the year 1150, Hildegard founded a monastery in Rupertsberg (near Bingen), in Germany. Her reported miracles and prophecies made her famous through-

out Europe: popes, kings, and priests sought her advice on political and religious issues. Sainthood came late for Hildegard; she was canonized only in 2012 by Pope Benedict XVI. Her highly original compositional style resembles Gregorian chant but is full of expressive leaps and melismas that clearly convey the meaning of the words.

MAJOR WORKS: A collection of poetry and visions entitled *Scivias* (*Know the Ways*) • A volume of religious poetry set to music (*Symphony of the Harmony of Celestial Revelations*) • A sung morality play (*The Play of the Virtues*) • Scientific and medical writings.

Because we know that Hildegard composed this praise song, it is *not* "Gregorian" chant—it is not part of the established repertory of praise song that was sanctioned in her day. The notion that *new* praise song could be used in the liturgy was very controversial at the time. How could a mere human come up with prayer melodies that would be appropriate for communication with God? This was all the more complicated for Hildegard, since many in the church held that women were unworthy to aspire to connection with the divine. She had to strike a balance between claiming divine inspiration and not appearing to be heretical or even devilish.

LISTENING GUIDE 2

Two Examples of Chant

Gregorian Chant: *Kyrie*   1:59

DATE: 10th century

GENRE: Kyrie plainchant, from the Ordinary of the Mass

PERFORMED BY: Schola Cantorum of Amsterdam; Wim van Gerven, director

What to Listen For

Melody Conjunct line in a small range, with wave-like motion.

Rhythm Free and nonmetric, following the flow of the words.

Texture Monophonic (a single line).

Form Repeated musical phrases that follow the text repetitions.

	TEXT	TRANSLATION	PERFORMANCE
0:00	Kyrie eleison.	Lord, have mercy upon us.	Sung three times.
0:27	Christe eleison	Christ, have mercy upon us.	Sung three times.
1:10	Kyrie eleison.	Lord, have mercy upon us.	Sung three times, with a varied final statement.

Hildegard of Bingen: *Alleluia, O virga mediatrix* (*Alleluia, O mediating branch*)   3:19

DATE: Late 12th century

GENRE: Alleluia, from the Proper of the Mass on feasts for the Virgin Mary

PERFORMED BY: Discantus; Brigitte Lesne, director

What to Listen For

Melody Unaccompanied conjunct line, with some expressive leaps and melismas.

Form Three-part structure ("Alleluia"-verse-"Alleluia").

Expression Dramatic leaps of a fifth, with high-range climaxes on important words.

Performing forces *A cappella* choir (voices alone), alternating between the soloist and the choir singing in unison.

TEXT	TRANSLATION	PERFORMANCE
0:00 Alleluia.	Alleluia.	Choral statement, very melismatic.
Verse		
0:31 O virga mediatrix	O mediating branch	Solo verse, with several melismas (sung by more than one singer on our recording).
sancta viscera tua mortem superaverunt,	Your holy flesh has overcome death,	Higher range, with neumatic text setting.
et venter tuus omnes creaturas illuminavit	and your womb has illuminated all creatures	
in pulchro flore de suavissima integritate	through the beautiful flower of your tender purity	
clausi pudoris tui orto.	that sprang from your chastity.	Melismatic at the end.
2:44 Alleluia.	Alleluia.	Choral response repeats the opening.

Expressive leap of a rising fifth and melisma on "mortem" (death):

mor - - - tem

▶|◀ **Reflect**

How did you respond to *Alleluia* after reading about where and by whom it was performed? Imagine the setting: how do you think the non-metric flow of the music might have enhanced the religious experience?

YOUR TURN TO EXPLORE

Consider how worship music is used today—popular styles such as Contemporary Christian or Christian Rap, among others. How do modern experiences of singing to communicate with the divine compare with the Hildegard example?

Storytelling Through Song: Troubadours and Medieval Court Culture

▶‖ **First, listen . . .**

to the secular song *Kalenda maya,* and focus on its structure. Can you hear the repeated music for each verse? Can you hear repeated music within each verse? How would you describe the form of the song?

The medieval German courtly love poet Heinrich von Meissen, called Frauenlob (champion of ladies), is pictured here with his musicians.

You have probably experienced the direct impact of a singer telling his or her emotional story with a simple melody and unobtrusive instrumental accompaniment; it's one of the more compelling images of Western musical culture, and indeed of many world cultures across millennia. It's therefore not surprising that the earliest written records we have in the West of secular music (that is to say, music not designed for worship) are by poet-musicians. These singer-songwriters continued unwritten traditions from centuries before *their* time, and helped to shape the conventions of song text and melody that continue to ours. We will focus on a musician from the songwriting tradition of Occitania, corresponding to present-day southern France: the troubadour Raimbaut de Vaqueiras.

MEDIEVAL MINSTRELS AND COURT MUSICIANS

Alongside the learned music of the cathedrals and choir schools grew a popular repertory of songs and dances that reflected every aspect of medieval life. Some musicians lived on the fringes of society, wandering among the courts and towns and entertaining audiences with juggling and other tricks as well

KEY POINTS

- Religious wars (the Crusades) and medieval explorations enabled an exchange of musical instruments and theoretical ideas about music between European and Asian cultures.

- Secular music arose in courts and was performed by aristocratic **troubadours** and **trouvères** in France, and by wandering minstrels in cities.

- Song texts focused on idealized love and the values of chivalry (a code of behavior).

- Songs were sung monophonically and played with improvised instrumental accompaniment. One popular type of dance song was called an **estampie**.

as songs and dances. While we know of their existence through descriptive accounts, their compositions have not survived, since they most likely didn't write down their music.

On a higher social level were the poet-musicians who flourished at the various courts of Europe and did write down their songs, using the notation systems that were being developed for plainchant. Those who lived in the region of southern France known as Occitania called themselves **troubadour** (or, in the case of women, **trobairitz**); those in northern France called themselves **trouvère**. Both terms mean the same thing: finders or inventors (in musical terms, composers). Similar terms were given to singer-songwriters in other regions of Europe. Some songs are attributed to members of the aristocracy and even royalty—among them King Richard the Lionheart of England, whose mother, the legendary Eleanor of Aquitaine (c. 1122–1204), presided over a famous court of poet-musicians.

Music in the singer-songwriter traditions accompanied dancing, banquets, and after-dinner entertainment at medieval courts. It was central to ceremonies, tournaments, civic processions, and military campaigns; music inspired warriors departing on the Crusades and welcomed them on their return. The poems ranged from simple ballads to love songs, political and moral ditties, war songs, chronicles of the Crusades, laments, and dance songs. They praised the virtues of the ruling classes in this age of chivalry: valor, honor, nobility of character, devotion to an ideal, and the quest for perfect love.

Like so many popular songs today, many of the lyrics described a man's unrequited, or unconsummated, passion. The object of his desire was generally unattainable, either because of her higher rank or because she was already wed to another; such love songs expressed idealized objectification-from-afar rather than mutually consensual tenderness. A few of them, attributed to women poet-musicians, express a female point of view—indicating that the theme of intense unrequited love was perceived as especially appealing to listeners, again a tendency that has lasted through the centuries.

In this thirteenth-century manuscript illumination, a French minstrel recites a poem to the lady Blanche of Castile, wife of King Louis VIII of France.

Raimbaut de Vaqueiras and the Troubadour Tradition

Raimbaut de Vaqueiras typifies the tradition of the courtly troubadour. Of his extant works, *Kalenda maya* (*The First of May*) is the most famous. This is a love song addressed to a noble lady—specifically Beatrice, daughter of his patron Boniface of Montferrat; the text celebrates the return of spring but also confirms the poet's pledge of honor, love, and service to the lady (LG 3).

Unlike in many songs we will hear later, the lines of the poem (and therefore the musical phrases) are irregular in length. The poet compares his devotion to that of well-known lovers (Eric and Enide) in an ancient epic poem; and at the end, he identifies the work as an **estampie** (estampida), a sung dance form common in late medieval France. The melody is in three sections, each of which is repeated, and the overall form is **strophic**—meaning the same melody is repeated with every stanza. Notice how the tune is balanced by phrases rising upward at the beginning and downward at the closing.

In His Own Words

❝ I have served you . . . with a glad heart; I have wooed ladies with you; and I have ridden at your side at war. . . . All good usage rules in your court: munificence and courting, elegant clothing and handsome armor, trumpets and games and viols and songs.❞

—Raimbaut de Vaqueiras

Medieval musicians playing a lute and nakers, both instruments of Arabic origin.

On our recording, we hear the dance version first, with a **rebec** (an early version of the violin; see p. 64) playing the tune, accompanied by a **pipe** (a three-holed, end-blown flute), **guitarra moresca** (a strummed string instrument introduced into Spain by the Moors), and small drums known as **nakers**. Not only the instruments but also the improvisational style and structure of *Kalenda maya* echo the sounds of Middle Eastern music, which Raimbaut certainly heard on his brave quest to the East.

The medieval manuscripts of *Kalenda maya* provide the poem, the melody, and an ambiguous indication of rhythm; notation had not yet become standardized. In other performances, you may hear the song in duple rather than triple meter, depending on the musicians' decision about the best "flow" for the music. Further, the original notation gives no indication of instrumental accompaniment: what we hear in performance comes from the historical research and creativity of

This French manuscript shows Raimbaut de Vaqueiras armed for battle.

Raimbaut de Vaqueiras (c. 1155–1207)

According to his *vida,* or biography written in the language of the troubadour, Raimbaut was of humble origin, the son of a "poor knight" from Provence, in southern France. As a young man, he entered the service of Marquis Boniface I of Montferrat, whose court was in northwestern Italy; he was later knighted for saving the life of his patron in a battle in Sicily. When Montferrat set off in 1202 on the Fourth Crusade to the Holy Land, Raimbaut did not accompany him, but he later joined the forces in Constantinople, where he wrote a famous epic describing the colorful events. It's likely that he was killed in battle there, alongside his patron. Thirty-five poems by Raimbaut survive, of which seven preserve the music as well.

twenty-first-century musicians. Something similar is true of many of the songs we find most meaningful today: the text and melody may be predominant in our minds, but the singer-songwriters and their collaborators carefully build a web of musical texture and timbre around them to intensify the effect on our emotions.

LISTENING GUIDE 3

 2:26

Raimbaut de Vaqueiras: *Kalenda maya (The First of May)*

DATE: Late 12th century

GENRE: Estampie (troubadour dance song)

PERFORMED BY: Martin Best Ensemble

What to Listen For

Melody A mostly conjunct line in a small range (an octave) and wavelike motion.

Rhythm Performed in a dance-like triple meter; other rhythmic interpretations are possible.

Form Strophic song: an instrumental (dance) introduction followed by four verses; the dance and verses all have the same music, three repeated phrases (**A-A-B-B-C-C**).

Performing forces Solo singer accompanied by a bowed string instrument (rebec), a strummed guitar, a pipe (three-holed end-blown flute), and drums (nakers).

Instrumental dance: Entire melody played once (**A-A-B-B-C-C**)

0:00	Solo rebec (phrase **A**).
0:07	Accompaniment with strummed guitar (on repeat of **A**).
0:12	Hand drum (nakers) accompaniment enters (on new phrase, **B**). Melody continues through phrase **C**, with more complex rhythms in the accompaniment; flutelike pipe enters at the end with an ostinato figure.

0:28   **Stanza 1,** with voice

Kalenda maya.	**A**
ni fueills de faia	
ni chans d'auzell ni flors de glaia	
non es qe m plaia,	**A**
pros dona gala	
tro q'un i snell mes sagier aia	
del vostre bell cors, qi.m retraia	**B**
plazer novell q'amors m'atraia	**B**
e jaia e.m traia vas vos	**C**
dona veraia.	
e chaia de plaia .lgelos.	**C**
anz qe.m n'estraia.	

Neither May Day nor the beech tree's leaves nor the song of birds nor gladiolus flowers are pleasing to me, noble and vivacious lady, until I receive a swift messenger from your fair person to tell me of some new pleasure that love brings me; and may I be joined to you and drawn toward you, perfect lady; and may the jealous fall stricken before I must leave you.

continued on next page

Stanza 2

0:56   Mabell'amia, / par Dieu non sia / qe ja.l gelos de mon danria, . . .

My sweet beloved, for the sake of God, may the jealous one never laugh at my pain, for his jealousy would be very costly if it were to separate two such lovers: for I would never be joyful again, nor would joy be of any benefit to me without you; I would set out on such a road that no one would ever see me again; on that day would I die, worthy lady, that I lost you.

Stanza 3

1:23   Con er perduda, / ni m'er renduda / donna, s'enanz non l'ai aguda? . . .

How shall my lady be lost, or restored to me, if she not yet be mine? For a man or woman is not a lover just by thinking so. But when a suitor is accepted as a lover, the reputation that he gains is greatly enhanced, and the attractive appearance causes much stir: but I have not held you naked nor conquered you in any other sense; I have only desired you and believed in you, without any further encourgement.

Stanza 6 (stanzas 4 and 5 not recorded)

1:52   Dona grazida, / qecs lauz'e crida / vostra valor q'es abellida . . .

Worthy lady, everyone praises and proclaims your merit which is so pleasing: and whoever would forget you places little value on life; therefore I worship you, distinguished lady, for I have singled you out as the most pleasing and the best, accomplished in worth, and I have courted you and served you better than Eric did Enide. Lord Engles [Boniface, marquis of Montferrat], I have constructed and completed the estampida.

▶│◀ **Reflect**

How do the instruments contribute to this mono-phonic song? Consider whether *Kalenda maya* seems more like a dance or a vocal song to you, and why.

YOUR TURN TO EXPLORE

Find an example of a stanza-based (strophic) song performed by a single individual—many contemporary singer-songwriters take this approach, but so do folk traditions of the United States and around the world. Pay attention to how (or whether) the singer changes her or his delivery in each stanza—through the melody, dynamics, vocal timbre, accompanying instruments, or other means. How does the musical delivery suit the text and implicit message of each individual stanza? How does it affect the impact of the song's overall story?

CHAPTER 15

Symbols and Puzzles: Machaut and the Medieval Mind

▶‖ First, listen …

to the medieval song *Ma fin est mon commencement*, and focus on the three vocal lines. Do the melodies seem equally matched to you, or is one more important than the others? How would you describe the interaction of the vocal lines in this song?

The Sphinx's riddle, Fermat's last theorem, cryptography, the "Da Vinci Code": we humans are fascinated by riddles and puzzles, maybe because they challenge us to think of possibilities beyond our current understanding. In the Western tradition, music has been linked with mathematics and geometry since antiquity. Ancient Greek mathematician Pythagoras was renowned for his musical experiments. In medieval times, the four topics (Quadrivium) considered essential to education were music, mathematics, geometry, and astronomy. Since then, musicians have remained involved in exploring the mathematical or geometrical implications of their art and conveying puzzles through sound.

The courtly love song tradition of the troubadours and trouvères continued into the early 1300s. Around the same time, musicians were experimenting with improvised polyphony: to make plainchant more grand, they added a second and even third simultaneous melody, following specific rules. As these simultaneous melodies became more elaborate, they were written down rather than added on the spot, and were eventually used in secular music as well.

In His Own Words

❝ Which creature walks on four legs in the morning, two legs in the afternoon, and three legs in the evening?"

—The Sphinx of Thebes

KEY POINTS

- Guillaume de Machaut was a poet-composer of the French **Ars nova** (new art) who wrote sacred music and polyphonic **chansons** (secular songs) set to fixed text forms (**rondeau, ballade, virelai**).

- Machaut's chanson *Ma fin est mon commencement* employs a palindromic form and an enigmatic text to display compositional craft and challenge the listener to careful listening and thinking.

MACHAUT AND THE FRENCH *ARS NOVA*

A polyphonic chanson is performed with voices and lute in this miniature representing the Garden of Love, from a Flemish manuscript of *Le Roman de la Rose* (c. 1500).

European contacts with Eastern cultures, along with developments in feudal social structure, inspired new concepts of life, art, and beauty. These changes were reflected in the musical style known as *Ars nova* (new art), which appeared in the early 1300s in France, and soon thereafter in Italy. The music of the French *Ars nova,* more refined and complex than music of the *Ars antiqua* (old art), which it displaced, ushered in developments in rhythm, meter, harmony, and counterpoint that transformed the art of music.

At the same time, writers such as Petrarch, Boccaccio, and Chaucer were turning from otherworldly ideals to human subjects; painters soon discovered the beauty of nature and the attractiveness of the human form. Similarly, composers like the French master Machaut turned increasingly from religious to secular themes. The influence of this great poet-composer was far-reaching, his music and poetry admired long after his death. He was also the first composer to self-consciously collect his works and leave them for posterity.

Chanson

Machaut's music introduced a new freedom of rhythm characterized by gentle syncopations and the interplay of duple and triple meters. In his secular works, he favored the **chanson**, which was generally set to a French courtly love poem written in one of several fixed text forms. These poetic forms— the **rondeau**, **ballade**, and **virelai**— established the musical repetition scheme of the chansons.

We will hear a rondeau by Machaut (LG 4) that presents us with both an enigmatic text and a hidden musical structure involving palindromes, words or phrases that read the same backward or forward (in music, this is referred to as retrograde movement). Machaut's text reiterates the refrain "My end is my beginning and my beginning is my end," a sentiment found in several biblical passages (e.g.,

Guillaume de Machaut (c. 1300–1377)

Machaut was the foremost poet-composer of the *Ars nova.* He took holy orders at an early age but worked much of his life at various French courts, including that of Charles, duke of Normandy, who subsequently became king of France.

Machaut's double career as cleric and courtier inspired him to write both religious and secular music. His own poetry embraces the ideals of medieval chivalry. One of his writings, a long autobiographical poem of more than 9,000 lines in rhymed couplets, tells the platonic love story of the aging Machaut and a young girl named Peronne. The two exchanged poems and letters, some of which the composer set to music. Machaut spent his final years as a priest and canon at the Cathedral of Reims, admired as the greatest musician and poet of the time.

MAJOR WORKS: Motets, chansons (both monophonic and polyphonic) • A polyphonic Mass (*Messe de Notre Dame*), one of the earliest complete settings of the Ordinary of the Mass.

LISTENING GUIDE 4   5:39

Machaut: *Ma fin est mon commencement*
(*My end is my beginning*)

DATE: Mid-14th century

GENRE: Polyphonic chanson (rondeau)

PERFORMED BY: Hilliard Ensemble; Paul Hillier, conductor

What to Listen For

Harmony Thin, sometimes hollow-sounding harmony; sections begin and end on octaves (same pitch).

Texture Three independent voices in mostly non-imitative polyphony.

Form Two sections (A and B) in a rondeau structure, performed ABaAabAB (uppercase for repeated refrain text, lowercase for new verses); the voices move in a palindrome, turning backward between the A and B sections.

Text Cryptic text that signals the retrograde (backward) movement of the palindrome.

	A SECTION		**B SECTION**
Triplum			
Cantus			
Tenor			

A SECTION	**B SECTION**
1, 4, 7: Ma fin est mon . . .	2, 8: Et mon commencement . . .
3: Est teneüre . . .	
5: Mes tiers . . .	6: Se retrograde . . .

		TEXT		**TRANSLATION**
0:00	Refrain	1. Ma fin est mon commencement	A	My end is my beginning
0:42		2. Et mon commencement ma fin	B	and my beginning my end
1:23	Partial verse	3. Est teneüre vraiement.	a	and my true tenor.
2:05	Partial refrain	4. Ma fin est mon commencement.	A	My end is my beginning.
2:47	Verse	5. Mes tiers chans trois fois seulement	a	My third part three times only
		6. Se retrograde et einsi fin.	b	moves backward and so ends.
4:10	Refrain	7. Ma fin est mon commencement	A	My end is my beginning
		8. Et mon commencement ma fin.	B	and my beginning my end.

Ecclesiastes 1:9–10: "The thing that hath been is that which shall be, and that which is done is that which shall be done. There is nothing new under the sun"). Thus, when we investigate the puzzles in Machaut's chanson, we must consider that their purpose was not merely to amuse but to carry a religious connotation as well.

As a priest and a canon at the Reims Cathedral, Machaut was certainly familiar with the famous octagonal labyrinth or maze built into the floor of this church, and with the ritual processions held on Easter and other holy days that traversed

The octagonal maze in the marble floor of the Cathedral of Amiens in France (1288) is similar to the one Machaut knew in Reims, which is now destroyed.

the maze, moving to the center and back, with retrograde motion in each direction symbolic of Christ's path through hell to resurrection. With this insight, we can appreciate all the more the palindromic structure of *Ma fin est mon commencement*, in which the two upper voices trade parts in retrograde at the center of the work (the cantus B section is the triplum A section in retrograde; the triplum B section is the cantus A section in retrograde), while the bottom voice, the Tenor, is a retrograde of itself at the midpoint. Although this musical puzzle cannot be easily heard, Machaut provides clues to its structure in his text.

Similar elements of balance and symmetry can be found in his other works as well. Indeed, the secular works of Machaut and his contemporaries in the *Ars nova* reflect a growing interest in both regularity and complexity of musical patterns. These sonic puzzles often require the listener to focus carefully, and listen several times to understand the nuances of both craft and expression. Like all puzzles, they engage the brain in novel ways, and feed our human desire for subtlety and complexity.

▶|◀ Reflect

After learning about the complexities of this polyphonic song—its text, musical form, and deeper meaning— did you hear the individual vocal lines differently when you listened again? How do you think listeners at a medieval court might have reacted to the song?

YOUR TURN TO EXPLORE

Many composers have created music that uses symbols, ciphers, or puzzles in either its construction or its text. Find a couple of examples (you might search for "canon," "palindrome," or "puzzle" together with a composer's name) and compare them. Can you hear the different elements come together? If a listener can't readily hear the construction of the puzzle, what might be its expressive purpose in the composer's mind?

Singing in Friendship: The Renaissance Madrigal

▶❙ First, listen ...

to *Fair Phyllis*, and pay careful attention to the words, which are clearly heard in this setting. Can you identify any places where the music "paints" the words? If so, how does this affect your listening experience?

When friends get together to celebrate, singing can't be far behind. Spontaneous social song is often monophonic throughout world cultures: everyone sings the same melody (think of "Happy Birthday"). Western culture has also developed a complex and widespread tradition of social part song, in which separate musical lines are combined into a harmonious whole— a fitting sonic image for friendship.

SOCIAL MUSIC-MAKING IN THE RENAISSANCE

In the Renaissance, while professional musicians entertained noble guests at court and civic festivities, more and more amateurs began making music in their homes. The music could be vocal— both unaccompanied and supported by instruments— or purely instrumental; indeed, in most prosperous homes you would find a lute (see illustration, p. 82) or a keyboard instrument. The study of music was considered part of the proper upbringing for a young girl or, to a lesser degree, boy. Partly as a result, women began to play prominent roles in the performance

In His Own Words

❝ And we will sit upon the rocks, / Seeing the shepherds feed their flocks, / By shallow rivers to whose falls / Melodious birds sing madrigals."

—Christopher Marlowe
(1564–1593)

KEY POINTS

- Both professional and amateur music-making expanded in the Renaissance through secular vocal and instrumental genres.

- Among the important secular genres were the **French chanson** and the **Italian madrigal,** the latter a sixteenth-century tradition that linked music and lyric poetry.

Madrigals usually feature expressive text setting, **word-painting**, and multiple meanings.

- **English madrigals**, such as those by John Farmer, were often simpler and lighter in style than their Italian counterparts.

A stylized sixteenth-century painting of four singers performing from music "part books." The couple in back are beating time. *Concert in the Open Air* (Italian School).

of music both in the home and at court (see p. 65). During the later sixteenth century in Italy, a number of professional women singers achieved great fame.

Two important secular genres arose from the union of poetry and music: the **French chanson** (an outgrowth of the medieval version we heard by Machaut) and the **Italian madrigal**. The intricate verse structures of French and Italian poetry helped shape these musical forms. The madrigal is known for the expressive device of **word-painting**—that is, making the music directly reflect the meaning of the words. An unexpected harsh dissonance, for example, might coincide with the word "death," or an ascending line might lead up to the word "heaven" or "stars." We will see how these so-called **madrigalisms** enhanced the emotional content of the music.

The Lute Player, by **Caravaggio** (1571–1610), accompanies himself while singing a madrigal.

THE MADRIGAL: LINKING MUSIC AND POETRY

The sixteenth-century **madrigal**, the most important secular genre of the era, was an aristocratic form of poetry and music that flourished first at the Italian courts as a favorite diversion of cultivated amateurs. The text consisted of a short poem of lyric or reflective character, often including emotional words for weeping, sighing, trembling, and dying, which the Italian madrigalists set suggestively. Love and unsatisfied desire were popular topics, but so were humor and satire, politics, and scenes of city and country life. The madrigal literature therefore presents a vivid panorama of Renaissance thought and feeling.

From the beginning, the Italian madrigal was an art form in which words and music were clearly linked. One of the most artful and influential composers of the late Italian madrigal tradition was Claudio Monteverdi (1567–1643), who famously declared that his music was designed to serve the expressive power of his texts.

John Farmer (c. 1570–1601)

The English composer Farmer was active in Dublin, Ireland, as an organist and master of the choirboys at Christ Church. In 1599, he moved to London and published his only collection of four-voice madrigals. Farmer used clever word-painting in these lighthearted works and helped shape the madrigal into a truly native art form.

MAJOR WORKS: English songs and madrigals (for four and six voices).

Just as Shakespeare adapted the Italian sonnet, so English composers developed the Italian madrigal into a native art form during the late sixteenth century and the reign of Elizabeth I (1559–1603). In their own madrigals, some English composers followed the late Italian model, setting dramatic love poetry in serious, weighty works, while others favored simpler texts in more accessible settings. New humorous madrigal types were cultivated, some with refrain syllables such as "fa la la." One of the most important English madrigal composers was John Farmer.

A shepherd and shepherdess at leisure in the field, depicted in 1627 by Dutch painter **Abraham Bloemaert** (1566–1651).

Farmer's *Fair Phyllis*

The pastoral text, lively rhythms, and good humor of *Fair Phyllis* (LG 5) make it a perfect example of the English madrigal. The poem tells of a shepherdess (Phyllis) being pursued by her lover, Amyntas (their names are stock ones for such rustic characters). The narrative brings their story to a happy conclusion with their amorous love play. English composers adopted the Italian practice of word-painting, allowing us to "hear" this charming story. While it's fun to listen to these madrigals, more fun is to "tell" the story in interactive social song—remember, this music was designed for friends to sing with each other, rather than for professionals to perform to an audience. The melodies are simple enough that you might be able to sing them yourself after you've heard them a few times. How does your connection to the story change when you tell it, rather than hearing it?

▶|◀ **Reflect**

How do you think Farmer's music fits the love story? In what ways is this music as playful as the text? How does the syllabic setting of the words help the listening experience?

YOUR TURN TO EXPLORE

Can you find examples of twenty-first-century part songs (whether in North America or elsewhere) that are designed for social singing rather than concert performance? Does the number of singers in a group affect the performance, in terms of hearing the words clearly or being able to follow the interaction of the voices? Is the effect different if the musical story is sung by a mixed-gender rather than single-gender group?

LISTENING GUIDE 5

 1:21

Farmer: *Fair Phyllis*

DATE: Published 1599

GENRE: English madrigal

PERFORMED BY: Quink Vocal Ensemble

What to Listen For

Rhythm Lively rhythms that follow emphases on words; first in duple meter, then shifting to triple (at "then they fell") and back to duple.

Texture Starts monophonic, then becomes polyphonic with some imitation between the voices; the last text line is sung homorhythmically.

Expression The music reflects the meaning of the words (word-painting), especially in the opening line ("sitting all alone") and in the second part ("up and down").

Performing forces Four equally important voices (SATB), *a cappella* (without instruments).

0:00   Fair Phyllis I saw sitting all alone,
        Feeding her flock near to the mountain side.
        The shepherds knew not whither she was gone,
        But after her [her] lover Amyntas hied.

0:24   Up and down he wandered, whilst she was missing;
        When he found her, oh, then they fell a-kissing.

0:48   Up and down . . .

Examples of word-painting

"Fair Phyllis I saw sitting all alone"—sung by soprano alone:

"Up and down"—descending line, repeated in all parts imitatively; shown in soprano and alto:

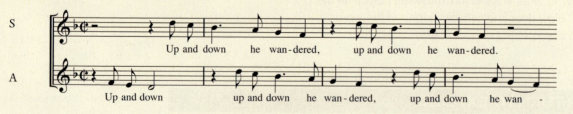

Remember Me: Personalizing the Motet in the Renaissance

▶❚❚ First, listen . . .

to *Ave Maria . . . virgo serena,* and think about how the vocal lines interact and copy each other. Does this feature help organize the work for the listener? How would you describe the imitation you hear?

> 66 We know by experience that song has great force and vigor to move and inflame the hearts of men to invoke and praise God with a more vehement and ardent zeal."
>
> —John Calvin

R eligious belief continued as a core aspect of identity in the Renaissance, even as the nature of that belief shifted to a more personal connection to the divine. This shift is perhaps most clearly reflected in the different artistic renditions of the Virgin Mary, on whom worshippers began to focus at this time. Medieval painting presented life through symbolism; the Renaissance preferred realism. Medieval painters posed their idealized figures impersonally, facing

Visual arts

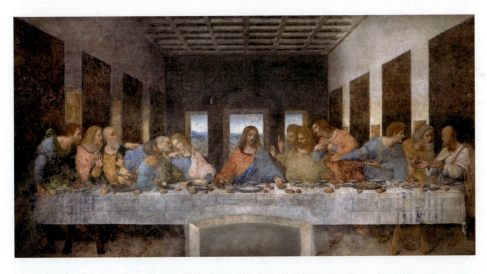

Leonardo da Vinci (1452–1519), whose remarkable *Last Supper* is the most reproduced religious painting of all time, was a contemporary of composer Josquin des Prez.

KEY POINTS

■ Renaissance sacred music was generally performed *a cappella* (for unaccompanied voices) and features a fuller, more consonant sound (with "sweet" thirds and sixths) than medieval music.

■ Josquin des Prez's *Ave Maria . . . virgo serena* is a **motet** to the Virgin Mary set in varied textural styles, which are designed to convey the changing meanings in the text.

Medieval and Renaissance artistic approaches.

LEFT: **Cimabue** (c. 1240–1302) aims to create an ideal effect, using magnificent colors, and there is an emotional distance between the characters that is in keeping with their distance from the worldly.

RIGHT: **Raphael** (1483–1520) shapes a more realistic environment, and the emotional bond between mother and child resonates with the faithful's trust that the Virgin will care for those who believe in her.

frontally; Renaissance artists developed profile portraiture and humanized their subjects. Space in medieval works was organized in a succession of planes that the eye perceived as a series of episodes, but Renaissance painters made it possible to see the whole simultaneously. They discovered the landscape, created the illusion of distance, and focused on the physical loveliness of the world. Echoing the visual arts, musicians helped to reinforce and intensify this newly personal approach to praise-through-beauty.

RENAISSANCE SACRED MUSIC

Humanism

The Renaissance marks the passing of European society from a predominantly religious orientation to a more secular one, and from an age of unquestioning faith and mysticism to one of growing reliance on reason and scientific inquiry. A new way of thinking centered on human issues and the individual. People gained confidence in their ability to solve their own problems and to order their world rationally, without relying exclusively on tradition or religion. This awakening, called **humanism**, was inspired by the ancient cultures of Greece and Rome, its writers and artworks.

In attempting to reconcile the needs of the individual with the primacy of the divine, musicians expanded their approaches to sung worship. In addition to the monophonic Gregorian chant that defined Catholic prayer, music for church services included hymns, motets, and polyphonic settings of the Mass. These were normally multivoiced and, especially in the early Renaissance era, based on preexisting music. They were sung by professional male singers trained from childhood in cathedral choir schools.

In His Own Words

❝ The better the voice is, the meeter [more fitting] it is to honor and serve God.❞

—William Byrd
(c. 1540–1623)

The vocal forms of Renaissance music were marked by smoothly gliding melodies conceived specially for the voice. In fact, the sixteenth century has come to be regarded as the golden age of the *a cappella* **style** (for voices alone, without instrumental accompaniment). Polyphony in such works was based on the principle of **imitation**: musical ideas are exchanged between vocal lines, the voices imitating one another so that a similar phrase is heard in different registers. (Imitation is different from a round in that the phrases sung by different voices in imitation are *similar* but not *identical*.) The result is a close-knit musical fabric capable of subtle and varied effects, in which each voice participates equally in the polyphonic prayer—a way to combine individual action with collaborative worship. In the matter of harmony, composers of the Renaissance leaned toward fuller chords. They turned away from the open fifths (missing the third of a triad) and octaves preferred in medieval times to the "sweeter" thirds and sixths. The use of dissonance in sacred music was carefully controlled.

A cappella **style**
Imitation

Polyphonic writing offered the composer many possibilities, such as the use of a fixed melody (**cantus firmus**) in one voice as the basis for elaborate ornamentation in the other voices. Triple meter had been especially attractive to the medieval mind because it symbolized the perfection of the Trinity. Renaissance composers, much less preoccupied with religious symbolism, showed a greater interest in duple meter.

Cantus firmus

Josquin des Prez and the Motet

In the Renaissance, one of the most popular genres was the **motet**—a sacred work with a Latin text, for use in the Mass and other religious services. The ability to combine newly written texts of praise with prescribed prayers was part of the appeal of the motet for composers, who were able to demonstrate their individual creativity through choice of text as well as musical invention. Motets in praise of the Virgin Mary were extremely popular because of the many religious groups all over Europe devoted to her, and also because of the potential for the faithful to identify with the powerful intimacy of the mother-child relationship.

The preeminent composers of motets from the early Renaissance (1450–1520) were from northern Europe, in particular present-day Belgium and northern France. Among these composers, we will consider Josquin des Prez, one of the great masters of sacred music.

In His Own Words

66 [Josquin] is the master of the notes. They have to do as he bids them; other composers have to do as the notes will."

—Martin Luther

Josquin des Prez (c. 1450–1521)

Josquin (as he is known) exerted a powerful influence on generations of composers to follow. After spending his youth in northern Europe, Josquin was employed for much of his varied career in Italy, at courts in Milan and Ferrara and in the papal choir in Rome. In Italy, he absorbed the classical virtues of balance and moderation, the sense of harmonious proportion and clear form, visible in the paintings of the era. Toward the end of his life, he returned to his native France, where he served as a provost at the collegiate church of Condé.

Josquin appeared at a time when the humanizing influences of the Renaissance were being felt throughout Europe. His music is rich in feeling, characterized by serenely beautiful melodies and expressive harmony.

MAJOR WORKS: Over 100 motets • At least 17 Masses • Many French chansons and Italian secular songs.

LISTENING GUIDE 6

 4:38

Josquin: *Ave Maria . . . virgo serena*
(Hail Mary . . . gentle Virgin)

DATE: 1480s?

GENRE: Latin motet

PERFORMED BY: La Chapelle Royale; Philippe Herreweghe, director

What to Listen For

Form Several sections, divided according to the strophes of the poem, each of which begins with "Ave."

Texture Imitative polyphony, with four equally important voices in changing combinations.

Harmony Consonant and sweet, with hollow-sounding cadences at the end of each section.

Text A rhymed, strophic prayer to the Virgin Mary; closes with a personal plea for mercy.

	TEXT	TRANSLATION	DESCRIPTION
0:00	Ave Maria, gratia plena, Dominus tecum, virgo serena.	Hail Mary, full of grace, The Lord is with you, gentle Virgin.	Four voices in imitation (SATB) quote a chant; duple meter.
0:45	Ave cujus conceptio Solemni plena gaudio Caelestia, terrestria, Nova replet laetitia.	Hail, whose conception, Full of solemn joy, Fills the heaven, the earth, With new rejoicing.	Two and three voices, later four voices; more homorhythmic texture.
1:21	Ave cujus nativitas Nostra fuit solemnitas, Ut lucifer lux oriens, Verum solem praeveniens.	Hail, whose birth Was our festival, As our luminous rising light Coming before the true sun.	Voice pairs (SA/TB) in close imitation, then four voices in imitation.
1:59	Ave pia humilitas, Sine viro fecunditas, Cujus annuntiatio, Nostra fuit salvatio.	Hail, pious humility, Fertility without a man, Whose annunciation Was our salvation.	Voice pairs (SA/TB); a more homorhythmic texture.
2:27	Ave vera virginitas, Immaculata castitas, Cujus purificatio Nostra fuit purgatio.	Hail, true virginity, Unspotted chastity, Whose purification Was our cleansing.	Triple meter; clear text declamation; homorhythmic texture.
3:04	Ave praeclara omnibus Angelicis virtutibus, Cujus fuit assumptio Nostra glorificatio.	Hail, famous with all Angelic virtues, Whose assumption was Our glorification.	Imitative voice pairs; return to duple meter.
3:59	O Mater Dei, Memento mei. Amen.	O Mother of God, Remember me. Amen.	Completely homorhythmic; text declamation in long notes, separated by rests.

Ave Maria . . . virgo serena (LG 6) is a prime example of how Josquin experimented with varied combinations of voices and textures to highlight different emotional aspects of the text. In this four-voice composition dedicated to the Virgin Mary, high voices engage in a dialogue with low ones, and imitative textures alternate with **homorhythmic** settings (in which all voices move together rhythmically). Josquin opens the piece with a musical reference to a preexisting chant for the Virgin, but soon drops this melody in favor of a freely composed form that is highly sensitive to the text. Notice that the equality and interdependence of the voices is highlighted by the frequent changes in the way voices are grouped, and that smaller groupings of two or three voices tend to build to the full ensemble at the ends of phrases.

Homorhythm

The final two lines of text, a personal plea to the Virgin ("O Mother of God, remember me"), is set in a simple texture that emphasizes the words, proclaiming the humanistic spirit of a new age. How do you think this direct appeal relates to the change in the depictions of the Virgin shown in the images on page 86? How does the full-chord sound that opens this section compare with the sound of the final "Amen," which is instead an open fifth?

▶️◀ Reflect

How has learning about Josquin's compositional techniques and reading this religious text helped you hear the work differently? Does the imitation of the polyphonic lines help underscore the words? How might Renaissance listeners have drawn meaning from the voices imitating each other?

A choir of men and boys sing sacred music from a choirbook, under the direction of composer Johannes Ockeghem (1410–1497).

YOUR TURN TO EXPLORE

The recording associated with our Listening Guide features a mixed-gender chorus of several voices to a part, but in the Renaissance, sacred music of this sort was almost exclusively sung by small all-male ensembles. Find a recording of this work (or another Josquin motet) by an all-male group (for example: the Hilliard Ensemble, The King's Singers, Chanticleer). How is the effect different from the version on your recording? Which do you find more expressive, and why?

Glory Be: Music for the Renaissance Mass

▶‖ **First, listen ...**

to the selection from Palestrina's *Pope Marcellus* Mass, focusing on how all the voices sing in the same rhythm. How does this feature help communicate the text? How would you describe the flow of the words?

D oes elaborate music in church distract worshippers from their focus on the scriptural text? Or does the sublime power of sound convey ultimate praise, and help the faithful envision the blessings of heaven? To this day, many consider unison song essential for building collective purpose, whether in worship or in other group activity—while others rely on the grandeur of polyphony to convey magnificence and glory, whether in church or in other places of celebration.

THE RENAISSANCE MASS

A similar debate was at the core of Christian reform in the 1500s: while Protestants argued for the simple unity of congregational singing, Catholics affirmed the power of professional choirs and complex textures, especially in polyphonic settings of the Mass.

With the rise of Renaissance polyphony, composers concentrated their musical settings on the Ordinary, the fixed portion that was sung daily. Its five prayers are the Kyrie, Gloria, Credo, Sanctus, and Agnus Dei. (Today, these sections are recited

KEY POINTS

- The most solemn ritual of the Catholic Church is the **Mass**, a daily service with two categories of prayers: the **Ordinary** (texts that remain the same for every Mass) and the **Proper** (texts that vary according to the day).

- Renaissance composers set texts from the Ordinary of the Mass (Kyrie, Gloria, Credo, Sanctus, Agnus Dei) for their polyphonic Masses.

- Reformers such as Luther and Calvin believed that monophonic congregational singing in the vernacular should define Christian worship, while the Catholic establishment preferred trained singers and polyphony.

- Giovanni Pierluigi da Palestrina's *Pope Marcellus* Mass foreshadowed the Council of Trent's recommendation for *a cappella* singing with clearly declaimed text.

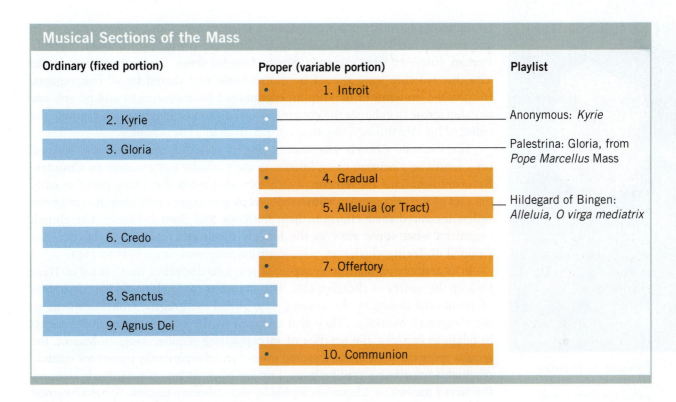

or sung in the vernacular, the language of the country, rather than in Latin—although in recent years there has been a resurgence of interest in the Latin Mass throughout the world.) The **Kyrie** (see LG 2) is a prayer for mercy that dates from the early centuries of Christianity, as its Greek text attests. This prayer is followed by the **Gloria** ("Glory be to God on high"), a joyful hymn of praise. The third section, the **Credo** ("I believe in one God, the Father Almighty"), is the confession of faith and the longest of the Mass texts. Fourth is the **Sanctus** ("Holy, holy, holy"), a song of praise, which concludes with "Hosanna in the highest." The fifth and last part of the Ordinary, the **Agnus Dei** ("Lamb of God, Who takes away the sins of the world"), is sung three times, with different words for its conclusion. The order of the Mass, with its Ordinary and Proper prayers, appears above. (Recall the *Alleluia* from the Proper of the Mass in Chapter 13.)

In His Own Words

❝ The Credo is the longest movement. There is much to believe."

— Igor Stravinsky

THE REFORMATION AND COUNTER-REFORMATION

Around the time of Josquin's death (1521), major religious reforms were spreading across northern Europe. In 1517, the Augustinian monk Martin Luther (1483–1546) launched the Protestant movement known as the **Reformation** with his Ninety-Five Theses—a list of reforms he proposed for the practices of the Catholic Church. Rather than adopt these new ideas, the church excommunicated him, and the rest is history.

Both Luther and another important reformer, John Calvin (1509–1564), believed that simple, monophonic **congregational singing** in the vernacular should

Portrait of the Protestant reformer Martin Luther, painted by **Lucas Cranach** (1472–1553).

In His Own Words

66 Among the various things which are suitable for man's recreation and pleasure, music is the first and leads us to the belief that it is a gift of God set apart for this purpose."

—John Calvin

be the basis of Christian worship. Calvin rejected polyphony as distracting from the essential focus on scriptural text: his followers (including the early Pilgrim/Puritan colonists who came to North America from England) embraced the idea that worship song should be monophonic and shared by all congregants. But Luther, an admirer of Josquin, encouraged *his* followers to add polyphonic worship music to enhance the congregational unison singing; we will examine the result of his idea through the music of J. S. Bach in a later chapter.

The Catholic Church was undergoing its own reform movement, focused on a return to Christian piety, known as the Catholic Reformation or **Counter-Reformation**. This movement, which extended from the 1530s into the early decades of the next century, witnessed sweeping changes in the church as religious orders increased their efforts to help the poor and combat heresy. The church organized what some view as the longest committee meeting in history: the **Council of Trent**, which met, with some interruptions, from 1545 to 1563.

In its desire to regulate every aspect of religious discipline, the Council of Trent took up the matter of church music. The attending cardinals noted the corruption of traditional chants by the singers, who added extravagant embellishments to the Gregorian melodies. They also objected to the use of certain instruments in religious services, the practice of incorporating popular songs in Masses, the secular spirit that had invaded sacred music, and the generally irreverent attitude of church musicians. In polyphonic settings of the Mass, the cardinals claimed, the sacred text was made unintelligible by the elaborate texture. Some advocated abolishing polyphony altogether and returning to Gregorian chant, but there were many music lovers among them who opposed so drastic a step.

The committee assigned to deal with the music problem issued only general recommendations in favor of a pure vocal style that would respect the integrity of the sacred texts, avoid virtuosity, and encourage piety. We will hear some of these traits in the glorious polyphony by the Italian master Giovanni Pierluigi da Palestrina.

Palestrina and the *Pope Marcellus* Mass

Palestrina's *Pope Marcellus* Mass was once thought to have been written to satisfy the Council of Trent's recommendations for polyphonic church music, but this is probably not true. Since the papal choir sang without instrumental

Giovanni Pierluigi da Palestrina (c. 1525–1594)

Palestrina (named for the town where he was born) worked as an organist and choirmaster at various Italian churches, including St. Peter's in Rome, where he spent the last twenty-three years of his life. He wrote largely sacred music—his output of Masses exceeds that of any other composer—and his music represents the pure *a cappella* style of vocal polyphony typical of the late Renaissance. He strove to make the words understood by properly accentuating them, thereby meeting the guidelines of the Catholic reform.

MAJOR WORKS: Over 100 Masses (including the *Pope Marcellus* Mass) • Madrigals and motets.

accompaniment, this Mass was most likely performed *a cappella*. It was written for six voice parts—soprano, alto, two tenors, and two basses, a typical setting for the all-male church choirs of the era. The highest voice was sung by boy sopranos or male falsettists (singing in falsetto, or head voice), and the alto part by male altos, or countertenors (tenors with very high voices).

LISTENING GUIDE 7

 5:50

Palestrina: Gloria, from *Pope Marcellus* Mass

DATE: Published 1567

GENRE: Gloria, from a setting of the Mass Ordinary

PERFORMED BY: The Sixteen; Harry Christophers, director

What to Listen For

Texture Monophonic opening; then mostly homorhythmic, with frequent changes in the combinations and density of voices.

Harmony Full, consonant harmony with six simultaneous voice parts.

Performing forces Six equally important voices (SATTBB), *a cappella* (without instruments); sung by an all-male sacred choir.

Text A hymn of praise; the second section of the Ordinary of the Mass.

	TEXT	NO. OF VOICES	TRANSLATION
0:00	Gloria in excelsis Deo	1	Glory be to God on high,
	et in terra pax hominibus	4	and on earth peace to men
	bonae voluntatis.	4	of good will.
	Laudamus te. Benedicimus te.	4	We praise Thee. We bless Thee.
	Adoramus te.	3	We adore Thee.
	Glorificamus te.	4	We glorify Thee.
	Gratias agimus tibi propter	5 / 4	We give Thee thanks for
	magnam gloriam tuam.	3 / 4	Thy great glory.
	Domine Deus, Rex caelestis,	4	Lord God, heavenly King,
	Deus Pater omnipotens.	3	God, the Father Almighty.
	Domine Fili	4	O Lord, the only-begotten Son,
	unigenite, Jesu Christe.	6 / 5	Jesus Christ.
	Domine Deus, Agnus Dei,	3 / 4	Lord God, Lamb of God,
	Filius Patris.	6	Son of the Father.
2:44	Qui tollis peccata mundi,	4	Thou that takest away the sins of the world,
	miserere nobis.	4	have mercy on us.
	Qui tollis peccata mundi,	4 / 5	Thou that takest away the sins of the world,
	suscipe deprecationem nostram.	6 / 4	receive our prayer.
	Qui sedes ad dexteram Patris,	3	Thou that sittest at the right hand of the Father,
	miserere nobis.	3	have mercy on us.
	Quoniam tu solus sanctus.	4	For Thou alone art holy.
	Tu solus Dominus.	4	Thou only art the Lord.
	Tu solus Altissimus.	4	Thou alone art most high.
	Jesu Christe, cum Sancto Spiritu	6 / 3 / 4	Jesus Christ, along with the Holy Spirit
	in gloria Dei Patris.	4 / 5	in the glory of God the Father.
	Amen.	6	Amen.

Palestrina worked at the Vatican in Rome, where **Michelangelo** (1475–1564) painted the famous Sistine Chapel ceiling. *The Creation of Adam* (c. 1511).

The Gloria from the *Pope Marcellus* Mass (LG 7) exhibits Palestrina's hallmark style— restrained, serene, and celestial. The opening line, "Gloria in excelsis Deo" ("Glory be to God on high"), is chanted by the officiating priest. For the remaining text, Palestrina constructed a polyphonic setting, balancing the harmonic and polyphonic elements so that the words are clearly audible, an effect that foreshadows the recommendations of the Council of Trent. His music is representative of the pure *a cappella* style of vocal polyphony of the later Renaissance. It reflects the Catholic Church's belief that heavenly sounds produced by trained professionals would be more spiritually powerful than the rough song of an untrained congregation—the precise opposite of Calvin's concept of a "musical priesthood of all the faithful."

▶◀ Reflect

Does understanding this work as church music change your impression of it? How might Renaissance worshippers have found the music an enhancement to the solemnity of a church service? Do you think it still conveys solemnity today, and if so, how?

YOUR TURN TO EXPLORE

Consider public events that involve "community spirit"—sports, political rallies, church services, etc. How is music used to foster that spirit? How do songs that are sung by the entire gathering differ from music played by professional musicians to "create the mood" at the event? Have you attended community events in which you were particularly inspired by the music? Was it participatory or listener-directed, or a combination of both?

Medieval and Renaissance Music

REPRESENTATIVE COMPOSERS

Hildegard von Bingen

Raimbaut de Vaqueiras

Guillaume de Machaut

Josquin des Prez

Giovanni Pierlugi da Palestrina

Claudio Monteverdi

John Farmer

IMPORTANT GENRES

chant

Mass

motet

chanson

madrigal

dance music

Listening Essentials

Melody: Small-range, modal, conjunct lines, moving toward smooth, arched lines (Renaissance sacred music).

Rhythm/meter: Free, nonmetric movement (early Middle Ages); mostly triple meter with syncopation (late Middle Ages); duple meter with a veiled pulse (Renaissance sacred music); dancelike movement (secular music).

Harmony: Open, hollow sonorities at cadences (Middle Ages); fuller-sounding chords moving toward major and minor tonality (Renaissance).

Texture: Monophonic (early Middle Ages); non-imitative polyphony (late Middle Ages); mixed textures, with much imitation (Renaissance).

Form: Strophic songs (secular music, late Middle Ages); structure follows the text (sacred music and much secular music, Renaissance).

Expression: Focus is on the text; use of word-painting.

Performing forces: Choir (sacred music); solo voices, sometimes doubled or substituted by string or wind instruments (secular music).

Listening Challenge

Now take the online Listening Challenge, where you'll listen to a mystery selection from the Renaissance era and answer questions about its elements: the character of the melody, the rhythmic movement and meter, the sound of the harmony, the form of the piece and its relationship to the text, the texture produced by the interweaving of the voices, and the likely genre. The style summary above may help guide your listening.

BAROQUE ERA

COMPOSERS AND WORKS

(1567–1643) Claudio Monteverdi
Operas and madrigals

Henry Purcell **(1659–1695)**
Dido and Aeneas

Antonio Vivaldi **(1678–1741)**
The Four Seasons

Johann Sebastian Bach **(1685–1750)**
Cantata *Wachet auf*
Orchestral Suite No. 3
"Little" Fugue in G Minor

George Frideric Handel **(1685–1759)**
Messiah

EVENTS

■ **1603** Death of Elizabeth I.

■ **1607** First settlement in Jamestown, Virginia.

■ **1611** King James Version of the Bible printed.

■ **1628** Dr. William Harvey explains the circulatory system.
Bay Psalm Book printed in Massachusetts.

■ **1643** Reign of Louis XIV begins.

■ **1649** Period of Commonwealth begins in England.

■ **1667** John Milton's *Paradise Lost* published.

■ **1687** Sir Isaac Newton's theory of gravitation published.

Reign of Louis XV begins. **1715** ■

George Washington born. **1732** ■

PART 3

Lionello Spada (1576–1622), *A Concert.*

The Baroque Era

▶❙ First, listen . . .

to *Alla hornpipe* from Handel's *Water Music,* and see how many musical traits described in Part 1 you can identify: for example, the shape of the melodic lines, how the rhythm is organized into a meter, whether the harmony is in a major or minor key, how the lines interact (the texture), how the Baroque instrument timbres sound different from modern ones, and how the dance is structured. Listen several times to try to pick up multiple elements, but don't worry about "getting it right" – this is your first chance to apply these basic principles to an example of Baroque-era music.

LISTENING OBJECTIVES

By the end of Part 3, you will be able to

- distinguish lyrical melodic lines with occasional leaps, ornaments (trills), and scalar patterns, set in a clear major or minor tonality.

- recognize how specific words are emphasized through distinctive musical gestures (such as melismas and leaps), how instrumental music can be highly virtuosic and theatrical, and the unique timbres of Baroque string and wind instruments.

- hear the steady rhythmic pulse throughout, set in a clear duple or triple meter, and how in vocal music the rhythm may move more freely to better express the words.

- note how the musical lines/voices interact, creating textures that vary from homophonic to highly polyphonic and imitative.

- define important vocal and instrumental genres that arose during this era, and recognize the different formal structures employed (including binary and ternary forms, and those featuring unifying themes).

Music as Exploration and Drama

> 66 These harmonic notes are the language of the soul and the instruments of the heart."
>
> —Barbara Strozzi
> (1619–1677)

Virtuosity

Music intensifies emotion. This may seem self-evident to us in the twenty-first century, but it was in the period that we are about to explore—the 1600s and early 1700s—that Europeans set out to develop musical approaches designed to "ramp up" various emotional states and help listeners experience their diversity more deeply.

Composers and performers became increasingly interested in how music could enhance the expression of words—most prominently through the development of a kind of musical theater called opera, but also through the training of specialized singers whose **virtuosity** (remarkable technical skill) made the amateur singing tradition of the Renaissance seem outdated and bland. Even more novel was a significant focus on the expressive power of musical instruments—not only in conjunction with voices, but on their own. While purely instrumental music existed before the 1600s, in the Baroque era it became much more prominent with the development of several new genres and the refinement of instrumental building and performance techniques.

During the early part of this period, musicians seemed almost giddy with the possibilities for intense expression, creating works that appear designed to swing between musical extremes. As time passed, such experimentation gave way to more predictable musical forms and procedures.

The Flemish painter **Peter Paul Rubens** (1577–1640) instills his paintings with high energy and drama. His voluptuous nudes, as in *Diana and Her Nymphs*, established the seventeenth-century ideal of feminine beauty.

"BAROQUE" ART AND CULTURE

The years between 1600 and 1750 represent a period of change, adventure, and discovery. The conquest of the New World stirred the imagination and filled the treasuries of Western Europe. The ideas of Galileo and Copernicus in physics and astronomy, of René Descartes in mathematics, and of Spinoza in philosophy were milestones in the intellectual history of Europe. The English physician William Harvey explained the circulation of the blood, and Sir Isaac Newton formulated the theory of gravity. Empires clashed for control of the globe.

There was appalling poverty and wasteful luxury, magnificent idealism and savage oppression. Baroque art—with its vigor, elaborate decoration, and grandeur—projected the pomp and splendor of the era. Indeed, the term "baroque" (applied in retrospect by later writers who saw this period as excessively extravagant) derives from a Portuguese word that originally meant "misshapen" or "distorted."

A comparison between the two depictions of the biblical figure David (right), one by Renaissance artist Michelangelo (1475–1564) and the other by Bernini (1598–1680), clearly reveals the Baroque love of the dramatic. The earlier sculpture is balanced, calm, reflective; on his shoulder is the sling with which he has just slain the giant Goliath, but the overall effect is static, poised. The Baroque David shows the young man in motion, every muscle in his body tensed in the act that will save his people. In like fashion, the Venetian school of painters and Northern masters such as Flemish artist Peter Paul Rubens captured the dynamic spirit of the new age, producing canvases ablaze in color and movement (see illustration opposite).

The Baroque was an era of absolute monarchy. Rulers throughout Europe modeled their courts on Versailles, a sumptuous palace on the outskirts of Paris. Louis XIV's famous declaration "I am the State" summed up a way of life in which all art and culture served the ruler. Courts large and small maintained elaborate musical establishments, including opera troupes, chapel choirs, and orchestras. Baroque opera, the favorite diversion of the aristocracy, told stories of the gods and heroes of antiquity, in whom the nobility and courtiers saw flattering likenesses of themselves.

The middle classes, excluded from the salons of the aristocracy, created a culture of their own. Their music-making took place in the home. It was for the middle classes that the comic opera and the novel, both genres filled with keen and witty observations on life, came into being. For them, painting abandoned its grandiose themes and turned to intimate scenes of bourgeois life. The Dutch School, embodying the vitality of a new middle-class art, reached its high point with Rembrandt and Jan Vermeer (see illustration on p. 100).

The Baroque was also an intensely devout period, with religion a rallying cry on some of the bloodiest battlefields in history. Protestants were centered in England, Scandinavia, Holland, and northern Germany, all strongholds of the rising middle class. On the Catholic side were two powerful dynasties: the French Bourbons and the Austrian-Spanish Hapsburgs, who fought one another as fiercely as they did their Protestant foes. Religion was an equally important part of life in the New World as well, both in the colonies of Protestant refugees who settled on the East Coast of North America and in the fervently Catholic Spanish and French colonies (Spanish in what is now Mexico, Central America, and the southwestern United States; French in Canada, the Mississippi valley, and the Gulf Coast).

Renaissance and Baroque sculptural approaches.

TOP: **Michelangelo** shows us David in contemplation (1501–04).

BOTTOM: In contrast, **Bernini** captures David in mid-slingshot (1623).

Creative artists played a variety of roles in Baroque society. Rubens was not only a famous painter but also an ambassador and friend of princes. The composer Antonio Vivaldi was also a priest, and George Frideric Handel an opera impresario. Artists usually functioned under royal or princely patronage, or, like Johann Sebastian Bach, they might be employed by a church or city administration. In all cases, artists were in direct contact with their public. Many musical works were created for specific occasions—an opera for a royal wedding, a dance suite for a court festivity, a cantata for a religious service—and for immediate use.

MAIN CURRENTS IN BAROQUE MUSIC

"The end of all good music is to affect the soul."
—Claudio Monteverdi

One of the most significant characteristics of the early Baroque style was a shift from a texture of several independent parts (polyphony) to one in which a single melody stood out (homophony).

A group of Florentine writers, artists, and musicians known as the Camerata (a name derived from the Italian word for "salon") first cultivated what they called "the new style" around 1600. The members of the Camerata were aristocratic humanists who aimed to resurrect the musical-dramatic art of ancient Greece. Although little was known of ancient music, the Camerata deduced that it must have heightened the emotional power of the text. Thus their "new style" consisted of a melody that moved freely over a foundation of simple chords.

A new kind of notation accompanied the "new style": since musicians were familiar with the basic harmonies, the composer put a numeral above or below the bass note, indicating the chord required (a kind of notation called **figured bass**; see music example on p. 113), and the performer filled in the necessary harmony. This system, known as **basso continuo**, provided a foundation over which a vocal or instrumental melody could unfold. It led to one of the most significant changes in all music history: the establishment of **major-minor tonality** (see Chapter 4). With this development, the thrust to the key note, or tonic, became the most powerful force in music. Each chord could assume its function in relation to the key center; and the movement between keys, governed by tonality, helped shape a musical structure. Composers were able to develop forms of instrumental music larger than had ever before been known.

Jan Vermeer is well known for his painting of bourgeois (middle-class) Dutch women playing keyboard instruments. *A Young Lady Seated at a Virginal*, c. 1670.

The Camerata's members engaged in excited discussions about their new homophonic music, which they also proudly named the "expressive style." The group soon realized that their approach could be applied not only to a short poem but also to an entire drama, fostering the most notable Baroque innovation: "drama through music," or what we now call **opera**.

The Hall of Mirrors in the French Royal Palace of Versailles exemplifies the Baroque love for elaborate decorations.

The elaborate scrollwork of Baroque architecture found its musical equivalent in the principle of continuous expansion of melody. A movement might start with a striking musical figure that would then be repeated and varied with seemingly infinite modifications, driven by rhythms that helped capture the movement of this dynamic age. In vocal music, wide leaps and chromatic tones helped create melodies that were highly expressive of the text.

Expressive devices

Baroque musicians used dissonant chords more freely, for emotional intensity and color. In setting poetry, for example, a composer might choose a dissonance to heighten the impact of a particularly meaningful word. The dynamic contrasts achieved in Renaissance music through varied imitative voicings gave way to a more nuanced treatment in the Baroque, allowing for a more precise expression of emotions, especially of the text. Dramatic *forte/piano* contrasts and echo effects were also typical of the era.

The Rise of the Virtuoso Musician

As the great musical instrument builders in Italy and Germany improved and refined their instruments, Baroque performers responded with more virtuosic (remarkably skilled) playing. Composers in turn wrote works demanding even more advanced playing techniques. Out of these developments came the virtuosic violin works of Antonio Vivaldi (see Chapter 23).

Instrumental virtuosity had its counterpart in the vocal sphere. The rise of opera brought with it the development of a phenomenal vocal technique, exemplified in the early eighteenth century by the **castrato**, a male singer who was castrated during boyhood in order to preserve the soprano or alto register

Castrato

of his voice for the rest of his life. What resulted, after years of training, was an incredibly agile voice of enormous range, powered by breath control unrivaled by most singers today. The castrato's voice combined the lung power of the male with the brilliance of the female upper register. Strange as it may seem to us, Baroque audiences associated this voice with heroic male roles. When castrato roles are performed today, they are usually sung in a lower register by a tenor or baritone, or in the original register by a countertenor or a woman singer in male costume.

Women, particularly singers, began to expand their role in music. Two early seventeenth-century Italian singers, Francesca Caccini and Barbara Strozzi (left), were among the earliest female composers to publish their works. Caccini stands out as the first woman to write an opera, and Strozzi was a prolific composer of both secular and sacred music. Some opera singers reached the level of superstars, such as the Italian sopranos Faustina Bordoni and Francesca Cuzzoni, who engaged in a bitter rivalry.

Improvisation played a significant role in Baroque music. In addition to elaborating on the simple harmonic foundation that was part of almost every musical work, musicians were expected to be able to improvise and add embellishments to what was written on the score, much like jazz or pop musicians today. Baroque music sounded quite different in performance from what was on the page.

An All-European Art

As great voyages of exploration opened up unknown regions of the globe, exoticism became a discernible element of Baroque music. A number of operas looked to faraway lands for their settings—Persia, India, Turkey, the Near East, Peru, and the Americas—offering picturesque scenes and dances that may not have been authentic but that delighted audiences through their appeal to the imagination.

Paradoxically, alongside the interest in exotic locales and regional traditions, the Baroque was a period in which there was significant exchange among national cultures. The sensuous beauty of Italian melody, the pointed precision of French dance rhythm, the luxuriance of German polyphony, the freshness of English choral song—these characteristic local traditions eventually blended into an all-European art that absorbed the best of each national style. For example, we will see how Handel, a German, wrote Italian opera for English audiences and gave England the oratorio. And it was precisely through this internationalization that, in the end, the Baroque gave way to a new set of stylistic priorities. An era of discovery and experimentation in which diversity and variety of musical expression was the ultimate goal eventually resulted in commonality of purpose and style, as Europeans became more and more interested in the elements that made humans equal rather than different.

Two professional singers of the era: Barbara Strozzi, painted (c. 1640) by **Bernardo Strozzi** (1581–1644); and the famous castrato singer Carlo Broschi, called Farinelli (1705–1782), by **Jacopo Amigoni** (1682–1752).

Performing Grief: Purcell and Early Opera

▶‖ **First, listen . . .**

to the aria known as Dido's Lament, from Purcell's *Dido and Aeneas*. At the beginning, you will hear a prominent bass-line melody that is introduced alone and then repeats throughout the aria. How does Purcell help you hear the repeats?

D ramatists and musicians who developed the tradition of sung drama—what we now call opera—understood music's power to intensify events; their aim was not realistic depiction but "hyper-reality." Both then and now, audiences knew that people don't sing to each other in real life. But characters in opera could convey strong emotions through music, making the experience of those emotions all the more compelling for the listener. The intense hyper-reality of sung drama has guaranteed its appeal and staying power for more than four centuries, and accounts for the use of music to enhance narrative multimedia (musical theater, film, video games) up to the present day.

THE COMPONENTS OF OPERA

An **opera** is a large-scale drama that is sung. It combines the resources of vocal and instrumental music—soloists, ensembles, chorus, orchestra, and sometimes ballet—with poetry and drama, acting and pantomime, scenery and costumes. To

KEY POINTS

- The most important new genre of the Baroque era was **opera**, a large-scale music drama that combines poetry, acting, scenery, and costumes with singing and instrumental music.

- The principal components of opera include the orchestral **overture**, solo **arias** (lyrical songs) and **recitatives** (speechlike declamations of the text), and ensemble numbers, including **choruses**.

- The text of an opera is called a **libretto**. The earliest opera libretti were based on mythology, epic poetry, and ancient history.

- Henry Purcell wrote *Dido and Aeneas*, based on *The Aeneid*, a Roman epic by Virgil. The closing Lament by Dido is a powerful expression of grief that reflects contemporary ideals about womanhood.

Set design for a Baroque opera based on the story of Dido and Aeneas, by Italian set designer **Giuseppe Galli da Bibiena** (1696–1757).

unify these diverse elements is a challenge that has attracted some of the most creative minds in the history of music. The plot and action are generally advanced through a kind of musical declamation, or speech, known as **recitative**. This vocal style is designed to imitate and emphasize the natural inflections of speech; its movement is shaped to the rhythm of the language.

Recitative gives way from time to time to the **aria** (Italian for "air" or "tune"), which releases through melody the tension accumulated in the course of the action. The aria is a song, usually of a highly emotional nature. It is what audiences wait for, what they cheer, what they remember. An aria, because of its tunefulness, can be effective even when sung out of context—for example, in a concert or on a recording. Arias can be "detached" in this way because they take place in "stop time"—the action is frozen and the character has the opportunity to dwell on a particular intense emotion. Words or groups of words, as well as musical phrases or even whole sections, are often repeated, as if the character were mulling them over in her or his mind. Once the aria ends, the action "un-freezes" and the drama returns to the "clock time" of recitative.

An opera may contain ensemble numbers—duets, trios, quartets, and so on—in which the characters pour out their respective feelings. The chorus may be used to back up the solo voices or may function independently. Sometimes it comments on the action, like the chorus of a Greek tragedy, and at other times is integrated into the action.

Overture   The orchestra sets the appropriate mood for the different scenes. It also performs the **overture**, heard at the beginning of most operas, which may introduce melodies from the arias. Each act of the opera normally opens with an orchestral introduction, and between scenes we may find interludes, or **sinfonias**.

Libretto   The composer works with a librettist, who creates the characters and the story line, with its main threads and subplots. The **libretto**, the text or script of the opera, must be devised to give the composer an opportunity to write music for the diverse numbers—recitatives and arias, ensembles, choruses, interludes—that have become the traditional features of this art form.

EARLY OPERA IN ITALY

An outgrowth of Renaissance theatrical traditions, early opera lent itself to the lavish spectacles and scenic displays that graced royal weddings and similar ceremonial occasions. A striking example of this tradition that is still performed and **Claudio Monteverdi**   recorded to this day is *Orfeo* (1607), composed by Claudio Monteverdi, who even in his own day was recognized for having solidified early experiments with drama-through-music (as it was called) into a mature and powerful new genre.

Spread of opera   By the time of Monteverdi's last opera, *The Coronation of Poppea* (1642), the first public opera houses had opened in Venice; opera was moving out of the palace and becoming a public and widespread entertainment. The accompanying orchestra, a string group with wind or brass instruments occasionally added for variety in timbre, became standard as Italian-style opera spread throughout Europe.

By the turn of the eighteenth century, Italian opera had gained wide popularity in the rest of Western Europe. Only in France was the Italian genre rejected; here, composers set out to fashion a French national style, in keeping with their strong traditions of court ballet and classical tragedy.

OPERA IN ENGLAND

In early seventeenth-century England, the **masque**, a type of entertainment that combined vocal and instrumental music with poetry and dance, became popular among the aristocracy. Later, in the period of the Commonwealth (1649–60), stage plays were forbidden because the Puritans regarded the theater as an invention of the devil. A play set to music, however, could be passed off as a "concert," and this is the tradition behind one of the earliest English operas (and certainly the most famous), Henry Purcell's *Dido and Aeneas* (LG 8).

Masque

Dido and Aeneas

Purcell's opera is based on an episode in Virgil's *Aeneid*, the ancient Roman epic that traces the adventures of the hero Aeneas after the fall of Troy. Since his contemporary audiences knew this Virgil classic, librettist Nahum Tate could compress the plot and suggest rather than fill in the details. Aeneas and his men are shipwrecked at Carthage on the northern shore of Africa. Dido, the Carthaginian

The Aeneid

Henry Purcell (1659–1695)

Purcell's standing as a composer gave England a leading position in the world of Baroque music. The London-born composer's career began at the court of Charles II (r. 1660–85) and extended through the turbulent reign of James II (r. 1685–88)—both Stuart kings—and into the period of William and Mary (r. 1689–1702). At these courts, Purcell held various posts as singer, organist, and composer. He wrote masques and operas for several venues.

Whether *Dido and Aeneas* was premiered at court or at the girls' boarding school where Purcell taught is unclear; we do know that it was performed in 1689 by his students at a school run by dancer Josias Priest. His incidental music for plays includes *Abdelazar (The Moor's Revenge)*, from which Benjamin Britten borrowed a dance as the basis for his *Young Person's Guide to the Orchestra* (see Chapter 11).

A truly international figure, Purcell wrote in many genres, assimilating the Italian operatic style along with the majesty of French music, all while applying his own lyrical gift to setting the English language to music.

MAJOR WORKS: Dramatic music, including *Dido and Aeneas* (1680s), *The Fairy Queen* (1680), and incidental music for plays (including *Abdelazar*, 1695) • Sacred and secular vocal music • Instrumental music, including fantasias, suites, and overtures.

Dido stabs herself with Aeneas's sword as he and his men sail out of the harbor. *The Death of Dido*, by **Andrea Sacchi** (1599–1661).

queen, falls in love with him, and he returns her affection. But Aeneas cannot forget that the gods have commanded him to continue his journey until he reaches Italy, since he is destined to be the founder of Rome. Much as he hates to hurt the queen, he knows that he must depart.

In the last act, the crew is ready to leave Carthage, although Aeneas has not yet told Dido of his imminent departure. Underlying the crew's festive mood is a growing chromaticism in the bass line that foreshadows Dido's Lament. Upon hearing of Aeneas's mission, a grief-stricken Dido decides her fate—death—in the moving recitative "Thy hand, Belinda," and the heartrending Lament that is the culminating point of the opera, "When I am laid in earth." In Virgil's poem, Dido mounts the funeral pyre, whose flames light the way for Aeneas's ships as they sail out of the harbor.

Dido's Lament unfolds over a five-measure **ground bass**, a repeated phrase that descends along the chromatic scale, often symbolic of grief in Baroque music. The repetitions of the text and music encourage the listener to dwell in the timelessness of the emotions performed through this scene. The scene also provides a powerful model for female grief, one considered appropriate by Purcell's society; but keep in mind that this was a model created by men based on male notions of suitable female behavior. This is another feature of opera, in common with all popular multimedia: it provides a reflection of what the librettist and composer wished their society to think about human character and interaction.

▶◀ Reflect

Now that you know more about the story of Dido and Aeneas, how do you think the Lament's ground bass helps to dramatize the emotions of that final scene?

YOUR TURN TO EXPLORE

Consider an example of one of your favorite "hyper-real" forms of narrative entertainment—science fiction/fantasy movie, TV show, video game. How is the more-than-real aspect conveyed? What role does music play in making the emotions more intense than "ordinary"? How does the music reinforce images and models of "ideal" (or "bad") behavior?

4:00

Purcell: *Dido and Aeneas*, Act III, Dido's Lament

DATE: 1680s

GENRE: Opera, English

BASIS: Virgil's *Aeneid*

CHARACTERS: Dido, queen of Carthage (soprano)   Belinda, Dido's serving maid (soprano)
Aeneas, adventuring hero (baritone)   Sorceress, Spirit, Witches, Sailors

PERFORMED BY: Lorraine Hunt Lieberson; Philharmonia Baroque Orchestra; Nicholas McGegan, conductor

What to Listen For

Melody In the speechlike recitative: chromatic, half-step movement and word-painting (on "darkness" and "death"). In the lyrical aria: some chromaticism and a descending line that portrays the text ("laid in earth").

Rhythm/meter Free movement in the recitative; slow, triple meter for the aria.

Harmony Aria is accompanied by a chromatic, descending bass line repeated eleven times (ground bass); it's set in a minor key to emphasize grief and death.

Form Aria is in two sections, each one repeated (**A-A-B-B**) over the ground bass.

Recitative: "Thy hand, Belinda," sung by Dido (accompanied by basso continuo only)   **0:57**

0:00   Thy hand, Belinda; darkness shades me.
       On thy bosom let me rest;
       More I would, but Death invades me;
       Death is now a welcome guest.

Aria: "When I am laid in earth," Dido's Lament   **3:03**

Basis: Ground bass, five-measure pattern in slow triple meter, descending chromatic scale, repeated eleven times:

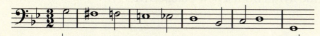

		SECTION	GROUND BASS STATEMENT NO.
0:57	**Instrumental introduction.**		1
1:09	When I am laid in earth, may my wrongs create	**A**	2
	no trouble in thy breast.		3
	When I am laid . . .	**A**	4
	no trouble . . .		5
2:17	Remember me, remember me, but ah, forget	**B**	6
	my fate, remember me, but ah, forget my fate.		7
	Remember me . . .	**B**	8
	forget my fate . . .		9
	Instrumental closing.		10
			11

Musical Sermons:
Bach and the Lutheran Cantata

> 66 I wish to make German psalms for the people, that is to say sacred hymns, so that the word of God may dwell among the people also by means of song."
>
> —Martin Luther

▶‖ First, listen . . .

to the fourth movement of Bach's Cantata *Wachet auf*, and consider the roles of the instruments and voices. Which do you think has the main melody and which is a countermelody (secondary tune) in this movement?

Bach worked for many years at Leipzig's St. Thomas Church and its famous choir school, seen in the background. Colored engraving from c. 1749.

One of the most important and lasting contributions that Martin Luther made to Western culture was the idea that musical worship belongs to the congregation. Both he and his fellow reformer John Calvin, as noted in Chapter 18, believed that the faithful should sing their praise collectively during the church service, rather than leaving song entirely to the priest and the choir. Unlike Calvin, however, Luther also believed that professional musicians—both singers and instrumentalists—had an important role in creating beautiful polyphony for the congregation to hear and reflect upon, much as the leader of the congregation played an important role in helping the faithful understand Scripture through sermons. As a sermon is an elaboration of a reading from the Bible, updating it for the congregation's contemporary concerns, the Lutheran cantata was an elaboration of the weekly hymn, allowing the congregation to understand the hymn from a new perspective.

THE LUTHERAN CHORALE AND CANTATA

Luther and his followers created weekly hymns (known as **chorales**) for their congregations to sing by composing (or sometimes recycling) simple and memorable melodies, and then writing German poetry in multiple stanzas that translated

KEY POINTS

- Lutheran musical worship is structured around congregational hymns, known as **chorales**, which are specific to each Sunday service.

- The **church cantatas** of Johann Sebastian Bach were mostly written for the Lutheran church service; they

are multimovement works with solo arias, recitatives, and choruses, all with orchestral accompaniment.

- Bach's cantata *Wachet auf* (*Sleepers, Awake*) is based on a well-known Lutheran chorale tune.

and/or interpreted passages in the Bible. Congregational singing of a specific chorale was (and still is) integrated into each weekly Lutheran service, along with the Gospel reading, prayers, and a sermon.

In these hymns, sung in unison by the congregation and in four-part harmony by the professional choir, the melody was in the soprano, where all could hear it and join in the singing. In this way, the chorales greatly strengthened the trend toward clear-cut melody supported by chords (homophonic texture).

Arrangements of chorales gradually expanded, so that instead of using every stanza of the chorale the same way, musicians and poets began to substitute some inner stanzas with new poetry, further elaborating their message. The resulting elaboration-of-chorale, a sort of musical sermon on the original hymn, is what we now call the **Lutheran cantata**.

BACH AND THE LUTHERAN CANTATA

In His Own Words

66 As Cantor of the St. Thomas School . . . I shall set the boys a shining example . . . serve the school industriously . . . bring the music in both the principal churches of this town into good estate . . . faithfully instruct the boys not only in vocal but also in instrumental music . . . arrange the music so that it shall not last too long, and shall . . . not make an operatic impression, but rather incite the listeners to devotion."

—J. S. Bach

Raised to serve Lutheran worship in his role as a professional musician, Johann Sebastian Bach was deeply familiar both with chorales and with the ways they could be elaborated. In his time, the cantata was an integral part of the church service, related, along with the sermon and prayers that followed it, to the Gospel reading for the day. Most Sundays of the church year required their own cantata, as did holidays and special occasions. Bach composed four or five such yearly cycles, from which only about two hundred works survive.

Bach's cantatas typically include five to eight movements, of which the first, last, and usually one middle movement are full-ensemble numbers—normally fashioned from the chorale tune—ranging from simple hymnlike settings to intricate fugues. Interspersed with the ensembles are solo or duet arias and recitatives, some of which may also retain the chorale melody or its text, or set new poetry that expands on the theme of the chorale.

Wachet auf (Sleepers, Awake)

Bach wrote his cantata *Wachet auf* (LG 9) in 1731, for the end of the church year. The reading of the Gospel for this church feast is the parable of the Wise and Foolish Virgins, in which the watchmen sound a call on the city wall above Jerusalem to the wise virgins to meet the arriving bridegroom (Christ). The biblical text (Matthew 25:1–3) clearly urges all Lutherans to prepare themselves spiritually for the second coming of Christ.

Bach builds his "musical sermon" on a hymn by Philipp Nicolai (1599), using its tune in three of the cantata's seven movements. The chorale is in a standard three-part structure known as **bar form** (**A-A-B**), in which the first section (**A**) is repeated with new words, and the second section (**B**) is rounded off with the same closing phrase as the first. The first movement is a grand chorale fantasia that features a majestic, marchlike motive signaling the arrival of Christ and an instrumental refrain that recurs between the vocal statements of the chorale. The fourth movement presents a unison chorale sung by the tenors against the watchman's memorable countermelody.

Bar form

Johann Sebastian Bach (1685–1750)

Bach is the culminating figure of the Baroque style and one of the giants in the history of music. Born at Eisenach, Germany, he was raised a Lutheran and followed the family vocation of organist. At the age of twenty-three, he was appointed to his first important position: court organist and chamber musician to the duke of Weimar. During his Weimar period (1708–17), Bach's fame as organ virtuoso spread, and he wrote many of his most important works for that instrument.

From 1717 to 1723, he served as composer for the prince of Anhalt-Cöthen, where he produced suites, concertos, sonatas for various instruments, and a wealth of keyboard music. Bach's two marriages produced at least nineteen off-spring, many of whom did not survive infancy; four of his sons became leading composers of the next generation.

Bach was thirty-eight when he was appointed to one of the most important music positions in Germany: cantor at St. Thomas Church in Leipzig. His duties were formidable (see quote on p. 109). He supervised the music for the city's four main churches, selected and trained their choristers, and wrote music for the daily services. He also served as director of the **collegium musicum**, a group of university students and musicians that gave regular concerts. In the midst of all this activity, Bach managed to produce truly magnificent works during his twenty-seven years in Leipzig (1723–50).

Two hundred or so church cantatas, the *St. John* and *St. Matthew Passions,* and the epic *Mass in B Minor* form the centerpiece of Bach's religious music, constituting a personal document of spirituality. Best known in his lifetime as an organist, Bach wrote organ compositions in both improvisatory and strict forms. His most important keyboard works are *The Well-Tempered Clavier,* forty-eight preludes and fugues in two volumes, and his last masterwork, *The Art of Fugue.* His orchestral music includes four suites of dance movements and the often-performed *Brandenburg Concertos.* Bach raised existing forms to the highest level rather than originating new forms. His mastery of contrapuntal composition, especially fugal writing, has never been equaled.

MAJOR WORKS: Sacred vocal music (over 200 church cantatas, four Passions, and the *Mass in B Minor,* 1749) • Four orchestral suites • Concertos (including six *Brandenburg Concertos*) • Solo sonatas and keyboard music (*The Well-Tempered Clavier, The Art of Fugue*) • Organ works, including the *Toccata and Fugue in D Minor.*

In *The Parable of the Wise and Foolish Virgins,* by **Peter von Cornelius** (1763–1867), the wise virgins greet Christ, the bridegroom.

The whole cantata reveals Bach's deep-rooted faith and his ability to communicate a meaningful spiritual message. The tune would still be resonating in the ears of the congregation as they sang the unison hymn later in the service, thereby deepening their appreciation for the words of the day's sermon.

▶❙◀ Reflect

How do you hear the two simultaneous melodies in the fourth movement now, after reading about Bach's plan in this cantata and his use of a well-known chorale tune? How would the Lutheran congregation of Bach's day have understood these two melodies? On which tune do you think they might have focused their attention?

YOUR TURN TO EXPLORE

Find recordings of a sacred song or hymn that has been reused/elaborated by musicians from different traditions (African American spirituals might be a good resource; for example, *Motherless Child*, *Swing Low, Sweet Chariot*, or *Amazing Grace*). How are different meanings of the song highlighted through different performances? Which ones do you think are more effective, and why?

LISTENING GUIDE 9 10:19

Bach: Cantata No. 140, *Wachet auf* (*Sleepers, Awake*), Nos. 1 and 4

DATE: 1731, performed in Leipzig

BASIS: Chorale (three stanzas) by Philipp Nicolai, in movements 1, 4, and 7

PERFORMED BY: American Bach Soloists; Jeffrey Thomas, director

OVERVIEW: 1. **Chorale fantasia** (stanza 1), E-flat major
2. Tenor recitative (freely composed), C minor
3. Aria: Soprano/bass duet (freely composed), C minor
4. **Unison chorale** (stanza 2), E-flat major
5. Bass recitative (freely composed), E-flat to B-flat major
6. Aria: Soprano/bass duet (freely composed), B-flat major
7. Chorale (stanza 3), E-flat major

continued on next page

Chorale tune
(A section)

Wa-chet auf, ruft uns die Stim - me   der Wäch-ter sehr_ hoch auf der
Mit - ter - nacht heißt die - se Stun - de;   sie   ru - fen uns_ mit hel - lem

Zin - ne,   wach auf, du Stadt Je - ru - sa - lem!
Mun - de: wo seid ihr klu - gen Jung - frau - en?

1. Chorale fantasia (chorus and orchestra)   6:06

What to Listen For

Melody Sopranos have a slow-moving chorale melody; other voices also reflect the shape of the chorale melody but more freely. The opening instrumental rising line represents the watchmen; a long melisma on "Alleluja!" occurs in the last section.

Rhythm/meter Triple meter punctuated by an insistent dotted rhythm in the orchestra, introduced in ritornello 1.

Form Three-part bar form (**A-A-B**), based on the chorale tune, preceded and reinforced by the instrumental ritornello (refrain).

Texture Polyphonic: alternation between the wind and string instruments; complex imitative polyphony in the lower voices, and contrasting slow chorale melody in the sopranos.

0:00   **Ritornello 1**, march-like dotted rhythm, alternating between violins and oboes:

A section

0:29   Wachet auf, ruft uns die Stimme   Awake! The voice of the
        der Wächter sehr hoch auf der Zinne,   watchmen calls us from high
        auf der Zinne,   on the tower,
        wach auf, du Stadt Jerusalem!   Awake, town of Jerusalem!

1:32   **Ritornello 2.**

        A section repeated (new text)

2:00   Mitternacht heisst diese Stunde,   Midnight is this very hour;
        sie rufen uns mit hellem Munde: they call to us with bright voices:
        Wo seid ihr klugen Jungfrauen?   where are you, wise virgins?

3:04   **Ritornello 3.**

        B section

3:24   Wohl auf, der Bräut'gam kommt,   Take cheer, the bridegroom comes,
        steht auf, die Lampen nehmt!   Arise, take up your lamps!
        Alleluja!   Alleluia!
        Macht euch bereit,   Prepare yourselves
        zu der Hochzeit,   for the wedding,
        Ihr müsset ihm entgegengehn!   You must go forth to meet him.

5:32   **Ritornello 4.**

4. Unison chorale

4:13

What to Listen For

Melody Tenors sing the chorale melody in unison, overlapping with a new, longer and repeating melody in the unison strings.

Form Three-part bar form (**A-A-B**), based on the chorale tune, preceded and reinforced by the instrumental ritornello.

Texture Non-imitative polyphony, in three contrasting simultaneous lines: the slow-moving chorale melody in the voices, a faster string melody, and a "walking" bass line.

Performing forces Multiple string instruments (violins, violas), tenor voices in unison, accompanied by basso continuo (cello, bass, organ).

0:00   **Ritornello 1**.

0:41   **A section**

Zion hört die Wächter singen,
das Herz tut ihr vor Freuden springen,
sie wachet und steht eilend auf.

Zion hears the watchmen singing,
for joy her very heart is springing,
she wakes and rises hastily.

1:11   **Ritornello 2**.

1:50   **A section** (new text)

Ihr Freund kommt vom Himmel prächtig,
von Gnaden stark, von Wahrheit mächtig,
ihr Licht wird hell, ihr Stern geht auf.

From resplendent heaven comes her friend,
strong in grace, mighty in truth,
her light shines bright, her star ascends.

2:20   **Ritornello 3**.

2:47   **B section**

Nun komm du werte Kron,
Herr Jesu, Gottes Sohn.
Hosiana!

Now come, you worthy crown,
Lord Jesus, God's own son.
Hosanna!

3:08   **Ritornello 4** (in minor).

3:29   **B section** (continues)

Wir folgen all
zum Freudensaal
und halten mit das Abendmahl.

We follow all
to the joyful hall
and share the Lord's supper.

Chorale tune in tenors set against countermelody in strings:

Textures of Worship:
Handel and the English Oratorio

▶❙❙ First, listen . . .

to the famous chorus "Hallelujah!" from Handel's *Messiah*, focusing on how the voices interact with each other and with the instruments. How does the composer emphasize the words through the musical texture, and how does he vary the way they are delivered?

Saint Philip Neri (1515–1595) promoted congregational singing in the oratory (prayer room) of the church.

Most of the music composed in Europe before the later 1700s enjoyed only a short arc of success: even the most highly esteemed works and composers fell into obscurity within one or two generations. George Frideric Handel's oratorios, and in particular *Messiah*, broke that trend: from their beginnings more than two and a half centuries ago, they have been performed continuously. Today, even small North American towns will feature a performance of *Messiah* every year as a staple of Christmastime celebrations; and larger urban centers often offer several performances, some incorporating audience sing-along during the most-loved choruses. The success of these works comes in part from their fitting the national mood during a time of British self-confidence, and in part from Handel's ingenuity in combining some of the most effective musical resources of his day as he invented an entirely new genre, the English oratorio. From their beginnings, Handel's oratorios have marked the meeting place of community worship with the grandeur and glory of power—political, sacred, and musical.

KEY POINTS

- The **oratorio** is a large-scale dramatic genre with a sacred text performed by solo voices, chorus, and orchestra; it is not staged or costumed.

- Originally conceived to put forth the message of the Catholic Church, the oratorio bears many similarities to opera.

- George Frideric Handel built his career as a composer of Italian-style opera; later in life, he invented the English oratorio, combining elements of Italian and English musical style.

- Handel's oratorios (including *Messiah*) have remained popular ever since the composer's day.

THE ORATORIO

The **oratorio**, one of the great Baroque sacred vocal genres, descended from the religious play-with-music of the Counter-Reformation. It took its name from the Italian word for "place of prayer," and early oratorios were sponsored by the Catholic Church in public meeting places as ways to convey its messages about faith to as wide an audience as possible. A large-scale musical work for solo voices, chorus, and orchestra, the oratorio was generally based on a biblical story and performed without scenery, costumes, or acting. The action was sometimes depicted with the help of a narrator, but in other ways oratorio was very much like opera on a religious theme—on purpose, since the Catholic Church wanted to propose oratorio as a more moral alternative to opera. Like operas, oratorios unfolded as a series of recitatives and arias, with duets, trios, and choruses.

Handel had become familiar with the Catholic oratorio during his musical study in Italy. After successfully becoming the leading producer of Italian opera in England, he decided to diversify his musical efforts. Unlike most musical genres, the first English oratorios can actually be determined, since Handel invented the genre by combining elements of Italian opera (and Catholic oratorio) with a grand choral style that had been associated with the English monarchy. And unlike the

George Frideric Handel (1685–1759)

If Bach represents the spirituality of the late Baroque, Handel embodies its worldliness. Born in the same year, the two giants of the age never met.

Handel was born in Halle, Germany, and attended the University of Halle. He then moved to Hamburg, where he played violin in the opera house orchestra and absorbed the Italian operatic style popular at the time. In 1706, he traveled to Italy, where he composed his first sacred works and Italian operas. Six years later, he settled permanently in London, where his opera *Rinaldo* had conquered the English public the year before.

Handel's great opportunity came in 1720 with the founding of the Royal Academy of Music, launched for the purpose of presenting Italian opera. For the next eight years, he was active in producing and directing his operas as well as writing them. When the Italian style fell out of favor, he turned from opera to oratorio, quickly realizing the advantages offered by a genre that dispensed with costly foreign singers and lavish scenery. Among his greatest achievements in this new genre were *Messiah* and *Judas Maccabaeus*. Shortly after his seventy-fourth birthday,

Handel collapsed in the theater at the end of a performance of *Messiah* and died some days later. The nation he had served for half a century accorded him its highest honor: a burial at Westminster Abbey.

Handel's rhythm has the powerful drive of the late Baroque. His melodies, rich in expression, rise and fall in great majestic arches. And with his roots in the world of the theater, Handel knew how to use tone color for atmosphere and dramatic expression. His more than forty operas tell stories of heroes and adventurers in ingenious musical settings, with arias that run the gamut from brilliant virtuosic displays to poignant love songs. His most important instrumental works are the concertos and two memorable orchestral suites, the *Water Music* (1717) and *Music for the Royal Fireworks* (1749).

MAJOR WORKS: Over 40 Italian operas (including *Rinaldo* and *Julius Caesar*) • English oratorios (including *Israel in Egypt, Judas Maccabeus,* and *Messiah*) • Other vocal music • Orchestral suites, including *Music for the Royal Fireworks* and *Water Music* • Keyboard and chamber music.

Catholic oratorio, the text (called **libretto**, as in opera) was written by trusted poets rather than by religious leaders. Just as important, English oratorios were not sponsored officially by the church: they were an entrepreneurial venture by Handel and his collaborators, designed to turn a profit.

Handel's oratorios quickly became popular: not only was the music grand and inspiring while still being memorable and singable, but the religious stories about a "chosen people" (most Handel oratorios tell Old Testament stories) were very appealing to an English public that saw economic expansion into its colonies as an indication of divine blessing. By a few decades after Handel's death, oratorio performances featuring hundreds of singers and instrumentalists (see illustration at left)—many times more than the composer would ever have envisioned—had become common. As the British Empire grew, and with it an increasing interest in choral singing throughout the English-speaking world, Handel's oratorios followed the empire's expansion.

London's Westminster Abbey is packed for this Handel performance on the centenary of his birth, as depicted by **Edward Edwards** (1738–1806).

Messiah

In the spring of 1742, the city of Dublin witnessed the premiere of what became one of the English-speaking world's best-loved works, Handel's *Messiah* (LG 10). The composer was reputed to have written the oratorio in only twenty-four days, working as if possessed. The story circulated of his servant finding him, after the completion of the "Hallelujah Chorus," with tears in his eyes. "I did think I did see all Heaven before me, and the Great God Himself!" he reportedly said. Such stories about divine inspiration and the genius composer's ability to create in an almost superhuman fashion helped to build the reputation of *Messiah* and oratorios like it.

The libretto is a compilation of biblical verses from the Old and New Testaments, set in three parts. The first part (the Christmas section) relates the prophecy of the coming of Christ and his birth; the second (the Easter section), his suffering, death, and the spread of his doctrine; and the third, the redemption of the world through faith. The orchestration features mainly strings; oboes and bassoons strengthen the choral parts, and trumpets and drums are reserved for special numbers.

The lovely soprano aria "Rejoice greatly, O daughter of Zion" is in three-part, or **A-B-A′**, form. In this type of **da capo aria**, the composer usually did not write out the third part (A′), since it duplicated the first, allowing the star singer the opportunity to ornament or elaborate the third part on the fly, a crowd-pleasing device in both opera and oratorio. For "Rejoice greatly," though, Handel did write out the last section, varying it considerably from the first. This may have been partly because he liked having as much control as possible over the expressive shape of the music, rather than leaving too many choices up to his performers. It may also have had to do with the fact that some of the first English oratorio performers were less skilled (especially in improvisation) than their Italian operatic counterparts, so Handel may have thought it prudent to give his singer as detailed a set of instructions as possible.

At the beginning of this aria, violins introduce an energetic figure that will soon be taken up by the voice. Notable are the melismatic passages on the word "rejoice." Throughout, the instruments exchange motives with the voice and help **Ritornello** provide an element of unity with the **ritornellos**, or instrumental refrains, that bring back certain passages.

The climax of *Messiah* comes at the close of the second part, the Easter section, with the familiar "Hallelujah Chorus." In this movement, we hear shifting textures in which the voices and text overlap and then come together to clearly declaim the text. Handel's extraordinary ability to combine tuneful melodies and intriguing textures with striking homorhythmic passages is most evident in this beloved chorus.

▶️◀ Reflect

How do the homorhythmic and imitative textures in this chorus affect how you hear the words? Do you always know which voice part is dominant? How does Handel use texture as an expressive device?

Newspaper notice for the first London performance of Handel's *Messiah*, on 23 March 1743.

YOUR TURN TO EXPLORE

Find a recording of a contemporary setting of a sacred text. How have the composer and performers chosen to use texture and other musical devices to bring out the spiritual aspects of the words that they, or their communities, find most important? Is the music designed to encourage participation by the community for which it has been designed, or is the expressive power left up to trained specialists?

LISTENING GUIDE 10   7:48

Handel: *Messiah*, Nos. 18 and 44

DATE: 1742

GENRE: Oratorio, in three parts

PERFORMED BY: Karen Clift, soprano; Boston Baroque; Martin Pearlman, conductor

PARTS: I: Christmas section
II: Easter section
III: Redemption section

Part I: Christmas Section / 18. "Rejoice greatly" (soprano aria)   4:15

What to Listen For

Melody Lyrical, virtuosic lines, with a long melisma to emphasize the word "rejoice"; second section is slower and in a minor key.

Text From the Old Testament book of Zachariah, on the coming of Christ.

Form Instrumental introduction (ritornello) sets up a three-part aria form (da capo, **A-B-A'**), with a shortened last section.

0:00	**Instrumental ritornello.**	Vocal theme presented in violins in B-flat major.
	A section	
0:16	Rejoice greatly, O daughter of Zion shout, O daughter of Jerusalem, behold, thy King cometh unto thee.	Disjunct rising line, melismas on "rejoice"; melody exchanged between soprano and violin.
	Instrumental ritornello.	Syncopated, choppy melody, ends in F major.

continued on next page

B section

1:30   He is the righteous Saviour and he shall
       speak peace unto the heathen.

Begins in G minor, slower and lyrical;
modulates to B-flat major.

A′ section

2:33   Rejoice greatly . . .

After an abridged ritornello, new melodic elaborations;
longer melismas on "rejoice."

Extended melisma on "rejoice" from the A′ section:

Part II: Easter Section / 44. "Hallelujah Chorus"   3:33

What to Listen For

Texture Varies from homorhythm (all voices moving together) to monophony to imitative polyphony ("And He shall reign forever").

Expression The varied textures and dynamics create dramatic tension; overlapping phrases move toward the climax.

Performing forces SATB chorus with voices in alternation, accompanied by the orchestra.

0:00   **Short instrumental introduction.**
       Hallelujah!

Four voice parts, homorhythmic at the opening.

0:24   For the Lord God omnipotent reigneth.

Textural reductions, leading to imitation and overlapping of text; builds in complexity, with imitative entries.

1:12   The kingdom of this world
       is become the Kingdom of our Lord
       and of His Christ;

Homorhythmic treatment, simple accompaniment.

1:29   and He shall reign for ever and ever.

Imitative polyphony, voices build from lowest to highest.

1:51   King of Kings and Lord of Lords.
       Hallelujah!

Women's voices introduce the text, punctuated by "Hallelujah"; closes in a homorhythmic setting with trumpets and timpani.

Opening of chorus, in homorhythmic style:

Grace and Grandeur: The Baroque Dance Suite

▶‖ **First, listen ...**

to the Gigue that closes Bach's Orchestral Suite No. 3, and pay special attention to the meter. Can you hear the pattern of the beats? Does the quick tempo make it easier or more difficult to follow the meter?

> 66 To enjoy the effects of music fully, we must completely lose ourselves in it."
>
> —Jean-Philippe Rameau (1683–1764)

Technology has always played a crucial role in the development of music. We have already encountered notational technologies (handwriting and print) that were essential to preserving and transmitting musical ideas. We now consider more closely the technologies of sound production: how musicians and craftspeople collaborated to imagine and manufacture increasingly sophisticated musical instruments.

Though humans have been involved in this creative practice since before recorded history, it was during the Baroque era that the Western tradition developed a remarkable focus on instruments and music written for them—a focus that eventually became the central feature of Western concert music in the following century. This flowering of instrumental music was encouraged by wealthy patrons who were eager to invest money and resources in magnificent displays. Since that time, elaborate instrumental music has often been used to convey grandeur on special occasions; most likely every time you have witnessed a grand celebration, it has been enhanced by graceful and powerful soundscapes made possible by the evolving technology of musical instruments.

KEY POINTS

- In the Baroque era, instruments were greatly improved and featured in several large-scale genres, including the **suite** (a collection of dances).

- Dances in a suite, usually all in the same key, are in binary form (**A-A-B-B**) or ternary form (**A-B-A**).

- J. S. Bach wrote four suites for orchestra in the French style, made up of dances popular in his day.

Baroque instruments, including a natural trumpet and timpani, in the Bach House, in Eisenach, Germany.

BAROQUE INSTRUMENTS

The seventeenth century saw a dramatic improvement in the construction of string instruments. Some of the finest violins ever built came from the North Italian workshops of Stradivarius, Guarneri, and Amati: to this day musicians seek them out, and pay millions of dollars for the best-made exemplars. The strings were made of gut rather than the steel used today. Gut, produced from animal intestines, yielded a softer yet more penetrating sound. In general, the string instruments of the Baroque resemble their modern descendants except for certain details of construction. Playing techniques, though, have changed somewhat, especially bowing.

While woodwind instruments were used primarily for loud outdoor events through the 1600s, in the late Baroque composers prized such instruments increasingly for color as builders expanded their range and subtlety. The penetrating timbres of the recorder, flute, and oboe, all made of wood at the time, were especially effective in suggesting pastoral scenes, while the bassoon cast a somber tone.

The trumpet developed from an instrument used for military signals to one with a solo role in the orchestra. It was still a "natural instrument"—that is, without the valves that would enable it to play in all keys—demanding real virtuosity on the part of the player. Trumpets contributed a bright sonority to the orchestral palette, to which the French horns, also natural instruments, added a mellow, huntlike sound. Timpani were occasionally added, furnishing a bass to the trumpets.

In recent years, a new drive for authenticity has made the sounds of eighteenth-century instruments familiar to us. Recorders and wooden flutes, restored violins with gut strings, and mellow-toned, valveless brass instruments are being played again, so that the Baroque orchestra has recovered not only its smaller scale but also its transparent tone quality.

THE BAROQUE SUITE

One of the most important instrumental genres of the Baroque was the **suite**, a group of short dances performed by the diverse array of instruments just described. It was a natural outgrowth of earlier traditions, which paired dances of contrasting tempos and character.

Dance types   The suite's galaxy of dance types, providing contrasting moods but all in the same key, could include the German **allemande**, the French **courante**, the Spanish **sarabande**, and the English **jig** (**gigue**), as well as a **minuet**, **gavotte**, lively **bourrée** or **passepied**, or jaunty **hornpipe**. Some dances were of peasant origin, bringing a touch of earthiness to their more formal surroundings. The suite sometimes opened with an overture, and might include other brief pieces with descriptive titles reflecting their origin in choreographed theatrical dance.

Binary and ternary form

Each piece in the Baroque suite was set either in **binary** form, consisting of two sections of approximately equal length, each rounded off by a cadence and each repeated (**A-A-B-B**); or in **ternary** form (**A-B-A**). In both structures, the **A** part usually moves from the home key (tonic) to a contrasting key (dominant), while the **B** part makes the corresponding move back. The two sections often share closely related melodic material. The form is easy to hear because of the modulation and the full stop at the end of each part.

The principle of combining dances into a suite could be applied to solo instrumental music (notably for harpsichord or solo violin) and to chamber ensembles, as well as to orchestral forces. It was an important precedent to the multimovement cycle that later became standard in Classical instrumental music.

Bach conducting a performance with his Collegium Musicum in Leipzig.

Bach's Orchestral Suite No. 3

Shortly after he arrived in Leipzig, J. S. Bach wrote a number of instrumental works meant for performance with the Collegium Musicum ensemble that he directed. This group of forty-to-fifty university students and professional musicians performed weekly concerts at Zimmerman's, a large coffeehouse in Leipzig with a hall that could accommodate some 150 audience members as well as an orchestra that included trumpets and timpani. A 1733 announcement from the coffeehouse noted the beginning of that year's series "with a fine concert. It will be maintained week by week, with a new clavicymbel [harpsichord] of a kind that has not been heard here before, and lovers of music as well as virtuosos are expected to be present."

Bach's four orchestral suites were among the repertory written for this group. The suites are in the French style: each opens with an overture, which is followed by a series of French dances that were popular across Europe. We will hear two movements from the Suite No. 3: first, the Air (popularly known as "Air on a G String"), featuring a gloriously serene melody carried by the first violin, with a reduced orchestra (two violins, viola, and basso continuo with cello and harpsichord). Richly ornamented, the asymmetrical melody unfolds over a steady, even bass line. The suite closes with a highly spirited Gigue, which adds a festive complement of oboes, trumpets, and timpani. Both movements are in binary form, with each of the two sections repeated (LG 11).

The Zimmermann Coffeehouse in Leipzig, where Bach's Collegium Musicum gave weekly concerts.

Bach's performances at Zimmerman's were early examples of the instrumental concert tradition, and were very popular both with locals and with visitors to Leipzig. Almost three centuries after they were first performed, Bach's orchestral suites continue to be a concert staple and a favorite with lovers of instrumental music. We need to hear only a few measures to understand why—they provide a perfect example of using technology (the latest instruments) for the most marvelous result possible.

▶◀ Reflect

Based on Bach's Gigue, what would you say is the general character of a gigue? How does it differ from other types of dances you know? How does Bach vary the expression while keeping a constant meter and tempo?

YOUR TURN TO EXPLORE

Find a performance of a band playing a march—the marches by John Philip Sousa are a great example of the genre. How do the changing timbres of the various instrument combinations compare with the timbres of Bach's Air and Gigue? How does the structure of the march resemble and differ from the binary form of the dances from Bach's suite? Why do you think these similarities and differences exist?

LISTENING GUIDE 11   7:24

Bach: Orchestral Suite No. 3, Air and Gigue

DATE:	1731
GENRE:	Dance suite for orchestra
PERFORMED BY:	Freiburger Barockorchester

MOVEMENTS:	Overture	Bourrée
	Air	**Gigue**
	Gavotte I and II	

Air   4:37

What to Listen For

Melody The serene, aria-like line is played by the first violin.

Form Two-part form, each section repeated (binary, **A-A-B-B**); the **B** section is longer than the **A** section.

Texture Homophonic texture focused on the melody, accompanied by a "walking bass" line and some moving lines in the lower strings.

Expression The graceful, singing melody, with expressive upward leaps and embellishments, unfolds in a slow tempo; the pace is marked by the moving basso continuo line (played by cello and harpsichord).

0:00   **A section**: rhapsodic and lyrical melody over a regularly moving cello line; strings only.

0:46   **A section** repeated.

1:31   **B section**: longer, with melodic phrases embellished and treated in sequence.

3:01   **B section** repeated.

Opening of the Air, the soaring solo violin melody accompanied by a "walking" bass in the continuo:

Gigue

2:47

What to Listen For

Rhythm/meter Fast-paced compound (6/8) meter that feels like a propelling duple pattern.

Harmony Bright D major; moves to the dominant key (A major), then returns to the tonic; highly consonant.

Texture Largely homophonic, with counterpoint created by the basso continuo line.

Performing forces Festive sound with oboes, trumpets, and timpani added to the strings; alternation of ideas between strings and winds (with percussion).

0:00   **A section**: vigorous dance with continuous motion as the strings and oboes exchange musical phrases with the trumpets.

0:27   **A section** repeated.

0:53   **B section**: longer, with some development of musical ideas as the music modulates to return to the tonic key.

1:46   **B section** repeated.

Opening of the violin and trumpet melody, played in octaves:

Sounding Spring: Vivaldi and the Baroque Concerto

66 [His playing] terrified me . . . he came with his fingers within a mere grass-stalk's breadth of the bridge, so that the bow had no room—and this on all four strings with imitations and at incredible speed."

—A contemporary musician describing Vivaldi's violin technique

▶‖ First, listen . . .

to the first movement from Vivaldi's *Spring* concerto from *The Four Seasons*, focusing on the music that returns throughout. How does this repetitive device help you follow the movement? How does Vivaldi provide contrast and variety?

How can sound mean something independently of words? Many of us today automatically refer to musical works as "songs," but as we know, the term is really only accurate when lyrics are involved. And one of the characteristics of the Western tradition is the complexity of its independent instrumental music. Separated from the need to follow the meanings and patterns of text, instrumental music can create meaning just through patterns of sound. However, even as they explored purely musical ways of fashioning "sound stories," composers frequently called on written language to help them, as well as their listeners, explore the possibilities for what music could mean. These explorations played out in especially interesting ways through the genre of the concerto.

THE BAROQUE CONCERTO

Contrast was as basic an element of Baroque music as unity. This twofold principle found expression in the **concerto**, an instrumental genre based on the opposition between two dissimilar bodies of sound. The concerto contrasted one or more "featured" instruments with a larger orchestral ensemble, an approach that lent itself to

KEY POINTS

- Baroque musicians developed the **concerto**, a genre that generally featured either a solo instrument or a small group of soloists set against a larger ensemble.

- First and last movements of concertos tended to follow a refrain-based structure known as **ritornello form**.

- Antonio Vivaldi, a virtuoso violinist, composed *The Four Seasons*, a well-loved set of solo violin concertos that exemplify **program music**.

experiments in sonority and virtuoso playing. A concerto usually consisted of three movements, in the sequence Allegro–Adagio–Allegro. The first and last movements tended to follow a loosely structured form based on the alternation between orchestral refrains and virtuosic outbursts by the soloist(s), which has taken on the Italian name for "refrain," **ritornello form**. This flexible form prepared the way for the more systematic structures in the concerto of the Classical and Romantic periods.

The concerto was first developed in the Italian peninsula in the late 1600s, but quickly spread north and was eagerly embraced by performers and patrons alike. J. S. Bach took the concerto to a new and almost encyclopedic level in his six *Brandenburg Concertos*. But of all the composers in the Baroque concerto tradition, Antonio Vivaldi was the most famous and the most prolific.

A concert by the girls of one of Venice's famous *ospedali*, or orphanages, by **Gabriele Bella** (1730–1799). Vivaldi taught music at the most prestigious of these institutions.

Program Music: Vivaldi's *The Four Seasons*

Vivaldi is in fact best remembered for his more than 500 concertos, about 230 of which are for solo violin, some with descriptive titles. He was active during a period that was crucially important to a new style in which instruments were liberated from their earlier dependence on vocal music. His novel use of rapid scale passages, extended arpeggios, and contrasting registers contributed decisively to the development of violin style and technique. And he played a leading part in the history of the concerto, effectively exploiting the contrast in sonority between large and small groups of players.

Antonio Vivaldi (1678–1741)

The son of a violinist, Vivaldi grew up in his native Venice. He was ordained in the church while in his twenties and became known as "the red priest," a reference to the color of his hair. For the greater part of his career, Vivaldi was *maestro de' concerti,* or music master, at the most important of the four music schools for which Venice was famous, the Conservatorio dell'Ospedale della Pietà. These schools were attached to charitable institutions established for the upbringing of orphaned children—mostly girls—and played a vital role in the musical life of Venetians. Much of Vivaldi's output was written for concerts at the school, which attracted visitors from all over Europe.

One of the most prolific composers of his era, Vivaldi also wrote, in addition to his many concertos, chamber music and operas as well as cantatas, an oratorio, and an extended setting of the *Gloria*, which is today one of his most performed works. His life came to a mysterious end: a contemporary Venetian account notes that the composer, who had once earned 50,000 ducats in his day (about $4 million today), died in poverty as a result of his extravagance.

MAJOR WORKS: Over 230 violin concertos, including *Le quattro stagioni* (*The Four Seasons*, c. 1725) • Other solo, double, triple, and orchestral concertos • Sinfonias • Vocal music, including operas and oratorios, Mass movements, and a *Magnificat*.

St. Cecilia, patroness of musicians, plays a Baroque violin in this painting by **Guido Reni** (1575–1642). There is no chin rest, so she plays it braced against her shoulder; her grip on the bow also differs from that of modern players.

Vivaldi's best-known work is *The Four Seasons*, a group of four solo violin concertos, each named for a season. We have observed the fondness for word-painting in Renaissance and Baroque vocal works, where the music is meant to portray the action and emotion described by the text. In *The Four Seasons*, Vivaldi applies this principle to instrumental music. While each concerto has an independent musical logic, it is also accompanied by a poem, describing the joys of that particular season. Each line of the poem is printed above a certain passage in the score; the music at that point mirrors graphically the action described. This literary link is called **program music**.

In the first movement of *Spring* (*La primavera*; LG 12), an Allegro in E major, both poem and music evoke the birds' joyous welcome to spring and the gentle murmur of streams, followed by thunder and lightning. The image of birdcalls takes shape in staccato notes, trills, and running scales; a storm is portrayed by agitated repeated notes answered by quickly ascending minor-key scales. Throughout, an orchestral ritornello (refrain) returns again and again (representing the general mood of spring) in alternation with the **episodes**, which often feature the solo violin. Ultimately, "the little birds take up again their melodious song" as we return to the home key. A florid passage for the violin soloist leads to the final ritornello.

In the second movement, a Largo in 3/4, Vivaldi evokes the poetic image of a goatherd who sleeps in a "pleasant, flowery meadow" with his faithful dog by his side. Over the bass line played by the violas, which sound an ostinato rhythm, he writes, "The dog who barks." In the finale, an Allegro marked "Rustic Dance," we can visualize nymphs and shepherds cavorting in the fields as the music suggests the drone of bagpipes. Ritornellos and solo passages alternate in bringing the work to a happy conclusion.

Like Bach, Vivaldi was renowned in his day as a performer rather than a composer. Today, he is recognized both as the "father of the concerto," having established ritornello form as its basic procedure, and as a herald of musical Romanticism in his use of pictorial imagery. In his compositions, we encounter an early attempt to empower instrumental music to create independent meanings apart from words and beyond the enhancement of dance.

▶|◀ Reflect

How do the ritornellos (refrains) help you follow the story (the program) of Vivaldi's concerto? If there were no story provided, could you make up your own to fit this music?

YOUR TURN TO EXPLORE

With a classmate or two, find an example of instrumental music with a title that describes some place or mood or activity. What specific elements of the music do you think were designed to convey that image? Did you and your classmate come up with the same imagery? What might account for similarities and differences in your interpretation? Can you think of ways that the composer or performers might have made the image even more compelling or clear?

LISTENING GUIDE 12   3:24

Vivaldi: *Spring*, from *The Four Seasons* (*La primavera, from Le quattro stagioni*), I

DATE: Published 1725 (Op. 8, No. 1)

PERFORMED BY: Rachel Podger, solo violin; Brecon Baroque

GENRE: Programmatic concerto for solo violin, based on an Italian sonnet:

No. 1: *Spring (La primavera)*	No. 3: *Autumn (L'autunno)*
No. 2: *Summer (L'estate)*	No. 4: *Winter (L'inverno)*

I. Allegro
Joyful spring has arrived,
the birds greet it with their cheerful song,
and the brooks in the gentle breezes
flow with a sweet murmur.

The sky is covered with a black mantle,
and thunder and lightning announce a storm.
When they fall silent, the little birds
take up again their melodious song.

II. Largo
And in the pleasant, flowery meadow,
to the gentle murmur of bushes and trees,
the goatherd sleeps, his faithful dog at his side.

III. Allegro (Rustic Dance)
To the festive sounds of a rustic bagpipe
nymphs and shepherds dance in their favorite spot
when spring appears in its brilliance.

I: Allegro, E major

What to Listen For

Melody The ritornello opens the work: a lively, memorable theme in two main sections (each with repeated phrases). Parts of this theme return throughout, alternating with flashy scales and trills by the solo violin.

Form The ritornello in the orchestra acts as a unifying refrain, alternating with contrasting episodes.

Performing forces Solo violin in dialogue with a small string orchestra, with the basso continuo (harpsichord) reinforcing them throughout.

Expression Soloist and orchestra provide a programmatic evocation of musical images from the poem (birds, brooks, breeze, storm).

Opening ritornello phrase:

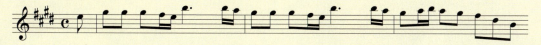

continued on next page

Closing ritornello phrase:

	DESCRIPTION	PROGRAM
0:00	Ritornello 1, in E major.	Spring
0:30	Episode 1; solo violin with birdlike trills and high running scales, accompanied by violins.	Birds
1:02	Ritornello 2.	Spring
1:09	Episode 2; whispering figures like water flowing, played by orchestra.	Murmuring brooks
1:31	Ritornello 3.	Spring
1:38	Episode 3 modulates; solo violin with repeated notes, fast ascending minor-key scales, accompanied by orchestra.	Thunder, lightning
2:03	Ritornello 4, in the relative minor (C-sharp).	Spring
2:12	Episode 4; trills and repeated notes in solo violin.	Birds
2:29	Ritornello 5, returns to E major; brief solo passage interrupts.	
2:56	Closing tutti (whole ensemble).	

Process as Meaning:
Bach and the Fugue

▶❙ First, listen ...

to the first minute of Bach's "Little" Fugue in G Minor; you will hear the main theme (the subject) four times. How is it recognizably the same each time, and how is it different? (Consider the range as a primary difference.)

> 66 He, who possessed the most profound knowledge of all the contrapuntal arts, understood how to make art subservient to beauty."
>
> —Carl Philipp Emanuel Bach (1714–1788), about his father, J. S. Bach

Instrumental music, in several contemporary traditions, often includes a component of improvisation: musicians will elaborate counterpoint on the spot, drawing on established conventions as well as their own creative imagination. Without the distraction of words, the listener's ear can focus on the shape and interaction of musical lines: this interaction provides the music's expressive resources and meaning. Thus, while some counterpoint-based music can be understood as individual "pieces" (which are always played the same way), counterpoint is also a process. And just like today's rock and jazz stars, the great composers of the past frequently *improvised* their polyphonic processes, so that the performer-composer and listener were more equal participants in the unfolding of meaning through sound.

KEYBOARD INSTRUMENTS IN THE BAROQUE ERA

Keyboard instruments, which are inherently suited to polyphonic performance, have been featured in Western music since the Middle Ages; in the 1600s, however, instruments such as the **organ** and **harpsichord** reached a new level of refinement. **Organ/harpsichord**

KEY POINTS

- The **organ** and **harpsichord** were the main keyboard instruments of the Baroque era.

- Keyboard players improvised and created free-form pieces called **preludes** or **toccatas**, followed by more structured works, such as **fugues**.

- *The Art of Fugue* is J. S. Bach's last and most comprehensive example of contrapuntal writing.

- Among Bach's many keyboard fugues, the "Little" G Minor Organ Fugue is among his most popular.

On this Baroque organ in St. Boniface Church, Arnstadt, Germany, the young virtuoso Bach performed the dedicatory recital in 1703.

These technological advances encouraged musicians to broaden their technique, and musicians' experiments likewise spurred instrument builders to new heights.

The harpsichord differs from the modern piano in two important ways. First, its strings are plucked by quills rather than struck with hammers, and its tone cannot be sustained like that of the piano, a product of the early Classical era. Second, the pressure of the fingers on the keys can produce subtle dynamic nuances but not the piano's extremes of loud and soft.

German builders of the 1600s and 1700s created organs with various sets of pipes, each with a sharply contrasting tone color, so that the ear could pick out the separate lines of counterpoint. The organ's multiple keyboards made it possible to achieve terraced levels of soft and loud. J. S. Bach was a sought-after consultant to church-organ builders, since he was renowned as an outstanding keyboard player. He was also famous for his ability to improvise at the organ or harpsichord—and his improvisations ranged from relatively free-form, with highly contrasting musical ideas and tempos (in what was often called a **toccata** or **prelude**), to a much more systematic working-out of a single musical thought (generally labeled fugue). Bach wrote out a number of his most successful improvisations, usually to serve as models for his students.

The toccata and prelude were designed to showcase the performer's dexterity and were often paired/contrasted with more systematically organized forms—you may know Bach's famous *Toccata and Fugue in D Minor*, which was the opening music for Disney's 1940 film *Fantasia* and has been heard in many films since. We will focus on the more tightly structured form, the fugue, since it illustrates the Baroque ideal of systematic elaboration of short musical ideas.

THE FUGUE AND ITS DEVICES

A **fugue** is a contrapuntal composition in which a single theme pervades the entire fabric, entering in one voice (or instrumental line) and then in another. The fugue, then, is based on the principle of **imitation**. Its main theme, the **subject**, constitutes the unifying idea, the focal point of interest in the contrapuntal web.

We have already encountered the fugue or fugal style in a number of works: in *The Young Person's Guide to the Orchestra*, by Britten; in Handel's choruses in *Messiah*; and in the opening movement of Bach's cantata *Wachet auf*. Though a fugue may be written for a group of instruments or voices, as in these works, Bach was most renowned for writing—and improvising—fugues for a solo keyboard instrument.

Subject and answer   The subject of the fugue is stated alone at the beginning in one of the voices—referred to by the range in which it sounds: soprano, alto, tenor, or bass. It is then imitated in another voice—this is the **answer**—while the first can continue with **Countersubject**   a **countersubject** (a different theme heard against the subject) or new material. When the subject has been presented in each voice once, the first section of the **Exposition**   fugue, the **exposition**, is at an end. From then on, the fugue alternates between

Contrapuntal Devices

Subject and answer (answer begins five notes higher, with intervals changed), from *The Art of Fugue*:

answer (on A)

subject (on D)

new material

Other contrapuntal devices:

Original   MELODY

Inversion   ᴹᴱᴸOᗡλ

Retrograde   YꓷOꓶƎM

Retrograde inversion   ⅄ꓷOꓶƎW

Augmentation   **M E L O D Y**

Diminution   MELODY

sections that feature entrances of the subject and **episodes**—interludes (lacking the subject) that serve as areas of relaxation.

Contrapuntal writing is marked by a number of devices used since the earliest days of polyphony. A subject can be presented in longer time values, often twice as slow as the original, called **augmentation** (see box above), or in shorter time values that go by faster, called **diminution**. The pitches can be stated backward (starting from the last note and preceding to the first), known as **retrograde**, or turned upside down (in mirror image), moving by the same intervals but in the opposite direction, a technique called **inversion**. Overlapping statements of the subject, called **stretto**, heighten the tension.

Episodes

Contrapuntal devices

BACH'S KEYBOARD FUGUES

Bach worked his entire life to refine his fugal technique, combining mastery of craft with creativity and beauty. Although every fugue follows the same principle, with an exposition that presents the subject in at least two (and usually three or

In *Fugue* (1925), by **Josef Albers** (1888–1976), the interlocking and parallel lines resemble the polyphonic textures of this genre.

more) voices, and then an alternation between returns of the subject and contrasting musical ideas, no two fugues are alike in detail. Indeed, the process of combining predictable material with fresh ideas is at the core of musical composition, and Bach was a master. *The Well-Tempered Clavier*, a collection of forty-eight preludes and fugues issued in two volumes and demonstrating a new system for tuning keyboard instruments that approaches our contemporary equal-semitone norm, is a testament to his skill. Bach intended the collection as a teaching aid, with each individual prelude and fugue demonstrating a different set of expressive and technical challenges for the aspiring keyboard player. His last demonstration of contrapuntal mastery was *The Art of Fugue*, a collection of fourteen fugues and four canons that systematically explores all the wizardry of fugal devices (see chart on p. 131).

"Little" Fugue in G Minor

Bach's Fugue for Organ in G Minor (generally called "Little" to distinguish it from a longer fugue in the same key) has long been acknowledged as a great teaching example; it was copied by hand many times during his day by students and admirers, and was republished in multiple copies when Bach's music was "rediscovered" a century after his death. The organist is tasked with playing all four simultaneous musical lines, or voices (designated soprano, alto, tenor, and bass, according to their range), three lines with hands on the keyboard (or keyboards; many organs have more than one keyboard, each of which can be associated with different pipes and therefore timbres) and one line with feet on the pedalboard (which is also associated with a different set of pipes). Bach was known for his extraordinary pedal technique, and for his ability to teach his students to move their feet as nimbly on the pedalboard as their fingers did on the keyboard.

The opening of the subject is very distinctive, outlining a minor triad; the middle part repeats with a slight variation to help the listener recognize the melody within the multivoice texture; and the end picks up steam in a flow of sixteenth notes to propel the music forward (LG 13).

Order of entries   As the exposition of this fugue begins, we hear the subject at the top of the range (soprano). When the alto enters with the answer (repeating the melody of the subject exactly, but lower), the soprano continues with a second melodic idea that will also return throughout the fugue: the countersubject, characterized by a trill and then continuous sixteenth notes with a distinctive adjacent-note pattern. After a few seconds of transition in which the subject is absent, Bach again introduces a subject-answer pair in successively lower voices (tenor, bass); the end of the subject is changed slightly in the bass (slowing down instead of speeding up) to provide a clearer cadence to close the exposition. When the bass voice enters, you may hear that the pedalboard uses pipes that have a different, more "brassy" timbre than those associated with the keyboard in our recording.

For the remainder of the fugue, Bach alternates modified returns of the subject with free material (episodes): he does not return to the subject in the original (tonic) key of G minor until the very end, after the longest episode of all. This

Exposition of "Little" G Minor Fugue

Measure	1	6	11	12	17	22—end of exposition
Soprano	**subject** G minor	counter-subject	transitional passage	new material	new material	closing cadence
Alto		**answer** D minor	transitional passage	counter-subject	new material	closing cadence
Tenor				**subject** G minor	counter-subject	closing cadence
Bass					**answer** D minor	closing cadence

decision to stay away from the home key until the end was one principal way that the composer/improviser could signal to his listeners when to expect the final section of a fugue. Another signal was placing the G minor subject in the low organ pedals, as Bach also does here, with a bold statement that leads through a brief rhythmic slow-down to the final cadence. The final chord, a major triad, jolts us from the contemplative minor-key setting; this shifting from minor to major at the end was a common feature in Baroque keyboard music.

Since all of Bach's keyboard music was designed to teach prospective students to refine their technique, this work can be understood as a stimulating dexterity exercise for both fingers and brain. Bach would have expected his advanced students to go on to improvise such processes on their own, as they demonstrated their professional independence.

LISTENING GUIDE 13

 4:04

Bach: "Little" Fugue in G Minor, BWV 578

DATE: 1703–07

GENRE: Fugue for organ in four voices (SATB)

PERFORMED BY: E. Power Biggs, organ

What to Listen For

Melody The subject is in three phrases, with the middle phrase repeated; the countersubject features a trill.

Harmony Begins in a minor tonality; the subject appears in a major mode in the middle of the fugue; the final cadence is on a major third.

Texture Four-part imitative polyphony, with a changing number of simultaneous musical lines.

Form Fugue in three parts: exposition, middle entries, closing section.

continued on next page

EXPOSITION

0:00   Soprano (subject).

0:18   Alto (answer; the soprano continues with the countersubject).

0:35   Brief transition, no subject.

0:41   Tenor (subject; the alto has the countersubject).

0:58   Bass (answer; the tenor has the countersubject); end of the subject is changed slightly.

MIDDLE ENTRIES

1:14   Episode, no subject.

1:25   Subject starts in the tenor, then continues in soprano after a brief pause.

1:43   Episode, no subject.

1:52   Subject in the alto, in B-flat major.

2:08   Episode, no subject.

2:20   Subject in the bass, in B-flat major.

2:36   Episode, no subject.

2:54   Subject in soprano, in C minor.

3:10   Longest episode, no subject.

CLOSING SECTION

3:40   Subject in the bass, in G minor.

3:54   Final chords, ending with a G major triad.

Fugue subject, in three phrases:

phrase 1   phrase 2   phrase 3

▶|◀ Reflect

How does Bach help you recognize the subject each time he introduces it? What are some of the ways he changes it? What do you think Bach's goal was in writing this fugue?

YOUR TURN TO EXPLORE

Seek out a recording (or better yet, a live performance) of an improvisation-oriented musician such as a rock guitarist or a jazz pianist. Listen for how the melody/harmony of each "standard tune" is first presented relatively straightforwardly, and then varied through several repetitions. How does the performer weave aspects of a recognizable melody through the texture as he/she improvises? Are there particular portions of the melody that are featured more prominently, and if so, why do you think this is?

MAJOR COMPOSERS

Henry Purcell
Antonio Vivaldi

Johann Sebastian Bach

George Frideric Handel

IMPORTANT GENRES

opera

Mass

oratorio

cantata

concerto

suite

dance music

fugue

PART 3 SUMMARY

Baroque Music

Listening Essentials

Melody: Continuous melody with wide leaps; chromatic notes for emotional effect; speechlike melody in recitative (opera and oratorio).

Rhythm/meter: One single rhythm predominates, with a steady, energetic pulse; freer movement in vocal music.

Harmony: A particular major or minor tonality, with brief excursions to other keys; chromatic harmony for expressive effect.

Texture: Homophonic texture (early Baroque) gives way to polyphonic, often imitative, texture (later Baroque).

Form: Binary form, ternary form, instrumental works with a returning, unifying theme (ritornello).

Expression: Emotional exuberance and theatricality; *forte/piano* contrasts and echo effects; focus on the text; performers were expected to improvise.

Performing forces: String orchestra, with added woodwinds and brass; organ and harpsichord provide harmonic continuity.

Listening Challenge

Now take the online Listening Challenge, where you'll listen to a mystery selection from the Baroque era and answer questions about its elements: the character of the melody, the rhythmic movement and meter, the tonality (major or minor) of the harmony, the genre and form, the texture produced by the interweaving of instrumental parts, any expressive devices you note (for example, use of dynamics, chromaticism, or virtuosity), and the timbre of Baroque string instruments.

135

CLASSICAL ERA

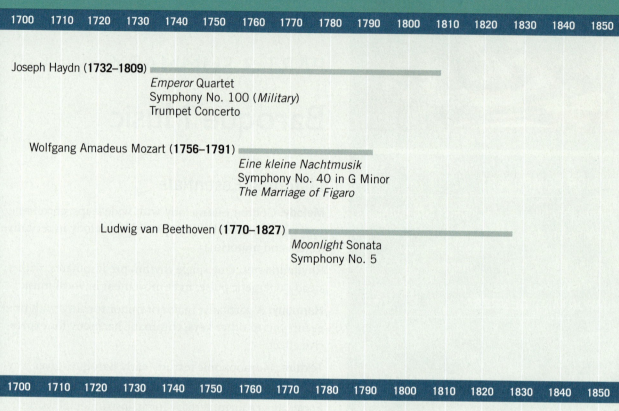

COMPOSERS AND WORKS

| 1700 | 1710 | 1720 | 1730 | 1740 | 1750 | 1760 | 1770 | 1780 | 1790 | 1800 | 1810 | 1820 | 1830 | 1840 | 1850 |

Joseph Haydn (**1732–1809**)

Emperor Quartet
Symphony No. 100 (*Military*)
Trumpet Concerto

Wolfgang Amadeus Mozart (**1756–1791**)

Eine kleine Nachtmusik
Symphony No. 40 in G Minor
The Marriage of Figaro

Ludwig van Beethoven (**1770–1827**)

Moonlight Sonata
Symphony No. 5

EVENTS

| 1700 | 1710 | 1720 | 1730 | 1740 | 1750 | 1760 | 1770 | 1780 | 1790 | 1800 | 1810 | 1820 | 1830 | 1840 | 1850 |

- **1715** Reign of Louis XV begins.
- **1732** George Washington born.
- **1752** Benjamin Franklin experiments with electricity.
- **1762** Catherine II crowned empress of Russia.
- **1771** First edition of *Encyclopaedia Britannica* printed.
- **1775** American Revolution begins.
- **1785** Friedrich von Schiller writes "Ode to Joy."
- **1789** French Revolution begins.
- **1796** Edward Jenner discovers vaccination for smallpox.
- **1804** Napoleon crowned emperor of France.
- **1815** Napoleon defeated at Battle of Waterloo.

Johann Nepomuk della Croce (1736–1819), *The Mozart Family,* at the piano.

Eighteenth-Century Classicism

▶‖ First, listen . . .

to the second movement from Haydn's Symphony No. 94 in G Major (*Surprise*), and see how many musical traits described in Part 1 you can identify: for example, the shape of the melodic lines; the organization of the rhythm into a meter; shifts between major and minor harmony; how repetition, contrast, and variation establish the form; and how instruments interact to weave the musical fabric, or texture. Listen several times to try to pick up multiple elements, but don't worry about "getting it right"—this is your first chance to apply these basic principles to an example of Classical-era music.

LISTENING OBJECTIVES

By the end of Part 4, you will be able to

- distinguish the music's balanced melodic lines and phrases, accompanied by diatonic harmonies in major or minor keys.

- hear the regular rhythmic movement, in clear duple or triple meters.

- perceive how the vertical, homophonic texture helps you focus on the melody.

- follow the unfolding of medium- and large-scale forms built around one or two main themes.

- define some of the main vocal and instrumental genres in the Classical era.

137

4

Music as Order and Logic

Some artistic movements can easily be pinpointed in time, those whose leaders make strong statements about the need for radical change. Classicism is not such a movement. In fact, in some ways classicism is a constant concern in Western culture, since its roots are in the values of order and reason expressed by the ancient Greeks and Romans, who laid the foundations for the very notion of European identity. Ideals of classicism have repeatedly resurfaced through the centuries, and in some cases have coexisted with other stylistic concerns. For example, French artists and musicians in the early 1700s never thought of their work as "baroque": they were the ones who introduced the term to disparage others who didn't share their "classical" sensibility.

The later 1700s were a time when classical ideals were especially strong in Europe, combined with a philosophical and intellectual movement known as the **The Enlightenment** **Enlightenment**, which stressed the centrality of reason in human experience. Artists and musicians strove to join the social push toward order and reason, developing works characterized by clarity and regularity of structure, and by an ideal of "natural simplicity." This tendency led to the development of an international musical style that was held up by subsequent generations as timeless, embodying the most perfect manifestations of musical logic. While previous styles had risen and fallen with fashion, the music of the Classical style was preserved and treasured even as later styles developed in contrast to its ideals—and this music continues to form the core of the Western concert tradition to this day.

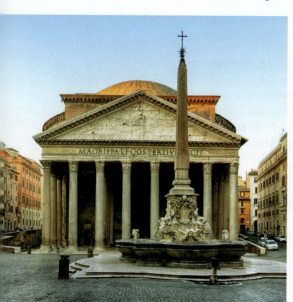

The Pantheon, in Rome (completed c. 126 CE), embodies the classical ideals of order and harmonious proportions.

CLASSICISM AND ENLIGHTENMENT CULTURE

The Classical era in music encompasses the last half of the eighteenth century and the early decades of the nineteenth (c. 1750–1825). During this era, the rule of strong aristocratic sovereigns continued throughout Europe. Louis XV presided over extravagant celebrations in Versailles, and Frederick the Great ruled in Prussia, Maria Theresa in Austria, and Catherine the Great in Russia. In such societies, the ruling class enjoyed its power through hereditary right. At the same time, a new economic power was growing through the Industrial Revolution, which gathered momentum in the mid-eighteenth century through a series of important inventions—from James Watt's improved steam engine and James Hargreaves's spinning jenny in the 1760s to Eli Whitney's cotton gin in the 1790s. These decades saw significant advances in science—Benjamin Franklin harnessed electricity, Joseph Priestley discovered oxygen, and Edward Jenner perfected vaccination—and intellectual life, with the publication of the French *Encyclopédie* and the first edition of the *Encyclopaedia Britannica*.

The eighteenth century has been called the Age of Reason as well as Enlightenment. Philosophers considered social and political issues in the light of reason and science, but they were also advocates for the rising middle class. The intellectual climate, then, was nourished by two contrasting streams. While Classical art captured the exquisite refinement of a way of life that was drawing to a close, it also caught the first wave of a new social structure that would emerge with the revolutionary upheavals at the end of the century.

Thomas Jefferson's design for the Rotunda of the University of Virginia, completed in 1826, reflects his admiration for classical architecture; note the similarities of this building with the Roman Pantheon (opposite).

Just as eighteenth-century thinkers idealized the civilization of the Greeks and Romans, artists revered the unity and proportions of ancient architecture and fine arts. In this spirit, Thomas Jefferson patterned the nation's Capitol, the University of Virginia (see illustration above), and his home at Monticello after Greek and Roman temples. His example spurred on a classical revival in the United States, which made Ionic, Doric, and Corinthian columns indispensable features of public buildings well into the twentieth century.

By the 1760s, though, a contrasting point of view was emerging in literature. **Romantic thought** The French philosopher Jean-Jacques Rousseau, sometimes called the "father of Romanticism," produced some of his most significant writings in these years. The first manifestation of the Romantic spirit in Germany was a literary movement known as *Sturm und Drang* (storm and stress).

By the end of the century, the old world of the aristocracy was beginning to give way to a new society of the people and to an era that produced some of the greatest artworks of Western culture. Thus, backward-looking classicism itself contained the seeds of what would become the most significant and self-conscious progressive redefinition of European culture.

ELEMENTS OF CLASSICAL STYLE

The Classical period in music is characterized best by the masters of the so-called Viennese School—Haydn, Mozart, Beethoven, and their successor Franz Schubert. **Viennese School** These composers worked in an age of great musical experimentation and discovery, when musicians took on new challenges: first, to explore thoroughly the possibilities offered by the major-minor system; and second, to perfect a large-scale form of instrumental music—now known as sonata-allegro form—that exploited those possibilities to the fullest degree. Having found this ideal structure, composers then developed it into the solo and duo sonata, the trio and quartet (especially the string quartet), the concerto, and the symphony.

Angelica Kauffmann (1741–1807), *Portrait of a Young Girl as a Bacchante*. This portrait displays the Classical interest in antiquity: a bacchante is a follower of Bacchus, the Roman god of wine.

The music of the Viennese masters is notable for its elegant, lyrical melodies. Classical melodies "sing," even those intended for instruments. They are usually based on symmetrical four-bar phrases marked by clearcut cadences, and they often move stepwise or by small leaps within a narrow range. Clarity is further provided by repetition and the frequent use of sequence (a pattern repeated at a higher or lower pitch). These devices make for balanced structures that are readily accessible to the listener.

The harmonies that sustain the melodies are equally clear. Chords are built from the seven tones of the major or minor scale (meaning they are diatonic) and therefore are firmly rooted in the key. The chords underline the balanced symmetry of phrases and cadences, and they form vertical columns of sound over which the melody unfolds freely, generally in a homophonic texture (a melody with accompanying harmony).

Much of the music is in one of the four basic meters—2/4, 3/4, 4/4, or 6/8—and moves at a steady tempo. If a piece or movement begins in a certain meter, it is apt to stay there until the end. Rhythm works closely with melody and harmony to make clear the symmetrical phrase-and-cadence structure of the piece. Well-defined sections establish the home (tonic) key, move to contrasting but closely related keys, and return to the home key. The result is the beautifully molded architectural forms of the Classical style, fulfilling the listener's need for both unity and variety.

Despite its aristocratic elegance, music of the Classical era absorbed a variety of folk and popular elements. This influence made itself felt not only in the German dances, minuets, and waltzes of the Viennese masters but also in their songs, symphonies, concertos, string quartets, and sonatas.

THE PATRONAGE SYSTEM

The culture of the eighteenth century thrived under the **patronage**, or sponsorship, of an aristocracy that viewed the arts as a necessary adornment of life. Music was part of the elaborate lifestyle of the nobility, and the center of musical life was the palace.

Detail of aristocratic performers in *The Concert*. Meissen porcelain from c. 1760.

The social events at court created a steady demand for new works from composers, who had to supply whatever their patrons wanted. Although musicians ranked little better than servants, their situation was not quite as depressing as it sounds. The patronage system actually gave musicians economic security and provided a social framework within which they could function. It offered important advantages to those who successfully adjusted to its requirements, as the career of Joseph Haydn clearly shows (see p. 146).

Opportunities for Women

While aristocratic women like Marie Antoinette, archduchess of Austria and wife of French king Louis XVI, continued their regular music studies, middle-class women also found a place as musicians under the patronage system. In Italy and

Map of Europe, 1763–89, showing major musical centers.

France, professional female singers achieved prominence in opera and in court ballets. Others found a place within aristocratic circles as court instrumentalists and music teachers, offering private lessons to members of the nobility.

Two women in particular, both associated with Wolfgang Amadeus Mozart, stand out as impressive keyboard players of the late eighteenth century. His sister, Maria Anna Mozart (1751–1829), known as Nannerl, was an accomplished pianist who as a child toured with Wolfgang, performing concertos and four-hand piano works (p. 137). Their father noted that Nannerl, at age twelve, played "so beautifully that everyone is talking about her and admiring her execution." A friend of Mozart's, the blind composer Maria Theresia von Paradis (1759–1824), was an excellent pianist and organist, renowned for her remarkable musical memory, which retained some sixty different concertos that she prepared for an extended European tour.

Maria Anna Mozart

Maria Theresia von Paradis

The public prominence achieved by these women was unusual for the era. However, the many engravings and paintings of the time illustrating music-making scenes make it clear that women participated frequently in performances at home, in aristocratic salons, and at court (p. 163). Ultimately, with the growth of the music trades, especially music printing and publishing, women found more professional opportunities open to them. And as more amateurs participated in music-making, women of the middle as well as upper classes found an outlet for their talents.

From Palace to Concert Hall

At this time, musical performances were beginning to move from the palace to the concert hall. The rise of the public concert gave composers a new venue (site) in which to perform their works. Haydn and Beethoven conducted their

Balthasar Wigand (1771–1846), a public concert of a Haydn oratorio in the Festival Hall of the University of Vienna (1808), honoring the composer.

own symphonies at concerts, and Mozart and Beethoven played their own piano concertos. The public flocked to hear the latest works—unlike modern (classical music) concertgoers who are interested mainly in music of the past. The eagerness of eighteenth-century audiences for new music surely stimulated composers to greater productivity.

While great virtuoso performers continued to be highly prized, the clarity and simplicity of the Classical style made it increasingly accessible to the informed amateur—whether through performance or through careful listening. More and more instrumental music was described in terms of dialogue and communication—whether between performers or between the composer and the public. As the idea of communication through instrumental storytelling became ingrained, the notion of using that communication to build a deep and intimate connection between the uniquely inspired composer-genius and the receptive listener grew more appealing to musicians and their audiences. This too was an essential element in the emerging Romantic sensibility, as we will see in the work of Beethoven and in the public response to Mozart's late compositions.

Musical Conversations: Haydn and Classical Chamber Music

▶‖ **First, listen . . .**

to the theme of the second movement of Haydn's *Emperor Quartet* (about a minute long), and focus on the interaction between the four instruments. What role does each play in presenting the theme?

You get together with some friends and begin a conversation on a topic of common interest. Members of your group will agree or disagree with each other, expand on others' perspectives, interrupt each other as things get more heated, all while keeping a friendly spirit going, with the goal of reaching a satisfactory conclusion. This is how eighteenth-century Europeans understood chamber music, and in particular the string quartet: the equal participation of various instruments was an essential aspect of a new sensibility. These were conversations without words, but they were just as purposeful, and just as structured, as real conversations might be. The way composers achieved this was through an emphasis on predictable musical forms, which would allow musicians and listeners alike to "follow the discussion" to its logical conclusion, and to profit, as Goethe's quote above suggests, from its artistic expression.

EXPANDING MUSICAL IDEAS

As noted in Chapter 6, a musical idea that is used as a building block in the construction of a composition is called a **theme**. Varying a theme's melodic outline, rhythm, or harmony is considered **thematic development**. This is one of the

Thematic development

KEY POINTS

- Form is the most important organizing element in **absolute music**, which has no specific pictorial or literary program.

- Musical ideas, or **themes**, are used as building blocks in a composition; these themes are made up of short melodic or rhythmic fragments known as **motives**.

- Themes can be expanded by varying the melody, rhythm, or harmony through **thematic development**; this usually happens in large-scale works.

- The Classical era is the golden age of **chamber music** (ensemble music for two to about ten performers, with one player per part). The **string quartet** (two violins, viola, and cello) was the most important chamber-music genre of the era.

- Joseph Haydn's *Emperor* Quartet features a famous set of variations on a hymn he wrote for the Austrian emperor.

Eighteenth-century engraving of the Esterháza Palace, where Haydn was employed. The palace was built in 1766 in imitation of Versailles.

Motive and sequence

most important techniques in composition and requires both imagination and craft on the part of the creator. In addition to its capacity for growth, a theme can be fragmented by dividing it into its constituent motives, a **motive** being its smallest melodic or rhythmic unit. A motive may grow into an expansive melody, or be treated in **sequence**—that is, repeated at a higher or lower level. Thematic development is generally too complex for short pieces, where repetition, a simple contrast between sections, and a modest expansion of material usually supply the necessary continuity. But thematic development is necessary in larger forms, where it provides clarity, coherence, and logic.

The development of thematic material—through extension, contraction, and repetition—occurs in music from all corners of the world. In considering the fugue by Bach (Chapter 24), we have already seen that musical structure and logic can unfold through a partly planned, partly improvised process.

The most prominent musicians of the Classical era were also excellent improvisers—both Mozart and Beethoven, for example, drew crowds when they improvised at the keyboard. However, the forms of the Classical style are composed-out and fixed: they indicate a fully worked-out rational argument, rather than a flexible process-in-motion like the one we encountered in Bach's fugue. Because this music is so dependent on the listener's expectation of recognizable structures, it's crucial for us to understand the conventions on which composers and listeners based musical meaning.

CLASSICAL FORMS

Absolute music

Every musical work has a form; it is sometimes simple, other times complex. In **absolute music**, where there is no prescribed story or text to hold the music together, form is especially important. The story is the music itself, so its shape is of primary concern for the composer, the performer, and the listener. Most instrumental works of the Classical era—symphonies, sonatas, concertos, string quartets, and other types of chamber music—follow a sequence of sections or

Multimovement Cycle: General Scheme			
Movement	**Character/Tempo**	**Form**	**Playlist**
First	Long, dramatic Allegro	Sonata-allegro	Mozart, *Eine kleine Nachtmusik*, I Symphony No. 40, I Beethoven, Symphony No. 5, I
Second	Slow, lyrical Andante or Adagio	Theme and variations or **A-B-A**	Haydn, *Emperor* Quartet, II Symphony No. 100 (*Military*), II
Third (optional)	Dancelike Allegro or Allegretto	Minuet and trio (18th c.) Scherzo and trio (19th c.)	Mozart, *Eine kleine Nachtmusik*, III Beethoven, Symphony No. 5, III
Fourth (last)	Lively, spirited Allegro or Vivace	Sonata-allegro (or rondo or sonata-rondo)	Beethoven, Symphony No. 5, IV Haydn, Trumpet Concerto, III

movements that is known as a **multimovement cycle**. We will briefly consider the overall characteristics of that cycle, and then dwell in turn (in this and the following chapters) on the formal conventions of each movement.

Multimovement cycle

The outline of the multimovement cycle above sums up the common practice of both the Classical and Romantic eras. It can help you build expectations and listening strategies, provided you remember that it is no more than a general scheme.

Each individual movement has an internal form that binds its different sections into one artistic whole. You have already learned two of the simplest forms: two-part, or binary (**A-B**); and three-part, or ternary (**A-B-A**). Rather than start with the customary form of the first movement of the cycle (sonata-allegro form), which is more intricate and will be the subject of a later chapter, we will begin with a less complex form, as exemplified by the second movement of a string quartet by Haydn.

This anonymous watercolor depicts a performance of a string quartet, the most influential chamber-music genre of the era.

The Second Movement: Theme and Variations

The second is usually the slow movement of the cycle, offering a contrast to the first movement—usually a spirited Allegro—and characterized by songful melodies. Typically, it is an Andante or Adagio in **A-B-A** or theme-and-variations form.

We have already noted that variation is an important procedure in music, but in one form—**theme and variations**—it is the ruling principle. Here, the theme is clearly stated at the outset and serves as the point of departure; it may be newly invented or borrowed (like the theme in Britten's *Young Person's Guide to the Orchestra*; see LG 1). The theme is likely to be a small two- or three-part idea, simple in character to allow room for elaboration.

Joseph Haydn (1732–1809)

Haydn was one of the most prolific composers of the Classical period. Born in the small Austrian village of Rohrau, he absorbed the folk songs and dances of his homeland. The beauty of his voice secured him a place as a choirboy at St. Stephen's Cathedral in Vienna.

In 1761, when he was twenty-nine, Haydn entered the service of the Esterházy, a family of enormously wealthy Hungarian princes famous for their patronage of the arts, with whom he remained for almost thirty years. The family palace of Eszterháza was one of the most splendid in Europe (see illustration, p. 144), and music played a central role in the constant round of festivities there. The musical establishment under Haydn's direction included an orchestra, an opera company, a marionette theater, and a chapel. His life exemplifies the patronage system at its best.

By the time Haydn reached middle age, his music had brought him much fame.

After his prince's death, he made two visits to England in the 1790s, where he conducted his works with phenomenal success. He died in 1809, revered throughout Europe.

It was Haydn's historic role to help perfect the new instrumental music of the late eighteenth century, as well as expand the orchestra's size and resources through greater emphasis on the brass, clarinets (new to the orchestra), and percussion. His expressive harmony, structural logic, and endlessly varied moods embody the mature Classical style.

MAJOR WORKS: Chamber music, including 68 string quartets (*Emperor*, Op. 76, No. 3) • Over 100 symphonies (including the 12 *London* symphonies, Nos. 93–104) • Concertos for violin, cello, harpsichord, and trumpet • Sacred vocal music (Masses, motets, and two oratorios, including *The Creation*) • 14 operas • Keyboard music (including 40 sonatas).

In His Own Words

66 I learned from Haydn how to write quartets. No one else can do everything—be flirtatious and be unsettling, move to laughter and move to tears—as well as Joseph Haydn."

—Wolfgang Amadeus Mozart

It is followed by a series of variations in which certain features of the original idea are retained while others are altered. Each variation sets forth the idea with some new modification—you might say in a new disguise—through which the listener glimpses something of the original theme.

Any musical element may be developed in the variation process. The melody may be varied by adding or omitting notes or by shifting the theme to another key—a favorite procedure in jazz, where the solo player embellishes a popular tune with a series of decorative flourishes. The chords that accompany a melody may be replaced by others; the shape of the accompaniment may be changed; note lengths, meter, or tempo can also be altered through rhythmic variation, and the texture may be enriched by interweaving the melody with new themes or countermelodies.

Chamber music, as we have seen, is music for a small ensemble—two to about ten players—with one player to a part. In this intimate genre, each instrument is expected to assert itself fully, but function as part of a team rather than as a soloist.

String quartet

The central position in Classical chamber music was held by the **string quartet**, which consists of two violins (a first and a second), a viola, and a cello. Because the string quartet was intended to be enjoyed by a small group of cultivated music lovers, composers did not need expansive gestures here. They could present their most private thoughts, and indeed, the final string quartets of Haydn, Mozart, and Beethoven contain some of their most profound music. Joseph Haydn, with his sixty-eight string quartets, played a central role in the evolution of this genre.

Haydn's *Emperor* Quartet

Haydn wrote most of his string quartets in sets of six, and his Op. 76 quartets are no exception. The third in the set is known as the *Emperor* because the second movement is based on a hymn Haydn wrote for the Austrian emperor Franz II. The invasion of Vienna by Napoleonic armies in 1796 raised a spirit of patriotism across Austria, to which Haydn responded with a musical tribute that became the country's national anthem, *Gott erhalte Franz den Kaiser* (*God Keep the Emperor Franz*). The hymn was sung in all the theaters of Vienna for the emperor's birthday on February 12, 1797; thanks to Haydn, Austria now had a moving anthem comparable to those of England (*God Save the King*) and France (*La Marseillaise*).

LISTENING GUIDE 14 6:46

Haydn: String Quartet in C Major, Op. 76, No. 3 (*Emperor*), II

DATE: 1797

PERFORMED BY: Gewandhaus Quartet

MOVEMENTS: I. Allegro; sonata-allegro form

II. Poco adagio, cantabile; theme and variations

III. Menuetto, Allegro; minuet and trio

IV. Finale, Presto; sonata-allegro form

II. Poco adagio

What to Listen For

Melody Memorable, lyrical melody in five regular phrases, two of which are repeated (a-a-b-c-c).

Form Theme (a five-phrase melody) and four variations, each with the same structure, followed by a four-measure coda.

Texture Homophonic opening; the movement becomes more polyphonic as it progresses.

Performing forces String quartet: two violins, viola, and cello.

Structure of the theme

Phrase a (repeated):

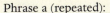

Phrase b:

Phrase c (repeated):

continued on next page

0:00   **Theme**: played by violin 1, with a simple chordal accompaniment.
1:19   **Variation 1**: theme played by violin 2 in a duet with high-range decorative figurations in violin 1.
2:28   **Variation 2**: theme played by the cello, accompanied by other instruments; grows more polyphonic.
3:46   **Variation 3**: theme played by the viola; syncopated accompaniment in violin 1; some chromaticism.
5:04   **Variation 4**: theme returns to violin 1, set in a polyphonic texture.
6:18   **Coda**: short closing with a sustained cello note, over which the other instruments fade out softly.

Austrian emperor Franz II, for whom Haydn wrote a birthday hymn. Anonymous, early nineteenth century.

Haydn wrote his Op. 76, No. 3, quartet a few months later, in the summer of 1797, using the imperial hymn as a basis for a majestic theme and variations in the slow movement (LG 14). He gives each player an equal chance to participate in the "conversation" about the hymn tune. After the tune is introduced by the first violin in a simple setting, each instrument takes its turn with the theme: the second violin, with an embroidered accompanying line played by its violin partner; the cello, with its deep and dignified tone; then the dark viola—Haydn's own instrument—with rich chromatic color. The fourth and final variation brings back the melody in a more complex polyphonic texture. This lyrical tune, thought to be based on a Croatian folk song, was a favorite of Haydn's and reportedly the last music played before his death.

As you listen to the variations that Haydn builds on the hymn to the emperor, think about the kinds of expectations that he would like you, as the listener, to have about this conversation—which is not only an interaction between four string-instrument-playing friends but also an interaction between Haydn and you.

▶❙◀ Reflect

How does Haydn change the role of each instrument through the multiple variations? Can you follow the melody throughout as it passes from instrument to instrument? What expressive "story" might that interaction tell?

YOUR TURN TO EXPLORE

Look for videos of performers from different chamber-music traditions—from the Classical era, but also jazz, country, rock, or hip-hop. In what way do these performers appear to be "performing friendship" through their music-making? What differences are there in the interactions or conversations between performers, and between performers and audience, in these various traditions?

The Ultimate Instrument: Haydn and the Symphony

▶|| **First, listen . . .**

for shifts between major and minor harmonies in the second movement of Haydn's Symphony No. 100. How do the major and minor harmonies correspond to changes in dynamics?

The palette of tone colors available to a symphony composer is remarkable. Even the most complex synthesizers cannot match the nuance of live instruments, especially when they are combined by the dozens into a carefully coordinated unit—the orchestra. It was during the Classical era that the notion of the orchestra as the "ultimate instrument" began to develop, and composers sought to realize their greatest expressive potential through this medium, which remains to this day (even as it has changed over the centuries) probably the most versatile and powerful musical resource of the Western tradition. While you can hear orchestral sounds (often electronically manipulated) in television and film, experiencing a symphony orchestra in person is so much more compelling than hearing it on a recording.

Early History of the Symphony

The **symphony**, which held the central place in Classical instrumental music, had its roots in the Italian opera **overture** of the early eighteenth century, an orchestral piece in three sections: fast-slow-fast. First played to introduce an opera, these three sections eventually became separate movements, to which the early German symphonists added a number of innovations. One was the use of a quick, aggressively rhythmic theme rising from low to high register with such speed that it

66 My Prince was always satisfied with my works. I not only had the encouragement of constant approval but as conductor of an orchestra I could make experiments, observe what produced an effect and what weakened it, and . . . improve, alter, make additions or omissions, and be as bold as I pleased."

—Joseph Haydn

In His Own Words

66 A symphony must be like the world; it must embrace everything."

—Gustav Mahler (1860–1911)

KEY POINTS

■ The **symphony**, a genre designed to demonstrate the expressive capabilities of a full orchestra, arose as one of the principal instrumental traditions during the Classical era.

■ The heart of the Classical orchestra (about thirty to forty players) was the strings, assisted by woodwinds, brass, and percussion.

■ Joseph Haydn wrote over 100 symphonies; among these, his last 12—the so-called *London Symphones*—are his masterpieces in the genre.

became known as a "rocket theme." Equally important was the use of drawn-out *crescendos* (called a "steamroller effect"), slowly gathering force as they built to a climax. Finally, composers added a dance movement, an elegant minuet.

THE CLASSICAL ORCHESTRA

The Classical masters established the orchestra as we know it today: an ensemble of the four instrumental families. The heart of the orchestra was the string family. Woodwinds provided varying colors and assisted the strings, often doubling them. The brass sustained the harmonies and contributed body to the sound, while the timpani supplied rhythmic life and vitality. The eighteenth-century orchestra numbered from thirty to forty players; thus, the volume of sound was still more appropriate for the salon than the concert hall. We will hear a movement from Haydn's Symphony No. 100 on eighteenth-century period instruments.

Classical composers created a dynamic style of orchestral writing in which all the instruments participated actively and each timbre could be heard. The interchange of themes between the various instrumental groups assumed the excitement of a witty conversation; in this, the Classical symphony also resembled the string quartet.

Haydn's Symphony No. 100 (*Military*)

Joseph Haydn contributed well over 100 symphonies to the genre, establishing the four-movement structure and earning himself the nickname "father of the symphony." His masterworks in the genre are his last set of 12, the so-called *London* Symphonies, commissioned for a concert series there. These late works

Natural horns (without valves) and woodwinds are seen in this painting of a small orchestra performing in an eighteenth-century Venetian palace.

LISTENING GUIDE 15

 5:33

Haydn: Symphony No. 100 in G Major (*Military*), II

DATE: 1794

PERFORMED BY: Hanover Band; Roy Goodman, conductor

MOVEMENTS: I. Adagio-Allegro; sonata-allegro form, G major
II. Allegretto; A-B-A′ form, C major

III. Moderato; minuet and trio, G major
IV. Presto; sonata-allegro form, G major

II: Allegretto

What to Listen For

Rhythm/meter Marchlike, in a regular duple meter.

Form Three-part form, with a varied return (**A-B-A'**); **A** is in rounded binary form, with two short repeated sections.

Harmony Begins in C major, shifts to C minor in the middle (**B**) section, and returns to C major for the last section (**A'**).

Performing forces Large orchestra, including woodwinds (oboes, flutes, and clarinets), trumpets, French horns, and Turkish percussion instruments (timpani, bass drum, cymbals, triangle).

0:00   **A section**—C major, rounded binary form ‖:a :‖:b a :‖
a = elegant, arched theme with grace notes; eight measures, with string and flute:

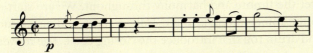

Repeated with oboes, clarinets, and bassoons.

0:29   **b** = eight+ four measures, theme developed from **a**, with strings and flute:

b + **a** phrases repeated with oboes, clarinets, and bassoons.

1:40   **B section**—C minor, "military" sound, with added percussion (triangle, cymbals, bass drum); begins with loud, C minor statement of **a**; mixes **a** and **b** themes with sudden dynamic changes:

2:45   **A′ section**—returns to C major, later adds percussion section; varied statements feature different instruments.

4:33   **Coda**—solo trumpet fanfare, followed by drum roll, leads to *fortissimo* chord in A-flat major; motive from theme **a** is repeated until the full orchestra closing.

The Main Hall of the Eszterháza Palace in Hungary (see p. 144), where the music master Haydn spent his summer months along with the court (eighteenth century).

abound in expressive effects, including syncopation, sudden *crescendos* and accents, dramatic contrasts of soft and loud, daring modulations, and an imaginative plan in which each family of instruments plays its own part.

Haydn's Symphony No. 100, the *Military*, was first presented in 1794 during his second London visit and was received enthusiastically by the British public. Its nickname comes from the composer's use of percussion instruments associated with Turkish military music—namely the triangle, cymbals, bass drum, and bell tree. The work also features a solo trumpet fanfare, another colorful military effect. Classical composers knew of these new instruments from the Turkish Janissary bands that performed in Vienna; after many centuries of wars between the Austrian Hapsburg Empire and the powerful Ottoman Empire, cultural exchanges between these political domains allowed Western Europeans the opportunity to hear, and adopt, these exotic sounds.

The Second Movement: **A-B-A′**

Haydn's *Military* Symphony features a memorable second movement (LG 15) that combines the concept of variations with a simple three-part, or ternary, structure that can be diagrammed as **A-B-A′**. The graceful opening theme is heard in various guises that alter the timbre and harmony throughout. We are startled by the sudden change to the minor mode in the middle section, and also struck by the trumpet fanfare and drum roll that introduce the closing coda. The movement ends with a victorious *fortissimo* climax.

As you listen to the contrasting melodies and timbres of this movement, think again about the notion of conversation that we explored in Chapter 25. What can Haydn "tell" you when he has so many more sonic resources at his disposal?

▶◀ Reflect

How do major and minor harmonies and dynamic shifts help you hear the **A-B-A′** form of this movement? What is the expressive effect of the changing harmonies and dynamics?

YOUR TURN TO EXPLORE

Look for (ideally video) recordings of instrumental ensembles, featuring at least ten musicians playing at least four different instruments, from various Western traditions—orchestras, wind bands, big-band jazz groups, rock-influenced "jam bands." How do the range and variety of timbres differ from ensemble to ensemble? In what ways are the musicians' interactions similar to and different from each other in these groups?

Expanding the Conversation: Mozart, Chamber Music, and Larger Forms

▶❙❙ **First, listen ...**

to the first movement of Mozart's serenade *Eine kleine Nachtmusik,* focusing on the main melodies. How many different tunes do you hear that return later in the movement? How might you describe the shape and character of each melody?

> ❝ People make a mistake who think that my art has come easily to me. Nobody has devoted so much time and thought to composition as I. There is not a famous master whose music I have not studied over and over."
>
> —Wolfgang Amadeus Mozart

All narrative and interactive genres—novels, plays, movies, video games—rely on a structural framework. Those following the narrative learn to understand the conventions of the genre, and the creators engage in a "conversation" with the reader/spectator/player through fulfilling or challenging his or her expectations. Your enjoyment of such genres hinges on your willingness to learn the structural conventions and understand the subtlety with which the creators are manipulating them. Sonata-allegro form, which we begin exploring in this chapter, quickly became a favorite resource for instrumental composers, since the musical story it can tell is significantly more dynamic than the one available through simpler forms (like, for example, theme and variations). Comprehending its principles and being able to follow its unfolding are essential for a deeper understanding of all instrumental music from this period onward: the form opens up opportunities for a profound conversation between composers, performers, and listeners. And if the string quartet can be understood as a conversation between four close friends, other genres of chamber music reveal a more wide-ranging discussion among a more diverse cohort; we will examine one such expanded conversation composed by Mozart.

In His Own Words

> ❝ Only when the form grows clear to you will the spirit become so too."
>
> —Robert Schumann

KEY POINTS

- The first movement of the Classical multimovement cycle is usually in a fast tempo and in **sonata-allegro form**, with three main sections: **exposition, development,** and **recapitulation.**

- The third movement is a triple-meter pair of dances, usually a **minuet and trio.**

- Wolfgang Amadeus Mozart, a child prodigy who started to write music before the age of five, contributed

to nearly all musical genres of the Classical era, including the symphony, sonata, concerto, chamber music, sacred music, and opera.

- One of Mozart's best-known chamber works is *Eine kleine Nachtmusik (A Little Night Music),* a serenade for strings.

MOZART'S *EINE KLEINE NACHTMUSIK*

Two popular expanded chamber genres in Mozart's day were the **divertimento** and the **serenade**. Both are lighter genres that were performed in the evening or at social functions. Mozart wrote a large variety of social music of this sort, the most famous of which is *Eine kleine Nachtmusik* (1787), a serenade for strings whose title means literally *A Little Night Music*. The work was most likely written for a string quartet supported by a double bass and was meant for public entertainment, in outdoor performance. The four movements of the version we know (originally there were five) are compact, intimate, and beautifully proportioned.

The First Movement: Sonata-Allegro Form

The most highly organized and often the longest movement in the multimovement cycle is the opening one, which is usually in a fast tempo such as Allegro and is written in **sonata-allegro form** (also known as **sonata form**). This movement establishes a home (tonic) key; then moves, or **modulates**, to another key; and ultimately returns to the home key. We may therefore regard sonata-allegro form as a drama between two contrasting key areas. In most cases, each key area is associated with a theme, which has the potential for development. The themes are stated, or "exposed," in the first section; developed in the second; and restated, or "recapitulated," in the third.

(1) The opening section of sonata-allegro form—the **exposition**, or statement—generally presents the two opposing keys and their respective themes. (In some cases, a theme may consist of several related ideas, in which case we speak of a theme group.) The first theme establishes the home key, or tonic. A **bridge**, or transitional passage, leads to a second theme in a contrasting key; in other words, the function of the bridge is to modulate. After the second theme, a closing section, sometimes with a new closing theme, rounds off the exposition in the contrasting key. In eighteenth-century sonata-allegro form, the exposition is repeated.

(2) Conflict and action, the essence of drama, characterize the **development**. This section may wander through a series of foreign keys, building up tension against the inevitable return home. The frequent modulations contribute to a sense of activity and restlessness. Here, the composer reveals the potential of the themes by varying, expanding, or contracting them, breaking them into their component motives, or combining them with other motives or with new material. When the development has run its course, the tension lets up and a bridge passage leads back to the key of the tonic.

(3) The beginning of the third section, the **recapitulation**, or restatement, is the psychological climax of sonata-allegro form. The return of the first theme in the tonic satisfies the listener's need for unity. The recapitulation restates the first and second themes more or less in their original form, but with one important difference from the exposition: both themes now remain in the tonic, thereby asserting the dominance of the home key. The movement often ends with a **coda**, an extension of the closing idea that leads to the final cadence in the home key.

The features of sonata-allegro form, summed up in the chart opposite, are present in one shape or another in many movements, yet no two pieces are exactly

Mozart composing at the keyboard, by **Johann Bosio**.

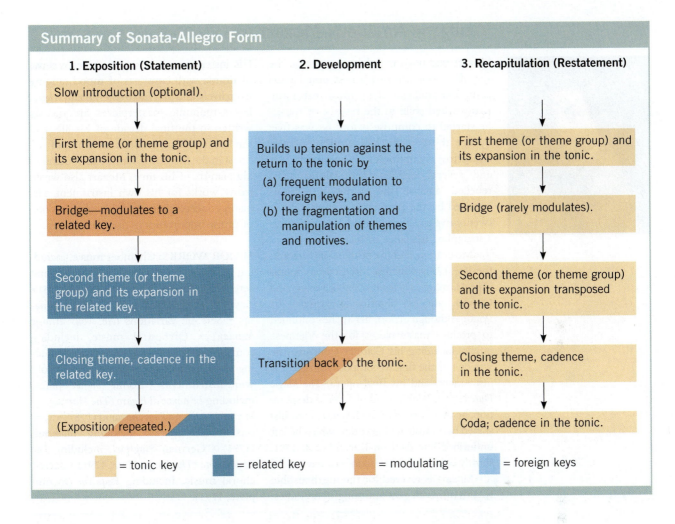

alike. What might at first appear to be a fixed plan actually provides a supple framework for infinite variety in the hands of the composer.

Let's examine how Mozart deploys sonata-allegro form in the first movement of *Eine kleine Nachtmusik* (LG 16). The movement opens with a strong, march-like theme that rapidly ascends to its peak (an example of a "rocket theme"), then turns downward at the same rate. Mozart balances this idea with an elegant descending second theme. The closing theme exudes a high energy level, moving the work into its short development; and the recapitulation brings back all the themes, ending with a vigorous coda.

The Third Movement: Minuet-and-Trio Form

In the Classical instrumental cycle, the third movement is almost invariably a **minuet and trio**. The minuet was originally a Baroque court dance whose stately triple (3/4) meter embodied the ideal of an aristocratic age. Since dance music lends itself to symmetrical construction, you often find in a minuet a clear-cut structure based on phrases of four and eight measures. The tempo ranges from stately to lively and whimsical.

Wolfgang Amadeus Mozart (1756–1791)

Mozart was born in Salzburg, Austria, the son of Leopold Mozart, an esteemed court composer-violinist. The most extraordinarily gifted child in the history of music, he started to compose before he was five; by age thirteen, he had written sonatas, concertos, symphonies, religious works, and several operas. The young artist rebelled against the social restrictions imposed by the patronage system, and at twenty-five established himself in Vienna as a struggling freelance musician.

Mozart reached the peak of his career in the late 1780s with his three comic operas (*The Marriage of Figaro, Don Giovanni,* and *Così fan tutte*) on librettos by Lorenzo da Ponte. Although in poor health, he continued to produce masterpieces for the Viennese public, including his Clarinet Concerto (he was one of the first to compose for this new instrument) and his final opera, *The Magic Flute* (1791). With a kind of fevered desperation, he then turned to the *Requiem*, commissioned by a music-loving count, which he left unfinished. He died on December 4, 1791, shortly before his thirty-sixth birthday.

Mozart is revered for the inexhaustible wealth of his elegant and songful melodies.

His instrumental music combines a sense of drama with contrasts of mood ranging from lively and playful to solemn and tragic. His symphonic masterpieces are the six written in the final decade of his life, and the last ten string quartets are some of the finest in the literature. One of the outstanding pianists of his time, Mozart also wrote many works for his own instrument. His piano concertos elevated this genre to one of prime importance in the Classical era.

MAJOR WORKS: Chamber music, including 23 string quartets • Divertimentos and serenades (*Eine kleine Nachtmusik,* K. 525) • Keyboard music, including 17 piano sonatas • Sets of variations (*Ah! vous dirai-je Maman*) • Orchestral music, including some 40 symphonies • Concertos, including 27 for piano, 5 for violin, others for solo wind instruments • Comic (*buffa*) operas, including *Le nozze di Figaro* (*The Marriage of Figaro,* 1786) and *Don Giovanni* (1787) • Serious (*seria*) operas, including *Idomeneo* (1791) • German *Singspiel*, including *Die Zauberflöte* (*The Magic Flute,* 1791) • Sacred choral music, including *Requiem* (incomplete, 1791).

The movement's name results from the custom of presenting two different dances as a group, the first repeated after the second (resulting in **A-B-A**). The dance in the middle was originally arranged for only three instruments, hence the name "trio," which persisted even after the customary setting for three had long been abandoned. At the end of the trio, you find the words **da capo** ("from the beginning"), signifying that the first section is to be played over again (as it was in the Baroque aria; see Chapter 21).

Each part of the minuet-trio-minuet in turn subdivides into two-part, or binary, form. The composer indicates the repetition of the subsections within repeat signs (||: :||). However, when the minuet returns after the trio, it is customarily played

Rounded binary form

straight through, without repeats (**a b**; see chart below). The second section of the minuet (**b**) or trio (**d**) may bring back the opening theme, making a **rounded binary form**.

Minuet (**A**)	Trio (**B**)	Minuet (**A**)
‖ : a : ‖ : b : ‖	‖ : c : ‖ : d : ‖	a b

The minuet and trio that makes up the third movement of *Eine kleine Nachtmusik* is marked by regular four-bar phrases set in rounded binary form (see p. 151).

The minuet opens brightly and decisively. The trio, with its polished, soaring melody, presents a lyrical contrast. The opening music then returns, satisfying the Classical desire for balance and symmetry.

While sonata-allegro and minuet and trio are different forms, they both rely on predictable principles of statement, contrast, and return that are at the core of the Classical style. Each movement of *Eine kleine Nachtmusik* provides a different perspective in a balanced, rational, yet inventive musical argument—the hallmark of Mozart's artistry.

▶|◀ Reflect

How does Mozart distinguish the two main melodies of the first movement's sonata-allegro form? How does the homophonic texture help you track these tunes?

Engraving of a couple dancing the minuet, from an eighteenth-century instruction book by **George Bickham** (c. 1706–1771).

YOUR TURN TO EXPLORE

Find video examples of dancing in contrasting traditions—for example, modern ballroom dance, country or square dancing, ballet, break-dancing or other hip-hop styles, Native American ceremonial dance, or a TV dance program. Can you notice patterns of statement, repetition, contrast, and return in the music that accompanies the dance? How is the musical logic of those formal elements reflected in the dancers' movements?

LISTENING GUIDE 16

  7:39

Mozart: *Eine kleine Nachtmusik* (*A Little Night Music*), K. 525, I and III

DATE: 1787

PERFORMED BY: Moscow Virtuosi; Vladimir Spivakov, conductor

MOVEMENTS: **I. Allegro; sonata-allegro form, G major**   **III. Allegretto; minuet and trio form, G major**
II. Romanza, Andante; sectional rondo form, C major   IV. Allegro; sonata-rondo form, G major

I: Allegro   **5:30**

What to Listen For

Melody A disjunct, ascending (rocket) theme then turns downward; the refined, descending second theme followed by a vigorous closing theme provide contrast.

Form Sonata-allegro form, in three sections: exposition, development, and recapitulation, with a short closing coda.

Texture Largely homophonic.

continued on next page

EXPOSITION

0:00   Theme 1—aggressive, ascending rocket theme, symmetrical phrasing, in G major:

Transitional passage, modulating.

0:46   Theme 2—graceful, contrasting theme, less hurried, in the key of the dominant, D major:

0:58   Closing theme—insistent, repetitive, ends in D major.
        Repeat of the exposition.

DEVELOPMENT

3:07   Short, begins in D major, manipulates theme 1 and closing theme; modulates, and prepares for the recapitulation in G major.

RECAPITULATION

3:40   Theme 1, in G major.

4:22   Theme 2, in G major.

4:34   Closing theme, in G major.

5:05   **Coda**—extends closing, in G major.

III: Allegretto   2:09

What to Listen For

Rhythm/meter Strong, rhythmic dance, in triple meter.

Form Two dances combined (minuet and trio); each is in binary form, with two repeated sections. The overall form is **A-B-A'** (minuet-trio-minuet), with the final **A'** leaving out the repeats.

0:00   Minuet theme, **A**—in accented triple meter, decisive character, in two sections (8 measures each), both repeated (rounded binary, || : a : || : b a : ||):

0:44   Trio theme, **B**—more lyrical and connected, in two sections (8 + 12 measures), both repeated (|| : c : || : d c : ||):

1:41   Minuet returns, **A'**, without repeats.

Intriguing Conversations: Mozart and Symphonic Innovation

▶‖ First, listen . . .

to the first movement of Mozart's Symphony No. 40, and focus your attention on the two distinct musical themes, introduced in the exposition. What kind of transformations do you hear as they reappear throughout the movement?

In our journey through the Western tradition, we are highlighting the common features among similar musical works, to help you perceive those traits in other music you may explore. In similar fashion, such companies as Spotify, Pandora, and Apple Music have built their presence in our lives by grouping music (both familiar and new) into categories that might appeal to us, and thus increase the time and money we spend on them. The Classical symphony is one such useful category; we can expect certain essential characteristics when we hear a symphony by a Classical composer. Yet the unexpected is part of what makes musical conversations especially intriguing. A compelling example is a symphony by Mozart that simultaneously conforms to and departs from the way listeners might expect a "Classical conversation" to go.

MOZART'S SYMPHONY NO. 40 IN G MINOR

This work represents the mingling of Classical and Romantic elements that marked the final decades of the eighteenth century. Its minor-key setting makes it especially moving; indeed, in Vienna it was given the label *Romantic*.

The first movement unfolds in a more extended sonata-allegro form than we have heard so far. As the sections are longer, with repetitions more spread out, listening to

KEY POINTS

- Mozart wrote forty-one symphonies; among the best known is Symphony No. 40 in G Minor (the *Romantic*), which mingles Classical and Romantic elements.

- The opening movement of Symphony No. 40 develops from a brief, three-note motive into an extended sonata-allegro form.

A performance of Mozart's Symphony No. 40 by the Mostly Mozart Festival Orchestra, conducted by Thierry Fischer, at Lincoln Center in New York City, August 2016.

it can help develop your musical memory. First we hear a dark rustling in the lower strings, over which a dynamic theme for the violins establishes the home key of G minor (LG 17). This theme flowers out of a three-note motive (short-short-long), built on a descending half step, that has great potential for growth and expansion and is as memorable as a line from a favorite song. The lyrical second theme, in a major key, provides comparative relaxation in the exposition's otherwise fast-paced drive, while the closing idea brings back the basic opening motive.

In the stormy development section, Mozart transforms his material in a variety of ways: by changing the melody and placing it in the bass; by adding a countermelody above it (remember a similar practice in the Bach fugue from Chapter 24); and by combining motives and expanding them through a descending sequence, or turning them upside down (that is, inverting them; see the chart on p. 131). The recapitulation follows the course of the exposition, with the second theme, now in G minor, taking on a more tender tone. A closing coda energetically confirms the home key.

Mozart's original orchestration featured flute, oboes, bassoons, and French horns added to the core of strings. Several years after he completed the work, however, he revised the score to include clarinets, a relatively new instrument then. This revised version is the one most often performed today.

LISTENING GUIDE 17   7:02

Mozart: Symphony No. 40 in G Minor, I

DATE: 1788; rev. 1791

PERFORMED BY: Prague Chamber Orchestra; Charles Mackerras, conductor

MOVEMENTS: **I. Allegro molto; sonata-allegro form, G minor**
II. Andante; sonata-allegro form, E-flat major
III. Allegro moderato; minuet and trio, G minor
IV. Allegro assai; sonata-allegro form, G minor

I: Allegro molto

What to Listen For

Melody The opening theme grows out of a three-note motive featuring a descending half step, which then leaps upward; the second theme is lyrical and descending in shape.

Rhythm/meter Lively duple meter, with a pervading rhythmic motive (short-short-long) heard throughout.

Form Sonata-allegro: two themes are presented in the exposition, varied in the development, and repeated (this time all in the tonic key) in the recapitulation.

Expression Dramatic, emotional, and dark; the minor key provides a melancholy color.

EXPOSITION

0:00   Theme 1—in G minor, a vigorous melody developed from a three-note motive (shaded), in the violins:

0:29   Bridge—a strong passage, building in a *crescendo*; modulates to the key of the relative major (B-flat).

0:44   Theme 2—in B-flat major; a lyrical, relaxed melody in woodwinds and strings:

1:14   Closing—based on the three-note motive from theme 1, leads to a final cadence in B-flat major.

1:44   Exposition repeated.

DEVELOPMENT

3:27   This short, compact section presents the three-note motive in new keys, in the bass part (bassoon and low strings), and as the focus of a string and woodwind dialogue, in inversion; the section returns to the tonic G minor.

RECAPITULATION

4:34   Theme 1—in G minor.

5:36   Theme 2—in G minor; the minor key now gives it a new character.

6:12   **Coda**—energetic extension of the closing, in G minor.

This "Romantic" symphony, by a composer usually associated with the Classical style, helps us recognize how musical traits ascribed to one particular period can sometimes be fluid. This is true especially when composers are experimenting at the margins of established practice: for example, by employing new instruments, choosing unconventional harmonies, or returning to earlier practices (as Mozart may be doing with his fugue-like passages in the development section). Balancing conventions that keep the audience grounded with surprises that keep them on their toes is what makes any artist an "intriguing conversationalist," regardless of his or her genre, style, or medium.

▶|◀ Reflect

How does Mozart differentiate the two main themes in the exposition, and how does he vary each one as the movement unfolds?

YOUR TURN TO EXPLORE

Find a familiar musical work or performance that you think "pushes the boundaries"— of a genre, style, performing practice, or other category. What aspects of the work are "typical" enough to make it fit in that category, and why do you consider them typical? What are some meaningful ways it pushes the boundaries of the category you've chosen? What would make that work or performance so far outside the "norm" that it belongs in a different category altogether?

29

Conversation with a Leader: Haydn and the Classical Concerto

▶‖ First, listen . . .

to the third movement of Haydn's Trumpet Concerto, and focus on the opening theme and its recurrences. How many times do you hear this melody, with its rising fourth, throughout the movement? Played by which instruments? How does this melody help you follow the movement?

I f chamber music in the Classical period was designed to convey a musical conversation among equals, the Classical **concerto** was closer to a political rally—an inspiring leader helping to advance a larger group to a common purpose. While the genre continued to display traits of the Baroque concerto, it was also influenced by the logic of the multimovement principle that governed other Classical genres like the string quartet and symphony. In the concerto, composers such as Haydn and Mozart relied on outstanding performers to provide the soloist's vitality, and sought to balance that energy with the complex collaboration of many unified voices.

MOVEMENTS OF THE CLASSICAL CONCERTO

During the Baroque era, "concerto" could refer to a solo group and orchestra or to a solo instrument and orchestra. The Classical era shifted the emphasis to the latter combination.

KEY POINTS

- Classical **concerto** form consists of three movements, alternating fast-slow-fast.

- The first movement is the longest and most complex, combining elements of Baroque ritornello procedure and sonata-allegro form.

- The last movement is fast and lively, often in **rondo** form, which is also a common form for the last movement of symphonies and other cyclic works.

- Haydn's lively Trumpet Concerto in E-flat Major, written for the new keyed trumpet, is a notable example of the genre.

The three movements of the Classical concerto follow the fast-slow-fast pattern established by Vivaldi. One unique feature is the **cadenza**, a virtuosic solo passage in the manner of an improvisation that comes toward the end of a movement. It creates a dramatic effect: the orchestra falls silent, and the soloist (for example, the pianist or violinist) launches into a free play of fantasy on one or more themes of the movement.

The Classical concerto begins with a first-movement form that adapts the principles of the Baroque concerto's ritornello procedure (based on a recurring theme) to those of sonata-allegro form. First-movement concerto form is sometimes described as a sonata-allegro form with a double exposition: the movement usually opens with an orchestral exposition, or ritornello, presenting several themes, followed by the soloist playing elaborated versions of these themes and often new material as well. The solo cadenza appears near the end of the movement, and a coda brings it to a close with a strong affirmation of the tonic key.

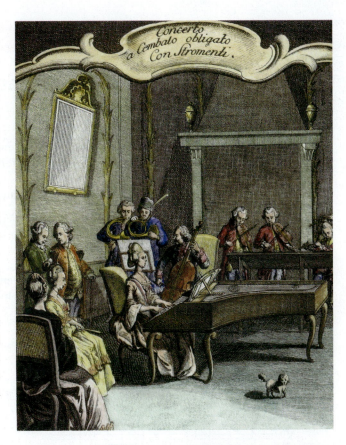

Engraving of a concerto performance (1777), with a female harpsichord soloist, by **Johann Rudolf Holzhalb** (1723–1806).

Rondo form

The Last Movement: Haydn's Concerto for Trumpet

The concerto, like the string quartet and symphony, often ends with a spirited **rondo**. The rondo is based on the recurrence of a musical idea—the theme, or refrain—in alternation with contrasting **episodes**, much like the ritornello procedure of the Baroque era. Its symmetrical sections create a balanced architecture that is satisfying aesthetically and easy to hear. In its simplest form, **A-B-A-C-A** (with **A** the catchy, dancelike refrain), the rondo is an extension of three-part form. As developed by the Classical masters, the rondo is more ambitious in scope, often taking a longer, arched form (**A-B-A-C-A-B-A**) generally described as **sonata-rondo** because of its combination of sonata-allegro form with the refrain principle of the rondo.

In addition to his symphonies and string quartets, Haydn also wrote some thirty-five concertos for various solo instruments. His Concerto for Trumpet in E-flat Major is considered one of his finest, written for an experimental trumpet with keys, not unlike a woodwind instrument, that allowed it to play in the instrument's full range with all diatonic and even chromatic notes of the scale (see p. 165). (The more modern, valved trumpet would be invented in 1801.) Haydn's concerto was first performed in 1800, after which the original manuscript was lost until 1929. Since its discovery, this work has been central to the repertory of every serious trumpet player.

In His Own Words

❝ The quality of tone of the trumpet is noble and brilliant; it comports with warlike ideas, with cries of fury, and of vengeance, as with songs of triumph; it lends itself to the expression of all energetic, lofty and grand sentiments.❞

—Hector Berlioz

LISTENING GUIDE 18 4:26

Haydn: Trumpet Concerto in E-flat Major, III

DATE: 1796; first performed 1800
PERFORMED BY: Wynton Marsalis, trumpet; National Philharmonic; Raymond Leppard, conductor
MOVEMENTS: I. Allegro; first-movement concerto form, E-flat major
II. Andante; **A-B-A** form, A-flat major
III. Allegro; sonata-rondo form, E-flat major

III: Allegro

What to Listen For

Melody Triadic, disjunct themes, featuring virtuoso arpeggios, leaps, trills, and scalar passages; the opening theme returns frequently.

Form Sonata-rondo, with two main ideas (plus a third) that alternate **A-B-A-B-A-C-A-B-A** (coda); **A** represents the ritornello (refrain).

Performing forces Solo keyed trumpet, with orchestra (strings, woodwinds, brass, and timpani).

0:00   **A section**—theme 1, heard softly in the violins, then full orchestra, in E-flat:

0:23   **B section**—theme 2, *sforzando* chord, then turns downward, in E-flat:

0:39   **A section**—trumpet enters with theme 1, with strings, then full orchestra, in E-flat; transition modulates to the dominant (B-flat).

1:09   **B section**—trumpet plays theme 2 in the dominant, then has virtuosic arpeggios, leading to a fermata.

1:52   **A section**—trumpet returns with a statement of theme 1, with flute obbligato.

2:06   **C section**—short developmental section, beginning with theme 1, featuring a modulatory passage in the strings and short motivic calls in the trumpet, on a rising fourth.

2:40   **A section**—trumpet and orchestra state theme 1, in dialogue with flutes, in the tonic.

2:56   **B section**—trumpet states, then elaborates theme 2 in a wide range, followed by a rapid octave passage:

3:29   **A section** (**coda**)—more contrapuntal and chromatic passages based on theme 1; trumpet has chains of trills, followed by a *fortissimo* rush to the end.

The concerto is set in a standard but compact three-movement form. It opens with an Allegro in first-movement concerto form that flaunts the new instrument's ability to play highly lyrical melodies and virtuosic passages. The second movement, in 6/8 meter, is pastoral in mood, and the third (last) movement is a brilliant sonata-rondo (LG 18).

There are some typical Haydn devices at play in the third movement, including unexpected turns of harmony and sudden dynamic contrasts (as in his *Military Symphony*, Chapter 26). Here, Haydn fully explores the new technical possibilities of the instrument, writing difficult passagework, fast octave leaps moving up the scale, and rapidly descending arpeggiated figures. There are two main themes: an energetic first idea that opens with a rising fourth, and a lighthearted second theme that turns downward. At the end, an extended coda offers a few last-minute surprises.

In this concerto, his last orchestral work, Haydn showed that he still had the capacity to employ novel ideas with great mastery, and to expand the Classical ideal of musical conversation to acknowledge a strong conversation leader—a "heroic" figure, in keeping with the emerging Romantic ideal.

Keyed trumpet, similar to the one for which Haydn wrote his Trumpet Concerto.

▶❙◀ **Reflect**

In this movement, Haydn actually presents two themes that reappear, combining the idea of rondo (one recurring theme) and sonata-allegro (two contrasting themes). How do theses two melodies differ from each other in shape and character? What other expressive devices does Haydn use in this movement?

YOUR TURN TO EXPLORE

Seek out videos of performances from different traditions that feature a soloist-leader—concertos from the Western orchestral tradition, but also (for example) rock bands, large jazz ensembles, or gospel groups. In what ways does the soloist interact with the larger ensemble? How does the leader appear to be "controlling" the musical conversation, and conversely, how is the larger ensemble providing structure and stability through musical repetition and return?

Personalizing the Conversation: Beethoven and the Classical Sonata

▶❚ **First, listen ...**

to the first movement of Beethoven's *Moonlight* Sonata, and listen for the device called arpeggio (broken chord) in the accompaniment to the melody: three pitches of a chord played one after the other (here, slowly) rather than all at once. How does the arpeggio pattern change throughout the movement?

While group conversations can be heated, our most intense interactions with friends tend to be one on one: this is where we reveal most about ourselves, and build the deepest emotional connections. Similarly, while quartets and other chamber music highlighted the group-conversational possibilities of the Classical style, the sonata was designed for a more intimate expressive space. Featuring one or two performers, it either gave amateurs the opportunity for one-to-one musical interactions or allowed a skilled professional the opportunity to communicate directly with the listener. It was especially through the sonata that Ludwig van Beethoven developed a style that has been valued as strikingly individual and meaningful from the time of his first performances. Beethoven's individuality, however, is evident because he developed it within a set of formal conventions against which he could "push"; if we do not understand these formal expectations, which his contemporaries had internalized, his intimate musical conversations with us cannot have the power and the passion that he envisioned.

THE SONATA IN THE CLASSICAL ERA

Haydn, Mozart, and their successors understood the term **sonata** as an instrumental work for one or two instruments, consisting of three or four contrasting

KEY POINTS

- Classical **sonatas** were set either for one solo instrument (usually the piano) or for duos (violin and piano, for example).

- Sonatas were sometimes designed for amateur performance in the home, but were also used by composer-performers as show pieces.

- The solo sonatas of Mozart and especially Ludwig van Beethoven are among the most significant in the keyboard literature.

- The *Moonlight* Sonata, perhaps Beethoven's best-known piano work, evokes the new Romantic style in its expressive manipulation of Classical conventions.

movements. The movements followed the basic order of the multimovement cycle that we have been exploring (see chart on p. 145).

In the Classical era, the sonata—for piano alone or for two instruments (violin or cello and piano)—became an important genre for amateurs in the home, as well as for composers like Mozart and Beethoven performing their own music at concerts. Beethoven's thirty-two piano sonatas, which span his entire compositional output, are among his most important works. The so-called *Moonlight* Sonata (LG 19) looks forward to the emotional expressiveness of the Romantic era.

A young Beethoven performs for Mozart. Engraving from the German School (early nineteenth century).

Ludwig van Beethoven (1770–1827)

Beethoven was born in Bonn, Germany. From age eleven, he supported his mother and two younger brothers by performing as an organist and harpsichordist. At twenty-two he moved to Vienna, where, although he was not attached to the court of a prince, the music-loving aristocrats helped him in various ways—by paying him handsomely for lessons or presenting him with gifts. He was also aided by the emergence of a middle-class public and the growth of concert life and music publishing.

When he was still in his twenties, Beethoven began to lose his hearing. His helplessness in the face of this affliction dealt a shattering blow to his pride: "How could I possibly admit an infirmity in the one sense that should have been more perfect in me than in others," he wrote to his brothers. Although he never regained his hearing and struggled with a sense of isolation, the remainder of his career was spent in ceaseless effort to achieve his artistic goals. He died at age fifty-six, famous and revered.

Beethoven is the supreme architect in music, a master in large-scale forms like the sonata and the symphony. His compositional activity fell into three periods. The

first reflected the Classical elements he inherited from Haydn and Mozart. The middle period saw the appearance of characteristics more closely associated with the nineteenth century: strong dynamic contrasts, explosive accents, and longer movements. In his third period, Beethoven used more chromatic harmonies and developed a skeletal language from which all nonessentials were rigidly pared away. It was a language that transcended his time.

Beethoven's nine symphonies, five piano concertos and Violin Concerto, thirty-two piano sonatas, seventeen string quartets, opera *Fidelio*, and the *Missa solemnis* are indispensable to their respective repertories.

MAJOR WORKS: Orchestral music, including nine symphonies (the "Ode to Joy" is featured in Symphony No. 9), overtures • Concertos, including five for piano and one for violin • Chamber music, including string quartets, piano trios, violin-piano sonatas, cello-piano sonatas, wind chamber music • 32 piano sonatas, including Op. 13 (*Pathétique*) and Op. 27, No. 2 (*Moonlight*) • Other piano music (*Für Elise*) • One opera (*Fidelio*) • Choral music, including *Missa solemnis* • Songs and one song cycle.

Beethoven's *Moonlight* Sonata

Shortly after Beethoven's death, the *Moonlight* Sonata was given its title by German poet Ludwig Rellstab, who likened the work to the moonlit scenery along Lake Lucerne in Switzerland. (Note that in this case the "program

---

LISTENING GUIDE 19   5:45

Beethoven: Piano Sonata in C-sharp Minor, Op. 27, No. 2 (*Moonlight*), I

DATE: 1801

PERFORMED BY: John O'Conor, piano

MOVEMENTS: I. Adagio sostenuto; modified song form, C-sharp minor
II. Allegretto; scherzo and trio, D-flat major
III. Presto agitato; sonata-allegro form, C-sharp minor

I: Adagio sostenuto

What to Listen For

Melody Poignant, singing melody that moves slowly in various ranges, after which short ideas are exchanged between the two hands.

Rhythm/meter An unrelenting arpeggiated, eighth-note pattern accompanies the very slow-moving melody, set in a duple meter.

Harmony Haunting, dark key of C minor, with shifting harmonies.

Expression Ethereal, dreamlike mood, with expressive, soft dynamics.

INTRODUCTION

0:00   Four-measure arpeggiated chords.

STROPHE 1

0:23   Melody in the right hand (shaded), with a dotted figure on a repeated note, accompanied by left-hand arpeggios, C-sharp minor; four-measure phrases:

0:48   Melody in a new key, expands and modulates.
1:12   New idea in dialogue between the two hands.
1:51   Melody returns, in a higher range.

MIDDLE SECTION

2:14   Motivic development of the dialogue, exchanged between the hands over a sustained-note pedal.

STROPHE 2

3:20   Returns to the opening melody and key center (C-sharp minor), followed by a short dialogue idea.

CODA

4:52   Closes with the melody stated in the bass on a repeated pitch (left hand).
        Resolution on a tonic cadence, with arpeggios and chords.

music" aspect of the piece was added by a listener, rather than the composer.) When Beethoven composed the sonata in 1801 (early in his career), he was enamored of a young pupil, Countess Giulietta Guicciardi. The sonata is dedicated to her, but since this dedication seems to have been a last-minute decision, the work is probably not a programmatic statement of his love (see illustration at right).

This work, one of a pair from Op. 27, breaks the formal molds—Beethoven called it a "fantasy-like sonata" (*sonata quasi una fantasia*), although he retained the typical three-movement format. In the dreamy first movement, one of the most famous of all his works, the melody sings continuously, moving through various keys and registers. A short contrasting idea intervenes between two statements of the melody. Though the form of this movement displays elements of development and recapitulation, it does not present the opposition of themes or keys typical of a first movement. Instead, it looks ahead to song forms favored by Romantic composers—indeed, it is almost a "song without words," a genre that arose in the generation following Beethoven.

The second movement is a gentle **scherzo** (quick-paced dance, a variant of the minuet) and trio set in a major key, providing necessary psychological relief between the emotionally charged opening movement and the stormy finale. The full force of Beethoven's dramatic writing is reserved for this closing movement, which he set in a full-blown sonata-allegro form.

Although Beethoven himself was not particularly enthusiastic about this sonata—"Surely I have written better things," he argued—it was an immediate success with audiences and remains one of the most beloved works in the Classical repertory. This may be partly because of a perception that Beethoven's musical ideas are "breaking out" of the conventions of the genre, making the intimacy of his message even more compelling.

Countess Giulietta Guicciardi, dedicatee of the *Moonlight* Sonata.

▶|◀ Reflect

Is the expressive effect of the arpeggios different when the melody is high-pitched as opposed to low-pitched? If so, how? How do changes in arpeggio patterns correspond to other striking moments in the movement?

YOUR TURN TO EXPLORE

Find video examples of solo piano performances, and contrast them with the ensemble conversations you have examined in other explorations. How are the performer's behavior, the setting, and the interaction with the audience different? Contrast solo performances of similar repertory by amateurs and professionals: besides the skill of the performer, what other aspects of the performance (self-presentation, connection with others, expressive gestures, and so on) are different?

Disrupting the Conversation: Beethoven and the Symphony in Transition

▶‖ First, listen ...

to the first movement of Beethoven's Symphony No. 5, and focus especially on the famous four-note motive at the beginning. How does this short rhythmic idea (short-short-short-long) evolve throughout the movement? How does Beethoven build new musical ideas from this basic motive?

> 66 I carry my thoughts about with me for a long time . . . before writing them down. I change many things, discard others, and try again and again until I am satisfied. . . . I turn my ideas into tones that resound, roar, and rage until at last they stand before me in the form of notes."
>
> —Ludwig van Beethoven

Even during his own lifetime, Beethoven was hailed as a genius, and his influence on the orchestral tradition that followed can be felt to the present day. His ability to disrupt the elegant, balanced musical conversation of the Classical era is seen as evidence of supreme inspiration, the mark of an artist who will say what he needs to say regardless of the effect on the social order. Indeed, the presence of "Beethoven the hero" in the imagination of Western culture has extended far beyond the concert hall—even if you had not encountered the name of any composer considered so far, you likely had heard of Beethoven. Yet this composer was also working carefully to balance the formal expectations of the tradition within which he had been trained with "strategic disruptions." His unique approaches do not entail rejecting the conventions of Classical form: in fact, formal considerations are absolutely essential to the meaning and power of his music. This transitional place between convention and disruption is one major element that keeps Beethoven's music so compelling more than two centuries after it was written.

The Theater an der Wien in Vienna, where (in 1808) Beethoven presented a concert that included his Fifth and Sixth Symphonies.

KEY POINTS

- Beethoven's music is grounded in the Classical tradition but pushes its limits in a way that helped define the emerging Romantic sensibility.

- Beethoven's nine symphonies exemplify his experiments with Classical conventions. Best known is his Fifth, built on a famous four-note motive that permeates all four movements.

Beethoven's funeral procession in 1827, a watercolor by **Franz Stoeber** (1760–1834).

BEETHOVEN'S SYMPHONIES

The symphony provided Beethoven with the ideal medium through which to address his public. His first two symphonies are closest in style to the two Classical masters who preceded him, but with his third, the *Eroica*, Beethoven began to expand the possibilities of the genre—the work was originally dedicated to Napoleon, and it was quickly interpreted as a personal narrative of individual heroism. The Fifth Symphony, which we examine here, is popularly viewed as a model of the genre. The finale of the Ninth (or *Choral*) Symphony, in which vocal soloists and chorus join the orchestra, is a setting of Friedrich von Schiller's "Ode to Joy," a ringing prophecy of the time when "all people will be brothers."

The Fifth Symphony

Perhaps the best-known of all symphonies, Beethoven's Symphony No. 5 can be heard not just as a standard four-movement cycle but as a unified whole that progresses from conflict and struggle to victorious ending. Now that we have examined individual movements in the cycle, we can tackle an entire symphony and consider both how it fits the parameters of the Classical cycle and how it pushes beyond them (LG 20).

The first movement, in a sonata-allegro form marked "Allegro con brio" (lively, with vigor), springs out of the rhythmic idea of "three shorts and a long" that dominates the entire symphony. This idea, perhaps the most commanding and recognizable gesture in the whole symphonic literature, is pursued with an almost terrifying single-mindedness in this dramatic movement. In an extended coda, the basic rhythm reveals a new fount of explosive energy. Beethoven described the motive as "Fate knocking at the door."

The second movement is a serene theme and variations, with two melodic ideas. Beethoven exploits his two themes with all the procedures of variation—changes in melodic outline, harmony, rhythm, tempo, dynamics, register, key, mode, and timbre. The familiar four-note rhythm (short-short-short-long) is sounded in the second theme, relating this movement to the first.

Third in the cycle is the scherzo, which opens with a rocket theme introduced by cellos and double basses. After a gruff, humorous trio in C major, the scherzo returns in a modified version, followed by a transitional passage to the final movement, in which the timpani sounds the memorable four-note motive.

Cyclical form The monumental fourth movement bursts forth without pause, once again bringing back the unifying rhythmic motive. This unification makes the symphony an early example of **cyclical form**, in which a theme or musical idea from one movement returns in a later one. Here, Beethoven unleashes not only a new energy and passion but also new instruments not yet part of the standard orchestra: piccolo, contrabassoon, and trombones all expand the ensemble's range and intensity. This last movement, in sonata-allegro form with an extended coda, closes with the tonic chord proclaimed triumphantly by the orchestra again and again.

Beethoven's career bridged the transition from the old society to the new. His commanding musical voice and an all-conquering will forged a link to the coming Romantic age.

LISTENING GUIDE 20

 31:34

Beethoven: Symphony No. 5 in C Minor, Op. 67

DATE: 1807–8

PERFORMED BY: Cleveland Orchestra; George Szell, conductor

MOVEMENTS: I. Allegro con brio; sonata-allegro form, C minor
II. Andante con moto; theme and variations (two themes), A-flat major
III. Allegro; scherzo and trio, C minor
IV. Allegro; sonata-allegro form, C major

I: Allegro con brio   7:31

What to Listen For

Melody The fiery opening four-note motive forms the basis for thematic development throughout the whole work; the second theme, by contrast, is lyrical.

Rhythm The four-note rhythmic idea (short-short-short-long) shapes this movement, and recurs in the others as well.

Form Concise sonata-allegro, with an extended coda; employs repetition, sequence, and variation techniques.

Harmony C minor, with dramatic shifts between minor and major tonality.

EXPOSITION

0:00   Theme 1—based on the famous four-note motive (short-short-short-long), in C minor:

0:06   Motive is expanded sequentially:

0:43   Expansion from four-note motive; horns modulate to the key of the second theme.

0:46   Theme 2—lyrical, in woodwinds, in E-flat major; heard against the relentless rhythm of the four-note motive:

basic rhythm

1:07   Closing theme—a rousing melody in a descending staccato passage, then the four-note motive.

1:26   Repeat of the exposition.

continued on next page

DEVELOPMENT

2:54   The beginning of the development is announced by a horn call.

3:05   Manipulation of the four-note motive through a descending sequence:

3:16   Melodic variation, interval of a third filled in and inverted.

4:12   Expansion through repetition leads into the recapitulation; music is saturated with the four-note motive.

RECAPITULATION

4:18   Theme 1—explosive statement in C minor begins the recapitulation.

4:38   Brief oboe cadenza.

5:15   Theme 2—returns in C major, not in the expected key of C minor.

5:41   Closing theme.

5:58   **Coda**—extended treatment of the four-note motive; ends in C minor.

II: Andante con moto   10:01

What to Listen For

Harmony Movement is in A-flat major, a key relationship (to C minor) that would be common in the Romantic era.

Meter Flowing triple meter.

Form Variation form, with two themes: the first one is smooth; the rising second theme is based on the four-note motive from movement 1. Rhythms, melodies, and harmony (major and minor) are then varied.

0:00   Theme 1—broad, flowing melody, heard in low strings:

0:52   Theme 2—upward-thrusting four-note (short-short-short-long) motive heard first in clarinets:

Brass fanfare follows.

1:57   Theme 1—embellished with running 16th notes, low strings:

3:52   Embellished with faster (32nd) notes in violas and cellos.

5:04   Melody exchanged between woodwind instruments (fragments of theme 1):

6:36   Melody shifts to minor, played staccato (detached version of theme 1):

8:10   **Coda**—*Più mosso* (faster), in the bassoon.

III: Scherzo, Allegro   5:27

0:00   Scherzo theme—a rising, rocket theme in low strings, sounds hushed and mysterious:

0:19   Rhythmic motive (from movement I) explodes in the horns, *fortissimo*:

1:59   Trio theme—in C major, in double basses, set fugally, played twice; contrasts with C minor scherzo:

2:30   Trio theme is broken up and expanded through sequences.
3:29   Scherzo returns, with varied orchestration, including pizzicato strings.
4:46   Transition to the next movement, with timpani rhythm from the opening four-note motive:

Tension mounts, orchestra swells to the heroic opening of the fourth movement.

IV: Allegro (without pause from movement III)   8:32

EXPOSITION

5:30   Theme 1—in C major, a powerful melody whose opening outlines a triumphant C major chord:

continued on next page

6:03   Lyrical transition theme in French horns, modulating from C to G major.

6:29   Theme 2—in G major, vigorous melody with rhythm from the four-note motive, in triplets:

6:55   Closing theme—featuring clarinet and violas, decisive.

DEVELOPMENT

7:30   Much modulation and free rhythmic treatment; brings back the four-note motive (short-short-short-long) from the first movement.

9:04   Brief recurrence, like a whisper, of the scherzo.

RECAPITULATION

9:39   Theme 1—in C major; full orchestra, *fortissimo*.

10:43   Theme 2—in C major, played by strings.

11:10   Closing theme, played by woodwinds.

11:38   **Coda**—long extension; tension is resolved over and over again until the final, emphatic tonic.

▶❙◀ Reflect

How effective do you find Beethoven's starting point (the four-note motive) for the whole symphony? Why is this musical idea so memorable? Can you imagine a different short motive that could serve as the basis for an entire symphony?

YOUR TURN TO EXPLORE

Find several references to Beethoven or his music (visual, literary, or sonic) in popular culture or commercial contexts. What is being said or shown or implied about the composer and his work? Can you determine how truthful/accurate or invented/mythical those claims or images might be? Why do you think those aspects of Beethoven are being highlighted? How is the mythology of Beethoven being used, and to whose advantage?

Making It Real: Mozart and Classical Opera

▶❚ First, listen . . .

to the Aria, Recitative, and Terzetto (Trio) from Act I of Mozart's opera *The Marriage of Figaro* and consider the differing vocal styles the composer employs. In what contrasting ways does the idea of a conversation come across in the recitative and the trio? How would you describe the melodic and rhythmic flow in each section?

> 66 I like an aria to fit a singer as perfectly as a well-tailored suit of clothes."
>
> —W. A. Mozart

Musical theater has never been, and never will be, about full-out realism: after all, people don't converse by singing. However, certain traditions of opera (just like certain traditions of film) have tried to convey realistic nuances in human interactions and emotions. And while some operas (and movies) reflect specific historical or cultural priorities (consider the 1939 film *Gone with the Wind*, for example), and thus may seem dated or old-fashioned to following generations, other works convey aspects of the human condition that easily cross boundaries of time and location. Mozart's comic operas fall in this latter category: more than two centuries after their premieres, they still rank high with modern producers and performers and always succeed with audiences. The characters are often not entirely "comic"—they are fleshed-out human beings, with contradictory emotions that shift and develop through the drama. The persuasive power of musical characterization is what makes Classical opera, especially in the hands of Mozart, truly the first "modern" tradition of musical theater.

CLASSICAL OPERA

Operas of the early eighteenth century accurately reflected the society from which they sprang. The prevalent form was ***opera seria***: "serious," or tragic, Italian opera, a highly formalized genre inherited from the Baroque that consisted mainly of

Opera seria

KEY POINTS

- In the Classical era, two types of Italian opera prevailed: ***opera seria*** (serious opera) and ***opera buffa*** (comic opera).

- While serious opera continued a tradition of idealized characters and plots, comic opera aimed

at a more realistic depiction of human concerns and emotions.

- Mozart's *The Marriage of Figaro* combines elements of serious and comic opera in a powerful dramatic work that is performed all over the world.

177

St. Michael's Square in Vienna, with the Burgtheater (center right), where Mozart's opera *The Marriage of Figaro* was first performed.

recitatives and arias specifically designed to display the virtuosity of star singers to the aristocracy. Its librettos, featuring stories of kings and heroes drawn from classical antiquity, were set again and again throughout the century.

Increasingly, however, audiences and artists moved toward a simpler style that reflected human emotions realistically. In Italy, this was called **opera buffa**, or comic opera. Initially, these works were seen merely as a less important counterpart to the more "socially elevated" serious tradition. Eventually the support of a rising merchant class with an increasing disposable income helped bring the comic tradition into the limelight. While serious opera was almost invariably in Italian, comic opera was generally in the local language of the audience (the vernacular), although Italian *opera buffa* was popular thoughout much of Europe. *Opera buffa* presented lively, down-to-earth plots rather than the remote concerns of gods and mythological heroes. It featured an exciting ensemble at the end of each act in which all the characters participated, instead of the succession of solo arias heard in the older style. And it abounded in farcical situations, humorous dialogue, and memorable tunes. As the Age of Revolution approached, comic opera became an important social force whose lively wit delighted even the aristocrats it satirized. *Opera buffa* spread quickly, steadily expanding its scope until it culminated in the works of Mozart.

Mozart's *The Marriage of Figaro*

In an effort to make a good impression on his emperor, Joseph II, Mozart chose to collaborate with prominent librettist Lorenzo da Ponte, and the result was three comic operas that are beloved by audiences around the world: *Così fan tutte* (*Women Are Like That*), *Don Giovanni*, and the work we will hear, *The Marriage of Figaro* (*Le nozze di Figaro*). *Figaro* was their first effort, and it was a risky one: the play it was based on, by French author Pierre Caron de Beaumarchais (1732–1799), had been banned in Vienna because of its depiction of common people being oppressed by the nobility. But Mozart and da Ponte changed the story's emphasis from political intrigue to love hijinks, making social critique secondary to complex musical slapstick, and the production was a great success.

In the story, Figaro, servant and right-hand man to the powerful Count Almaviva, and his beloved Susanna, servant to the Countess, are about to marry; but Susanna is being pursued by the Count, a notorious womanizer. Da Ponte retained Beaumarchais's premise that the Count wishes to claim his "right of first night" with Susanna—the semi-fictional right of a nobleman to sleep with the spouse of a servant on her wedding night—but made the Count somewhat more sympathetic by having him want Susanna to fall in love with him first. In the play, Figaro's anger is directed at the wrongful power of the Count, while in the opera he's more jealous of Susanna, afraid she might really fall for the Count. The opera could thus be played with knowing laughter and socially safe references to women's betrayal of men.

The Countess in turn is jealous of the Count. And adding to the two couples' woes (which will all be resolved at the end) is the character of Cherubino, a teenage boy who falls in love with every woman he sees, with whom both Susanna and the Countess are clearly enchanted (resulting in further jealousy from Figaro and the Count). While the play's Cherubino is a younger version of the Count and represents the sins of the nobility, in *Figaro* he is an entirely appealing figure, often at the center of the most complicated comic situations.

When we first meet Cherubino, he's in Susanna's room, singing an aria to the Countess about his lovesick state: "I don't know what I am, what I'm doing; first I seem to be burning, then freezing; every woman makes me change color" (LG 21). Mozart wrote the role (sometimes called a trouser role) for a mezzo-soprano who dresses as a man, to convey the character of a teenager whose voice has not yet changed. The aria is followed by recitative, the rapid-fire, talky kind of singing accompanied by simple harmonies whose main function is to advance the plot—similar to spoken dialogue in a Broadway musical.

Now the action moves quickly. The Count arrives to arrange a tryst with Susanna, and Cherubino hides behind a large armchair. The music master Basilio, who delights in uncovering other people's secrets, comes looking for the Count, who also tries to hide behind the chair. Cherubino stealthily slips onto the chair and Susanna covers him with a throw. Basilio, who knows the Count is hiding, slyly provokes him to step forward by suggesting that Cherubino is wooing the Countess. In the trio that follows ("Cosa sento!"), Susanna is anxious to get both men to leave, the Count is angry but also tries to soothe and seduce her, and the devious Basilio is enjoying himself. At one point the Count flings off the throw to reveal the sheepish boy, and the trio resumes even more intensely.

Mozart's ability to match the demands of a dramatic situation with musical forms is fully evident in this trio, which resembles sonata form in its presentation, development, and recapitulation of themes. His extraordinary skill in conveying emotional realism, in both solo and ensemble numbers, is what makes his characters so believable and compelling. In *Figaro* and other comic operas, Mozart holds a mirror up to society and points out the contradictions inherent in separating people based on class and gender. This is another reason why his operas still speak so strongly to modern audiences: they can easily be understood to contain messages about social unfairness and the rights of individuals, ideas that appeal to enlightened audiences everywhere.

"The Count discovers the Page." Detail of an illustration from Beaumarchais's comedy *Le mariage de Figaro*. The engraving (c. 1784) is after **Jacques Philippe Joseph de Saint-Quentin**.

LISTENING GUIDE 21

 10:41

Mozart: *The Marriage of Figaro*, Act I, excerpts

DATE OF WORK: 1786

GENRE: *Opera buffa*

LIBRETTIST: Lorenzo da Ponte

BASIS: Play by Pierre Caron de Beaumarchais

PERFORMED BY: Patrizia Ciofi (soprano; Susanna), Simon Keenlyside (baritone; Count), Angelika Kirchschlager (mezzo-soprano; Cherubino), Kobie van Rensburg (tenor; Basilio); Concerto Köln; René Jacobs, conductor

continued on next page

Aria (Cherubino)   2:51

What to Listen For

Melody A descending scale pattern (**A**) with quick rhythms then becomes more passionate and lyrical (**B**); after a repeat of the opening scale pattern, a transition leads to a more intense emotional build (**C**), which is repeated and varied with a final flourish.

Form **A-B-A-C-C'** (the final **C** is abridged).

Performing forces Mezzo-soprano voice supported by a small orchestra—mostly strings, with horns, bassoon, and clarinets adding variety and timbral contrast.

Expression Breathless, intense, and almost obsessive in repetition—reflecting the whirlwind passion of a lovestruck teenager.

A—quick rhythms (in E-flat):

Non so   più co - sa son, co - sa fac - cio,

B—more lyrical (in B-flat):

So   lo ai   no - mi d'a - mor di di - let - to,

A—return (in E-flat).

C—begins quietly, then builds and modulates:

Par - lo d'a - mor ve - glian - do.

0:00	**A**	Non so più cosa son, cosa faccio,	I don't know what I am, what I'm doing;
		or di foco, ora sono di ghiaccio,	first I seem to be burning, then freezing;
		ogni donna cangiar di colore,	every woman makes me change color,
		ogni donna mi fa palpitar.	every woman I see makes me shake.
0:17	**B**	Solo ai nomi d'amor, di diletto,	Just the words "love" and "pleasure"
		mi si turba, mi s'altera il petto,	bring confusion; my breast swells in terror,
		e a parlare mi sforza d'amore	yet I am compelled to speak of love
		un desio ch'io non posso spiegar.	by a force which I cannot explain.
0:44	**A**	Non so più cosa son . . .	I don't know what I am . . .
1:03	**C**	Parlo d'amor vegliando,	I speak of love while waking,
		parlo d'amor sognando,	I speak of love while dreaming,
		all'acqua, all'ombra, ai monti,	to the water, to shadows, to mountains,
		ai fiori, all'erbe, ai fonti,	to the flowers, the grass, and the fountains,
		all'eco, all'aria, ai venti,	to the echo, to the air, to the winds
		che il suon de'vani accenti,	which carry the idle words
		portano via con se.	away with them.
1:37	**C'**	Parlo d'amor . . .	I speak of love . . .
		E se non ho chi m'oda,	And if there is no one to listen,
		parlo d'amor con me!	I'll speak of love to myself!

(Seeing the Count in the distance, Cherubino hides behind the chair.)

Recitative (Susanna, Count, Basilio)   3:43

What to Listen For

Melody In a rapid, syllabic style without a distinct melodic shape; focus is on the text.

Performing forces Three characters in turn—Susanna (soprano), the Count (bass), and Basilio (tenor)—accompanied in our performance by a reproduction of a piano from Mozart's day (fortepiano) and a cello.

Expression Occasional pauses and slight musical emphases at key words in the story, but otherwise the musical expression is secondary to the dialogue and the action that's building between the characters.

0:00 Susanna quickly hides Cherubino behind a big armchair in her room as the Count arrives . . .

0:07 The Count starts putting his moves on Susanna; she tries to shoo him away, but he presses and insists . . .

1:17 We hear Basilio offstage; the Count hides behind the armchair; Cherubino quickly scoots to the front, and Susanna covers him with a cloth . . .

1:39 Basilio enters ("Susanna, God keep you in health. Have you by any chance seen the Count?") and begins hinting broadly about the Count's love for her (he probably knows the Count is hiding somewhere nearby) and eventually about Cherubino's love for the Countess. Susanna denies everything and tries to get him to shut up and leave, but he keeps at it ("Tell that boy not to look at the Countess like that, because everyone's saying . . .").

3:38 The Count can't take it anymore, and jumps out from behind the armchair ("*What* is everyone saying?!?"). Basilio is delighted that he's flushed him out ("oh goody"), and we go straight into the trio.

Terzetto (Trio; Count, Basilio, Susanna) 4:07

What to Listen For

Melody The Count tends to grandiose and pompous statements, Susanna is alternatively anxious and angry, and Basilio is devious and mealy-mouthed.

Form Through-composed, with short sections repeated, modified, and rearranged for dramatic development.

Texture Three voices in various overlapping combinations, with both imitative and contrasting ideas; mostly polyphonic, with moments of melody-plus-accompaniment homophony.

Expression Orchestral instruments reinforce the characters' emotional roller-coaster and their almost slapstick comedic-dramatic interactions as they struggle to hide or reveal their secrets.

The Count—angry:

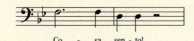

Basilio and the Count—comforting Susanna, who has fainted:

Basilio—gossiping, to the (slowed down) tune of Cherubino's aria:

COUNT	
0:00	Cosa sento! Tosto andate, e scacciate il seduttor!	I heard it all! Go at once, throw the seducer out!

COUNT

Cosa sento! Tosto andate, I heard it all! Go at once,
e scacciate il seduttor! throw the seducer out!

BASILIO

In mal punto son qui giunto; I have come at an unfortunate moment;
perdonate, o mio signor. forgive me, o my lord.

SUSANNA

Che ruina! me meschina! What a catastrophe! I am ruined!
Son' oppressa dal dolor! Pain grips my heart!

continued on next page

COUNT

Tosta andate, andate . . .	Go at once, go . . .

BASILIO

In mal punto . . .	I have come . . .

SUSANNA

Che ruina!	What a catastrophe!

BASILIO

. . . son qui giunto;	. . . at an unfortunate moment;

COUNT

. . . e scacciate il seduttor.	. . . and throw the seducer out.

BASILIO

. . . perdonate, o mio signor.	. . . forgive me, o my lord.

SUSANNA

Me meschina!	I am ruined!
Me meschina!	I am ruined!
Son' oppressa dal dolor.	Pain grips my heart.

BASILIO, COUNT (*supporting Susanna*)

Ah! già svien la poverina!	Ah! The poor girl's fainted!
Come, oh Dio! le batte il cor.	Oh God, how her heart is beating.

BASILIO

Pian, pianin, su questo seggio—	Gently, gently on to the chair—

(*taking her to the chair*)

SUSANNA (*coming to*)

Dove sono? Cosa veggio?	Where am I? What's this I see?
Che insolenza! andate fuor.	What insolence! Leave this room.

BASILIO, COUNT

Siamo qui per aiutarvi, . . .	We're here to help you, . . .

BASILIO

. . . è sicuro il vostro onor.	. . . your virtue is safe.

COUNT

. . . non turbarti, o mio tesor.	. . . do not worry, sweetheart.

BASILIO

Ah, del paggio, quel che ho detto,	What I was saying about the page
era solo un mio sospetto.	was only my own suspicion.

SUSANNA

E un'insidia, una perfidia,	It was a nasty insinuation,
non credete all'impostor.	do not believe the liar.

COUNT

1:54 Parta, parta il damerino, . . .	The young skirt-chaser must go, . . .

SUSANNA, BASILIO

Poverino!	Poor boy!

COUNT

. . . parta, parta il damerino.	. . . the young skirt-chaser must go.

SUSANNA, BASILIO

Poverino!   Poor boy!

COUNT (*sarcastically*)

Poverino! poverino!   Poor boy! Poor boy!
ma da me sorpreso ancor!   But I caught him yet again!

SUSANNA

Come?   How?

BASILIO

Che?   What?

SUSANNA

Che?   What?

BASILIO

Come?   How?

SUSANNA, BASILIO

Come? che?   How? What?

COUNT

2:11   Da tua cugina,   At your cousin's house
        l'uscio jer trovai rinchiuso,   I found the door shut yesterday.
        picchio, m'apre Barbarina   I knocked and Barbarina opened it
        paurosa fuor dell'uso.   much more timidly than usual.
        Io, dal muso insospettito,   My suspicions aroused by her expression,
        guardo, cerco in ogni sito,   I had a good look around,
        ed alzando pian, pianino,   and very gently lifting
        il tappeto al tavolino,   the cloth upon the table,
        vedo il paggio.   I found the page.

        (Imitating his own action with the dress over the chair, he reveals the page.)
        Ah, cosa veggio?   Ah, what do I see?

SUSANNA

Ah! crude stelle!   Ah! wicked fate!

BASILIO

Ah! meglio ancora!   Ah! better still!

COUNT

2:55   Onestissima signora, . . .   Most virtuous lady, . . .

SUSANNA

Accader non può di peggio.   Nothing worse could happen!

COUNT

. . . or capisco come va!   . . . now I see what's happening!

SUSANNA

Giusti Dei, che mai sarà!   Merciful heaven, whatever will happen?

BASILIO

Così fan tutte . . .   They're all the same . . .

continued on next page

SUSANNA

Giusti Dei! che mai sarà
Accader non può di peggio,
ah no! ah no!

Merciful heaven! Whatever will happen?
Nothing worse could happen!
ah no! ah no!

BASILIO

. . . le belle,
non c'è alcuna novità,
cosí fan tutte.

. . . the fair sex,
there's nothing new about it,
they're all the same.

COUNT

Or capisco come va,
onestissima signora!
or capisco, ecc.

Now I see what's happening,
most virtuous lady!
Now I see, *etc.*

BASILIO

Ah, del paggio, quel che ho detto,
era solo un mio sospetto.

What I was saying about the page
was only my own suspicion.

SUSANNA

Accader non può di peggio, ecc.

Nothing worse could happen, *etc.*

COUNT

Onestissima signora, ecc.

Most virtuous lady, *etc.*

BASILIO

Così fan tutte, ecc.

They're all the same, *etc.*

▶|◀ Reflect

How do characters in this scene express their
emotions through music, and how do they move
the action ahead musically? How effective do
you find these two contrasting singing styles—
recitative and aria—in opera?

YOUR TURN TO EXPLORE

The Marriage of Figaro has been produced countless times. Find productions of this
opera that emphasize a particular aspect of the design, characters, or plot. (One
example that you might seek out is a 1990 production by Peter Sellars, reset in
New York City's Trump Tower, stressing elements of political commentary and the "de-
cay of the upper classes." How do the singers' vocal qualities, their interaction with
each other and the orchestra, and staging choices create different dramatic nuances?

MAJOR COMPOSERS

Joseph Haydn

Wolfgang Amadeus
  Mozart

Ludwig van
  Beethoven

IMPORTANT GENRES

opera

oratorio

Mass

symphony

concerto

string quartet

solo sonata

Classical-Era Music

Listening Essentials

Melody: Symmetrical melody in balanced phrases and cadences; tuneful and diatonic.

Rhythm/meter: Rhythmic clarity, with regular recurring accents; dance rhythms popular.

Harmony: Diatonic harmony favored, tonic-dominant relationships are expanded and become the basis for large-scale forms.

Texture: Largely homophonic, with a focus on vertical chords.

Form: Medium-scale binary and large-scale ternary forms predominant; sonata-allegro form developed.

Expression: Emotional balance and restraint; improvisation is limited to cadenzas; continuously changing dynamics, through *crescendo* and *decrescendo*.

Performing forces: Thirty-to-forty-piece orchestra of strings, with a few woodwinds and some brass.

Listening Challenge

Now take the online Listening Challenge, where you'll listen to a mystery selection from the Classical era and answer questions about its elements: the character of the melodies, the rhythmic movement and meter, the harmony (major or minor), the form of the movement, the texture produced by the interweaving of instrumental lines, and expressive devices such as dynamics, chromaticism, and virtuosity.

ROMANTIC ERA

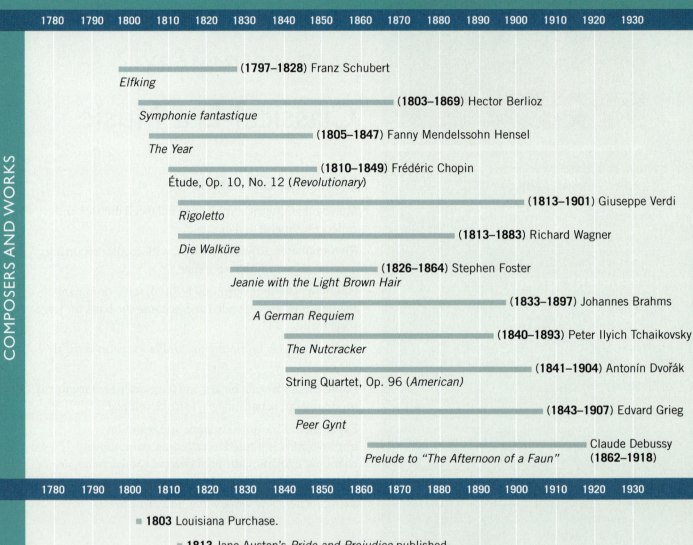

| | 1780 | 1790 | 1800 | 1810 | 1820 | 1830 | 1840 | 1850 | 1860 | 1870 | 1880 | 1890 | 1900 | 1910 | 1920 | 1930 |

COMPOSERS AND WORKS

(1797–1828) Franz Schubert
Elfking

(1803–1869) Hector Berlioz
Symphonie fantastique

(1805–1847) Fanny Mendelssohn Hensel
The Year

(1810–1849) Frédéric Chopin
Étude, Op. 10, No. 12 (*Revolutionary*)

(1813–1901) Giuseppe Verdi
Rigoletto

(1813–1883) Richard Wagner
Die Walküre

(1826–1864) Stephen Foster
Jeanie with the Light Brown Hair

(1833–1897) Johannes Brahms
A German Requiem

(1840–1893) Peter Ilyich Tchaikovsky
The Nutcracker

(1841–1904) Antonín Dvořák
String Quartet, Op. 96 (*American*)

(1843–1907) Edvard Grieg
Peer Gynt

Claude Debussy
Prelude to "The Afternoon of a Faun" **(1862–1918)**

| | 1780 | 1790 | 1800 | 1810 | 1820 | 1830 | 1840 | 1850 | 1860 | 1870 | 1880 | 1890 | 1900 | 1910 | 1920 | 1930 |

EVENTS

■ **1803** Louisiana Purchase.

■ **1813** Jane Austen's *Pride and Prejudice* published.

■ **1815** Napoleon defeated at Waterloo.

■ **1829** Louis Braille invents printing for the blind.

■ **1830** Tuba first used in an opera score.

■ **1840** Saxophone developed by Adolph Sax.

■ **1859** Charles Darwin's *Origin of Species* published.

■ **1861** American Civil War begins.

■ **1862** Victor Hugo's novel *Les misérables* published.

■ **1877** Thomas Edison invents the cylinder phonograph.

Paris World Exhibition. ■ **1889**

PART 5

Auguste Renoir (1841–1919), *Yvonne and Christine Lerolle at the Piano.*

The Nineteenth Century

▶‖ First, listen . . .

to *Hungarian Dance No. 1* by Johannes Brahms, and see how many musical traits described in Part 1 you can identify: for example, the shape of the melodic lines, the rhythmic and metric treatment, whether the piece is in a major or minor key, its overall structure, which instruments are used, and any expressive devices that make it sound exotic. Listen several times to try to pick up multiple elements, but don't worry about "getting it right"—this is your first chance to apply these basic principles to an example of Romantic-era music.

LISTENING OBJECTIVES

By the end of Part 5, you will be able to

- distinguish the era's wide-ranging melodies, which often feature chromatic inflections.

- hear the variety and flexibility of the rhythm.

- recognize increasingly chromatic harmonies and expanded concepts of tonality.

- follow the changing textures within a composition.

- perceive large-scale forms that are built around one or two main themes, and are often programmatic, with literary or pictorial associations.

- identify new instruments added to the orchestra, providing more variety in tone colors and dynamic possibilities.

- identify some of the main vocal and instrumental genres in the Romantic era.

187

5

Music as Passion and Individualism

I f the time frame of Classicism is hard to pin down, Romanticism is one of the artistic trends for which beginnings can be most readily identified, since it was a self-conscious break from the ideals of the Enlightenment. The artistic movement really comes into its own through music in the early decades of the 1800s. Indeed, it is a musician—Ludwig van Beethoven—who is often identified as the first great creative Romantic, and whose influence looms to the present day as an embodiment of passionate individual expression. Many of the common tenets of Romanticism are still very much with us: the artist struggling against rather than working within society and convention; the need for art to unsettle rather than soothe; the belief that works display their creator's distinctive originality and self-expression.

AN AGE OF REVOLUTIONS

The Romantic era grew out of the social and political upheavals that followed the French Revolution in the last decade of the 1700s. The revolution signaled the transfer of power from a hereditary landholding aristocracy to the middle class. This change, firmly rooted in urban commerce and industry, emerged from the Industrial Revolution, which brought millions of people from the country into the cities. The new society, based on free enterprise, celebrated the individual as never before. The slogan of the French Revolution—"Liberty, Equality, Fraternity"— inspired hopes and visions to which artists responded with zeal. Sympathy for the oppressed, interest in peasants, workers, and children, faith in humankind and its destiny, all formed part of the increasingly democratic character of the Romantic period, and inspired a series of revolutions and rebellions that gradually led to the modern political landscape of Europe.

The spirit of the French Revolution is captured in *Liberty Leading the People*, by **Eugène Delacroix** (1798–1863).

Romantic Writers and Artists

Romantic poets and artists rebelled against the conventional concerns of their Classical predecessors and were drawn instead to the fanciful, the picturesque, and the passionate. These men and women emphasized intense emotional expression and were highly aware of themselves as individuals apart from all others. "I am different from all the men I have seen," proclaimed philosopher Jean-Jacques Rousseau. "If I am not better, at least I am different." In Germany, a group of young writers created a new kind of lyric poetry that culminated in the art of Heinrich Heine, who became a favorite poet of Romantic composers. A similar movement in France was led by Victor Hugo, the country's greatest prose writer. In England, the revolt against the formalism of the Classical age produced an outpouring of emotional lyric poetry that reached its peak in the works of Lord Byron, Percy Bysshe Shelley, and John Keats.

The newly won freedom of the artist proved to be a mixed blessing. Confronted by a world indifferent to artistic and cultural values, artists felt more and more cut off from society. A new type emerged: the bohemian, a rejected dreamer who starved in an attic and shocked the establishment through peculiar dress and behavior. Eternal longing, regret for the lost happiness of childhood, an indefinable discontent that gnawed at the soul—these were the ingredients of the Romantic mood. Yet the artist's pessimism was based in reality. It became apparent that the high hopes fostered by the French Revolution were not to be realized overnight. Despite the brave slogans, all people were not yet equal or free. The short-lived optimism gave way to doubt and disenchantment, a state of mind that was reflected in the arts and in literature.

An exotic harem in northern Africa, painted by **Delacroix**: *The Women of Algiers* (1834).

The nineteenth-century novel found one of its great themes in the conflict between the individual and society. Hugo dedicated *Les misérables* "to the unhappy ones of the earth." His novel's hero, Jean Valjean, is among the era's memorable discontented (well known from the 1985 musical and 2012 film of the same name). Some writers sought escape by glamorizing the past, as Walter Scott did in *Ivanhoe* and Alexandre Dumas *père* in *The Three Musketeers*. A longing for far-off lands inspired the exotic scenes that glow on the canvases of Jean-Auguste Dominique Ingres and Eugène Delacroix (top right). The Romantic world was one of "strangeness and wonder": the eerie landscape we meet in Samuel Taylor Coleridge's poem *Kubla Khan*, the isolation we feel in Nathaniel Hawthorne's novel *The Scarlet Letter*, and the supernatural atmosphere we encounter in Edgar Allan Poe's poem *The Raven*.

In *The Laundress,* by **Honoré Daumier** (1808–1879), a burdened-down laundress helps her child up the steps from the Seine River in Paris.

ROMANTICISM IN MUSIC

The Industrial Revolution brought with it the means to create more affordable and responsive musical instruments, as well as the technical improvements that strongly influenced the sound of Romantic music.

As music moved from palace and church to the public concert hall, orchestras increased in size. Naturally, this directly influenced the sound. New instruments such as the piccolo, English horn, tuba, and contrabassoon added varied timbres and extended the high and low ranges of the orchestra. The dynamic range also expanded—sweeping contrasts of very loud (*fff*) and very soft (*ppp*) lent new drama to the music of the Romantics. And as orchestral music developed, so did the technique of writing for instruments. **Orchestration**

The rallying cry of the French people, as depicted in a 1993 performance in Madrid of the stirring musical *Les Misérables*; the show is adapted from Victor Hugo's 1862 novel of the same name.

became an art in itself. Composers now had a palette as broad as those of painters, and they used it to create mood and atmosphere and to evoke profound emotional responses. With all these developments, it was no longer feasible to direct an orchestra from the keyboard or the first violin desk, as had been the tradition in the eighteenth century, and thus a central figure—the conductor—was needed to guide the performance.

In order to communicate their intentions as precisely as possible, composers developed a vocabulary of highly expressive terms. Among the directions frequently encountered in nineteenth-century scores are *dolce* (sweetly), *cantabile* (songful), *dolente* (sorrowful), *maestoso* (majestic), *gioioso* (joyous), and *con amore* (with love, tenderly). A new interest in folklore and a rising tide of nationalism inspired composers to make increased use of the folk songs and dances from their native lands. As a result, a number of national styles—Spanish, Polish, Russian, Bohemian, Scandinavian, and eventually American—flourished, greatly enriching the melodic, harmonic, and rhythmic language of music (see map on p. 219).

The exotic attracted composers as well as artists and writers. Russian, German, and French composers turned for inspiration to the warmth and color of Italy and Spain and to the glamour of Asia and the Far East. French and Italian opera composers also drew on exotic themes, notably Giuseppe Verdi in *Aida*, set in Egypt; and Giacomo Puccini in the Japanese-inspired *Madame Butterfly*.

This chromolithograph from around 1865 shows the Royal Pavilion at Brighton, England, with its Islamic domes and minarets reflecting the nineteenth-century fascination with Eastern culture. Designed by **John Nash** (1752–1835).

Romantic Style Traits

Above all, nineteenth-century musicians tried to make their instruments "sing." Melody was marked by a lyricism that gave it an immediate appeal, and it is no accident that themes from Romantic symphonies and concertos have been transformed into popular songs, and that tunes by composers such as Frédéric Chopin, Verdi, and Peter Ilyich Tchaikovsky have enjoyed an enduring popularity with the public.

Composers employed combinations of pitches that were more chromatic and dissonant than those of their predecessors, allowing for emotionally charged and highly expressive harmony. They expanded the instrumental forms they had inherited from the Classical masters to give their ideas more time to play out. A symphony by Haydn or Mozart takes about twenty minutes to perform; one by Johannes Brahms lasts at least twice that long. Where Haydn wrote more than a hundred symphonies and Mozart more than forty, Franz Schubert (following the example of Beethoven) wrote nine, and Brahms four.

Romantic harmony and form

New orchestral forms emerged as well, including the one-movement symphonic poem, the choral symphony, and works for solo voice with orchestra. In many of these works, we can see how music in the nineteenth century drew steadily closer to the other arts. Even in their purely orchestral music, Romantic composers captured with remarkable vividness the emotional atmosphere that surrounded poetry and painting.

Nineteenth-century music was linked to dreams and passions—to profound meditations on life and death, human destiny, God and nature, pride in one's country, desire for freedom, the political struggles of the age, and the ultimate triumph of good over evil. These intellectual and emotional associations brought music into a commanding position as a link between the artist's most personal thoughts and the realities of the outside world.

Virtuoso violinist Niccolò Paganini, painted in 1832 by **Delacroix**.

The Musician in Society

The newly democratic societies liberated composers and performers. Musical life now reached the general populace, since performances took place in the public concert hall as well as in the salons of the aristocracy. Where eighteenth-century musicians had belonged to a glorified servant class and relied on aristocratic patronage and the favor of royal courts, nineteenth-century musicians, supported by the new middle class, met their audience as equals; they could make a living in their profession. Indeed, as solo performers began to dominate the concert hall, whether as pianists, violinists (Niccolò Paganini, right), or conductors (Franz Liszt, both pianist *and* conductor; p. 204), they became "stars" who were idolized by the public.

Although composition remained largely a man's province, a few women broke away from tradition and overcame social stereotypes to become successful composers. Among them were Clara Wieck

A public orchestral concert in Hungary, including a woman harpist. Nineteenth century.

Schumann, a talented performer and composer of piano, vocal, and chamber music, and Fanny Mendelssohn Hensel, known for her songs and piano music and also for the salon concerts she hosted in her home (see Chapter 36). We will see too that women exerted significant influence as patrons of music or through their friendships with composers. Novelist George Sand played a key role in Chopin's career, as did Princess Carolyne Sayn-Wittgenstein in Liszt's. Nedezhda von Meck is remembered as the mysterious woman who supported Tchaikovsky in the early years of his career and made it financially possible for him to compose. These activities highlight the crucial, but largely private, contributions of women to music in this era.

With the creation of a lucrative musical market for both the home and the concert hall, debates arose about the relationship between art and commerce. While some composers (such as songwriter Stephen Foster) were exploited by the growing publishing industry, others (such as opera composer Giuseppe Verdi) were savvy businessmen and helped to establish economic models that benefit musicians in modern times.

In the later 1800s, distinctions widened between "light music" for entertainment and "art music" for serious listening, a separation that gradually led to categories of "popular" and "classical" music in the century to come. So paradoxically, while access to music became much more democratic, there arose a distinction between "highbrow" and "lowbrow" in musical repertories. But this only happened later in the century: the early and middle Romantic period was a time of expansion for all aspects of music, and musicians became more important to the imagination of society than ever before.

Musical Reading: Schubert and the Early Romantic Lied

▶‖ **First, listen . . .**

to Schubert's song *Elfking*. Without worrying about the words, note the changes in tone of the voice and its interaction with the piano. How does the singer suggest a dialogue between different characters?

> **"** Out of my great sorrows I make my little songs."
>
> —Heinrich Heine

I f a song is meaningful to us, we may have a tendency to identify the words as carrying that meaning. But those words are sung, not spoken, and if someone were to read them, we would likely not find the effect nearly as compelling. This is the power and paradox of song: while it's easy to focus on the text, the music carries the subtle intensity. Some songs rely on simple musical elements, highlighting the predominance of the voice; others employ greater complexity of melody, texture, and timbre, providing multiple resources for the expression of emotion. Within the music you listen to on a regular basis, you can probably identify a wide range of approaches to text and music. Becoming aware of these different treatments will increase your understanding of the expressive potential of song.

THE LIED

Though songs have existed throughout the ages, the **art song** as we know it today was a product of the Romantic era. The **Lied** (plural, **Lieder**), as the new genre was called, is a German-texted solo song, generally with piano accompaniment. Prominent composers in this tradition were Franz Schubert, Robert Schumann,

KEY POINTS

- Typical Romantic song structures include **strophic** and **through-composed** forms; some songs fall between the two, into a **modified strophic** form.

- The German **art song**, or **Lied**—for solo voice and piano—was a favored Romantic genre.

- The poetry of the Lied projects themes of love and nature; favored poets were Johann Wolfgang von Goethe and Heinrich Heine.

- Franz Schubert wrote more than 600 Lieder and two masterful **song cycles**. *Elfking (Erlkönig)*, a through-composed Lied based on a Danish legend related in a dramatic poem by Goethe, is one of his most famous songs.

The immense appeal of the Romantic art song was due in part to the increased popularity and availability of the piano. A lithograph by **Achille Devéria** (1800–1857), *In the Salon.*

and Johannes Brahms, as well as Fanny Mendelssohn Hensel and Clara Wieck Schumann.

In some repertories, the words for a song are newly written; in others, composers choose preexisting poetry for their musical settings. Composers of the Lied were especially dedicated to the latter method, often releasing "competing" musical settings from the outpouring of poetry that marked German Romanticism. Johann Wolfgang von Goethe (1749–1832) and Heinrich Heine (1797–1856) were two leading figures among a group of poets who, like Wordsworth, Byron, Shelley, and Keats in England, favored short, personal, "lyric" poems. Overall, Romantic poems range from tender sentiment to dramatic balladry; common themes are love, longing, and the beauty of nature. Some composers, like Schubert and Robert Schumann (1810–1856), wrote groups of Lieder that were unified by a narrative thread or descriptive theme, known as a **song cycle**.

Another circumstance that made the art song popular was the emergence of the piano as the preferred household instrument of the nineteenth century. Voice and piano together infused the short lyric form with feeling and made it suitable for amateurs and artists alike, in both the home and the concert hall.

Types of Song Structure

In the nineteenth century, two main song structures prevailed. One was **strophic** form, in which the same melody is repeated with every stanza, or strophe, of the poem; hymns, carols, as well as most folk and popular songs are strophic. This form sets up a general atmosphere that accommodates all the stanzas, all sung to the same tune.

The other song type, **through-composed**, proceeds from beginning to end without repetitions of whole sections. Here the music follows the story line, changing according to the text. This makes it possible for the composer to mirror every shade of meaning in the words.

In an intermediate type that combines features of the other two, the same melody may be repeated several times, with new material introduced when the poem requires it. This is considered a **modified strophic** form, similar to what we heard in the lovely first movement of Beethoven's *Moonlight* Sonata (Chapter 30).

In His Own Words

66 [With a good poem] you immediately get a good idea; melodies pour in so that it is a real joy. With a bad poem you can't get anywhere; you torment yourself over it, and nothing comes of it but boring rubbish."

— Franz Schubert

SCHUBERT AND THE LIED

Franz Schubert was a young songwriting prodigy who composed more than six hundred Lieder in his short life. While some of his songs (like *Elfking*, examined below) were performed in concert settings, most of his career was built on intimate musical performances in friends' and sponsors' homes, for which Schubert would write not only Lieder but also dances and chamber works. His gift for melodic writing and the subtle interactions he created between vocal part and accompaniment have made his Lieder a staple of the art-song repertory for both amateurs and professionals ever since.

Franz Schubert (1797–1828)

Schubert was born in Vienna and educated at the Imperial Chapel, where he sang in the choir that later became the famous Vienna Boys' Choir. Although his father hoped he would pursue a career in teaching, Schubert fell in with a small group of writers, artists, and fellow musicians who organized a series of concerts, called Schubertiads, where the young composer's newest works could be heard. One of his friends claimed that "everything he touched turned to song."

He wrote *Elf king*, as well as other great songs, when he was still a teenager. This work won him swift public recognition; still, he had difficulty finding a publisher for his instrumental works, and he was often pressed for money, selling his music for much less than it was worth. His later works, including the song cycle *Winter's Journey*, sound a somber lyricism that parallels his struggle with life, made worse by being afflicted with syphilis. Schubert's dying wish, at age thirty-one, was to be buried near the master he worshipped—Beethoven; his wish was granted.

Schubert's music marks the confluence of the Classical and Romantic eras. His symphonies and chamber music are Classical in their clear forms. In his songs, though, he was wholly the Romantic, writing beautiful melodies that match the tone of the poetry he set. To his earlier masterpieces he added, in the final year of his life, a group of profound works that includes the String Quintet in C, three piano sonatas, and thirteen of his finest songs.

MAJOR WORKS: More than 600 Lieder, including *Erlkönig* (*Elf king*, 1815), *Die Forelle* (*The Trout*, 1817), and the song cycles *Die schöne Mullerin* (*The Lovely Maid of the Mill*, 1823) and *Winterreise* (*Winter's Journey*, 1827) • Nine symphonies, including the *Unfinished* (No. 8, 1822) • Chamber music, including quintets, string quartets, piano trios • Piano sonatas • Seven Masses • Other choral music • Operas and incidental music.

Elfking (Erlkönig)

This masterpiece of Schubert's youth (LG 22) captures the Romantic "strangeness and wonder" of the poem, a celebrated ballad by Goethe, in which a father and his sick child are riding through a forest on a windy night. *Elf king* is based on a Danish, legend that whoever is touched by the king of the elves must die.

Schubert (walking at left) on an outing in the Austrian countryside with his friends (known as Schubertians), painted by one of them (also at left), **Leopold Kupelwieser** (1796–1862).

The legend of *The Elfking* (c. 1860), as portrayed by **Moritz von Schwind** (1804–1871), a good friend of Schubert's.

The eerie atmosphere of the poem is first established by the piano. Galloping triplets are heard against a rumbling figure in the bass. This motive, perhaps suggesting a horse's pounding hooves (or maybe a child's fast heartbeat?), pervades the song, helping to unify it. The poem's four characters—the narrator, father, child, and seductive elf—are all sung by one singer but vividly differentiated through changes in the melody, register, harmony, rhythm, and accompaniment. The child's terror is suggested by clashing dissonance and a high vocal range. The father calms his son's fears with a more rounded vocal line, sung in a low register. And the Elfking cajoles the child in suavely melodious phrases set in a major key.

The song is through-composed; Schubert chose to avoid stanza-based repetition, instead changing the accompaniment for each stanza of Goethe's poem, and shaping his music to follow the action of the story with a steady rise in tension—and pitch—that builds almost to the end. The work of an eighteen-year-old, *Elfking* was a milestone in the history of musical Romanticism: Schubert chose it as his first work to be published (though he had written many other songs), and it quickly became one of the most popular songs of the nineteenth century.

Schubert and the other great song composers created a unity of expression between text and music (and voice and piano) that enhanced the words of the poems they chose, giving them meanings beyond what their poets had envisioned. This is the nature of song, and the reason why we still thrill at its power.

LISTENING GUIDE 22

 4:00

Schubert: *Elfking* (*Erlkönig*)

DATE: 1815

GENRE: Lied

PERFORMED BY: Thomas Quasthoff, baritone; Charles Spencer, piano

What to Listen For

Melody Wide ranging; each character sings in a different range: the narrator in a middle register, father in a low register, son in a high register, and Elfking also in a middle register.

Rhythm/meter Duple meter, with triplets in the piano throughout; a more lilting feeling for the Elfking.

Harmony Minor key, with shifts to major for the Elfking.

Expression Fast tempo projects a mood of urgency; dramatic dialogue; the son's terror is expressed through increased dissonance.

0:00   Piano introduction—minor key and rapid repeated octaves in triplets set the mood, simulating horse's hooves:

TEXT	TRANSLATION
Narrator (minor mode, middle range)	

0:23
Wer reitet so spät durch Nacht und Wind?	Who rides so late through night and wind?
Es ist der Vater mit seinem Kind;	It is the father with his child;
Er hat den Knaben wohl in dem Arm,	he has the boy close in his arm,
Er fasst ihn sicher, er hält ihn warm.	he holds him safely, he keeps him warm.

Father (low range)

"Mein Sohn, was birgst du so bang dein Gesicht?"   "My son, why do you hide your face in fear?"

Son (high range)

"Siehst, Vater, du den Erlkönig nicht?   "Father, don't you see the Elfking?
Den Erlenkönig mit Kron' und Schweif?"   The Elfking with his crown and train?"

Father (low range)

"Mein Sohn, es ist ein Nebelstreif."   "My son, it is a streak of mist."

Elfking (major mode, melodic)

1:29
"Du liebes Kind, komm, geh mit mir!	"You dear child, come with me!
Gar schöne Spiele spiel' ich mit dir;	I'll play very lovely games with you.
Manch' bunte Blumen sind an dem Strand;	There are lots of colorful flowers by the shore;
Meine Mutter hat manch' gülden Gewand."	my mother has some golden robes."

Son (high range, frightened)

1:51
"Mein Vater, mein Vater, und hörest du nicht,	"My father, my father, don't you hear
Was Erlenkönig mir leise verspricht?"	the Elfking whispering promises to me?"

Father (low range, calming)

"Sei ruhig, bleibe ruhig, mein Kind;   "Be still, stay calm, my child;
In dürren Blättern säuselt der Wind."   it's the wind rustling in the dry leaves."

Elfking (major mode, cajoling)

2:13
"Willst, feiner Knabe, du mit mir geh'n?	"My fine lad, do you want to come with me?
Meine Töchter sollen dich warten schön;	My daughters will take care of you;
Meine Töchter führen den nächtlichen Reih'n	my daughters lead the nightly dance,
Und wiegen und tanzen und singen dich ein."	and they'll rock and dance and sing you to sleep."

Son (high range, dissonant outcry)

2:31
"Mein Vater, mein Vater, und siehst du nicht dort,	"My father, my father, don't you see
Erlkönigs Töchter am düstern Ort?"	the Elfking's daughters over there in the shadows?"

Father (low range, reassuring)

"Mein Sohn, mein Sohn, ich seh' es genau,   "My son, my son, I see it clearly,
Es scheinen die alten Weiden so grau."   it's the gray sheen of the old willows."

continued on next page

Elfking (loving, then insistent)

3:00   "Ich liebe dich, mich reizt deine schöne Gestalt,   "I love you, your beautiful form delights me!
       Und bist du nicht willig, so brauch' ich Gewalt."   And if you're not willing, then I'll use force."

Son (high range, terrified)

3:00   "Mein Vater, mein Vater, jetzt fasst er mich an!   "My father, my father, now he's touching me!
       Erlkönig hat mir ein Leids gethan!"   The Elfking has done me harm!"

Narrator (middle range, speechlike)

3:26   Dem Vater grausets, er reitet geschwind,   The father shudders, he rides swiftly,
       Er hält in Armen das ächzende Kind,   he holds the moaning child in his arms;
       Erreicht den Hof mit Müh und Noth: with effort and urgency he reaches the courtyard:
       In seinen Armen das Kind war todt.   in his arms the child was dead.

Melody of son's dissonant outcry on
"My father, my father":

Mein   Va - ter,   mein   Va - ter,

▶|◀ Reflect

How does Schubert use the voice and piano to lead you on this emotional journey? How do the vocal and instrumental timbres each contribute to the drama of the song?

YOUR TURN TO EXPLORE

Consider a couple of your favorite songs. Are they strophic, through-composed, or modified strophic? Why do you think the songwriters have chosen those particular forms? Do they differentiate the stanzas? How are instruments used to reinforce musical repetitions and to help underline key moments?

Marketing Music:
Foster and Early "Popular" Song

▶‖ First, listen . . .

for phrase structure in Foster's *Jeanie with the Light Brown Hair*. What similarities and contrasts can you hear in the phrases? What overall structure unfolds over the entire song?

> 66 Weep no more my lady, / Oh! Weep no more today; / We will sing one song for the old Kentucky home, / For the old Kentucky home far away."
>
> —Stephen Foster

What makes a song successful? Some melodies have become so beloved and familiar that we no longer associate them with an individual composer— for example, "Happy Birthday," which you probably have sung countless times without knowing that it was likely composed by sisters Patty and Mildred J. Hill in the early 1890s. This is one meaning of "popular"—we think of "Happy Birthday" as belonging to "the people." Another meaning connects to the idea of success: some music has brought great financial profit, partly because it has been carefully marketed. These two meanings of "popular" intersect in the songs of Stephen Foster, whose music has long saturated North American culture. Foster helped build a powerful musical industry in the nineteenth-century United States, while earning very little profit from the skyrocketing sales of his sheet music. The accessibility of his songs laid the foundation for the enormous international influence of North American musical culture in the following century.

Music in Early North America:
Cultivated and Vernacular

European immigrants to the Americas brought with them cultivated repertories such as operas, chamber music, and symphonies. Along with this imported "high art," they also began to develop traditions of lighter music—for dancing, singing

KEY POINTS

- Nineteenth-century songwriters in the united States combined elements of European art song and opera with other traditions to create commercially successful "popular" music.

- Songs often were popularized through **minstrel shows**, which were racially charged theatrical variety shows.

- The **minstrel** and **parlor songs** of Stephen Foster (including *Jeanie with the Light Brown Hair*) were very successful during his lifetime and remain so today.

Posters advertising minstrel shows often used images of performers both in blackface costume (onstage) and in more formal poses (above), perhaps to reassure audiences of the "proper" nature of the show.

at home, and public events like parades. These traditions were thought of as vernacular, more connected to new notions of "American popular identity." However, there was not yet a clear split between "classical" and "popular" music in the nineteenth century; the various traditions were mutually influential, and audiences would often encounter them in the same spaces and even performed by the same ensembles.

STEPHEN FOSTER, PARLOR SONG, AND MINSTRELSY

The songs of Stephen Foster exemplify the intersection between the vernacular American spirit and the European art tradition. Foster was familiar with the Italian operas that were popular among the upper classes, and was also aware of the great financial success of nostalgic "folk songs" that helped second- and third-generation Anglo immigrants fantasize about an ideal Old Country their grandparents had left. He blended the two traditions in his **parlor songs**, which are often sweet, sentimental, and nostalgic; we will consider one, *Jeanie with the Light Brown Hair*. Though many of Foster's songs were designed for amateur performance in the parlor (a reception or gathering place) of a middle-class home, several became popular through a very prominent and uniquely North American nineteenth-century musical tradition: the minstrel show.

Minstrelsy can be unpleasant for modern audiences to face: the shows featured white performers in blackface, acting out idealized "scenes from the plantation" that were vastly different from the realities of slave life. Minstrelsy is one of the first traditions that revealed white Americans' fascination with—and misunderstanding of—African Americans, and because of its widespread popularity in the 1800s, it shaped stereotyping of African American culture well into the twentieth century.

Two examples of Foster's songs written for or incorporated into minstrel shows are *Camptown Races*, in which a slave sings of his happy time betting on horses, and *Old Folks at Home* ("Way down upon the Swanee River"). Though Foster himself was sympathetic toward the Abolitionist cause and wanted his "plantation songs" to inspire compassion for the plight of slaves, it was they rather than his parlor songs that earned him most of his income.

A Song by Foster

Jeanie with the Light Brown Hair (LG 23) was written in 1853–54, just after the composer separated from his wife. In his sketchbook, the original title was not "Jeanie" but "Jennie," from Jane Denny McDowell's name. The tone is bittersweet, wishing for days gone by, and draws on the then-popular tradition of Anglo-Irish folk song. The song, like most of Foster's, is strophic and set for solo voice and piano, thereby meeting the growing need for parlor music appropriate for amateurs. The brief cadenza before the return of the opening music marks a moment of free

Stephen Foster (1826–1864)

Foster grew up outside Pittsburgh, where he spent much of his life, and attended Jefferson College (now Washington & Jefferson College). Rather than completing his degree, he moved to Cincinnati, where he wrote his first hit song, *Oh! Susanna*. Many of Foster's early songs were for the blackface minstrel shows that were popular during this era. From 1847 on, he was under contract with the Christy Minstrels, who specialized in performing blackface shows. For them, he wrote some of his most enduring songs, including *Camptown Races* and *Old Folks at Home*. Later he turned to parlor songs, like *Jeanie with the Light Brown Hair*. These songs, evoking themes of lost youth and happiness, reflect his desire to write

more serious music. Although Foster did not spend much time in the South, it is thought that *My Old Kentucky Home*, today the state song of Kentucky, was inspired by Harriet Beecher Stowe's antislavery novel *Uncle Tom's Cabin*.

Foster was perhaps the first American to make a living as a professional songwriter, but composers in this era made little profit from their publications. After he and his wife separated, Foster moved to New York, where he wrote his famous song *Beautiful Dreamer*, conceived in the style of an Italian air. He died there at age thirty-seven, a penniless alcoholic, victim to a fall in a cheap New York hotel room. Today, Foster's songs are much better known than he is.

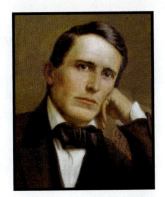

interpretation for the performer. Though we might be tempted to read this as a personal narrative expressing Foster's own nostalgia, we must also keep in mind that Foster was not a singer and would have expected the song to be performed primarily by amateurs in their homes, each of whom would bring her or his own interpretation of the object of the melancholy "dreaming."

Unlike some other Foster songs, *Jeanie* was not a huge success during his lifetime. However, it reached millions nearly a century later when, in 1941, a dispute broke out over licensing fees charged by companies that owned the rights to newly composed music, and some radio broadcasters chose to air older music that would cost them less to play. Thus, economic considerations once again helped to make this song even more "popular."

The title page to *Jeanie with the Light Brown Hair* (1854).

▶|◀ **Reflect**

How does the **A-A′-B-A″** form make this song accessible to amateur performers? What expressive qualities do you think helped to make it so popular in Foster's time? Could it still be considered a "popular song" today?

YOUR TURN TO EXPLORE

What can you find out about the economic networks that support musicians or bands? How do you suppose the musicians' creative choices (country, rap, folk-rock) have influenced their commercial distribution? Do you think technologies have influenced these creative choices, and if so, how?

LISTENING GUIDE 23

 1:27

Foster: *Jeanie with the Light Brown Hair*

DATE: 1854

GENRE: Parlor song

PERFORMED BY: Wolodymyr Smishkewych, tenor; Yonit Lea Kosovske, square piano

What to Listen For

Melody A wavelike line, descending then ascending; syllabic text-setting.

Harmony Major key, with a simple block- and broken-chord accompaniment.

Form A-A'-B-A" song form within each strophe (only one is performed).

0:00	**Piano introduction**
0:12	**Verse**

I dream of Jeanie with the light brown hair, Borne, like a vapor, on the summer air!	**A section**
I see her tripping where the bright streams play, Happy as the daisies that dance on her way.	**A′ section** (varied)
Many were the wild notes her merry voice would pour, Many were the blithe birds that warbled them o'er;	**B section**
Oh! I dream of Jeanie with the light brown hair, Floating like a vapor, on the soft summer air.	**A″ section** ends the song (ascending cadence on "Oh!").

1:13   **Piano postlude**

Opening of verse, with descending melodic line:

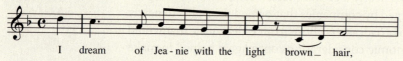

I dream of Jea-nie with the light brown_ hair,

B section, with wavelike line:

Ma-ny were the wild notes her mer-ry voice would pour.

Fire and Fury at the Keyboard: Chopin and Romantic Piano Music

▶❚❚ First, listen . . .

to Chopin's *Revolutionary* Étude, and focus on the expressive qualities you hear. Which elements do you feel contribute most to the descriptive name *Revolutionary*? How do they support the emotional mood of the piece?

> **❝** To be a great composer, one needs an enormous amount of knowledge, which . . . one does not acquire from listening only to other people's works, but even more from listening to one's own."
>
> —Frédéric Chopin

Of all musical instruments, the piano is the most central to the Western musical tradition. From the nineteenth century onward, the instrument was increasingly hailed as equally suited to amateurs and professionals, to the home and to the concert hall. Before the arrival of recorded sound, families and communities alike gathered around the piano to make and hear music. Learning to play was long a staple of refined education, and you may have taken at least a few lessons yourself. One of the most valued aspects of the piano is its suitability for polyphonic and homophonic textures, whether on its own or by accompanying voices or instruments. It can also create a variety of dynamic and resonant effects. Today the piano is still considered the most expressive instrument available to most musicians, and we owe this to the skilled individuals who refined the technologies of construction and performance in the early nineteenth century.

THE NINETEENTH-CENTURY PIANO

The rise in popularity of the piano helped shape the musical culture of the Romantic era. It proved especially attractive to amateurs because melody and harmony could be performed on one instrument, as they couldn't on strings or

KEY POINTS

- Technical improvements to the nineteenth-century piano led to the development of the modern concert grand piano.

- Polish composer Frédéric Chopin dedicated his entire compositional output to the piano; he is said to have originated the modern piano style.

- Chopin's works include **études** (virtuosic study pieces), meditative nocturnes, preludes, and dances (especially

Polish mazurkas and polonaises), as well as piano sonatas and concertos. His music calls for the use of **rubato**, or "robbed time."

- The *Revolutionary* Étude (Op. 10, No. 12) is one of Chopin's most popular works; its highly emotional quality has been linked to the composer's distress over his native Poland's war with Russia.

A Parisian salon concert depicted by **James Tissot** (1836–1902).

winds. The piano thus played a crucial role in the taste and experience of the new mass public.

Hardly less important was the rise of the virtuoso pianist. At first, the performer was also the composer; Mozart and Beethoven introduced their own piano concertos to the public. With the developing concert industry, however, a class of virtuoso performers arose whose only function was to dazzle audiences by playing music composed by others.

The nineteenth century saw a series of crucial technical improvements that led to the development of the modern concert grand, mandated by Romantic composers' quest for greater power and dynamic range. Piano manufacturing eventually moved from the craft shop to the factory, allowing a huge increase in production at a significantly reduced cost. A standardized instrument was developed that had a metal frame supporting increased string tension, as well as an improved mechanical action and extended range of notes—from five octaves to seven or more. At the Paris Exhibition of 1867, two American manufacturers took the top awards, one of them Steinway, maker of some of today's finest pianos. By the early twentieth century, the piano had become a universal fixture in the homes of middle-class and upper-class families.

THE SHORT LYRIC PIANO PIECE

Caricature of virtuoso pianist Franz Liszt, to whom Chopin dedicated his études.

With its ability to project melodious and dramatic moods within a compact form, the short lyric piano piece, or **character piece**, was the instrumental equivalent to the song. Composers adopted new and sometimes fanciful terms for such works. Some titles—"Prelude," "Intermezzo" (interlude), "Impromptu" (on the spur of the moment), and "Nocturne" (a night piece), for example—suggest free, almost improvisational forms. The **étude**, once considered a technical study piece, rose to new heights of virtuosity in the hands of Frédéric Chopin and Franz Liszt. Many composers produced keyboard versions of dances like the Polish mazurka and polonaise and the Viennese waltz, as well as the lively scherzo. They sometimes chose more descriptive titles for character pieces that depict a mood or scene, such as "Wild Hunt," "The Little Bell," and "Forest Murmurs" (all by Liszt).

Frédéric Chopin (1810–1849)

Chopin was born outside Warsaw to a French father and a Polish mother. He studied at the Conservatory of Warsaw, but in 1831 left for Paris, where he spent the remainder of his career. Paris in the 1830s was the center of the new Romanticism, and the circle in which Chopin moved included the most famous composers, writers, and artists in France.

Through the virtuoso pianist Franz Liszt, Chopin met the novelist George Sand, with whom he had a long relationship. He spent his summers at Sand's estate in Nohant, where she entertained prominent artists and writers. These were productive years for the composer, although his health grew progressively worse and his relationship with Sand ran its course from love to conflict, jealousy, and hostility. He died of tuberculosis in Paris at the age of thirty-nine.

Chopin's works, central to the pianist's repertory, include four epic ballades, the thoroughly Romantic Sonatas in B-flat Minor and B Minor, and two piano concertos. The nocturnes are melancholic and meditative. The preludes are visionary fragments, and in the études, which crown the literature of the study piece, Chopin's piano technique is transformed into poetry. The mazurkas, derived from a Polish peasant dance, evoke the idealized landscape of his youth, and the polonaises revive the stately processional dance in which Poland's nobles hailed their kings.

MAJOR WORKS: Two piano concertos • Piano music, including four ballades, three sonatas, preludes, études, mazurkas, polonaises, scherzos, waltzes, impromptus, and nocturnes • Chamber music, all with piano • Songs.

Nineteenth-century composers who refined the piano miniature—Schubert, Chopin, Liszt, Felix Mendelssohn, Fanny Mendelssohn Hensel, Robert and Clara Schumann, and Brahms—showed inexhaustible ingenuity in exploring the technical resources of the instrument and its potential for expression.

Étude, Op. 10, No. 12 (*Revolutionary*), by Chopin

Chopin's music, rooted in the heart of Romanticism, made this era the piano's golden age. His style was entirely his own—there is no mistaking it for any other—and he remains one of the most original artists of the nineteenth century. His entire creative life revolved around the piano, and he is credited with originating the modern piano style. Chopin's music calls for the use of **rubato**, or "robbed time," in which certain liberties are taken by the performer without upsetting the basic pulse. He taught his students that the left hand should remain steady while the right-hand melody might hesitate a little here and hurry forward there. We will hear one of the composer's most popular works—the so-called *Revolutionary Étude* (LG 24)—although the mood and propulsion of this particular piece may make any rubato more difficult to hear.

Chopin composed his first set of études—twelve virtuoso showpieces—between 1829 and 1832, while on a European tour: first to Vienna, where he stayed for eight months, and then on to Paris, where he remained for the rest of his life. Just one week after his arrival in the Austrian capital, he learned of the disastrous

November Uprising in Warsaw 1830, by **Georg Benedikt Wunder** (1786–1858).

Polish uprising in Warsaw against Russian domination. The homesick musician wanted to return to his native land, but was advised by family and friends to stay away. In Paris salons, where he was already famous as a composer and pianist, he met the virtuoso pianist Franz Liszt, to whom he dedicated his étude collection.

Chopin's études, generally regarded as the finest of the genre, explore a wide range of technical problems for the pianist; but far more than practice studies, they are established works for the concert repertory—albeit not for every pianist. The German critic Ludwig Rellstab found them highly difficult, noting that "those who have distorted fingers may put them right by practicing these studies, but those who have not should not play them . . . without having a surgeon at hand."

The last étude in the set, dubbed the *Revolutionary,* is believed to have been inspired by the composer's strong feelings for his homeland and for the Polish cause. The work is a stormy outpouring of emotions, from beginning to end: while the left hand races through dazzling sixteenth-note figurations, the right hand delivers an impassioned dotted-rhythm melody that develops increasing rhythmic complexities. The brooding, C minor key contributes to the feeling of conflict throughout; the coda suggests resolution, but then a torrential downpour of notes drives the piece toward its forceful final chords—the last one, surprisingly, in C major.

When Poland was finally defeated, Chopin wrote: "All this has caused me so much pain. Who could have foreseen it!" Schumann praised the expressive depth of Chopin's music, suggesting he was a "poet." And to this day, his music is revisited around the world by pianists of all abilities, each finding a unique way to revitalize the composer's extraordinary connection with this most technologically versatile of instruments.

LISTENING GUIDE 24   2:39

Chopin: Étude, Op. 10, No. 12 (*Revolutionary*)

DATE: c. 1831

GENRE: Étude for solo piano

PERFORMED BY: Maurizio Pollini, piano

What to Listen For

Rhythm/meter Duple meter, with steady, virtuosic sixteenth-note figurations in the left hand and a dotted-rhythm melody that explores triplets, syncopations, and cross-rhythms.

Harmony Dark minor key, with many chromatic inflections; an abrupt C major closing chord.

Form Modified strophic form (**A–A′**), with variations, and coda.

Expression Fiery and emotional; wide-ranging figurations performed at a rapid-fire pace, with large dynamic contrasts and a haunting theme; the tension is briefly released in a subdued (*sotto voce*) coda before a powerful closing.

0:00   **Introduction**
Dramatic chords, followed by rushing, descending passages.

0:13   **A section** (marked *Allegro con fuoco,* with fire)
Dotted-figure theme in C minor, played in octaves, above constantly swirling sixteenth notes.

0:32   Main theme returns, played much more softly.

1:04   Accented descending chords, played *fortissimo,* with swirling figurations in the left hand.

1:24   **A′ section**
Main theme returns in a dotted-triplet pattern; rhythm grows increasingly complex.

1:54   The accented descending chords return.

2:19   **Coda** (marked *sotto voce,* or softly)
Quiet chords, gently ascending, are followed by a sudden *fortissimo,* rushing passage, marked *appassionato,* closing with strong chords, the last one in C major.

▶◀ Reflect

How do the étude's expressive elements affect your response to it? Why might this work deserve the title *Revolutionary*?

YOUR TURN TO EXPLORE

Compare videos of different keyboard players, ideally performing the same Chopin piece. Try to find a work that's more lyrical than our étude, perhaps a nocturne or mazurka, and listen closely for any rubato. Do the performers choose the same tempo, both overall and at specifc "rubato" moments? How do different performers' choices reveal different notions of expressiveness? How do pianists' physical movements differ, and how does this movement create different ideas of "singing through the piano"?

Musical Diaries: Hensel and Programmatic Piano Music

66 I have called my piano pieces after the names of my favorite haunts . . . they will form a delightful souvenir, a kind of second diary."

—Fanny Mendelssohn Hensel

▶|| First, listen . . .

to the piano piece *September: At the River*, by Fanny Mendelssohn Hensel, noting any programmatic elements you perceive. What mood and possible story can you hear in this piece?

In telling our story about the musical past, we've been focusing on composers, largely because written-down compositions constitute the most precise evidence we have of musical activity before the invention of sound recording at the end of the 1800s. But other types of individuals have been essential to music from even before the beginnings of notation: for example, performers have brought written compositions to life, teachers have passed on both performance skills and compositional savvy, and patrons have provided musicians with career-promoting opportunities. While social assumptions about women long discouraged them from composing (and limited their public performances), they were crucial teachers and sponsors of music from the earliest days of the European tradition. Considering their roles is important, since it can help us remember that composition and performance are only two aspects of musical activity, and that teaching and active sponsorship are still just as crucial to a musical work's success.

WOMEN AND MUSIC IN NINETEENTH-CENTURY SOCIETY

In this era, women made great strides in establishing careers as professional musicians and public advocates for musical innovation. This path was now possible through the broadening of educational opportunities: in public conservatories, women could receive training as singers, instrumentalists, and even composers.

KEY POINTS

■ While women in the nineteenth century were discouraged from composing by social convention, they played an essential role as patrons, sponsors, and teachers, as well as coordinating musical activity in the home.

■ Fanny Mendelssohn Hensel, sister of Felix Mendelssohn and an important sponsor of his music, was a talented pianist and composer, known today for her Lieder and piano music, including the autobiographical cycle *The Year* (*Das Jahr*).

Likewise, the rise of the piano as the favored chamber instrument, both solo and with voice or other instruments, provided women of the middle and upper classes with a performance outlet that was socially acceptable. Indeed, as music for the home increased in importance with the mass-marketing of instruments and sheet music, such music-making was increasingly associated with female social graces. This made instruction on the piano and other amateur-friendly instruments more and more desirable; and increasingly women became piano teachers as well as students, since it was considered a little scandalous for a man to be in close proximity—let alone physical contact—with an unrelated woman.

Although composition remained largely a man's province, some women broke away from tradition and overcame social stereotypes to become successful composers. Among them were Fanny Mendelssohn Hensel, known for her songs, piano music, and chamber works; and Clara Wieck Schumann, a talented performer and composer of piano, vocal, and chamber music. Both, however, were only tentatively encouraged by their male relatives. Women also exerted a significant influence as patrons of music or through their friendship with composers. We noted earlier that novelist George Sand enabled Chopin to focus on his creative work during their sometimes stormy relationship. Several women of the upper class, including Fanny Mendelssohn, presided over musical salons where composers could gather to perform and discuss their music.

Miss Elizabeth Bennet plays the pianoforte for Mr. Darcy and a friend, from an 1895 edition of Jane Austen's *Pride and Prejudice* (originally published 1813), illustrated by **Charles Edmond Brock** (1870–1938).

Fanny Mendelssohn Hensel and the Piano Miniature

The music of Fanny Hensel has been neglected until recent years, when she was lifted from the shadow of her famous brother to reveal her genuine talents. Well educated in music and recognized in her lifetime as a gifted composer, she remained reluctant to make her compositions public. Her story enhances our modern-day understanding of the challenges faced by women musicians in the Romantic era.

Hensel's music room in her Berlin residence (1849) features her grand piano at right. Watercolor by **Julius Eduard Wilhelm Helfft** (1818–1894).

A Piano Cycle: *The Year (Das Jahr)*

Hensel's cycle of piano works entitled *The Year* shows her at the pinnacle of her artistry. This set of twelve pieces, each named for a month of the year, and one postlude was once thought to be a kind of travel diary, documenting her year-long trip to Italy in 1839–40. But with the discovery in 1989 of a lost manuscript in her hand, missing for nearly 150 years, scholars have found a deeper meaning in the works. Each miniature piece is prefaced by a poetic epigram and a painting by her husband, Wilhelm Hensel, and is written on different-colored paper. The poems and artwork seem to suggest the passage of time or the seasons of one's life, perhaps her own. The cycle is unified through recurring motives, tonal schemes, and references to the works of other composers, including her brother Felix.

Fanny Mendelssohn Hensel (1805–1847)

Fanny Mendelssohn was born into a highly cultured family (her grandfather, Moses Mendelssohn, was a leading Jewish scholar/philosopher). She was especially close to her younger brother Felix, a renowned composer and conductor.

Raised in Berlin, Fanny learned piano from her mother and studied theory and composition with the well-known composer Carl Friedrich Zelter. Because of her gender, however, she was actively discouraged from pursuing music as a career. Her father cautioned her to focus on "the only calling for a young woman—that of a housewife." In 1829, Fanny married the court artist Wilhelm Hensel. She remained active during the following years as a composer, pianist, and participant in the regular salon concerts held each Sunday at the Mendelssohn residence, which she eventually organized. She died suddenly of a stroke on May 13, 1847, while preparing to conduct a cantata written by her brother.

Having lost his dearest companion, Felix died just six months later.

Although she wrote several large-scale works, including a piano trio and a string quartet, Hensel's output was dominated by Lieder, choral part songs, and piano music, notably *The Year* (*Das Jahr*), a set of twelve character pieces. Most of her compositions were intended for performance at the family's Sunday musical gatherings. Her solo vocal music is highly lyrical, and her choice of Romantic poets and complex piano writing place her in the mainstream of the Lieder tradition. Her piano music reflects a strong interest in Bach's contrapuntal procedures.

MAJOR WORKS: Instrumental music, including an orchestral overture, a string quartet, and a piano trio • Over 125 piano works: sonatas, preludes and fugues, and character pieces, including *Das Jahr* (*The Year*, 1841) • Vocal music, including four cantatas and part songs for chorus, and over 250 Lieder.

We will consider the character piece entitled *September: At the River* (LG 25), which is accompanied by a drawing of a bare-footed woman by the stream and several poetic lines from Goethe: "Flow, flow, dear river, / Never will I be happy." This melancholic idea is captured in the haunting, meandering melody, sounded below a stream of notes signifying the flowing river. The piece takes us on a daring journey through distant key centers, unfolding in a typical three-part form of statement-departure-return, framed by a brief introduction and coda. *The Year* was never published in its entirety; in her lifetime, indeed, only *September* was included in Fanny's collection of piano works and without its literary and visual details. The musical and extra-musical links in this set make it a significant large-scale venture for the composer, who reached a new level of achievement that even her brother had not yet attained in his piano works.

In Her Own Words

66 I want to admit how terribly uppity I've been and announce that six 4-part Lieder . . . are coming out next. . . . My choir has enjoyed singing them . . . and I've made every effort to make them as good as possible."

—Fanny Mendelssohn Hensel

▶◀ Reflect

What devices does Hensel use in this character piece to make the music descriptive? How effective is the musical storytelling?

YOUR TURN TO EXPLORE

In contemporary society, are certain musical styles, traditions/genres, and/or instruments associated more with women than with men, or vice versa? If so, why? How do different ideals of gender in your community play out in the way music is performed, created, or supported?

LISTENING GUIDE 25

 3:02

Hensel: *September: At the River*, from *The Year (Das Jahr)*

DATE: 1841

GENRE: Character piece, from a programmatic cycle of 12

PERFORMED BY: Sarah Rothenberg, piano

What to Listen For

Melody The slow-paced melody, in the piano's middle range, is set against fast-moving, churning notes; much chromaticism.

Rhythm/meter A lilting 6/8 meter, with constant running eighth notes; some rubato (push and pull of the beat) in the performance.

Form Ternary (**A-B-A'**) form, with a short introduction and coda.

Harmony Minor key, with modulations to distant keys in the middle; very chromatic.

Introduction

0:00   Gentle, flowing 16th notes, punctuated by chords and octaves; slows down before the next section.

A section

0:12   Wistful, slow-moving melody in the middle register, in B minor, accompanied by constantly flowing fast notes and bass chords (melody notes are circled):

More movement in the main melody; grows chromatic and modulates; slows into next section, growing louder.

B section

1:23   Melody moves more quickly, in a new key, with more emphasis under a churning accompaniment. Grows louder and more chromatic, with high-range octaves exchanging a three-note idea with the main melody; builds in a swirling *crescendo*.

A' section

1:56   Returns to the main melody, in B minor, but with more chromaticism; octave chords make a long descent to the tonic.

Coda

2:38   Introduction returns; fast-moving notes with chords; dies away *pianissimo*.

Personal Soundtracks: Berlioz and the Program Symphony

▶|| **First, listen . . .**

to the first two minutes of the *March to the Scaffold* from Berlioz's *Symphonie fantastique.* Pay special attention to the different instrument families you hear. How does the composer use instruments to develop the main theme and contrast it with another melody?

A s we walk through campus wearing our headphones or earbuds, we might think of the music playing on our portable player as a personal soundtrack, a musical accompaniment to our everyday life. Of course, when we choose our playlists, we pick from favorite songs we have purchased, rather than creating our own soundscapes from scratch. In an era before recording technology, those who wanted a "soundtrack" for their lives had to compose it themselves. One extraordinary example comes from the work of Hector Berlioz, who combined his musical creativity with the idea of personal storytelling and raised program music to a new level.

In His Own Words

66 The painter turns a poem into a painting; the musician sets a picture to music."

—Robert Schumann

ROMANTIC PROGRAM MUSIC

Music often evokes specific ideas or visual images. Sometimes these are the products of the listener's imagination, but other times they are intended by the composer. Schumann's quote above aptly suggests how a composer might think when creating such a work. The genre that evokes images and ideas became known as **program music**, or instrumental music with literary or pictorial associations. The program is supplied by the composer, either in the title or in an explanatory note. A title such as *King Lear* (by Berlioz), for example, suggests specific characters and events, while *Pièces fugitives* (*Fleeting Pieces*, by Clara Schumann) merely labels the

KEY POINTS

- Many Romantic composers cultivated **program music**—instrumental music with a literary or pictorial association supplied by the composer—over **absolute music.**

- Hector Berlioz's *Symphonie fantastique* is a five-movement **program symphony** unified by a recurring theme (*idée fixe*) that represents the composer's beloved.

mood or character of the work. Program music is distinguished from **absolute music**, or pure music, which consists of musical patterns that are designed without intended literary or pictorial meanings, like Beethoven's Fifth Symphony.

Program music was especially important during the nineteenth century, when musicians became sharply conscious of the connection between their art and the world around them. Adding a programmatic title brought music closer to poetry and painting, and helped composers relate their own work to the moral and political issues of their time. The passion for program music was so strong that it invaded even the most revered form of absolute music, the symphony. We will examine Berlioz's monumental **program symphony**, the *Symphonie fantastique*.

Berlioz and the *Symphonie fantastique*

"To render my works properly requires a combination of extreme precision and irresistible verve, a regulated vehemence, a dreamy tenderness, and an almost morbid melancholy."

The flamboyance of Victor Hugo's poetry and the dramatic intensity of Eugène Delacroix's painting found their musical counterpart in the works of Hector Berlioz, whose music is intense, bold, and passionate. He was the first great proponent of musical Romanticism in France.

Berlioz wrote his best-known program symphony when he was twenty-seven, basing its story on his personal life. His score describes "a young musician of morbid sensibility and ardent imagination, in . . . lovesick despair, [who] has poisoned himself with opium. The drug, too weak to kill, plunges him into a heavy sleep accompanied by strange visions. . . . The beloved one herself becomes for him a melody, a recurrent theme that haunts him everywhere."

The symphony's recurrent theme, called an ***idée fixe*** (fixed idea), acts as a musical thread unifying the five diverse movements, though its appearances are varied in harmony, rhythm, meter, tempo, dynamics, register, and instrumental color. This type of unification, called **thematic transformation**, serves the huge, expansive form of Berlioz's symphony. These transformations take on literary as well as musical significance, as the following description by Berlioz shows.

The Program

I. *Reveries, Passions*. "[The musician] remembers the weariness of soul, the indefinable yearning he knew before meeting his beloved. Then, the volcanic love with which she at once inspired him, his delirious suffering . . . his religious consolation." The Allegro section introduces a soaring melody, the fixed idea.

II. *A Ball*. "Amid the tumult and excitement of a brilliant ball he glimpses the loved one again." This dance movement is in ternary (three-part) form. In the middle section, the fixed idea reappears in waltz time.

III. *Scene in the Fields*. "On a summer evening in the country he hears two shepherds piping. The pastoral duet, the quiet surroundings . . . all unite to fill his heart with a long-absent feeling of calm. But she appears again [*idée fixe*]. His heart contracts. Painful forebodings fill his soul." The composer said that his aim in this pastoral movement was to establish a mood of "sorrowful loneliness."

Berlioz's *idée fixe* was inspired by the Shakespearean actress Harriet Smithson (1800–1854).

Idée fixe

Listeners flee Berlioz's bombastic orchestra, in a satirical engraving from 1846.

Hector Berlioz (1803–1869)

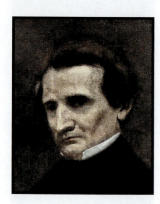

Berlioz was born in southern France. His father, a well-to-do physician, expected the boy to follow in his footsteps, but the Romantic revolution was brewing in Paris, and Berlioz, under the spell of such artists as Victor Hugo and Eugène Delacroix, followed his dream to study music. He became a huge fan of Beethoven and of Shakespeare, to whose plays he was introduced by a visiting English troupe. Berlioz fell madly in love with an actress in this troupe, Harriet Smithson: "I became obsessed by an intense, overpowering sense of sadness," he wrote. "I could not sleep, I could not work, and I spent my time wandering aimlessly about Paris and its environs."

In 1830, Berlioz won the coveted Prix de Rome, which gave him an opportunity to work in Italy. That same year, he composed the *Symphonie fantastique*, his most celebrated work. After returning from Rome, he began a hectic courtship of Harriet Smithson, whom he married, only to realize it was Shakespeare he had loved rather than Harriet.

Berlioz's works, showing the favorite literary influences of the Romantic period, draw on Goethe, Lord Byron, and especially Shakespeare, the source for his overture *King Lear*, his opera *Béatrice et Bénédict*, and his dramatic symphony *Romeo and Juliet*. It was in the domain of orchestration that Berlioz's genius asserted itself most fully. His scores, calling for the largest orchestra that had ever been used, abound in novel effects and discoveries, revealing him as one of the boldest innovators of the nineteenth century.

MAJOR WORKS: Orchestral music, including overtures (*King Lear*) and program symphonies (*Symphonie fantastique* and *Romeo et Juliette*) • Choral music, including a *Requiem* Mass • Three operas, including *Les Troyens* (*The Trojans*) • Nine works for solo voice and orchestra • Writings about music, including an orchestration treatise.

IV. *March to the Scaffold*. "He dreams that he has killed his beloved, that he has been condemned to die and is being led to the scaffold. . . . At the very end the fixed idea reappears for an instant, like a last thought of love interrupted by the fall of the blade."

V. *Dream of a Witches' Sabbath*. "He sees himself at a witches' sabbath surrounded by a host of fearsome spirits who have gathered for his funeral. Unearthly sounds,

Francisco Goya (1746–1828) anticipated the passionate intensity of Berlioz's music in this painting of the *Witches' Sabbath*, c. 1819–23.

groans, shrieks of laughter. The melody of his beloved is heard, but it has lost its noble and reserved character. It has become a vulgar tune, trivial and grotesque. It is she who comes to the infernal orgy. A howl of joy greets her arrival. She joins the diabolical dance. Bells toll for the dead. A burlesque of the *Dies irae*. Dance of the witches. The dance and the *Dies irae* combined."

The last two movements are perfect examples of the Romantic era's preoccupation with the grotesque and the supernatural. In the fourth (LG 26), a diabolical march in minor, the theme of the beloved appears at the end in the clarinet, and is cut off by a grim *fortissimo* chord. In this vivid portrayal of the story, we clearly hear the final blow of the guillotine blade, the head rolling, and the resounding cheers of the crowd.

In the final movement, Berlioz sounds an infernal spirit that nourished a century of satanic operas, ballets, and symphonic poems. The mood is heightened by the introduction of the traditional religious chant Dies irae (Day of Wrath) from the ancient Mass for the Dead, scored for the bassoons and tubas.

This composition is an extraordinary example of the Romantic desire to reflect the intensity of personal experience through music, but it also opens up the essential paradox of program music: if you heard the *March to the Scaffold* without knowing its title or its descriptive program, would you understand the story it's supposed to tell? Can the music convey meaning without the story?

LISTENING GUIDE 26   4:37

Berlioz: *Symphonie fantastique*, IV

DATE:	1830
GENRE:	Program symphony with five movements
PERFORMED BY:	Baltimore Symphony Orchestra; David Zinman, conductor
PROGRAM:	A lovesick artist in an opium trance is haunted by a vision of his beloved, which becomes an *idée fixe* (fixed idea).
MOVEMENTS:	I. *Reveries, Passions:* Largo; Allegro agitato e appassionato assai (lively, agitated, and impassioned)
	II. *A Ball:* Valse, Allegro non troppo
	III. *Scene in the Fields:* Adagio
	IV. *March to the Scaffold*: Allegretto non troppo
	V. *Dream of a Witches' Sabbath:* Larghetto, Allegro assai

IV. *March to the Scaffold*

What to Listen For

Melody Two main march themes (**A** and **B**), each strongly accented.

Timbre Prominent timpani in the march; instruments play in unusual ranges.

Form Sonata-like, with two themes introduced, then developed and recapped.

Expression Diabolical mood; minor key with sudden dynamic changes; the idea of the beloved at the end (clarinet solo) is followed by a sudden chord (representing the beheading).

continued on next page

0:00   Opening motive: muted horns, timpani, and pizzicato low strings;
forecasts syncopated rhythm of a march (theme **B**):

0:24   Theme **A**—an energetic, downward minor scale in low strings, then violins (with bassoon countermelody):

1:31   Theme **B**—diabolical march tune, played by brass and woodwinds:

1:56   Developmental section:
  Theme **B**—in brass, accompanied by strings and woodwinds.
  Theme **A**—soft, with pizzicato strings.
  Theme **B**—brass, with woodwinds added.
  Theme **A**—soft, pizzicato strings, then loud in brass.
3:02   Theme **A**—full orchestra statement in original form, then inverted (now an ascending scale).
4:05   Fixed idea in clarinet ("a last thought of love"), marked "as sweetly and passionately as possible,"
followed by a loud chord that cuts off the melody ("the fall of the blade"):

Pizzicato bass notes, possibly depicting the fall of the head, are followed by loud, triumphant chords that close
the movement.

▶⏮ Reflect

How does the change in instrumentation for the two themes
affect you as a listener? Do the separate instrumentations
continue throughout the movement? What happens at the
end? What do you think Berlioz is trying to convey through
the contrasts in theme and timbre?

YOUR TURN TO EXPLORE

What excerpts from your favorite music might you use to tell a story about yourself and
your emotional life? List the songs or pieces. How might you want to modify the music
(its tempo, instrumentation, texture, etc.) to convey your emotions more precisely?
How would you try to make sure a listener would understand your story accurately?

Sounding a Nation: Grieg and Orchestral Nationalism

▶‖ **First, listen ...**

to the opening of Grieg's *Hall of the Mountain King,* from *Peer Gynt.* What expressive devices does the composer employ to develop and vary the melody?

> 66 I dipped into the rich treasures of native folk song and sought to create a national art out of this hitherto unexploited expression of the folk soul of Norway."
>
> —Edvard Grieg

One of the most important roles that music plays in all human societies is building community cohesion. Since the nineteenth century, the notion of community has been strongly tied to the concept of nationality: a distinctive culture and heritage shared by people who live in a common territory. But although individuals are associated with a nation by birth or immigration, they can choose whether or not—and how—to highlight that association through their music. While this concern was especially important in nineteenth-century Europe, aspects of musical nationalism still play a role in building communities today; for example, compositions are often commissioned for presidential inaugurations, such as the variations on the Shaker tune *Simple Gifts* written by film composer John Williams for Barack Obama's inauguration in 2009.

VARIETIES OF ORCHESTRAL PROGRAM MUSIC

One type of program music came out of the opera house, where the overture, a rousing orchestral piece in one movement, served as an introduction to an opera (or a play). Some operatic overtures became popular as separate concert pieces, which in turn pointed the way to a new type of **concert overture** not associated with opera: a single-movement concert piece for orchestra that might evoke a

Concert overture

KEY POINTS

- Prominent types of Romantic program music include the **concert overture**, **incidental music** to a play, and the **symphonic poem** (a one-movement work).

- Political unrest throughout Europe stimulated schools of nationalistic composers in Russia, Scandinavia, Spain, England, and Bohemia.

- Edvard Grieg looked to the folklore of his native Norway in many of his works. His incidental music for *Peer Gynt* was written to accompany a play by Henrik Ibsen about this folk legend, then was excerpted into an independent suite.

217

Shakespeare's play *A Midsummer Night's Dream* inspired this fanciful canvas by **Henry Fuseli** (1741–1825), *Titania and Bottom* (c. 1790).

land- or seascape, or embody a patriotic or literary idea, like Tchaikovsky's *Romeo and Juliet*.

Another type of program music, **incidental music**, usually consists of an overture and a series of pieces performed between the acts of a play and during important scenes. The most successful pieces of incidental music were arranged into suites (such as Felix Mendelssohn's *A Midsummer Night's Dream*). This use of music to enhance spoken drama was influential in the development of musical accompaniment to silent film at the very end of the 1800s, and in the tradition of film soundtracks after the 1920s.

Eventually, composers felt the need for a large orchestral genre that would serve the Romantic era as the symphony had served the Classical. Liszt created the **symphonic poem**, the nineteenth century's most original contribution to large forms. A symphonic poem is program music for orchestra in one movement, with contrasting sections that develop a poetic idea (like Debussy's *Prelude to "The Afternoon of the Faun,"* Chapter 44), suggest a scene, or create a mood. It differs from the concert overture, which usually retains a traditional Classical form, by having a much freer structure. The symphonic poem (also called **tone poem**) gave composers the flexibility they needed for a big single-movement work. It became the most common type of orchestral program music through the second half of the century.

MUSICAL NATIONALISM

"I grew up in a quiet spot and was saturated from earliest childhood with the wonderful beauty of Russian popular song. I am therefore passionately devoted to every expression of the Russian spirit. In short, I am a Russian through and through!"

—PETER ILYICH TCHAIKOVSKY

In nineteenth-century Europe, political conditions so encouraged the growth of nationalism that it became a decisive force within the Romantic movement. The pride of conquering nations and the struggle for freedom of suppressed ones gave rise to strong emotions that inspired the works of many creative artists.

Romantic composers expressed their nationalism in a variety of ways. Some based their music on the songs and dances of their people, others wrote dramatic works based on folklore or peasant life—for example, the Russian fairy-tale operas and ballets of Tchaikovsky. And some wrote symphonic poems and operas celebrating the exploits of a national hero, a historic event, or the scenic beauty of their country: Bedřich Smetana's *The Moldau* is a popular tone poem depicting the river that was the lifeblood of the emerging state of Bohemia.

In associating music with the love of homeland, composers sought to give expression to the hopes of millions of people. The political implications were not lost on the authorities. During the Second World War, for example, the Nazis outlawed the playing of Chopin's polonaises in Warsaw and Smetana's descriptive symphonic poems in Prague because of the powerful symbolism behind these works.

Several regions throughout Europe gave rise to a national voice through music. In particular, the Russian school produced a circle of young musicians called "The Mighty Five" (or "The Mighty Handful"), whose members sought to free themselves from the older sounds of the German symphony, French ballet, and Italian opera and express a true Russian spirit. England and Spain produced nationalistic composers as well whose music was intended to echo the souls of their countries (see map below).

A SCANDINAVIAN NATIONALIST: EDVARD GRIEG

Among nationalist composers of the nineteenth century, the Norwegian master Edvard Grieg stands out for his ability to capture the essence of his country's folklore and dance through music. It was his goal to create an art that was accessible to all the public.

Schools of Musical Nationalism in Europe

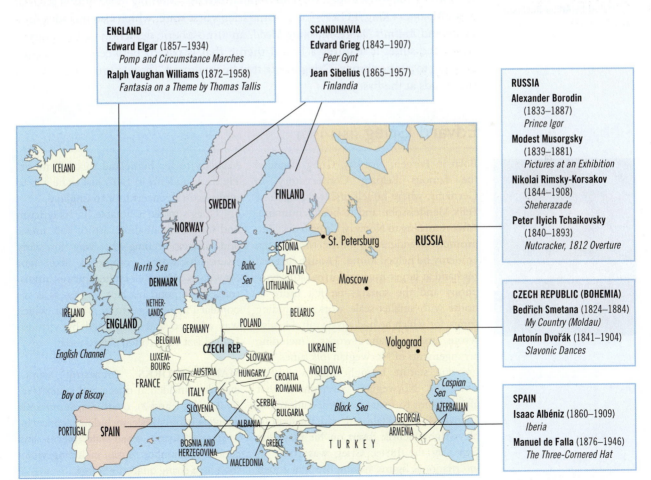

ENGLAND
Edward Elgar (1857–1934)
Pomp and Circumstance Marches
Ralph Vaughan Williams (1872–1958)
Fantasia on a Theme by Thomas Tallis

SCANDINAVIA
Edvard Grieg (1843–1907)
Peer Gynt
Jean Sibelius (1865–1957)
Finlandia

RUSSIA
Alexander Borodin
(1833–1887)
Prince Igor
Modest Musorgsky
(1839–1881)
Pictures at an Exhibition
Nikolai Rimsky-Korsakov
(1844–1908)
Sheherazade
Peter Ilyich Tchaikovsky
(1840–1893)
Nutcracker, 1812 Overture

CZECH REPUBLIC (BOHEMIA)
Bedřich Smetana (1824–1884)
My Country (Moldau)
Antonín Dvořák (1841–1904)
Slavonic Dances

SPAIN
Isaac Albéniz (1860–1909)
Iberia
Manuel de Falla (1876–1946)
The Three-Cornered Hat

The King of the Trolls, from Ibsen's *Peer Gynt* as illustrated by **Arthur Rackham** (1867–1939).

Peer Gynt, Suite No. 1

Peer Gynt, a play by Henrik Ibsen based on a Norwegian folk tale, premiered in Christiana, Norway, in 1876. Like most folk tales, the story presents a strong moral message. Peer is an idle and boastful youth; his mother Åse reprimands him for his laziness, which caused him to lose his bride-to-be Ingrid to another. At her wedding, however, Peer abducts Ingrid, only to abandon her later. He runs away to a forest, where he seduces a young girl who turns out to be a daughter of the Mountain King, ruler of the trolls. When her sisters find out she is pregnant, they vow to avenge her, but Peer manages to escape them. Now an outlaw, he builds a cottage in the woods, where Solveig, a girl he once loved, comes to live with him. Life seems safe for a while, but when Peer's mother dies, he sets off on a series of fantastical adventures; on the shores of North Africa, he cavorts with the Arabian girl Anitra, who performs a sultry dance for him. Peer finally returns home many years later to find Solveig, now a middle-aged woman, still faithful to him.

At Ibsen's invitation, Grieg composed some twenty-two pieces, including preludes and dances, as incidental music for the play. Not altogether happy with the result, he later extracted eight of the movements and combined them—in a different order—into two orchestral suites, of four movements each.

Two of the most endearing and popular pieces—*Morning Mood* and *In the Hall of the Mountain King* (LG 27)— are from Grieg's first suite, which also includes *Åse's Death* and *Anitra's Dance. Morning Mood,* an atmospheric depiction of the sunrise, opens the suite. It features a lyrical theme that is passed between instruments, building to a long climax. Grieg wrote that he imagined "the sun breaking through the clouds at the first *forte.*"

Edvard Grieg (1843–1907)

Born in Bergen, Norway, Grieg attended the famous Leipzig Conservatory in Germany, where he fell under the spell of Felix Mendelssohn and Robert Schumann. After returning to Norway, Grieg worked to promote Scandinavian music through an academy he helped found. Though he tried his hand at larger musical forms—the symphony and the sonata—he felt more at home with smaller-scale works, including songs, for which he had a lyric gift. He also wrote many piano works, including arrangements of Norwegian folk tunes. His growing stature brought him a stipend from the Norwegian government that allowed him to focus on composition and an invitation to collaborate with the famous playwright Henrik Ibsen on his play *Peer Gynt.* By the 1880s, Grieg was truly an international figure, having brought much

visibility to his homeland through music. He died suddenly in 1907, just as he was to embark on a concert tour to England.

Grieg's music is notable for its lyricism and for his nationalistic use of folk music and dances, leading the way for early twentieth-century composers like Igor Stravinsky. His well-crafted piano miniatures are among his best works, as is his popular Piano Concerto in A Minor, which was admired and performed by virtuoso Franz Liszt and is often played today.

MAJOR WORKS: Orchestral works, including incidental music and suites (*Peer Gynt,* Nos. 1 and 2), overtures, symphonic dances • Piano music, including a concerto, a sonata, many small-scale pieces and dances • Chamber music, including violin sonatas, a string quartet • Songs.

In the Hall of the Mountain King was conceived as grotesque ballet music—a march for the wild troll daughters of the Mountain King. The girls taunt and threaten Peer for seducing one of them, with the insistent theme growing louder and faster as they chase him. The crashing final chords signify the collapse of the mountain on top of the trolls.

Though these excerpts from the *Peer Gynt* Suite share the common orchestral language of the nineteenth century, this strikingly expressive work, like other nationalist program music, draws on the unique imagery and folk traditions of the composer's homeland. Can you "hear" the imagery of Norway that Grieg means to convey?

LISTENING GUIDE 27

 6:21

Grieg: *Peer Gynt*, Suite No. 1 (Op. 46), excerpts

DATE: 1874–75 (play); 1888 (suite)

GENRE: Incidental music to a play by Henrik Ibsen

PERFORMED BY: New York Philharmonic; Leonard Bernstein, conductor

MOVEMENTS: *Morning Mood*   *Anitra's Dance*
Åse's Death   ***In the Hall of the Mountain King***

What to Listen For

Morning Mood

Melody Dreamy melody in an inverted arch shape, with decorative grace notes.

Rhythm/meter A lilting 6/8 meter.

Performing forces Pastoral instruments (flute, oboe, horn) are prominent.

In the Hall of the Mountain King

Rhythm/meter Duple-meter march; short, staccato notes and offbeat accents.

Form A single theme repeated over and over; closing coda.

Performing forces Pizzicato strings and staccato woodwind effects; offbeats in brass and percussion.

Morning Mood   3:50

A section

0:00   A flowing melody is exchanged between flute and oboe, with sustained string chords; builds in a *crescendo*:

0:49   Full orchestral statement, marked *forte*; continues to build, then dies down;
cello motive leads to a new *crescendo*.

B section

1:29   Reaches a climax, then cellos alternate with higher strings in sudden dynamic changes;
builds in a *crescendo*, then *decrescendo*; a brief shift to the minor.

continued on next page

A′ section

1:59   French horn has the main theme, accompanied by wavering woodwinds.

2:12   Louder statement in low strings and woodwinds.

2:32   Horn introduces a slower statement of the theme in violins, answered by clarinet.

Coda

2:45   A quiet mood, with trills in woodwinds; solo French horn.

3:17   Flute has the theme, slowing, then bassoon; tranquil chords in strings; closing chords in full orchestra with a soft timpani roll.

In the Hall of the Mountain King   2:31

0:00   An eerie theme is heard six times, played softly in low pizzicato strings and bassoons:

0:55   Theme continues in violins, answered by woodwinds, with strong off beat accents.

1:11   Pizzicato theme moves to a higher range in violins, grows louder and a little faster; answered by oboes and clarinets.

1:26   Louder statement accompanied by a bowed-string spinning figure.

1:40   Full orchestra at *fortissimo*, with strong accents.

1:52   Brass is prominent as the music speeds up and is more accented.

Coda

2:12   Sudden chords, alternating with running passages; a timpani roll leads to the final chord.

▶|◀ Reflect

How does Grieg build tension through changes in timbre and tempo throughout *In the Hall of the Mountain King?* How successful do you think he is in evoking the imagery from the story? Which variation do you find most expressive, and why?

YOUR TURN TO EXPLORE

What kinds of musical repertories do you think best represent the communities with which you identify? Are those communities shaped by regional or ethnic identity, and does their music reflect those identities? If you are a fan of a particular musician or group, what characteristics do your fellow fans share, and how does the music reinforce those common elements?

Nationalism Crosses the Ocean: Dvořák and Late Romanticism in the USA

▶‖ **First, listen . . .**

to the first movement of Dvořák's *American* String Quartet, focusing on the opening melody. How does it sound different from other melodies we've heard in nineteenth-century works? What do you think might account for this difference?

> 66 When I wrote this quartet in the Czech community of Spillville in 1893, I wanted to write something for once that was very melodious and straightforward, and dear Papa Haydn kept appearing before my eyes, and that is why it all turned out so simply. And it's good that it did."
>
> Antonín Dvořák, writing about his *American* String Quartet

M usical nationalism in the nineteenth century was often described as a way to hold a composer's regional traditions—the distinctive folk melodies of his or her "people," for example—equal in expressive power to the acknowledged great tradition of German art music. But the question of how to express national identity in music was more complex in a nation like the United States, composed of immigrants from various European regions, descendants of slaves shipped from Africa, and members of Native American tribes. In the 1890s, a famous European "nationalist" composer, Antonín Dvořák, became the figurehead for intense debate about the definition of American music. And more than a century later, discussions about the nature and future of concert music in the United States still regularly evoke his name.

MUSIC IN A NATION OF IMMIGRANTS

European immigrants who populated the United States in multiple waves maintained their languages (German, Swedish, Czech) and continued to perform or write music in the traditions of their native lands (see Chapter 34). There were

KEY POINTS

- European immigrant composers looked to both Native American and African American musics in their efforts to establish a national American school.

- One of these composers was Antonín Dvořák, who, while teaching music in New York City, challenged American composers to embrace the "folk songs" of America.

- Dvořák's *New World* Symphony and String Quartet, Op. 96 (dubbed *American*), both written while he was in the United States, draw on scales typical of African American spirituals as well as his native Central European folk music.

also efforts to create music that would rival the "high culture" institutions of Europe. But what would be the defining characteristics of a musical language in a nation of diverse peoples, rather than one composed of families grounded in the land for many generations? A number of musicians of European descent chose Indian themes, though these were based on stereotypical notions of Native American music rather than an accurate understanding. Others drew on African American traditions; German immigrant composer Henry Schoenefeld suggested in 1890 that the "American school will be based upon the Negro melodies of the South, as the Russians have founded the Russian school by looking to the Slav melodies." Still others argued for an international style, often couched in terms of "universality"; but their models were based on German or Anglo-American traditions. The cultural racism that had defined citizenship around white identity within the U.S. Constitution was still shaping a definition of "universal" that excluded nonwhites.

Into this ongoing debate stepped Antonín Dvořák, recruited in 1892 by Jeanette Thurber, founder of the National Conservatory of America, to be the conservatory's director. Dvořák had become well known both as a practitioner of German absolute music and as a champion of musical nationalism in his native Prague. As he prepared to take his post, he told a London newspaper, "America will have to reflect the influence of the great German composers, just as all countries do." But once in New York, when he listened to his African American composition students—most notably Harry T. Burleigh—perform spirituals from their communities, he was struck by the music's expressive potential. His symphony titled *From the New World,* written the following year, was, he said, grounded in "the spirit of Negro and Indian melodies."

In the summer of 1893, Dvořák traveled with his family to Spillville, Iowa, home to a community of Bohemian immigrants. From there he wrote to a friend: "You probably know that the children arrived safely in America. As soon as they

St. Wenceslaus Church in Spillville, Iowa, where Dvořák spent the summer of 1893.

got here, we left New York for Spillville for our summer holidays. It's a Czech settlement. There are Czech church services and a school—so it seems as if we were in [Bohemia]." Dvořák felt at ease in Spillville, as he indicated in a later letter: "I liked to be among these people and they all liked me as well, especially the elderly citizens, who were pleased when I played 'O God, we bow before Thee' or 'A thousand times we greet Thee' for them on the church organ." In Spillville, he wrote an entire string quartet in just a few days, and it was premiered shortly after the *New World* Symphony the following January. It quickly became known as the "Negro Quartet" (now it's called the *American Quartet*) because critics felt that it borrowed ideas from African American traditions. But is that really the case?

Antonín Dvořák (1841–1904)

Dvořák was born in Bohemia (now part of the Czech Republic). At sixteen, he moved to Prague, where he secured a position playing viola in the Czech National Theater under the baton of Bedřich Smetana, a notable Czech nationalist composer. In 1874, he resigned his orchestra post to devote himself to composing, in which he was much encouraged by Johannes Brahms. Later, he took up a position as professor of composition at the Conservatory of Prague, where he was able to exert an important influence on the musical life of his country.

In 1891, Jeannette Thurber, who ran the National Conservatory of Music in New York City, invited Dvořák to become its director. His stay in the United States was highly productive, resulting in, among other works, his *New World* Symphony (No. 9), which drew inspiration from African American spirituals. During his time in the United States, Dvořák challenged American composers to embrace "the beautiful and varied themes" that are "the folk songs of America." Several of his students did just so, including Harry T. Burleigh, who published a land-mark collection of spirituals arranged as art music. After three years in New York, Dvořák returned to his beloved Bohemia and spent his remaining years in Prague. He died at sixty-three, revered throughout his native land as a national artist.

Dvořák's great gift for melody, love of native folk tunes, and solid craftsmanship enabled him to shape musical ideas into large forms notable for their clarity. His operas, many based on Czech themes, are the most strongly national of his country. His symphonies reflect a mastery of Classical procedures, and the Cello Concerto is a crowning achievement in that instrument's repertory.

MAJOR WORKS: Orchestral music, including nine symphonies (No. 9, *From the New World*, 1893), symphonic poems, other symphonic works (*Slavonic Dances*, 1878/87) • Concertos, including one for cello • Vocal music, including 14 operas • Choral music (including a *Requiem*, 1890) • Chamber music (*American* String Quartet) • Songs • Keyboard music, including dances and character pieces.

Dvořák's *American* String Quartet

The melodies Dvořák chose for his quartet make significant use of the five-note **pentatonic scale**, rather than a seven-note major or minor scale. Pentatonic scales do occur frequently in African American spirituals, but they are also characteristic of folk traditions of Bohemia and central Europe in general; so the composer may have had either an American or a Czech association in mind. The first movement, unusually, is almost entirely homophonic: the primary melodies presented by one string instrument, with unobtrusive accompaniment in the other three. The effect is thus "melodious and straightforward," as Dvořák described it. Yet the movement is very much part of the tradition that had passed from Haydn (see quote at beginning of the chapter) through Beethoven, Schubert, and Johannes Brahms, following a clear sonata-allegro form (LG 28). Its key of F major, long associated with the countryside, contributes to the wistfulness of the folk-infused pentatonic melodies.

Is this quartet about American nationalism via African American empowerment, or is it a nostalgic fantasy of blissful Bohemian isolation in remote cornfields?

Pentatonic scale

DR. DVOŘÁK INSTRUCTING AN AMERICAN COMPOSER.

Cartoon of Dvořák instructing a student at the National Conservatory in New York City.

Absolute music allows for many interpretations. And it is perhaps appropriate that this striking musical contribution to conversations about national identity in the United States should have been conceived within an immigrant community that had chosen not to integrate into the U.S. mainstream, one that likely saw itself as Bohemian at least as much as American.

▶|◀ Reflect

How do the first and second themes of this movement provide opportunity for contrasting emotions? How does Dvořák shape your emotional experience through their development? What might be the benefits and drawbacks of thinking of the quartet as "American" music?

YOUR TURN TO EXPLORE

Find two or three separate arrangements of a song from a folk tradition—like *Amazing Grace, Greensleeves,* or *La cucaracha.* How does each arrangement create a balance between the simple folk melody and the added music—is the arrangement homophonic or polyphonic? Is the original melody modified, and if so, how? In what way do you think each arrangement is faithful to the traditional melody, or to the cultural tradition from which it is derived? Which one do you consider most musically expressive, and why?

LISTENING GUIDE 28   9:38

Dvořák: String Quartet in F Major, Op. 96 (*American*), I

DATE: 1893

GENRE: String quartet

PERFORMED BY: Pavel Haas Quartet

MOVEMENTS: I. **Allegro ma non troppo; sonata-allegro form, F major**
II. Lento; sectional form (**A-A-B-B-C-C-A′**), D minor
III. Molto vivace; scherzo and trio, F major/minor
IV. Finale: Vivace ma non troppo; sonata-rondo form, F major

What to Listen For

Melody First theme is arpeggiated and pentatonic; second theme, more stepwise with ornaments, also uses the pentatonic scale.

Texture Mostly homophonic; melody is passed from instrument to instrument as the others provide accompaniment; moments of imitation.

Harmony The pentatonic scale is ambiguous—between major and minor; the main key areas are related by thirds rather than fifths (F major / A major in the exposition, F major / A-flat major / F major in the recapitulation).

Form Sonata-allegro form, with a long transition between the first and second themes and an extended development.

EXPOSITION

0:00   Theme 1, in F major and based on the pentatonic scale, is played by the viola, then by the first violin; accompanied by oscillating thirds and arpeggios in the cello.

First violin with theme:

0:24   Transition begins with repetitions of the final notes of theme 1; after an elaboration of short motives from theme 1, the music modulates to A minor.

0:54   Short rhythmic motives are passed back and forth; dramatic contrasts in dynamics.

1:39   Theme 2, in A major, is played by the first violin, ornamented; other instruments provide slow, quiet chords.

DEVELOPMENT

2:25:   Snatches of theme 1 and rhythmic motives from the transition are passed back and forth between instruments.

4:05   Theme 2 returns in varied and expanded form, again with the first violin most prominent.

4:53   Theme 1 again, with variations on the opening section in a dialogue between instruments.

6:12   *Fugato* section: all four instruments play short motives in imitation, with the solo first violin fading out at the end.

RECAPITULATION

6.48   Theme 1 in F major, first played by the viola then by the first violin.

7:12   A new cello solo in A-flat major begins the transition.

8:26   Theme 2, back in F major, now alternates between the first violin in a low range and the cello in its highest range.

9:02   **Coda**—short, based on motives from the transition.

Multimedia Hits: Verdi and Italian Romantic Opera

▶❙❙ First, listen . . .

to the Quartet from Verdi's *Rigoletto* without worrying about the meaning of the words. How does Verdi convey the different moods of the characters? What emotion do you think each character is trying to express?

A portrait of Swedish soprano Jenny Lind (1820–1887).

Music is an essential component of contemporary multimedia, whether films, television shows, or video games. Hit songs are often associated with them—and so it was from the beginning of what we might call commercially sucessful multimedia, which arose in the Italian theatrical tradition in the 1800s. Before the age of recording, catchy excerpts from operas were marketed in arrangements, whether for the home (piano four-hands, voice and guitar) or for public places (wind band medleys). This allowed the music to saturate its culture, becoming popular in both the economic and the social sense. In the process, it became connected to the social aspirations of its audiences, providing emotional reinforcement to political messages—another important role played by music to this day.

WOMEN AND NINETEENTH-CENTURY OPERA

Successful multimedia has always relied on the draw of star performers, and this was true of the Italian musical-theatrical tradition—opera—from its early days. By the time of Mozart, fashion had shifted from the castrati toward the more

KEY POINTS

- Romantic opera developed distinct national styles in Italy, Germany, and France, and women singers excelled in all styles.

- Both *opera seria* (serious opera) and *opera buffa* (comic opera) were favored in Italy; they marked the peak of the **bel canto** (beautiful singing) style.

- Giuseppe Verdi is best known for his operas, which embody the spirit of Romantic drama and passion. His *Rigoletto*, based on a play by Victor Hugo, is one of the most performed operas today.

Milan's famous opera house La Scala (c. 1850), where some of Verdi's operas premiered.

"natural" voices of female sopranos, and from that point on, women opera singers were among the most prominent performers of their time, in demand throughout Europe and the Americas. One international star was Jenny Lind (p. 228), famous for her roles in operas by the Italians Gaetano Donizetti and Vincenzo Bellini, among others. A concert artist as well, Lind made her American debut in 1850 in a tour managed with immense hoopla by circus impresario P. T. Barnum. During her tour, Lind sang both Italian operatic excerpts and American parlor songs, emphasizing the flexibility between art and popular music in nineteenth-century North America.

VERDI AND ITALIAN OPERA

"Success is impossible for me if I cannot write as my heart dictates!"

Italy in the nineteenth century still recognized the opposing genres of *opera seria* (serious opera) and *opera buffa* (the Italian version of comic opera), legacies of an earlier period. One of the most important composers of this era was Gioachino Rossini (1792–1868), whose masterpieces include *Il barbiere di Siviglia* (*The Barber of Seville*, 1816) and *Guillaume Tell* (*William Tell*, 1829). These operas marked the high point of a **bel canto** (beautiful singing) style, characterized by florid melodic lines delivered by voices of great agility and purity of tone.

Verdi was the consummate master of nineteenth-century Italian opera. In his case, time, place, and personality were happily merged. He inherited a rich

In His Own Words

❝ It seems to me that the best material I have yet put to music is *Rigoletto*. It has the most powerful situations, it has variety, vitality, pathos; all the dramatic developments result from the frivolous, licentious character of the Duke. Hence Rigoletto's fears, Gilda's passion, etc., which give rise to many dramatic situations, including the scene of the quartet."

—Giuseppe Verdi

Giuseppe Verdi (1813–1901)

Born in a small town in northern Italy, Verdi got off to an early start by writing operas for Milan's La Scala opera house. After the tragic deaths of his daughter, baby son, and young wife in 1838–40, the distraught composer wrote no music for months. Then one night he met the director of La Scala, who insisted he take home a libretto about Nebuchadnezzar, king of Babylon. Verdi returned to work, and the resulting opera, *Nabucco,* launched him on a spectacular career.

Italy at the time was liberating itself from Austrian Hapsburg rule, and Verdi identified himself with the national cause. His works took on special meaning for his compatriots; the chorus of exiled Jews from *Nabucco* became an Italian patriotic song that is still sung today. In 1848, Verdi began an association with soprano Giuseppina Strepponi, whom he later married, and proceeded to produce one masterpiece after another. At seventy-three, he completed *Otello,* his greatest lyric tragedy. And in 1893, on the threshold of eighty, he astonished the world with *Falstaff* (a comic opera based on *The Merry Wives of Windsor*). In all, he wrote twenty-eight operas.

Verdi's favorite literary source was Shakespeare, whose plays inspired *Macbeth, Otello,* and *Falstaff. La traviata* is based on *La dame aux camélias* by Alexandre Dumas, and *Il trovatore* on a fanciful Spanish play. *Aida,* a monumental work commissioned in 1870 by the ruler of Egypt to mark the opening of the Suez Canal, premiered in Cairo. On his death, Verdi left his fortune to a home for aged musicians (Casa Verdi) that he founded in Milan and that still exists today.

MAJOR WORKS: 28 operas, including *Macbeth* (1847), *Rigoletto* (1851), *Il trovatore* (*The Troubadour,* 1853), *La traviata* (*The Lost One,* 1853), *Un ballo in maschera* (*The Masked Ball,* 1859), *Don Carlos* (1867), *Aida* (1871), *Otello* (1887), and *Falstaff* (1893) • Vocal music, including a *Requiem* Mass.

Rigoletto's costume for a production at the Paris Opera on February 27, 1885.

musical tradition, his capacity for growth was matched by extraordinary energy, and he was granted a long life in which to engage fully his creative gifts. He also came into his professional peak at a time when music publishers were helping to build markets for composers who were willing to work closely with them on licensing and other commercial ventures.

Verdi's music was adopted by those who supported political independence for Italy, which was then under Austrian rule. The intensity of his compositions and the potential for some of the stories to be read as calls for liberation made him a figurehead for the Italian unification movement—though Verdi himself was only mildly political: he agreed to serve in the senate of newly unified Italy, but retired after only one term. The combination of appealing melodies, intense dramatic situations, and savvy marketing by his publisher Ricordi made Verdi's music a national soundtrack for the new Italian spirit. Every town in Italy, no matter how small, has a street bearing Verdi's name, and his operas are still the most frequently performed around the world.

Rigoletto

The epitome of Romantic drama and passion, Verdi's music for *Rigoletto* communicates each dramatic situation with profound emotion. A play by Victor Hugo, an acknowledged leader of French Romanticism, was Verdi's source of inspiration.

The setting is a Renaissance-era ducal court in northern Italy. The plot revolves around lechery, deceit, and treachery. At a ball in the Duke's palace, the hunchbacked jester Rigoletto taunts a nobleman, whose wife is the object of the Duke's wandering eye, while another nobleman places a curse on the Duke for compromising his daughter's honor and on Rigoletto for making a joke of it. Unbeknown to Rigoletto, his daughter Gilda will be the Duke's next conquest, despite the fact that the jester has kept her in seclusion. Through complicated trickery involving the Duke and some conspirators, Gilda is carried off from Rigoletto's house. The jester then plots his revenge—to kill the Duke—with the assassin Sparafucile and his sister Maddalena. In the last act, Maddalena lures the Duke to a lonely tavern where Rigoletto forces Gilda to watch through a window as the man she loves woos Maddalena. The jester arranges to send Gilda away, dressed as a man, but she deceives her father and sacrifices herself for the unworthy man she loves. About to dispose of the sack containing what he believes is the Duke's body, Rigoletto is horrified to find Gilda in the sack instead. He recalls the curse one last time, as Gilda dies in his arms.

In Act III, the Duke sings the best known of Verdi's tunes, "La donna è mobile" ("Woman is fickle"), a simple but rousing song accompanied by a guitarlike orchestral strumming (LG 29). The orchestra previews the catchy melody, which is heard numerous times in a strophic setting that brings back the opening text as a refrain.

The quartet that follows shortly is a masterpiece of operatic ensemble writing, as Verdi himself noted ("In His Own Words," p. 229). Each character presents a different point of view: the Duke woos Maddalena in a lovely bel canto–style melody; Maddalena answers with a laughing line in short notes; Gilda, watching from outside, is heartbroken as she laments her lost love; and Rigoletto swears vengeance for his beloved daughter.

These two show-stopping numbers ensured the immediate success of *Rigoletto*. It remains one of the most frequently performed operas of the international repertory—and every Italian singer can belt out "La donna è mobile." Verdi's music is simultaneously great art and powerful pop.

Lithograph depicting the quartet scene from *Rigoletto*, from an 1863 performance in Paris. Rigoletto and his daughter Gilda, on the left, watch the Duke and Maddalena inside the tavern.

▶️◀ Reflect

How does the dramatic situation of the tavern scene in *Rigoletto* play out through the vocal melodies and polyphonic interactions of the four characters in the Quartet? What role does the orchestra play in helping you feel their emotions? To which character do you connect most closely in musical terms, and why?

YOUR TURN TO EXPLORE

Identify a song or instrumental track made popular through films, TV, or video games. Search online to determine how the music has been circulated or "remixed" outside the film/show/video itself. How well does the music work in a new context—does its expressive quality change without the framework of the original story?

LISTENING GUIDE 29

 8:13

Verdi: *Rigoletto*, Act III, excerpts

FIRST PERFORMANCE:	1851, Venice
LIBRETTIST:	Francesco Maria Piave
BASIS:	*Le roi s'amuse*, a play by Victor Hugo
PERFORMED BY:	Roberto Alagna (Duke), Dimitri Kavrakos (Sparafucile), Renato Bruson (Rigoletto), Andrea Rost (Gilda), Mariana Pentcheva (Maddalena); Orchestra del Teatro alla Scala; Riccardo Muti, conductor
MAJOR CHARACTERS:	The Duke of Mantua (tenor)
	Rigoletto, the Duke's jester, a hunchback (baritone)
	Gilda, Rigoletto's daughter (soprano)
	Sparafucile, an assassin (bass)
	Maddalena, Sparafucile's sister (contralto)

What to Listen For

Aria

Melody Soaring tenor line, with accented notes.

Rhythm/meter Triple-meter, "oom-pah-pah" accompaniment; some rubato.

Form Two strophes, framed by an orchestral ritornello that unifies the aria.

Quartet

Melody Dialogue between characters; then a simpler, square melody at "Bella figlia."

Texture Non-imitative polyphony; each character displays a different expressive quality.

Form (second part) **A-B-A'-C** + coda.

Aria: "La donna è mobile" (Duke)   **2:43**

0:00   Orchestral ritornello previews the Duke's solo; opening melody of aria:

(The Duke, in a simple cavalry officer's uniform, sings in the inn;
Sparafucile, Gilda, and Rigoletto listen outside.)

Duke

0:12 La donna è mobile	Woman is fickle
qual piuma al vento,	like a feather in the wind,
muta d'accento,	she changes her words
e di pensiero.	and her thoughts.
sempre un amabile	Always lovable,
leggiadro viso,	and a lovely face,
in pianto o in riso,	weeping or laughing,
è menzognero.	is lying.
La donna è mobile, *etc.*	Woman is fickle, *etc.*

1:01   **Orchestral ritornello.**

1:11 È sempre misero	The man's always wretched
chi a le s'affida,	who believes in her,
chi lei confida	who recklessly entrusts
mal cauto il core!	his heart to her!
pur mai non sentesi	And yet one who never
felice appieno	drinks love on that breast
chi su quel seno	never feels
non liba amore!	entirely happy!
La donna è mobile, *etc.*	Woman is fickle, *etc.*

(Sparafucile comes back in with a bottle of wine and two glasses, which he sets on the table;
then he strikes the ceiling twice with the hilt of his long sword. At this signal, a laughing young woman
in Gypsy dress leaps down the stairs: the Duke runs to embrace her, but she escapes him. Meanwhile
Sparafucile has gone into the street, where he speaks softly to Rigoletto.)

Quartet (first part): "Un dì" (Duke, Maddalena, Gilda, Rigoletto)   **5:29**

Duke

2:44 Un dì, se ben rammentomi,	One day, if I remember right,
o bella, t'incontrai . . .	I met you, O beauty . . .
Mi piacque di te chiedere,	I was pleased to ask about you,
e intesi che qui stai.	and I learned that you live here.
Or sappi, che d'allora	Know then, that since that time
sol te quest'alma adora!	my soul adores only you!

Gilda

Iniquo!	Villain!

Maddalena

Ah, ah! . . . e vent'altre appresso	Ha, ha! . . . And perhaps now
le scorda forse adesso?	twenty others are forgotten?

continued on next page

Ha un'aria il signorino da vero libertino . . .	The young gentleman looks like a true libertine . . .

Duke (*starting to embrace her*)

Sí . . . un mostro son . . .	Yes . . . I'm a monster . . .

Gilda

Ah padre mio!	Ah, Father!

Maddalena

Lasciatemi, stordito.	Let me go, foolish man!

Duke

Ih che fracasso!	Ah, what a fuss!

Maddalena

Stia saggio.	Be good.

Duke

E tu sii docile, non fare tanto chiasso. Ogni saggezza chiudesi nel gaudio e nell'amore.	And you, be yielding, don't make so much noise. All wisdom concludes in pleasure and in love.

(*He takes her hand, vowing his love for her. Outside, Rigoletto reveals the unfaithful lover to
Gilda as the dialogue continues, leading to the famous quartet below.*)

Quartet (second part): "Bella figlia"

Overall form: **A-B-A′-C** plus coda
How characters interact in the ensemble and how they fit into the musical structure:

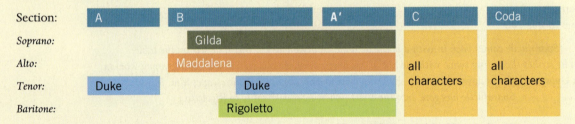

Opening melody of "Bella figlia," sung by the Duke:

	Duke		**Section**
4:15	Bella figlia dell'amore, schiavo son de' vezzi tuoi; con un detto sol tu puoi le mie pene consolar. Vieni, e senti del mio core il frequente palpitar . . .	Beautiful daughter of love, I am the slave of your charms; with a single word you can console my sufferings. Come, and feel the quick beating of my heart . . .	**A**

Section

Con un detto sol tuo puoi
le mie pene consolar.

With a single word you can
console my sufferings.

(Many text lines repeated.)

Maddalena

5:19   Ah! ah! rido ben di core,
chè tai baie costan poco.

Ha! Ha! I laugh heartily,
for such tales cost little.

B

Gilda

Ah! cosí parlar d'amore . . .

Ah! To speak thus of love . . .

Maddalena

Quanto valga il vostro gioco,
mel credete, sò apprezzar.

Believe me, I can judge
how much your game is worth.

Gilda

. . . a me pur l'infame ho udito!

. . . I too have heard the villain so!

Rigoletto (*to Gilda*)

Taci, il piangere non vale.

Hush, weeping is of no avail.

Gilda

Infelice cor tradito,
per angoscia non scoppiar. No, no!

Unhappy, betrayed heart,
do not burst with anguish. Ah, no!

Maddalena

Son avvezza, bel signore,
ad un simile scherzare.
Mio bel signor!

I'm accustomed, handsome sir,
to similar joking.
My handsome sir!

Duke

6:01   Bella figlia dell'amore, etc.
Vieni!

Beautiful daughter of love, etc.
Come!

A′

Rigoletto

Ch'ei mentiva sei sicura.
Taci, e mia sarà la cura
la vendetta d'affrettar.
sì, pronta fia, sarà fatale,
io saprollo fulminar.
taci, taci . . .

You are sure that he was lying.
Hush, and I will take care
to hasten vengeance.
Yes, it will be swift and fatal,
I will know how to strike him down.
Hush, hush . . .

All characters

Repeated text from above.

C

7:27   **Coda,** featuring all characters.

Coda

Total Art: Wagner and German Romantic Opera

▶‖ First, listen . . .

to the famous *Ride of the Valkyries,* from Wagner's *Die Walküre,* and think about the mood Wagner creates in this passage. What musical devices and instruments help paint this mood?

Through Hollywood blockbusters, we have become accustomed to being "told" by the movie soundtrack when a character is in danger from an evil-doer or monster, or when we should start crying. Films and TV shows have also taught us to associate musical ideas with specific characters, so that we can be made aware that someone on screen is thinking about an absent character through the appearance of that character's music in the soundtrack. We owe this supremely effective resource to the work of Richard Wagner, who established the idea that multimedia can convey multiple meanings at once: words may be telling us one thing, and the music may be adding something else that is more subtle. Contemporary composers have repeatedly credited Wagner's concept of "leitmotif," which we will explore in this chapter, with opening up opportunities to create powerful musical reinforcement in film, TV, and computer gaming.

WAGNER AND GERMAN MUSICAL THEATER

Nineteenth-century Germany had no long-established opera tradition, as Italy and France did. The immediate predecessor of German Romantic opera was the *Singspiel,* a light or comic drama with spoken dialogue like Mozart's *The Magic Flute* (*Die Zauberflöte*). One element that characterized German musical theater of the

KEY POINTS

- In Germany, the genre *Singspiel* (light, comic drama with spoken dialogue) gave way to more serious works, including Richard Wagner's **music dramas**, which integrated music, poetry, drama, and spectacle.

- Wagner's music dramas are not sectional (with arias, ensembles, and the like) but are continuous, unified by **leitmotifs**, or recurring themes, that represent a person, place, or idea. His most famous work is the four-opera cycle *The Ring of the Nibelung.*

Richard Wagner (1813–1883)

Wagner was born in Leipzig, Germany. After studying briefly at the University of Leipzig, he gained practical experience conducting in provincial theaters. At twenty-three, he married the actress Minna Planer, and began to produce his first operas. He wrote the librettos himself, as he did for all his later works, unifying music and drama more than anyone had before.

Wagner's early opera *Rienzi* won a huge success in Dresden. With his next three works, *The Flying Dutchman, Tannhäuser,* and *Lohengrin,* Wagner chose subjects derived from medieval German epics. In them, he displayed a profound feeling for nature, employed the supernatural as an element of the drama, and glorified the German land and people. In 1849, after a failed revolution in Dresden, Wagner fled to Switzerland, where he set forth his theories of the music drama, the name he gave his complete integration of theater and music. He proceeded to put theory into practice in the cycle of four music dramas called *The Ring of the Nibelung,* and two more— *Tristan and Isolde* and *Die Meistersinger von Nürnberg.*

Wagner soon won the support and admiration of the young monarch Ludwig II of Bavaria, who commissioned him to complete the *Ring* and helped him build a theater to present his music dramas, which ultimately became the Festival Theater at Bayreuth. And the composer (now separated from Minna) found a woman he considered his equal in will and courage— Cosima, the daughter of his old friend Franz Liszt. She left her husband and children in order to join him.

The Wagnerian gospel spread across Europe as a new art-religion. The *Ring* cycle was completed in 1874 and presented to worshipful audiences at the first Bayreuth Festival two years later. Wagner's final work was *Parsifal* (1877–82), based on the legend of the Holy Grail.

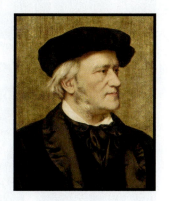

MAJOR WORKS: 13 operas (music dramas), including *Rienzi* (1842), *Der fliegende Holländer* (*The Flying Dutchman,* 1843), *Tannhäuser* (1845), *Lohengrin* (1850), *Tristan und Isolde* (1865), *Die Meistersinger von Nürnberg* (*The Mastersingers of Nuremberg,* 1868), and *Parsifal* (1882) • Cycle of music dramas: *Der Ring des Nibelung* (*The Ring of the Nibelung*), consisting of *Das Rheingold* (*The Rhine Gold,* 1869), *Die Walküre* (*The Valkyrie,* 1870), *Siegfried* (1876), and *Götterdämmerung* (*The Twilight of the Gods,* 1876) • Orchestral music • Piano music • Vocal and choral music • Writings: *Art and Revolution; The Art Work of the Future.*

early 1800s was **melodrama**: scenes with spoken dialogue or minimal singing, but striking orchestral accompaniment to intensify the dramatic effect of the words.

The greatest figure in German opera, and one of the most significant in the history of the Romantic era, was Richard Wagner. Historians often divide the period into before and after Wagner. The course of post-Romantic music is unimaginable without the impact of this complex and fascinating figure. We will consider his music drama *Die Walküre* (*The Valkyrie,* which includes the famous *Ride of the Valkyries*), part of his cycle *The Ring of the Nibelung.*

The Ring of the Nibelung

Wagner did away with the concept of separate arias, duets, ensembles, choruses, and ballets, developing an "endless melody" that was molded to the natural inflections of the German language, more melodious than the traditional recitative but

A Valkyrie on her winged horse, in a design (c. 1876) by **Carl Emil Doepler**.

freer and more flexible than the traditional aria. He conceived of opera as a total artwork (in German, *Gesamtkunstwerk*) in which the arts of music, poetry, drama, and visual spectacle were fused together, each element created and controlled by his creative genius: a **music drama**.

The orchestra became its focal point and unifying element, fashioned out of concise themes—the **leitmotifs**, or "leading motives," that recur throughout a work, undergoing variation and development like the themes and motives of a symphony. The leitmotifs carry specific meanings, suggesting in a few notes a person, an emotion, an idea, an object. Through a process of continual transformation, they trace the course of the drama, the changes in the characters, their experiences and memories, and their thoughts and hidden desires.

Wagner based his musical language on chromatic harmony, which he pushed to its then farthermost limits. Chromatic dissonance gives his music its restless, intensely emotional quality. Never before had unstable pitch combinations been used so eloquently to portray states of the soul.

The story of *The Ring of the Nibelung* centers on the treasure of gold that lies hidden in the depths of the Rhine River, guarded by three Rhine Maidens. Alberich the Nibelung, who comes from a hideous race of dwarfs that inhabit the dark regions below the earth, tries to make love to the maidens. When they repulse him, he steals the treasure and makes it into a ring that will bring unlimited power to its owner. Wotan, father of the gods (for whom Wednesday, or Wotan's Day, is named), tricks Alberich out of the ring, whereupon the dwarf pronounces a terrible curse: may the ring destroy the peace of mind of all who gain possession of it, may it bring them misfortune and death.

Thus begins the cycle of four dramas that ends only when the curse-bearing ring is returned to the Rhine Maidens. Gods and heroes, mortals and Nibelungs, intermingle freely in this tale of betrayed love, broken promises, magic spells, and general corruption brought on by the lust for power. Wagner freely adapted the story from the myths of the Norse sagas and the legends associated with a medieval German epic poem, the *Nibelungenlied*. (Norse mythology and Wagner's *Ring* were also the inspiration for J. R. R. Tolkien's epic *Lord of the Rings* and for the popular movies based on that literary work, as well as for many role-playing games.)

Die Walküre (The Valkyrie)

Die Walküre, the second work in the cycle, revolves around the twin brother and sister Siegmund and Sieglinde, the offspring of Wotan by a mortal. Their love is not only incestuous but also adulterous, for she has been forced into a loveless marriage with the grim chieftain Hunding, who challenges Siegmund to battle. The second act opens with a scene between Wotan and Brünnhilde, one of his nine daughters, called Valkyries. The Valkyries' perpetual task is to circle the battlefield on their winged horses and swoop down to gather up the fallen heroes, whom they bear away to the great hall of Valhalla, where they will sit forever feasting with the gods. At the insistence of Wotan's wife Fricka (the goddess of marriage), Wotan acknowledges that Siegmund has violated the holiest law of the universe and sadly realizes that he must die in combat with Hunding. Brünnhilde decides to disobey her father's command to let Hunding win the duel by shielding Siegmund. But Wotan appears and holds out his spear, upon which Siegmund's sword is shattered. Hunding then buries his own spear in Siegmund's breast. Wotan, overcome by his son's death, turns a ferocious look upon Hunding, who falls dead. Then the god hurries off in pursuit of the daughter who dared to defy his command.

Act III opens with the famous *Ride of the Valkyries*, a vivid orchestral picture of the nine warrior maidens on their way from the battlefield back to Valhalla, carrying fallen heroes slung across the saddles of their winged horses (LG 30; see illustration on p. 238). This prelude features some of Wagner's most brilliant scoring. The rustling strings and woodwinds give way to the memorable "Ride" theme (familiar from movie soundtracks and even commercials), which is sounded repeatedly by a huge and varied brass section through a dense orchestral texture that builds to several climaxes beneath the warriors' voices.

Arthur Rackham's drawing portrays Brünnhilde asleep in a ring of fire.

Brünnhilde is the last Valkyrie to arrive, carrying Sieglinde and several fragments of Siegmund's sword. Sieglinde wants to die, but Brünnhilde tells her she must live to bear his son, who will become the world's mightiest hero. Brünnhilde remains to face her father's wrath. Her punishment is severe: she is to be deprived of her godhood, Wotan tells her, to become a mortal. He will put her to sleep on a rock, and she will fall prey to the first mortal who finds her. Brünnhilde begs him to soften her punishment: let him at least surround the rock with flames so that only a fearless hero will be able to penetrate the wall of fire. Wotan relents and grants her request. He kisses her on both eyes, which close at once. Striking the rock three times, he invokes Loge, the god of Fire. Flames spring up around the rock (above right), and the "magic fire" leitmotif is heard, followed by the "magic sleep" and "slumber" motives. "Whosoever fears the tip of my spear shall never pass through the fire," he sings, as the orchestra announces the theme of Siegfried, the fearless, yet-unborn son of Sieglinde who in the third music drama will force his way through the flames and awaken Brünnhilde with a kiss.

While the action in this final scene is fairly static, Wagner brings together several strands of meaning through the interaction of the leitmotifs, even introducing us to a character (Siegfried) who has not even been born. Wotan does not name Siegfried, but the striking brass motive names him through music, and prepares us to meet him on the following night (Wagner conceived the *Ring* to be performed on four consecutive evenings). Contemporary film composers such as John Williams also have used this foreshadowing device (in the *Star Wars* films, for example; see Chapter 54), introducing early in the film subtle musical references that prepare us for a full "reveal" later on.

▶|◀ Reflect

How does the complex polyphony help convey the action taking place during the *Ride of the Valkyries*? How are the different musical lines and instruments each contributing to the story of the opera?

YOUR TURN TO EXPLORE

Consider an instance of epic-scale multimedia—the *Star Wars* or *Lord of the Rings* movie "cycles," or an MMORPG like World of Warcraft or RuneScape. Can you identify leitmotifs associated with situations, characters, key objects? Do they evolve along with the characters as the drama progresses, and if so, how? How do you think the use of leitmotifs helps shape the dramatic/gaming experience?

LISTENING GUIDE 30   5:51

Wagner: *Die Walküre* (*The Valkyrie*), Act III, Opening and Finale

DATE: 1856; first performed 1870, in Munich

GENRE: Music drama: second in a cycle of four (*The Ring of the Nibelung*)

PERFORMED BY: Theo Adam, bass; Staatskapelle Dresden

CHARACTERS: Wotan, father of the gods (bass-baritone)
Brünnhilde, his favorite daughter (soprano)
Valkyries, the nine daughters of Wotan

Act III, scene 1: *Ride of the Valkyries*   1:17

What to Listen For

Melody Swirling strings and woodwinds, then the famous "Ride" leitmotif ascends, and is repeated many times.

Rhythm/meter Lively dotted rhythm in 9/8 for the "Ride" leitmotif.

Performing forces Expanded orchestra, most notably: eight French horns, bass trumpet, multiple trombones, Wagner tubas and contrabass tuba; piccolos, English horn, and bass clarinet; cymbals, triangle, glockenspiel, gong; and six harps.

0:00	Orchestral prelude, marked *Lebhaft* (Lively), in 9/8 meter.
	Rushing string figure alternates with fast wavering in woodwinds, then
0:08	insistent dotted figure begins in horns and low strings.
	Swirling string and woodwind lines, accompanied by dotted figure.
0:22	Famous "Ride" motive, heard first in a minor key in the horns:

0:34   "Ride" motive is now heard in a major key in the trumpets.
        Four-note dotted motive exchanged between low and high brass instruments, heard above the swirling idea.
1:04   "Ride" motive heard *fortissimo*, as curtain opens.
        (Four Valkyries, in full armor, have settled on the highest peak above a cave.)

Act III, closing of scene 3: Wotan and Brünnhilde   4:34

What to Listen For

Melody   Three recurring themes (leitmotifs); "endless" melody; a forceful descending trombone melody.

Rhythm/meter   Broad, duple meter; majestic feeling.

Performing forces   Bass voice (Wotan) with orchestra; focus on trombones (in calling Loge); woodwinds and French horns (in magic fire music); harps (in magic sleep music); and brass (in Siegfried theme).

*(Wotan clasps Brünnhilde's head in his hands. He kisses her long on the eyes.
She sinks back with closed eyes, unconscious in his arms. He gently bears her to a low
mossy mound . . . and lays her upon it. He looks upon her and closes her helmet; his eyes rest on the
form of the sleeper, whom he covers with the great shield of the Valkyrie. He turns slowly away,
then again turns around with a sorrowful look.)*

(He strides with solemn decision to the middle of the stage and directs the point of his spear toward a large rock.)

0:00   A forceful trombone passage precedes Wotan's invocation of Loge, god of Fire:

Wotan's evocation of Loge:

Wotan

0:08   Loge, hör'! Lausche hieher!   Loge, listen! Harken here!
        Wie zuerst ich dich fand, als feurige Gluth,   As I found you first, a fiery blaze,
        wie dann einst du mir schwandest,   as once you vanished from me,
        als schweifende Lohe;   a random fire;
        wie ich dich band, bann' ich dich heut'!   as I allied with you, so today I conjure you!
        Herauf, wabernde Lohe,   Arise, magic flame,
        umlod're mir feurig den Fels!   girdle the rock with fire for me!
                    (He strikes the rock thrice with his spear.)
        Loge! Loge! Hieher!   Loge! Loge! Come here!
        *(A flash of flames issues from the rock, which swells to an ever-brightening fiery glow. Bright shooting
        flames surround Wotan. With his spear he directs the sea of fire to encircle the rock; it presently spreads
        toward the background, where it encloses the mountain in flames.)*

continued on next page

1:03   "Magic fire" music, heard in full orchestra:

1:40   "Magic sleep" motive, evoked in descending chromatic line in woodwinds:

1:53   "Slumber" motive, heard in woodwinds:

Wotan (*singing to "Siegfried" motive*)

2:03   Wer meines Speeres Spitze fürchtet,   Whosoever fears the tip of my spear
durchreite das Feuer nie!   shall never pass through the fire!

(*He stretches out the spear as a spell. He gazes sadly on Brünnhilde. Slowly he turns to depart.*
He turns his head again and looks back. He disappears through the fire.)

2:34   Brass in *fortissimo* announce the "Siegfried" motive; long orchestral closing:

Embracing Death: Brahms and the Requiem

▶❚ **First, listen . . .**

to the fourth movement from Brahms's *German Requiem*, focusing on its structure. How many times do you hear the opening music return? And how many contrasting episodes do you perceive? How would you outline the form of this movement?

> ❝ I speak through my music. The only thing is that a poor musician such as myself would like to believe that he was better than his music."
>
> –Johannes Brahms

We often turn to music for comfort in times of trouble. "When all hope is gone," sings Elton John, "sad songs say so much." Many also seek spiritual sustenance in music— and these two strands combine in the **Requiem**, or Mass for the Dead, a genre long cultivated by musicians in the Western tradition. Although the Catholic Church specifies certain texts and prayers for the Requiem Mass, composers have often customized these for their own spiritual tendencies and expressive goals. Several musicians of the nineteenth century wrote unique *Requiems*. Johannes Brahms, in particular, chose texts that were purposefully detached from specific religious practice, trying for a message that would comfort grieving listeners regardless of their faith. In this chapter, we examine a work that Brahms called *A German Requiem* (though he considered calling it "A Requiem for People")—both as representative of the Romantic-era choral repertory and as an early example of successful interfaith music.

ROMANTIC CHORAL MUSIC

The nineteenth century witnessed a spreading of the democratic ideal and an enormous expansion of the audience for music. This climate was uniquely favorable to choral singing, a group activity enjoyed by increasing numbers of amateur music lovers that played an important role in the musical life of the Romantic era.

KEY POINTS

- Choral music grew in popularity during the Romantic era and provided an artistic outlet for the middle classes.

- Favored genres in the nineteenth century include part songs (unaccompanied secular songs for three or four voice parts), the oratorio, the Mass, and the **Requiem Mass**.

- Brahms's *German Requiem*, set to biblical texts chosen by the composer, is a masterpiece of the Romantic choral repertory.

In the nineteenth century, enormous choral and orchestral forces were a common sight, as in this engraving of the opening concert at St. Martin's Hall, London, in 1850.

Part songs

Choral music offered people an ideal outlet for their artistic energies. Although the repertory centered on the great choral heritage of the past, a vast literature of secular choral pieces also appeared. These works, settings for chorus of lyric poems in a variety of moods and styles, were known as **part songs**—that is, songs with three or four voice parts. Most of them were short melodious works, easy enough for amateurs. They gave pleasure both to the singers and to their listeners, and played an important role in developing the new audience of the nineteenth century.

Large-scale choral works

Among the large-scale genres of choral music in the nineteenth century were the Mass, the Requiem Mass, and the oratorio. Though all three were originally intended to be performed in church, by the nineteenth century they had found a wider audience in the concert hall. This is certainly the case with Brahms's *Requiem*, which is far removed from the traditions of the Catholic Church that gave birth to the genre.

BRAHMS'S *GERMAN REQUIEM*

A German Requiem was rooted in the Protestant tradition into which Brahms was born. Its aim was to console the living and lead them to a serene acceptance of death as an inevitable part of life, hence its gentle lyricism. Brahms chose his text from the Old and New Testaments: from the Psalms, Proverbs, Isaiah, and Ecclesiastes as well as from the writings of Paul, Matthew, Peter, and John, and the book of Revelation. He was not religious in the conventional sense. nor was he affiliated with any particular church. He was moved to compose his *Requiem* by the deaths first of his teacher and friend Robert Schumann, then of his mother, whom he idolized; but the piece transcends personal emotions and endures as a song of mourning for all humanity.

Written for soloists, four-part chorus, and orchestra. *A German Requiem* is in seven movements arranged in a formation resembling an arch: there are connections between the first and last movements, between the second and sixth, and

Johannes Brahms (1833–1897)

Born in Hamburg, Germany, Brahms early on developed what would be a lifelong affection for folk music, collecting songs and folk sayings throughout his life. Brahms had the good fortune to study with Robert Schumann at Düsseldorf, who recognized in his pupil a future leader of the circle dedicated to absolute music. Robert and his wife Clara took the young musician into their home, and their friendship opened up new horizons for him.

The death of Brahms's mother in 1865 inspired him to write his *German Requiem,* with biblical texts that he selected himself, in her memory. He ultimately settled in Vienna, where, at age forty, he began writing his great symphonic works. During these years, he became enormously successful, the acknowledged heir of the Viennese masters. The declining health of his dear friend Clara Schumann gave rise to his *Four Serious Songs.* Her death deeply affected the composer, already ill with cancer. He died ten months later and was

buried in Vienna, near Beethoven and Schubert.

Brahms's four symphonies are unsurpassed in the late Romantic period for their breadth of conception and design. In his two piano concertos and violin concerto, the solo instrument is integrated into a full-scale symphonic structure. Brahms gorgeously captured the intimacy of chamber-music style, and is an important figure in piano music as well. As a song writer, he stands in the direct succession from Schubert and Schumann, with about two hundred solo songs.

MAJOR WORKS: Orchestral music, including four symphonies, variations, overtures • Four concertos (two for piano, one for violin, one double concerto for piano and violin • Chamber music, including piano trios and quartets • Duo sonatas • Piano music, including sonatas, character pieces, dances, variations • Choral music, including A *German Requiem* (1868) and part songs • Lieder, including *Wiegenlied* (*Lullaby*).

between the third and fifth. That leaves the fourth movement, the widely sung chorus "How lovely is Thy dwelling place," as the centerpiece.

This movement is based on a verse from Psalm 84 (LG 31). The first two lines of the psalm are heard three times, separated by two contrasting sections that present the other lines. The form, therefore, is **A-B-A′-C-A′**. The first two sections move largely in quarter notes, but the third section (**C**) moves more quickly.

This vigorous rhythm better suits the line "die loben dich immerdar" (that praise Thee evermore), with much expansion on "immerdar." With the final reappearance of the **A** section, the slower tempo returns. Marked *piano* and *dolce* (soft and sweet), this passage serves as a coda that brings the piece to its gentle and serene close.

Brahms's approach to the Requiem is especially unusual in that he chooses to comfort the living rather than dwell on the fate of the dead: he omits the intense references to religious judgment (for example, the Dies irae) found in the Catholic

Brahms's study and personal library in Vienna, in a nineteenth-century painting.

Requiem Mass. Perhaps because of its focus on divine compassion outside of a specific sectarian message, his *German Requiem* was quickly embraced across Europe among many communities of faith. It is still among the best-known and most frequently performed of Brahms's works, sought after in large part for its power to console those of us who are left contemplating how to continue after loved ones have passed.

▶|◀ Reflect

How might patterns of returning melody and words in this movement resemble the way we return to and reflect on our memories of lost loved ones? What about Brahms's choices of melody, dynamics, combination of voices and instruments, or other musical qualities do you find comforting? What other emotions does the movement evoke in you?

YOUR TURN TO EXPLORE

Find an example of a musical work designed to reflect on a tragic event and/or offer comfort or hope to those who have witnessed it. If words are incorporated, where are they from, and what kind of imagery do they evoke? How is music used to reinforce particular words or bring out specific meanings? What instrumental (and vocal) forces are used, and why do you think that particular instrumentation was chosen? What musical (as opposed to word-related) elements might be intended to express the intensity of sorrow, or foster the lightness of hope?

LISTENING GUIDE 31 5:54

Brahms: *A German Requiem*, IV

DATE: 1868

GENRE: Protestant Requiem, in seven movements

PERFORMED BY: Vienna Philharmonic; Nikolaus Harnoncourt, director

IV: Mässig bewegt (at a moderate tempo)

What to Listen For

Melody Lyrical, wavelike choral melody that returns, rondo-like, to unify the form.

Harmony Changes between major and minor keys to follow the text.

Expression Emotional expressions of loss and acceptance of death through word-painting and harmonic shifts.

Text Based on Psalm 84 (in the Protestant Bible; 83 in the Vulgate, or Latin Bible).

Opening melody—clarinets and flutes begin with inverted first phrase of the chorus:

0:00	**Orchestral introduction**.		
0:08	Wie lieblich sind deine Wohnungen, Herr Zebaoth!	How lovely is Thy dwelling place, O Lord of Hosts!	**A**—a flowing, arched melody in an SATB homophonic setting (in E-flat major); text is repeated in the tenors; then in the other voices.
1:27	Meine Seele verlanget und sehnet sich nach den Vorhöfen des Herrn;	My soul longs and even faints for the courts of the Lord;	**B**—shift to the minor mode, builds fugally from lowest to highest voices;
2:04	mein Leib und Seele freuen sich in dem lebendigen Gott.	my flesh and soul rejoice in the living God.	sudden accents on first beat of measures, with plucked strings; climax on "lebendigen."
2:49	Wie lieblich . . . Wohl denen, die in deinem Hause wohnen,	How lovely . . . Blessed are they that live in Thy house,	**A′**—opening returns in E-flat major, with new text and varied melody.
3:55	die loben dich immerdar!	that praise Thee evermore!	**C**—martial quality, faster movement; voices declaim polyphonically.
4:51	Wie lieblich . . .	How lovely . . .	**A′**—coda-like return of opening material; soft orchestral closing.

Poetry in Motion: Tchaikovsky and the Ballet

> 66 Dance is the hidden language of the soul."
>
> —Martha Graham

▶❙ First, listen . . .

to the *Dance of the Sugar Plum Fairy,* from Tchaikovsky's *Nutcracker,* focusing on the overall structure of the dance. Which musical elements or instruments help you follow the form? Does this sound like dance music to you?

A French court dancer from the era of Louis XIV.

Out of movement, dance weaves an enchantment all its own. We watch with amazement as dancers synchronize their actions to the music, performing pirouettes and intricate footwork with the utmost grace, and leaps that seem to triumph over the laws of gravity. Their bodies are their instruments, which they must keep in excellent shape in order to perform the gymnastics required of them. They create moments of elusive beauty, made possible only by total control of their muscles. It is this combination of physical and emotional factors, blended with the expressive resources of music, that marks the distinctive power of choreographed dance.

THE BALLET

Beginning in the Renaissance, the choreographed dance known as **ballet** was central to lavish festivals and theatrical entertainments presented at the courts of kings and dukes. Royal weddings and other celebrations were accompanied by spectacles with scenery, costumes, and staged dancing known as *intermedio* in Italy, **masque** in England, and *ballet de cour* in France, notably at the court of Louis XIV.

The eighteenth century saw the rise of ballet as an independent art form. French ballet was preeminent in the early nineteenth century, then Russian ballet came into its own—helped along considerably by the arrival in 1847 of French-born Marius Petipa, the great choreographer at St. Petersburg. Petipa

KEY POINTS

- **Ballet** became an independent dramatic form in the eighteenth and nineteenth centuries, particularly in France and Russia.

- The ballets of Russian composer Peter Ilyich Tchaikovsky—*Swan Lake, Sleeping Beauty*, and *The Nutcracker*—remain central to the repertory today.

Peter Ilyich Tchaikovsky (1840–1893)

The son of a Russian government official, Tchaikovsky entered the newly founded Conservatory of St. Petersburg at the age of twenty-three. He was immediately recommended by composer Anton Rubinstein, director of the school, for a teaching post in the new Moscow Conservatory, and his twelve years in Moscow saw the production of some of his most successful works.

Extremely sensitive by nature, Tchaikovsky was subject to attacks of depression. The social stigma associated with being a homosexual may have led him to marry a student at the conservatory; they soon separated. Good fortune followed when in 1877 Nadezhda von Meck, the wealthy widow of an industrialist, sent Tchaikovsky money to go abroad, and launched him on the most productive period of his career. Bound by the rigid conventions of her time and class, von Meck had to be certain that her enthusiasm was for the artist, not the man; hence she stipulated that she never meet the recipient of her patronage.

Tchaikovsky was the first Russian whose music appealed to Western tastes— it was performed in Vienna, Berlin, and Paris—and in 1891 he was invited to

participate in the inaugural concert of Carnegie Hall in New York. Two years later, he conducted his *Pathétique* Symphony in St. Petersburg, where the work met with a lukewarm reception. He died within several weeks, at the age of fifty-three, and the tragic tone of his last work led to rumors that he had committed suicide. More likely he contracted cholera from tainted water.

Although Tchaikovsky declared, "I am Russian through and through!," he also came under the spell of Italian opera, French ballet, and German symphony and song. These he joined to the strain of folk melody that was his heritage as a Russian, imposing on this mixture his sharply defined personality.

MAJOR WORKS: Eight operas, including *Eugene Onegin* (1878) • Three ballets: *Swan Lake* (1877), *The Sleeping Beauty* (1890), and *The Nutcracker* (1892) • Orchestral music, including seven symphonies (one unfinished), three piano concertos, a violin concerto, symphonic poems (*Romeo and Juliet*), and overtures (*1812 Overture*) • Chamber and keyboard music • Choral music • Songs.

created the dances for more than a hundred works, invented the structure of the classic ***pas de deux*** (dance for two), and brought the art of staging ballets to unprecedented heights.

TCHAIKOVSKY AND *THE NUTCRACKER*

The giant of Russian ballet in the later nineteenth century was Peter Ilyich Tchaikovsky, who had a natural affinity for the theater. His three ballets—*Swan Lake, The Sleeping Beauty,* and *The Nutcracker*, all choreographed by Petipa— were quickly established as basic works of the Russian repertory. We will hear excerpts from the popular ballet that's performed every Christmas all over the world, *The Nutcracker.*

Act I takes place at a Christmas party during which two children, Clara and Fritz, receive a nutcracker from their godfather. After the children have gone to bed, Clara returns to gaze at her gift, falls asleep, and begins to dream. First she is terrified to see mice scampering around the tree. Then the dolls she has received come alive and fight

A traditional Russian nutcracker—a toy soldier who comes alive in Tchaikovsky's ballet.

Mikhail Baryshnikov as the Nutcracker Prince fights the Mouse King in an American Ballet Theater production of *The Nutcracker.*

a battle with the mice, which reaches a climax in the combat between the Nutcracker and the Mouse King (left). Clara helps her beloved Nutcracker by throwing a slipper at the Mouse King, who is vanquished. The Nutcracker then becomes a handsome Prince, who sweeps Clara away with him.

Act II finds them in Confiturembourg, the land of sweets, ruled by the Sugar Plum Fairy. The Prince presents Clara to his family, and a celebration follows, with a series of dances that reveal all the attractions of this magic realm (LG 32). The dances are accompanied by colorful instruments; Tchaikovsky wrote to his publisher that he had discovered a new one in Paris, "something between a piano and a glockenspiel, with a divinely beautiful tone, and I want to introduce it into the ballet." The instrument was the **celesta,** whose timbre perfectly suits the Sugar Plum Fairy's dance. In the *Trepak* (Russian Dance, featuring the famous Cossack squat-kick; see p. 57), the orchestral sound is enlivened by a tambourine. Other exotic dances follow, from Arabia and China, climaxing with the *Waltz of the Flowers.*

This engaging work conjures up everything we have come to associate with the Romantic ballet. It is an example of the way music has been combined with movement in the Western tradition to tell stories that are both more precise than instrumental program music and more subtle and nuanced than opera and song.

▶️◀ Reflect

How does the three-part (ternary) form of the Fairy's dance satisfy listeners' need for the familiar and also desire for change? How does the recognition of a passage you've already heard affect your appreciation of the piece?

LISTENING GUIDE 32 2:56

Tchaikovsky: *The Nutcracker,* Two Dances

DATE:	1892
GENRE:	Ballet (from which an orchestral suite was made)
BASIS:	E. T. A. Hoffmann story, expanded by Alexandre Dumas *père*
CHOREOGRAPHER:	Marius Petipa
PERFORMED BY:	Philadelphia Orchestra; Eugene Ormandy, conductor

SEQUENCE OF DANCES:		
March	*Chinese Dance*
Dance of the Sugar Plum Fairy	*Dance of the Toy Flutes*
Trepak	*Waltz of the Flowers*
Arab Dance	

Dance of the Sugar Plum Fairy: Andante non troppo   1:44

What to Listen For

Rhythm/meter Bouncy duple meter.
Form Three-part form (**A-B-A**).

Performing forces Bell-like timbre of the celesta, accompanied by bass clarinet and pizzicato strings.

A section

0:00   Short introduction (four measures) of pizzicato strings.

0:08   Main theme introduced by celesta, staccato in a high range (in dialogue with bass clarinet):

B section

0:39   Brief section with arched lines in woodwinds and celesta, answered by strings.

A section

1:11   Solo celesta leads back to the main theme, accompanied by staccato strings. Closes with a loud pizzicato chord.

Trepak (*Russian Dance*): **Tempo di trepak, molto vivace (very lively)**   1:12

What to Listen For

Rhythm/meter Lively peasant dance in a heavily accented duple meter; includes an *accelerando* (getting faster).
Form **A-B-A** with texture (contrapuntal) contrast in the **B** section.

Performing forces Tambourine featured with strings and woodwinds; a trumpet fanfare near the end.

A section

0:00   Lively dance tune in strings, repeated in full orchestra:

B section

0:27   Brief diversion in the same rhythmic style, melody in the low strings.

A section

0:47   Return of the dance tune; quickens at the end, with trumpet fanfare and syncopations.

YOUR TURN TO EXPLORE

Find two videos of dancers from separate traditions (for example, classical ballet, modern dance, tap, jazz and/or Broadway dance, hip-hop)—some extraordinary performers you might look for are Rudolf Nureyev, Savion Glover, Bob Fosse, Katherine Dunham, Lil Buck. Note how the dancer varies and repeats movements, the variety of melodic ideas in the music, and the way the music and movement are synchronized. Do you think the dancer is conveying a story through her/his moves, and if so, how would you describe it? If not, what do you think the dancer is conveying?

Mythical Impressions: Program Music at the End of the Nineteenth Century

66 For we desire above all—nuance / Not color but half-shades! / Ah! nuance alone unites / Dream with dream and flute with horn."

—Paul Verlaine (1844–1896)

▶️ First, listen . . .

to the first two minutes of Debussy's *Prelude to "The Afternoon of a Faun,"* focusing on the changing instruments and timbres. Which timbres are distinct, and which are difficult to discern? How is this use of the orchestra different from other orchestral textures we have encountered?

There is something about mythological characters that speaks both to essential human nature and to the mystery of the supernatural. They can serve as a resource for a musician, poet, or painter to pull us out of the ordinary, give us a glimpse into the possible. Mythological themes have been especially promi-nent in Western multimedia, from the sung plays of ancient Greece to contem-porary film and role-playing games. A striking example is provided by one of the most famous works of the later 1800s, Claude Debussy's *Prelude to "The Afternoon of a Faun,"* which we will examine in this chapter. Looking backward to ancient mythology and forward to new sound worlds and expressions, it reflects the subtle perspectives of several creative minds through words, sounds, and movement.

SYMBOLISM AND IMPRESSIONISM IN PARIS

In the 1860s, breaking with what they considered the static grandiosity of contemporary art, Impressionist painters tried to capture on canvas the fresh-ness of their first impressions and the continuous change in the appearance of

KEY POINTS

- **Impressionism** in music is characterized by modal and exotic scales (chromatic, whole tone, and pentatonic), unresolved dissonances, tone combinations such as ninth chords, rich orchestral color, and free rhythm, all generally cast in small-scale programmatic forms.

- The most important French Impressionist composer was Claude Debussy. His orchestral work *Prelude to*

"The Afternoon of a Faun" was inspired by a Symbolist poem, and later choreographed by the great Russian dancer Vaslav Nijinsky.

- Debussy and his contemporaries were highly influenced by non-Western and traditional music styles heard at the Paris World Exhibition of 1889.

their subjects through varied treatment of light and color. A hazy painting by Claude Monet, *Impression: Sunrise*, completed in 1867, was rebuffed by the academic salons of Paris (see illustration below), and **Impressionism** quickly became a term of derision. However, Monet's luminous painting style was eagerly embraced by Parisian artists such as Edgar Degas (right) and Auguste Renoir (p. 187). We will see how composers like Debussy tried to emulate the use of color and iridescence that characterize this new style.

A parallel development in poetry was similarly influential to French composers: the Symbolist movement sought to evoke poetic images through suggestion rather than description, through symbol rather than statement. This literary revolt against tradition gained prominence in the works of French writers Stéphane Mallarmé and Paul Verlaine, both of whom were strongly influenced by the American poet Edgar Allan Poe. Through their experiments in free verse forms, the Symbolists were able to achieve in language an abstract quality that had once belonged to music alone.

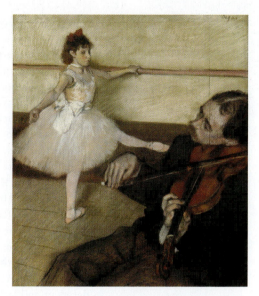

The Dance Lesson (1879), watercolor by French Impressionist **Edgar Degas** (1834–1917).

TRANSLATING IMPRESSIONS INTO SOUND

Inspired by the Impressionist and Symbolist movements, a number of French composers of the later 1800s also attempted to break from tradition in order to experiment with greater subtlety and ambiguity. The major-minor system, as we saw, is based on the pull of the active tones to the tonic, or rest tone. Impressionist composers regarded this as a formula that had become too obvious. In their works, we do not hear the triumphal final cadence of the Classical-Romantic period, in which the dominant chord is resolved to the tonic chord with the greatest possible emphasis. Instead, more subtle harmonic relationships come into play. Rather than viewing dissonance as a momentary disturbance, composers began to use dissonance as a goal in itself, freeing it from the need to resolve. They taught their listeners to accept tone combinations that had formerly been regarded as inadmissible, just as the Impressionist painters taught people to see colors in sky, grass, and water they had never seen there before. Composers made use of the entire spectrum of notes in the chromatic scale, and also explored the whole-tone scale and others derived from various non-Western musics heard at the 1889 Paris World Exhibition.

The Impressionists took painting out of the studio and into the open air; their subject was light. **Claude Monet** (1840–1926). *Impression: Sunrise.*

Freed from a strong tonal center and rigid harmonic guidelines, composers experimented with new tone combinations such as the **ninth chord**, a set of five notes in which the interval between the lowest and highest tones is a ninth. The

Claude Debussy (1862–1918)

The most important French composer of the late nineteenth–early twentieth century, Debussy was born near Paris and entered the Paris Conservatory when he was eleven. Within a few years, he was shocking his professors with bizarre harmonies that defied the rules. He was only twenty-two when his cantata *The Prodigal Son* won the coveted Prix de Rome. By this time, he had already realized his future style.

The 1890s, the most productive decade of Debussy's career, culminated in the opera *Pelléas and Mélisande*, based on the Symbolist drama by the Belgian poet Maurice Maeterlinck. At first, *Pelléas* was attacked as being decadent and lacking in melody and form, but this opera made Debussy famous. His energies sapped by the ravages of cancer, Debussy died in March 1918, during the bombardment of Paris.

Like artist Claude Monet and writer Paul Verlaine, Debussy considered art to be a sensuous experience. "French music," he declared, "is clearness, elegance, simple and natural declamation . . . aiming first of all to give pleasure." His fame rests on a comparatively small output; *Pelléas and Mélisande* is viewed by many as his greatest achievement. Among his orchestral compositions, the *Prelude to "The Afternoon of a Faun"* became a favorite with the public early on, as did *The Sea (La mer)*.

Many of his piano pieces demonstrate an interest in non-Western scales and instruments (he regarded sonata-allegro form as an outmoded formula), which he first heard at the Paris Exhibition in 1889. Debussy also helped establish the French song (*mélodie*) as a national art form. His settings of the French Symbolist poets Verlaine and Mallarmé are exquisite and refined.

MAJOR WORKS: Orchestral music, including *Prélude à "L'après midi d'un faune"* (*Prelude to "The Afternoon of a Faun,"* 1894), *Nocturnes* (1899), *La mer* (*The Sea*, 1905) • Dramatic works, including the opera *Pelléas et Mélisande* (1902) and a ballet • Chamber music, including a string quartet and various sonatas • Piano music, including two books of preludes (1909–10, 1912–13) • Songs, choral music, and cantatas.

effect was one of hovering between tonalities, creating elusive effects that evoke the misty outlines of Impressionist painting.

These floating harmonies demanded the most subtle colors, and here composers learned new techniques of blending timbres from their counterparts in art. Painters juxtaposed brush strokes of pure color on the canvas, leaving it to the eye of the viewer to do the mixing. Debussy similarly replaced the lush, full sonority of the Romantic orchestra with veiled sounds: flutes and clarinets in their dark, velvety registers, violins in their lustrous upper range, trumpets and horns discreetly muted; and over the whole, a shimmering gossamer of harp, celesta, triangle, glockenspiel, muffled drum, and brushed cymbal. One instrumental color flows into another close by, as from oboe to clarinet to flute, in the same way that Impressionist painting moves from one color to another in the spectrum, from yellow to green to blue.

Debussy's *Prelude to "The Afternoon of a Faun"*

Vaslav Nijinsky in the ballet *Afternoon of a Faun*. Design by **Léon Bakst** (1866–1924).

Debussy's best-known orchestral work was inspired by a pastoral poem by Symbolist writer Stéphane Mallarmé describing the faun, a mythological forest creature that is half man, half goat, and symbolizes raw sensuality. Debussy intended his music to be a series of "backdrops" that would illustrate the faun and his actions. We can thus consider this work a coming together of visual Impressionism and textual Symbolism through sound (LG 33).

The work follows the familiar pattern of statement-departure-return (**A-B-A'**), yet the progression is fluid and rhapsodic, with a relaxed rhythm. We first hear a flute solo in the lower register. The melody glides along the chromatic scale, narrow in range and languorous. Glissandos on the harp usher in a brief dialogue in the horns, a mixture of colors never heard before.

Next, a more decisive motive emerges, marked "en animant" (growing lively). This is followed by a third theme, an impassioned melody that carries the piece to an emotional climax. The first theme then returns in an altered guise. At the close, antique cymbals (small disks of brass whose rims are struck together gently and allowed to vibrate) play *pianissimo*. "Blue" chords (with lowered thirds and sevenths) are heard on the muted horns and violins, sounding infinitely remote. The work dissolves into silence, leaving us, and the faun, in a dreamlike state.

Nymph costume for the ballet *Afternoon of a Faun.*

Debussy's symphonic poem was widely performed (as far away as Boston in 1902), but it gained even more prominence when it was choreographed by the great Russian dancer Vaslav Nijinsky (about whom we will learn more in Chapter 45). Nijinsky himself danced the role of the faun (see illustration opposite), and his sensuous cavorting among the nymphs caused a scandal in Paris: this choreography is often viewed as a turning point in modern ballet. Nijinsky's choreography helped make Debussy's work all the more successful, but it also introduced a problem: to what extent does the meaning added by a dancer/choreographer "shape" the interpretation of a musical work? Does a storytelling choreography go against the subtlety and vagueness of Debussy's Symbolist/Impressionist approach?

LISTENING GUIDE 33

 9:45

Debussy: *Prelude to "The Afternoon of a Faun"* (*Prélude à "L'après-midi d'un faune"*)

DATE: 1894

GENRE: Symphonic poem

PERFORMED BY: New Philharmonia Orchestra; Pierre Boulez, conductor

What to Listen For

Melody A lyrical, sinuous melody; chromatic at the opening and closing.

Rhythm/meter Free-flowing rhythms; a sense of floating, lacking a pulse; middle section is more animated.

Form Loose **A-B-A'** structure.

Performing forces Strings (with two harps), woodwinds, French horns, and antique cymbals provide an unprecedented mixture of timbres.

continued on next page

Opening of poem, by Stéphane Mallarmé:

Ces nymphes, je les veux perpétuer.	These nymphs I would perpetuate.
Si clair	So light
Leur incarnat léger, qu'il voltige dans l'air	their gossamer embodiment, floating on the air
Assoupi de sommeils touffus.	inert with heavy slumber.
Amais-je un rêve?	Was it a dream I loved?

A section

0:00   Opening chromatic melody in flute; passes from one instrument to another, accompanied by muted strings and a vague sense of pulse:

B section

2:48   Clarinet introduces a more animated idea, answered by a rhythmic figure in cellos.

3:16   New theme with livelier rhythm in solo oboe, builds in a *crescendo*:

4:34   Contrasting theme in woodwinds, then strings, with syncopated rhythms, builds to a climax:

A′ section

6:22   Abridged return, in a varied setting.

▶◀ Reflect

How does Debussy use new kinds of blended timbre and melodic shapes to convey exotic and mysterious effects? In what ways might his expressive goal be similar to that of contemporaneous Symbolist poets or Impressionist artists? What story do you hear in this work?

YOUR TURN TO EXPLORE

Pick a movie, TV show, or video game that includes music and draws on mythology. How are specific elements like timbre, melody, and harmony used to reinforce certain characters or dramatic moments? How do you think those musical choices contribute to the simultaneously real/unreal quality of mythology?

Romantic-Era Music

REPRESENTATIVE COMPOSERS

Franz Schubert

Stephen Foster

Fanny Mendelssohn Hensel

Frédéric Chopin

Edvard Grieg

Hector Berlioz

Johannes Brahms

Antonín Dvořák

Giuseppe Verdi

Richard Wagner

Peter Ilyich Tchaikovsky

Claude Debussy

IMPORTANT GENRES

solo song (Lied)

opera

symphonic poem

program symphony

incidental music

Requiem Mass

symphony

concerto

string quartet

ballet

piano miniature

Listening Essentials

Melody: Expansive, flowing, and wide-ranging melodies, with chromatic inflections and dramatic leaps.

Rhythm/meter: Rhythmic diversity and elasticity; use of tempo rubato.

Harmony: Increased chromaticism, within expanded concepts of tonality.

Texture: Homophonic (early nineteenth century); increasingly polyphonic in later part of the century.

Form: Forms expanded; continuous and miniature programmatic forms developed.

Expression: Emphasis on intense emotions and moods; wide-ranging dynamics and high levels of virtuosity; interest in the bizarre and macabre.

Performing forces: New instruments (English horn, piccolo, harp, tuba, valved brass) introduced into the orchestra; piano predominant as a solo instrument.

Listening Challenge

Now take the online Listening Challenge, where you'll listen to a mystery selection from the Romantic era and answer questions about its elements: the nature of the melodic line and whether it's in a major or minor key; the rhythmic and metric movement; the form of the piece and how repetition helps organize it; which instruments play the melody; and whether expressive musical devices evoke specific imagery.

THE MODERN ERA

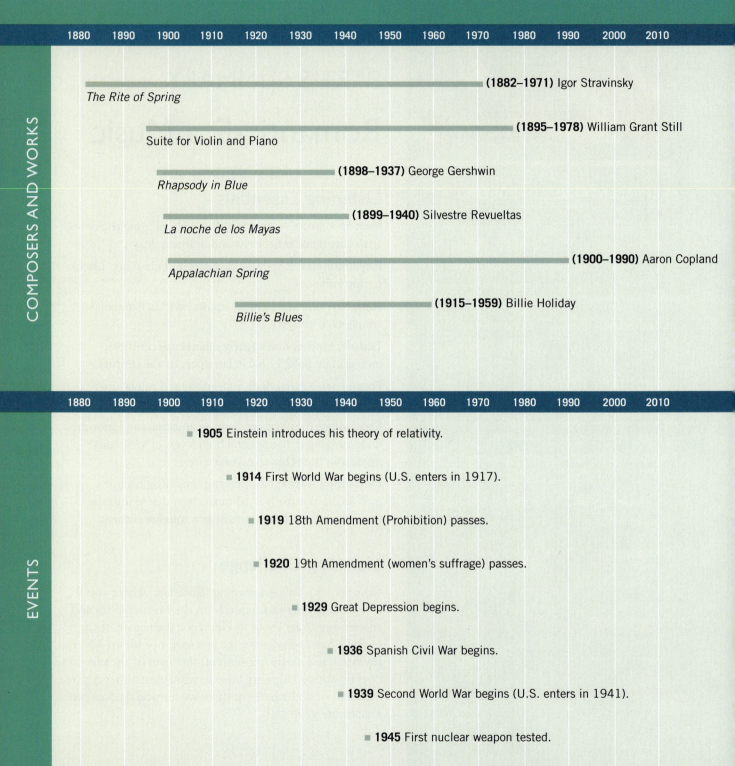

COMPOSERS AND WORKS

| 1880 | 1890 | 1900 | 1910 | 1920 | 1930 | 1940 | 1950 | 1960 | 1970 | 1980 | 1990 | 2000 | 2010 |

(1882–1971) Igor Stravinsky
The Rite of Spring

(1895–1978) William Grant Still
Suite for Violin and Piano

(1898–1937) George Gershwin
Rhapsody in Blue

(1899–1940) Silvestre Revueltas
La noche de los Mayas

(1900–1990) Aaron Copland
Appalachian Spring

(1915–1959) Billie Holiday
Billie's Blues

EVENTS

| 1880 | 1890 | 1900 | 1910 | 1920 | 1930 | 1940 | 1950 | 1960 | 1970 | 1980 | 1990 | 2000 | 2010 |

1905 Einstein introduces his theory of relativity.

1914 First World War begins (U.S. enters in 1917).

1919 18th Amendment (Prohibition) passes.

1920 19th Amendment (women's suffrage) passes.

1929 Great Depression begins.

1936 Spanish Civil War begins.

1939 Second World War begins (U.S. enters in 1941).

1945 First nuclear weapon tested.

PART 6

Pablo Picasso, *Still Life with Guitar* (1924).

Twentieth-Century Modernism

▶❙ First, listen . . .

to the *Hoedown* movement from Aaron Copland's ballet *Rodeo,* and see how many musical traits described in Part 1 you can identify: for example, the nature of the melodic lines; the complexity of the rhythm/meter and the texture; instances of consonance and dissonance in the harmony, and how they contribute to the expression; the overall structure; and which instruments (including percussion) are featured. Listen several times to try to pick up multiple elements, but don't worry about "getting it right"—this is your first chance to apply these basic principles to an example of modernist-era music.

LISTENING OBJECTIVES

By the end of Part 6, you will be able to

- distinguish the era's wide-ranging, disjunct melodies—sometimes influenced by folk music and jazz—accompanied by dissonant harmonies that move away from tonality.

- hear the complexity of the rhythm, with much syncopation and changing meters, and polyphonic textures in which lines move linearly.

- recognize the crisp, lean orchestral sound, with unusual instrumental combinations and some instruments playing in extreme ranges.

- perceive the wide-ranging dynamics and high levels of virtuosity that help to provide a new means of expression.

- identify the era's tightly structured forms, some of which derive from earlier eras.

Making Music Modern

66 The entire history of
modern music may be
said to be a history of the
gradual pull-away from the
German musical tradition
of the past century."

—Aaron Copland

MODERNISMS

Much of the twentieth century was characterized by artists' self-conscious attempts to make their art "modern," not only expressing their own creative visions but suggesting progressive directions for others to follow. This led to purposeful departures from tradition, which have been labeled with a variety of "isms"—Expressionism, futurism, Fauvism, serialism, neo-Classicism, and so on. What these "isms" all have in common is a concern with "making art new." Yet the particular strategies through which individuals tried to make music modern were often quite different from one another. This is why it can be useful to think of multiple musical modernisms, each serving a different creative purpose. We will examine several of them in the chapters to come.

Most modernists did share a wish to reject nineteenth-century models and a suspicion of popular or mass culture. The twentieth century, however, was also a time when sound recording made vernacular traditions ever more prominent, and modernist musicians often grappled with this powerful cultural phenomenon—sometimes rejecting it, other times integrating some aspects of popular music and culture into their search for the new.

LEFT: The powerful
abstraction of African
sculpture strongly influenced
European art.

RIGHT: **Henri Rousseau**
(1844–1910) found his
subject matter in distant
places, as in *The Sleeping
Gypsy* (1897).

Early Modernist Art

Just as European and American societies saw great changes in the era from 1890 to 1940, so did the arts witness a profound upheaval. A first wave of modernist attitudes took hold just before the First World War (1914–18), when European

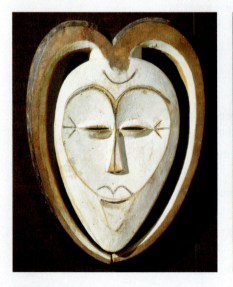

Ceci n'est pas une pipe.

LEFT: In *Girl Running on a Balcony*, by **Giacomo Balla** (1871–1958), art portrays movement.

RIGHT: *The Treachery of Images*, by **René Magritte** (1898–1973), confronts our perception of reality: the caption means "This is not a pipe." As Magritte said, "Just try to stuff tobacco in it."

Spanish artist **Joan Miró** (1893–1983) explores the surrealist world of dreams through the distortion of shapes. *Dutch Interior I.*

arts tried to break away from overrefinement and capture the spontaneity and freedom from inhibition that was associated with primitive life (though artists often had an idealized notion of "exotic" cultures outside Europe; see the Rousseau illustration opposite). Likewise, some composers turned to what they perceived as the revitalizing energy of non-Western rhythm, seeking fresh concepts in the musics of Africa, Asia, and eastern Europe.

In the years surrounding the war, two influential arts movements arose: **futurism**, whose manifesto of 1909 declared an alienation from established institutions and a focus on the dynamism of twentieth-century life; and **Dadaism**, founded in Switzerland in 1916. The Dadaists, mainly writers and artists who reacted to the horrors of the war's bloodbath, rejected the concept of art as something to be reverently admired. To make their point, they produced works of absolute absurdity. They also reacted against the excessive complexity of Western art by trying to recapture the simplicity of a child's worldview. Following their example, the French composer Erik Satie (1866–1925) wrote music in a simple, "everyday" style.

The Dada group, with artists like Marcel Duchamp, merged into the school of **surrealism**, which included Salvador Dali and Joan Miró (at right), both of whom explored the world of dreams. Other styles of modern art included **Cubism**, the Paris-based style of painting in geometric patterns embodied in the works of Pablo Picasso (see p. 259), Georges Braque, and Juan Gris; and **Expressionism**, which made a significant impact on music of the early twentieth century.

Expressionism

While French artists explored radiant impressions of the outer world through Impressionism, their German counterparts preferred digging down to the depths of the psyche. As with Impressionism (Chapter 44), the impulse for the Expressionist movement came from painting. Artists such as Edvard Munch

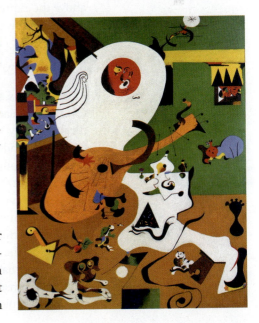

Arnold Schoenberg's Expressionist painting *The Red Gaze* (1910) is highly reminiscent of Edvard Munch's *The Scream* (1893).

In His Own Words

66 The old romanticism is dead; long live the new!"

—Arnold Schoenberg

(famous for *The Scream*) influenced the composer Arnold Schoenberg (1874–1951) and his disciples Alban Berg and Anton Webern (as well as writers like Franz Kafka), just as the Impressionist painters influenced Debussy.

The musical language of Expressionism favored hyperexpressive harmonies, extraordinarily wide leaps in the melody, and the use of instruments in their extreme registers. Expressionist music soon reached the boundaries of what was possible within the major-minor system. Inevitably, it had to push beyond. Schoenberg in fact advocated doing away with tonality altogether by giving the twelve tones of the chromatic scale equal importance—thus creating **atonal** music. Atonality entirely rejected the framework of key. Consonance, according to Schoenberg, was no longer capable of making an impression; atonal music moved from one level of dissonance to another, functioning always at maximum tension, without areas of relaxation. He eventually developed a unifying principle through a technique known as **serialism**, or **twelve-tone** music, in which all twelve tones of the chromatic scale are arranged in a particular order (**row**) throughout a piece.

Neo-Classicism

One way of rejecting the nineteenth century was to return to earlier eras. Instead of revering Beethoven and Wagner, as the Romantics had done, composers began to emulate the great musicians of the early eighteenth century—Bach, Handel, and Vivaldi—and the detached, objective style often associated with their music. **Neo-Classical** composers turned away from the symphonic poem and the Romantic attempt to bring music closer to poetry and painting. They preferred absolute to program music, and they focused attention on craftsmanship and balance, a positive affirmation of the Classical virtues of objectivity and control but also of twentieth-century ideals of progress through science. They revived a number of older forms such as toccata, fugue, concerto grosso, and suite, while retaining the traditional symphony, sonata, and concerto. They valued the formal above the expressive; accordingly, the new classicism, like the old, strove for purity of line and proportion.

The Americas and the Avant-Garde

As Europeans rejected their own Romantic past, Americans saw the opportunity to take the lead in defining the future in the new "American century." The cultural diversity of North America provided many resources to inspire modernist musicians, and their different backgrounds and goals—both creative and social-political—brought them to a variety of styles (some incorporating folk music, blues, and jazz) that we will explore.

As in previous movements, modernism was both a reaction against the past and a distillation of it. The movement transformed a culture and allowed for endless experimentation. One of the elements of modernist art and music is the concept of the **avant-garde**, a French term originally used to describe the part of an army that charged first into battle. Artists who identify as avant-garde distinguish themselves from traditional "high culture" and from mass-market taste, seeking to explore true creativity by breaking from social and artistic conventions.

FEATURES OF EARLY MUSICAL MODERNISM

*"To study music, we must learn the rules.
To create music, we must break them."*

—Nadia Boulanger (1887–1979)

The New Rhythmic Complexity

Twentieth-century music enriched the standard patterns of duple, triple, and quadruple meter by exploring the possibilities of nonsymmetrical patterns based on odd numbers: five, seven, eleven, or thirteen beats to the measure. In nineteenth-century music, a single meter customarily prevailed through an entire movement or section. Now the metrical flow shifted constantly (**changing meter**), sometimes with each measure. Formerly, one rhythmic pattern was used at a time. Now composers turned to **polyrhythm**, the simultaneous use of several patterns. As a result of these innovations, Western music achieved something of the complexity and suppleness of Asian and African rhythms. This revitalization of rhythm is one of the major achievements of early twentieth-century music.

Composers also enlivened their music with materials drawn from popular styles. Ragtime, with its elaborate syncopations, traveled across the Atlantic to Europe. The rhythmic freedom of jazz captured the ears of a great many composers, who strove to achieve something of the spontaneity of that popular style.

The New Melody and Harmony

Nineteenth-century melody is fundamentally vocal in character: composers tried to make the instruments sing. In contrast, early twentieth-century melody is conceived in relation to instruments rather than the voice, abounding in wide leaps and dissonant intervals. Composers have greatly expanded our notion of what a melody is, rejecting the neatly balanced phrase repetitions of earlier music and creating tunes and patterns that would have been inconceivable before the early 1900s.

No single factor sets off early twentieth-century music from that of the past more decisively than the new conceptions of harmony. The triads of traditional harmony gave way to stacked chords with more and more notes added, eventually forming highly dissonant chords of six or seven notes; these created multiple streams of harmony, or **polyharmony**. The new sounds burst the confines of traditional tonality and called for new means of organization, extending or replacing the major-minor system.

The Emancipation of Dissonance

Throughout the history of music, as listeners became increasingly tolerant of new sounds, one factor remained constant: a clear distinction was drawn between dissonance (the element of tension) and consonance (the element of rest). Consonance was the norm, dissonance the temporary disturbance. In many twentieth-century

The infinite looping and interlacing of colorful circles in **Robert Delaunay**'s (1885–1941) *Endless Rhythm* (1934) is suggestive of the new rhythmic energy of the modernist movement.

Irregular lines and sudden leaps, comparable to those found in early modernist melodies, characterize this vista from Arches National Park in Utah.

works, however, tension became the norm. A dissonance could serve even as a final cadence, provided it was less dissonant than the chord that came before; in relation to the greater dissonance, it was judged to be consonant. Twentieth-century composers emancipated dissonance by freeing it from the obligation to resolve to consonance. Their music taught listeners to accept tone combinations whose like had never been heard before.

Orchestration

The rich sonorities of nineteenth-century orchestration gave way to a leaner, brighter sound, played by a smaller orchestra. Instrumental color was used not so much for atmosphere as for bringing out the form and the lines of counterpoint. The string section, with its warm tone, lost its traditional role as the heart of the orchestra; attention was focused on the more penetrating winds. The emphasis on rhythm brought the percussion group into greater prominence, and the piano, which in the Romantic era was preeminently a solo instrument, found a place in the orchestral ensemble.

Modernist musical culture was above all individualistic: in seeking out the new, composers tried to distinguish their approach not just from the past but from other competing visions of the musical future. Musicians belonging to the high-art tradition were also keenly conscious of the growing presence of mass culture, and grappled with the extent to which vernacular styles could coexist with (or be assimilated into) their creative visions. And even as they rejected Romanticism, modernists shared concerns about national identity and artistic independence founded by that revolutionary nineteenth-century movement.

Intersecting lines and bold blocks of color mirror modernist orchestration in this work: *Composition in Red, Yellow, and Blue* (1937–42), by **Piet Mondrian** (1872–1944).

Calculated Shock: Stravinsky and Modernist Multimedia

▶‖ **First, listen . . .**

to the first minute of Stravinsky's *Rite of Spring*, considering the rhythmic flow and the harmony. How does the composer jolt you as a listener? What mood is evoked in this selection?

66 I hold that it was a mistake to consider me a revolutionary. If one only need break habit in order to be labeled a revolutionary, then every artist who has something to say and who in order to say it steps outside the bounds of established convention could be considered revolutionary."

—Igor Stravinsky

I n every human society, dance plays important social, expressive, and/or religious roles. While dancing faded out of most Christian ritual during the Middle Ages, much Western music since has been designed for dancing, whether simple social types or more elaborate choreographies that tell a story. Much multimedia today involves dance (music videos are perhaps the most striking example), which helps to emphasize important aspects of the music and also provides complementary meanings.

THE RITE OF SPRING: COLLABORATIVE MULTIMEDIA

The art of ballet (Chapter 43) was significantly revitalized with the career of the impresario Serge Diaghilev (1872–1929), whose Paris-based dance company, the Ballets Russes, opened up a new chapter in the cultural life of Europe. He surrounded his dancers—the greatest were Vaslav Nijinsky and Tamara Karsavina—with productions worthy of their talents. He invited artists such as Picasso and Braque to paint the scenery, and commissioned the three ballets—*The Firebird*, *Petrushka*, and *The Rite of Spring*—that catapulted Russian composer Igor Stravinsky to fame.

Ballets Russes

KEY POINTS

- Modernist approaches to art, music, and dance were combined by Paris's Ballets Russes under the leadership of impresario Serge Diaghilev.

- Russian composer Igor Stravinsky revitalized rhythm by increasing its complexity—using, for example, **polyrhythms** and **changing meters**.

- Stravinsky's early works, including his ballets *The Firebird*, *Petrushka*, and *The Rite of Spring*, are strongly nationalistic; the last evokes rites of ancient Russia through new instrumental combinations and the percussive use of dissonance, as well as polyrhythmic and polytonal writing.

Valentine Hugo's (1887–1968) sketches of the *Sacrificial Dance* from the ballet *The Rite of Spring*, choreographed by Nijinsky.

The Rite of Spring was designed as a fully integrated modernist multimedia spectacle, with an innovative choreography by Vaslav Nijinsky (whose provocative way with Debussy's music had helped build "buzz" for the Ballets Russes; see p. 255) and experimental stage designs by renowned artist Nicholas Roerich. Nijinsky's choreography was considered as groundbreaking as Stravinsky's music: it involved dancers creating jerky and irregular movements with individual limbs, jumping up and down in place, and forming rotating geometric patterns onstage (see illustrations at left and opposite).

Audience members at the premiere, held on May 29, 1913, at the swanky Parisian Théâtre des Champs-Élysées, had been primed for a work that would push the envelope of dance and music. And reaction to the ballet was immediate that first night: mild protests as soon as the initial dissonant notes sounded soon turned to an uproar. Cries of "Shut up!" were heard around the theater from both supporters and detractors, and one critic barked obscenities at the elegantly dressed ladies who found the work offensive: finally the dancers couldn't hear the music, and the show had to be interrupted. When the dust settled, the reactions ranged from "magnifique" to "abominable."

Yet several more performances were given that season, none of which were greeted with such a hullabaloo. And there is some evidence that the management of the Ballets Russes "seeded" some of the individuals who disrupted the premiere, trying to ensure press coverage. While Stravinsky was publicly incensed with the disrespect that had been shown his music, he must have been aware of its shocking and unsettling quality. The very fact that the work was received negatively by traditionalists made him the darling of the avant-garde, providing crucial support for his rise to prominence as a modernist composer.

Musical Innovation

For more than half a century, Stravinsky reflected several main currents in twentieth-century music. First through his ballets, he was a leader in the revitalization of rhythm in European art music. He is also considered one of the great orchestrators, his music's sonority marked by a polished brightness and a clear texture. *The Rite of Spring*, subtitled "Scenes of Pagan Russia," not only embodies the cult of primitivism that so startled its first-night audience, but also sets forth a new musical language characterized by the percussive use of dissonance, as well as polyrhythms and polytonality.

Though later modernist principles would call for more bare-bones ensembles, here the size of the orchestra is monumental. Stravinsky often uses the full force of the brass and percussion to create a barbaric, primeval sound and gives the strings

Igor Stravinsky (1882–1971)

Born in Russia, Stravinsky grew up in a musical environment and studied composition with Nikolai Rimsky-Korsakov. His music attracted the attention of impressario Serge Diaghilev, who commissioned him to write a series of ballets (*The Firebird, Petrushka, The Rite of Spring*) that launched the young composer to fame. The premiere of *The Rite of Spring* in 1913 was one of the most scandalous in music history. Just a year later, however, when presented at a symphony concert, it was received with enthusiasm and deemed a masterpiece. When war broke out in 1914, Stravinsky took refuge first in Switzerland and then in France. With the onset of the Second World War, he decided to settle his family in Los Angeles; he became an American citizen in 1945. His later concert tours around the world made him the most celebrated figure in twentieth-century music. He died in New York in 1971.

Stravinsky's musical style evolved throughout his career, from the post-Impressionism of *The Firebird* and the primitivism of *The Rite of Spring* to the controlled Classicism of his mature style (*Symphony of Psalms*), and finally to the twelve-tone method of his late works (*Agon*). In his ballets, which are strongly nationalistic, Stravinsky invigorated rhythm, creating a sense of furious and powerful movement. His lustrous orchestrations are so clear that, as Diaghilev remarked, "one can see through [them] with one's ears."

MAJOR WORKS: Orchestral music, including *Symphonies of Wind Instruments* (1920) and *Symphony in Three Movements* (1945) • Ballets, including *L'oiseau de feu* (*The Firebird*, 1910), *Petrushka* (1911), *Le sacre du printemps* (*The Rite of Spring*, 1913), *Agon* (1957) • Operas, including *Oedipus Rex* (1927) • Other theater works, including *L'histoire du soldat* (*The Soldier's Tale*, 1918) • Choral music, including *Symphony of Psalms* (1930) and *Threni: Lamentations of the Prophet Jeremiah* (1958) • Chamber music • Piano music • Songs.

percussive material such as pizzicato and successive down-bow strokes. The overall impact of the orchestration is harsh and loud, with constantly changing colors. Some of Stravinsky's melodies quote Russian folk songs, and the remaining melodic material, often heard in short fragments, uses limited ranges and extended repetition in a folk-song-like manner. Similarly, within each scene, he minimizes harmonic changes through the use of ostinatos, pedal points, and melodic repetition.

The most innovative and influential element of *The Rite of Spring* is the energetic interaction between rhythm and meter. In some scenes, a steady pulse is set up, only to serve as a backdrop for unpredictable accents or melodic entrances. In other passages, the concept of a regular metric pulse is totally abandoned as downbeats occur seemingly at random. With this ballet, Stravinsky freed Western music from the traditional constraints of metric regularity.

The *Introduction*'s writhing bassoon melody, played in its uppermost range, depicts the awakening of the Earth in spring (LG 34). The *Dance of the Youths and Maidens* then erupts with a series of violent chords, with unpredictable accents that veil any clear sense of meter. These dissonant chords alternate with folklike melodies, as the music builds to a loud, densely textured climax.

The Kirov Ballet performs "The Glorification of the Chosen One" from Stravinsky's *Rite of Spring,* with costumes and choreography reconstructed from the original production.

We get a brief respite in the *Game of Abduction*, as another folk melody is introduced; but the level of activity quickly becomes chaotic, replete with seemingly random accents. The primitive atmosphere continues to the culminating *Sacrificial Dance* that closes Part II, during which the young girl—the "chosen one"—dances herself to death in a frenzy.

Stravinsky capitalized on the scandal-success of *The Rite of Spring* by having the work performed only orchestrally, detaching it from its original multimedia project. Indeed, he (deceptively) began to claim that the music had always been the driving reason behind the project: that choreography and staging had been afterthoughts. Today, *The Rite* stands as one of the landmarks in twentieth-century symphonic literature. But it never would have come about had it not been for the Ballets Russes and the opportunity the group gave Stravinsky to collaborate on pathbreaking multimedia.

▶|◀ Reflect

What effect do the unpredictable accents and shifting meters in *The Rite of Spring* have on you? How does the extreme dissonance support the ballet's story? What elements do you think audiences of the time may have found shocking, and why?

YOUR TURN TO EXPLORE

Consider the music videos for one of your favorite songs, or any video of music you consider especially meaningful that adds a story line (not just images of musicians playing). How does the dancing or story line help bring out specific elements of the music? Are there aspects of the music/song that you think are obscured or made less effective by the addition of the video/dancing? How might you change the "video track" to bring out different aspects of the music, perhaps ones that you would find more significant?

LISTENING GUIDE 34   4:34

Stravinsky: *The Rite of Spring (Le sacre du printemps)*, Part I, excerpts

DATE: 1913

GENRE: Ballet (often performed as a concert piece for orchestra)

BASIS: Scenes of pagan Russia

SCENARIO: Nicholas Roerich and Igor Stravinsky

CHOREOGRAPHY: Vaslav Nijinsky

PERFORMED BY: Philharmonia Orchestra; Esa-Pekka Salonen, conductor

Introduction (closing measures)

What to Listen For

Melody Disjunct, floating folk-song melody.

Expression Haunting mood, representing the awakening of the earth; in a very slow tempo (*Lento*).

Timbre Bassoon playing in a high range, with solo clarinets and pizzicato strings.

0:00   Folk tune played by the bassoon, from the opening:

0:12   Pizzicato rhythmic figure in violins:

0:19   Clarinet flourish, followed by a sustained string chord.
0:22   Violin figure returns to establish the meter for the next section.

Dance of the Youths and Maidens

What to Listen For

Melody Russian folk-song melodies alternate with dissonant, nonmelodic blocks of sound.

Rhythm/meter Basic duple pulse with very irregular accents; constant eighth-note motion.

Texture Dense, complex polyphony.

Performing forces Huge orchestra, with expanded brass, woodwind, and percussion sections.

0:30   Strings play harsh, percussive chords, reinforced by eight horns, with unpredictable accents:

0:37   English horn plays the pizzicato motive from the *Introduction*.
0:42   Brief return of the opening accented chords.
0:45   Motives combine with new ideas. Strings continue their chords; English horn repeats its four-note motive; loud brass interruptions and a descending melodic fragment.

continued on next page

1:02   Return of the opening accented chords.

1:10   Bassoon plays syncopated folk melody, over accented string chords:

1:38   Steady eighth-note pulse; a four-note motive alternates between the English horn and trumpet; scurrying motives in the winds and strings, and sustained trills.

1:50   Four-note motive (English horn, then violins) and sustained trills; low string instruments hit the strings with the wood of their bows (*col legno*).

1:58   French horn and flute introduce a folklike melody; the texture thickens with activity:

2:16   Flutes repeat the theme from above.

2:29   New melody appears in trumpets with parallel chords:

2:42   Texture is abruptly reduced; accents of the opening section return; frenetic activity continues.

2:50   Melody in piccolo, then in flutes and strings; unpredictable accents, scurrying activity, and an expanding texture lead to the climax.

Game of Abduction

What to Listen For

Melody Frenetic, scurrying melodic figures and horn calls; a brief folk tune is heard.

Rhythm/meter Meter not established; fast tempo and unpredictable accents.

Harmony Harshly dissonant, with crashing chords.

Timbre Quickly shifting instrumental colors.

3:16   Sustained chords, hurrying string sounds, and syncopated accents.

3:20   Woodwinds and piccolo trumpet introduce a folk theme; texture is dense with constantly changing activity and timbres:

3:29   Horns introduce a new motive, alternating the interval of a fourth:

3:48   New thematic idea, in a homorhythmic texture and changing meters:

3:56   Horn motive returns.

4:07   Timpani and full orchestra alternate strong beats; irregular accents.

4:24   Series of loud chords and a sustained trill end the movement.

American Intersections: Jazz and Blues Traditions

▶❙❙ **First, listen ...**

to the song *Billie's Blues*, focusing on its form (after the very brief introduction). Can you feel a sense of regularity to its structure, with regular cadences? How many sections can you discern?

> ❝ All riddles are blues,
> And all blues are sad,
> And I'm only mentioning
> Some blues I've had."
>
> —Maya Angelou (1928–2014)

Some call jazz the "American classical music," and there's no question that the tradition has been associated with the United States for more than a century. Primary antecedents of jazz were West African musical traditions brought to this continent by slaves and developed (sometimes in secret) to both maintain continuity with a lost homeland and provide a creative distraction from hard labor. But jazz was also heavily influenced by Euro-American vernacular traditions, partly through the tradition of minstrelsy (see Chapter 34), and music from the Americas. Jazz bands played for the popular dances (such as ragtime) that swept the country from the 1890s into the 1940s. As the century wore on, many musicians attempted fruitful "cross-pollinations" between jazz and blues, another tradition rooted in black culture, as well as between jazz and Euro-American cultivated music (as we will see in the case of George Gershwin). Jazz has since taken many forms, and it remains one of the most vibrant and powerful musical traditions of our day, evolving along with the multifaceted culture of the United States.

Painter **Romare Bearden** (1911–1988) pays tribute to singer Bessie Smith in his colorful collage *Empress of the Blues* (1974).

KEY POINTS

- The roots of **jazz** lie in West African traditions, Western popular and art music, and African American ceremonial and work songs.

- **Blues**, a genre based on three-line text stanzas set to a repeating harmonic pattern, was an essential factor in the rise of jazz.

- Louis Armstrong (trumpet player, singer) was associated with **New Orleans–style jazz**, characterized by a small ensemble improvising simultaneously.

- Armstrong's groundbreaking improvisatory style was a huge influence on jazz musicians, including singer Billie Holiday.

- The 1930s saw the advent of the **swing** (or **big-band**) **era** and the brilliantly composed jazz of Duke Ellington.

- By the late 1940s, big-band jazz gave way to smaller group styles, including bebop, cool jazz, and West Coast jazz; Latin American music also influenced later jazz styles.

ROOTS OF JAZZ AND BLUES

Eighteenth-century slaves from Africa's west coast, often called the Ivory or Gold Coast, brought to America such singing styles as call and response and distinctive vocal inflections. In the next century, black music also embraced dancing and the singing of **work songs** (communal songs that synchronized the rhythm of work), **ring shouts** (religious rituals that involved moving counterclockwise in a circle while praying, singing, and clapping hands), and **spirituals**. The art of storytelling through music and praise singing (glorifying deities or royalty) were other traditions retained by slaves that contributed to the rich African American repertories.

In the years after the Civil War, a new style of music arose in the South, especially in the Mississippi Delta: country, or rural, blues, performed by a male singer and, by the turn of the century, accompanied by a steel-string guitar. This music voiced the difficulties of everyday life. A **blues text** typically consists of a three-line stanza whose first two lines are identical. The vocal lines featured melodic "pitch bending," or **blue notes**, sung over standard harmonic progressions (**chord changes**)—usually twelve (or occasionally sixteen) bars in length. Among the greatest blues singers were Charlie Patton (c. 1891–1934), Bessie Smith (1894–1937), and, more recently, B. B. King ("King of the Blues," 1925–2015). Blues style derives from the work songs of Southern blacks, but may also owe some elements to the folk songs of poor Euro-Americans in the Southern Appalachians—one example of the complexity of identifying purely African American musical traditions.

Blue notes

New Orleans Jazz

The sheet-music cover for the popular fox trot *La jazzbandette* (1921), published in Paris.

Blues was an essential factor in the development of the **New Orleans jazz** tradition. This city, which had long facilitated interaction across races and cultures, was where jazz gained momentum through the fusion of **ragtime** (a highly syncopated dance style) and blues with other traditional styles—spirituals, work songs, and ring shouts, but also Caribbean and Euro-American styles. There, in Congo Square, slaves met in the pre–Civil War era to dance to the accompaniment of drums, gourds, mouth harps, and banjos. Their music featured a strong underlying pulse with syncopations and polyrhythm. Melodies incorporated African-derived techniques such as rhythmic interjections, vocal glides, and percussive sounds made with the tongue and throat, and were often set in a musical scale with the lowered third, fifth, or seventh of a major scale.

New Orleans ensembles depended on the players' improvisation to create a polyphonic texture. One of the greats of New Orleans jazz was trumpet player and singer Louis "Satchmo" Armstrong (1901–1971), a brilliant improviser who transformed jazz into a solo art that presented improvised fantasias on chord changes. Armstrong's instrumental-like approach to singing (**scat-singing**), his distinctive inflections, and his improvisatory style were highly influential to jazz vocalists, including Billie Holiday, one of the leading singers in jazz history.

Billie Holiday (1915–1959)

Known as Lady Day, Holiday was born in Philadelphia and grew up in Baltimore. In 1928, with barely any formal education, she moved to New York, where she probably worked as a prostitute. Around 1930, Holiday began singing at clubs in Brooklyn and Harlem, and was discovered three years later by a talent scout who arranged for her to record with the white clarinetist Benny Goodman. This first break earned her $35.

By 1935, Holiday was recording with some of the best jazz musicians of her day. As her popularity increased, she was featured with several prominent big bands—making her one of the first black singers to break the color barrier and sing in public with a white orchestra. She recorded her most famous song in 1939—*Strange Fruit*, about a Southern lynching. With its horrible images of blacks dangling from trees, the song resonated with blacks and whites alike and became a powerful social commentary on black identity and equality.

By the 1940s, Holiday's life had deteriorated, the result of alcohol, drug abuse, and ill-chosen relationships with abusive men. She began using opium and heroin, and was jailed on drug charges in 1947. Her health—and her voice—suffered because of her addictions, although she still made a number of memorable recordings. She died of cirrhosis of the liver in 1959, at the age of forty-four.

SELECTED RECORDINGS: *God Bless the Child* and *Billie's Blues*, both on the album *Lady Day: The Best of Billie Holiday; Fine & Mellow* and *Strange Fruit*, on the album *Strange Fruit*.

THE JAZZ SINGER BILLIE HOLIDAY

Holiday had a unique talent that was immediately recognized by other musicians. "You never heard singing so slow, so lazy, with such a drawl," one bandleader reminisced. Although she had never received formal vocal training, she had a remarkable sense of pitch and a flawless delivery—a style she learned from listening to her two idols, Bessie Smith and Louis Armstrong. We will hear a song that Holiday wrote and recorded in 1936, *Billie's Blues* (LG 35), and performed regularly throughout her career. It's a twelve-bar blues, with a short introduction and six choruses—a **chorus** is a single statement of a melodic-harmonic pattern, like a twelve-bar blues or thirty-two-bar popular song—some of which are instrumental. The first verse (chorus 2) is a typical three-line strophe, but as the work progresses, the form becomes freer. In the vocal choruses, Holiday demonstrates her masterful rhythmic flexibility and talent for jazz embellishments (scoops and dips on notes). In this performance, we hear Artie Shaw's creative clarinet improvisations and Bunny Berigan's earthy, "gutbucket" trumpet playing (displaying an unrestrained, raspy quality of tone).

Holiday's song exemplifies the intersection between jazz and blues, and also the connection between jazz and dance, since the regular phrases and repeating structure are perfectly suited to the popular dances of the time. Most jazz of the first half of the 1900s was performed in dance clubs, and patrons would be as likely to dance to Holiday's song as they would to listen (opposite).

In the 1930s and 40s, early jazz gave way to the **swing**, or **big-band**, **era**. Bands needed arranged and composed music—that is, written down, rather than

Billie Holiday, with jazz trumpeter Louis Armstrong in the 1947 film *New Orleans*.

Big-band jazz

improvised—and one musician who played a major role in its development was Edward Kennedy "Duke" Ellington (1899–1974), whose group first went on the road in 1932 and remained popular until his death. His unique big-band style of jazz won over a wide audience, both black and white, who danced away their cares in clubs and hotel ballrooms across the country.

In 1939, Ellington began a collaboration with Billy Strayhorn (1915–1967), a classically trained pianist who served as an arranger and composer for the band; together they achieved unparalleled success with their music. Their most notable collaboration, *Take the A Train*, became the band's signature tune.

LISTENING GUIDE 35 2:38

Holiday: *Billie's Blues*

DATE: Recorded 1936

GENRE: 12-bar blues

PERFORMED BY: Billie Holiday, vocal; Bunny Berigan, trumpet; Artie Shaw, clarinet; Joe Bushkin, piano; Dick McDonough, guitar; Pete Peterson, bass; Cozy Cole, drums

What to Listen For

Melody Syncopated lines, with pitch inflections; laid-back feeling, free improvisations.

Harmony Same progression of chords (I-IV-I-V-I) for each chorus.

Form 12-bar blues (introduction and six choruses); choruses 2, 3, and 6 are vocal.

Performing forces Holiday, vocal; with trumpet, clarinet, piano, guitar, string bass, and drums.

0:00	**Introduction** (4 bars)—bass, guitar, and piano.	
0:07	**Chorus 1**—ensemble (12 bars).	
0:32	**Chorus 2**—vocal (12 bars):	Lord, I love my man . . .
		[repeated text line]
		But when he mistreats me . . .

Opening of first vocal chorus, showing syncopated line, with upward slide at the end:

0:56	**Chorus 3**—vocal (12 bars):	My man wouldn' gimme . . .
		[new text without repeated lines]
1:21	**Chorus 4**—solo clarinet improvisation (12 bars).	
1:45	**Chorus 5**—solo trumpet improvisation (12 bars).	
2:11	**Chorus 6**—vocal (12 bars):	Some men like me . . .
		[new text without repeated lines]

BEBOP, COOL, LATIN JAZZ

By the end of the 1940s, musicians were rebelling against big-band jazz and developing new styles. **Bebop** (also known as **bop**) was an invented word mimicking the two-note trademark phrase of this new style of fast tempos and complex harmonies. Trumpeter Dizzy Gillespie (right), saxophonist Charlie Parker, and pianist Thelonious Monk were among the leaders of the bebop movement in the 1940s. Over the next two decades, the term "bebop" came to include sub-styles such as cool jazz, West Coast jazz, hard bop, and soul jazz. Trumpeter Miles Davis was the principal exponent of **cool jazz**, a laid-back style characterized by dense harmonies, lowered levels of volume, moderate tempos, and a new lyricism. **West Coast jazz** was a small-group, cool-jazz style featuring mixed timbres (one instrument for each color, often without piano) and contrapuntal improvisations.

Dizzy Gillespie playing his custom-made trumpet, with raised bell.

Latin American music has always been highly influential in the development of jazz, chiefly its dance rhythms and percussion instruments (for example, conga drum, bongos, and cowbells). In the 1930s and 40s, bandleaders such as Xavier Cugat brought Latin dance music—especially the rumba—into the mainstream. Duke Ellington's band recorded two hit Latin numbers: *Caravan* (1937, featuring Puerto Rican trombonist Juan Tizol), and *Conga Brava* (1940). Latin elements were integral to the bebop style of the late 1940s, and the next decades saw strong Brazilian as well as Cuban influences on jazz. We will see that these influences were significant in musical theater as well, particularly in the shows of Leonard Bernstein (Chapter 53).

In the last century, many strands of jazz have developed, and there are controversies about whether some of them can legitimately be labeled jazz. There is no question, however, that jazz is among the most vibrant and original North American contributions to the modern musical soundscape.

▶️◀ Reflect

Count the measures of this twelve-bar blues carefully as you listen to each chorus, both vocal and instrumental. How does this structure provide a sense of predictability? How do the performers create surprise within the structure, and what effect does this have on you?

YOUR TURN TO EXPLORE

Find an example of a jazz performance by one of the renowned singers of the twentieth century (like Ella Fitzgerald or Louis Armstrong) or a more recent jazz singer (like Diana Krall). How does the singer's approach to syncopation and blue notes and other elaborations compare with the one taken by Holiday in *Billie's Blues?* How do the instrumentalists interact with the singer? How do any extended instrumental solos compare with the ones on our recording? If you find a video recording, what is the venue for the performance (concert hall, dance club?), and how is the performer interacting with the audience (and what is the audience response)?

Modern America: Still and Musical Modernism in the United States

▶‖ **First, listen . . .**

to the first minute of the third movement of Still's Suite for Violin and Piano, focusing on the melody and harmony. How does Still's approach to melody and harmony sound different from those you have learned to recognize? Which elements help give this style its unique sound?

H ow can or should music reflect the identity of a composer? Romanticism introduced the ideal of autobiographical expression by the creative individual, and nationalism added the question of group identity, leaving artists to struggle with striking a balance between those two mandates. The 1920s and 30s were a time when African American artists in many media banded together to identify creative outlets for blacks that would both pay tribute to their heritage and recognize individual excellence regardless of race or ethnicity. One of the most prominent and successful musicians who joined this effort, William Grant Still, is now regarded as a pioneer both in the search for a "modern American sound" and in opening a wider range of musical opportunities for African Americans.

In His Own Words

66 Life is for the living,
Death is for the dead,
Let life be like music,
And death a note unsaid."

—Langston Hughes

THE HARLEM RENAISSANCE

In the early 1900s, economic opportunity brought increasing numbers of African Americans to New York City, and specifically to the northern part of Manhattan called Harlem. By the beginning of the economic boom of the 1920s, a contemporary poet referred to Harlem proudly as "not merely a Negro colony or community, [but] a city within a city, the greatest Negro city in the world." Building on a growing sense of a new black cultural identity, a book of essays called *The*

KEY POINTS

- American composers of the early twentieth century sought to define a unique tradition of American modernism.

- The **Harlem Renaissance** was a cultural movement in the 1920s and 30s that highlighted African American contributions to the country's cultural heritage.

- African American composer William Grant Still broke numerous racial barriers in the art-music tradition. His Suite for Violin and Piano looks to three black visual artists for inspiration.

William Grant Still (1895–1978)

Still grew up in Little Rock, Arkansas. His parents, both educators, encouraged his early music studies on violin. He left college to work as a professional musician in Memphis and then New York, earning a reputation as an arranger for radio and musical theater, while continuing his classical music studies with French-born composer Edgard Varèse. Still deliberately moved away from the avant-garde, however, to find his original voice in the music of his black cultural heritage.

His first symphony, the *Afro-American*, was premiered in 1931 by the Rochester Philharmonic Orchestra: the first symphony by an African American composer to be performed by a major American orchestra. The symphony brought him numerous commissions from major orchestras, including the New York Philharmonic. In 1934, he won a Guggenheim Fellowship and moved to Los Angeles, where he wrote film and television scores. An opera, *Troubled Island*, was produced by the New York City Opera in 1949, marking another first for an African American composer. Still was recognized with many honorary degrees during his last years, and collaborated on music for such popular TV series as *Gunsmoke* and *Perry Mason*. He remained in Los Angeles until his death in 1978. In his music, Still looked to writers and artists of the Harlem Renaissance for inspiration, including the renowned poet Langston Hughes, whose libretto he set for *Troubled Island*, on the struggles of the Haitian people.

MAJOR WORKS: Orchestral music, including four symphonies (No. 1, *Afro-American Symphony*, 1930) • Orchestral suites • Film scores • Stage works, including four ballets (*La Guiablesse*, 1927; *Sahdji*, 1930) • Eight operas, including *Troubled Island* (1937–49) • Chamber music, including Suite for Violin and Piano (1943) • Vocal music, including *Songs of Separation* (1949) and spiritual arrangements • Piano music • Choral music.

New Negro was published in 1925, edited by philosopher Alain Locke, a Harvard graduate who became the first African American Rhodes scholar. Locke and the other authors of *The New Negro* encouraged their fellow black artists to look to Africa for inspiration on how to shape their American future, and the essays spoke about racial equality and pride in black cultural heritage.

The ideas from the essays in *The New Negro* are credited with sparking the so-called **Harlem Renaissance**, a literary, artistic, and sociological movement that highlighted African American intellectual life in the 1920s and 30s. The most important literary figure associated with the movement was Langston Hughes (1902–1967), a poet and novelist whose works, depicting the struggles of working-class blacks, radiated black pride. A frequent visitor to the Harlem jazz clubs, Hughes wrote verse that imitated the rhythms and flow of jazz, thus devising a new kind of poetry that was understood as uniquely African American. Most jazz musicians, including Duke Ellington and Billie Holiday (Chapter 46), gained early recognition performing in Harlem clubs as well, one of which was the famous Cotton Club. Black musicians uniformly rejected the stereotyped images that had been popular in minstrel shows and worked to break down the long-standing prejudice against all black artists. Among these crusaders was William Grant Still, whose artistic efforts were focused on fashioning an art-music tradition that would fuse modernist and African American creative concerns.

Sargent Johnson (1888–1967) focused his art on African American racial identity, as in *Mother and Child* (c. 1932; chalk on paper).

Still's Suite for Violin and Piano

Gamin, a sculpture by **Augusta Savage** (1892–1962). Savage played a significant role in the Harlem Renaissance.

In choosing the genre of the suite, which had long been part of the European dance and programmatic tradition, Still was able to draw on an established genre (one that reflected the modernist neo-Classical trend) and also to evoke images that he felt exemplified the artistic efforts of black America in a progressive way. He based each movement on a different artwork by African American artists. The spirited first movement was inspired by the sculpture *African Dancer* by Richmond Barthé, a noted Harlem Renaissance artist. The second movement evokes the expressive mood of *Mother and Child* by Sargent Johnson (p. 277), one of the first Californian black artists to achieve fame. And the rhythmically charged closing movement reflects the impish humor of *Gamin* by Augusta Savage, the most prominent African American woman artist of her day. Her sculpture (at left) captures the confident image of a street-smart kid in Harlem ("gamin" suggests a street urchin).

The movements of the suite all employ modal harmonies and melodies featuring lowered thirds and sevenths, typical of the blues. Throughout his career, Still favored blues as source material for his music, explaining that "they, unlike spirituals, do not exhibit the influence of Caucasian music." The last movement of the suite (LG 36) zips along with a flashy and syncopated violin line accompanied by an insistent bass that resembles the jazz piano style known as **stride**. Sometimes called "Harlem stride piano," this style evolved from ragtime and features a regular four-beat pulse with right-hand chords on the second and fourth beats. The movement unfolds in sections, sometimes engaging the piano and violin in a call-and-response exchange, but it keeps returning to the opening exuberant idea, varied with ornamentation and dazzling glissandos in the violin.

Not all members of the concert music establishment embraced blues and jazz as compositional resources. And while the Harlem Renaissance was a powerful cultural moment for the growth of black cultural prestige, its supporters were more interested in fostering musical traditions that they understood as more thoroughly African American—blues, jazz, and spirituals—than in encouraging the development of modernist art music. Today there are still too few African Americans involved in shaping the idea of an American art-music tradition; though as the twenty-first century progresses, a lively interaction of musical styles and repertories is helping to bring a wider range of voices into that dialogue.

▶|◀ Reflect

How successful do you think Still was in combining elements of art music and popular music? How do you think the sculpture *Gamin* influenced his idea of a "program" for this movement?

YOUR TURN TO EXPLORE

Seek out works by African American art-music composers of the twentieth and twenty-first centuries. (Three examples are Will Marion Cook, Undine Smith Moore, and Olly Wilson; how might you go about finding more?) How have these individuals chosen to incorporate their heritage into their compositions? Are their approaches to racial/ethnic heritage different from Still's, or from the way European or Euro-American composers have used their own heritage as inspiration?

LISTENING GUIDE 36 2:07

Still: Suite for Violin and Piano, III

DATE: 1943

GENRE: Suite for violin and piano

PERFORMED BY: Lynn Chang, violin; Vivian Taylor, piano

MOVEMENTS: I. Majestically and vigorously (based on Richmond Barthé's *African Dancer*)

II. Slowly and expressively (based on Sargent Johnson's *Mother and Child*)

III. Rhythmically and humorously (based on Augusta Savage's *Gamin*)

III: Rhythmically and humorously

What to Listen For

Melody Bluesy, short, syncopated ideas, with flatted third and seventh scale degrees; ideas exchanged between violin and piano.

Harmony Modal, with blues chords; piano plays a "stride" bass and insistent ostinatos.

Expression Playful and humorous; evokes image of the cocky street kid depicted in the sculpture.

0:00   Four-measure introduction in piano, with ostinato bass and offbeat chords.

0:05   Violin enters with a syncopated line, a four-measure idea in fragments, with stride piano accompaniment:

0:26   Rising line to a new syncopated violin idea, accompanied by a syncopated, more active piano part.

0:35   Low-range, repeated-note idea in violin, against moving piano line.

0:45   Piano takes over low-range melody, with violin playing double stops.

0:56   Opening motive returns, varied, in violin; piano is more syncopated.

1:06   Humorous repeated-note exchange between piano and violin.

1:17   Opening motive returns in violin, includes glissando and more active piano accompaniment.

1:27   Repeated-note idea is developed in violin.

1:38   Recapitulation of opening, including the brief piano introduction.

1:59   **Coda**, with rising violin line, then triumphant double-stop chords and glissando to the last chord.

Modern Experiments: Gershwin and "Cultivated Jazz"

66 Jazz has contributed an enduring value to America in the sense that it has expressed ourselves."

—George Gershwin

▶❘❘ First, listen ...

to Gershwin's *Rhapsody in Blue,* and focus on the main melodies. How many do you hear, and how would you describe the differences between them?

In His Own Words

66 My *Rhapsody in Blue* represents what I have been striving for since my earliest composition. I wanted to show that jazz is an idiom not to be limited to a mere song and chorus. . . . Jazz is not merely a dance; it comprises bigger themes and purposes. It may have the quality of an epic."

—*George Gershwin*

Throughout our survey so far, we have seen how music is an essentially collaborative art, and this is nowhere more true than in the multifaceted tradition of jazz, which is defined primarily around performers adding their distinctive interpretations to a preexisting musical framework. Some songs have become jazz "standards," attracting performers because of their memorable melodies and harmonic structures, and resulting in hundreds or even thousands of creative reworkings. Among the most talented composers of such tunes was George Gershwin, one of several musicians of the mid-1900s (both African American and Euro-American) who attempted to bring the jazz tradition forward not only as a booming commercial enterprise but also as a distinctive kind of cultivated music. Gershwin's all-too-short life was dedicated to the proposition that jazz could be as expressive an art form as any European-derived tradition; his "cultivated jazz" compositions were not only creatively outstanding but also financially successful and influential on other musicians. Yet Gershwin was criticized both for "whitewashing" an African American tradition and for introducing commercial music into the lofty halls of art—joining a long, still-continuing line of artists who have been accused of "selling out" the purity of a musical heritage.

FROM SONG PLUGGING TO THE CONCERT HALL

Gershwin first broke into the music business as a "song plugger" who demonstrated and sold sheet music on New York's Tin Pan Alley. Many of those songs made some reference to ragtime or jazz, though the songs themselves followed structural and melodic conventions

KEY POINTS

- George Gershwin built international fame through his Tin Pan Alley songs, musical theater productions, and "jazzy" compositional and performance style.

- Seeking to unite elements of jazz and the European concert tradition, Gershwin composed several hybrid works, including his very popular *Rhapsody in Blue.*

George Gershwin (1898–1937)

Gershwin grew up in Manhattan, where he worked for a Tin Pan Alley publisher, playing and singing new releases for customers. "This is American music," he told one of his teachers. "This is the kind of music I want to write." He had his first big hit in 1920, with the song *Swanee*, recorded by Al Jolson.

During the 1920s, Gershwin won international acclaim with *Rhapsody in Blue*, premiered in 1924 by the Paul Whiteman Orchestra. This was followed by his *Concerto in F* and the tone poem *An American in Paris*. He also had a string of hit musicals, beginning with *Lady, Be Good* (1924), his first collaboration with his brother Ira, who wrote many of his song lyrics. Gershwin wrote enduring film scores, including *Shall We Dance* (featuring the song *They Can't Take That Away from Me*), starring Fred Astaire and Ginger Rogers. His folk opera *Porgy and Bess* is perhaps his masterpiece. He died of a brain tumor in 1937, at not quite thirty-nine.

In his music, Gershwin achieves an appealing rhythmic vitality through the use of syncopation, blue notes, and an "oom-pah" accompaniment typical of jazz piano style. His harmonic language extends from diatonic to very chromatic, with sudden shifts in tonality. His melodies range from declamatory to highly lyrical, and his forms are typical blues and song structures. No master has achieved this union of styles—popular and classical, vernacular and art—more successfully than Gershwin.

MAJOR WORKS: Orchestral works, including *Rhapsody in Blue* (1924, for piano and jazz band), *Concerto in F* (1925), and *An American in Paris* (1928) • Piano music • More than 30 stage works, including *Lady, Be Good* (1924), *Girl Crazy* (1930), *Of Thee I Sing* (1931), and *Porgy and Bess* (1935) • Songs for films, including *Shall We Dance* (1937) • Other songs (such as *Swanee, 'S Wonderful, Embraceable You, The Man I Love*).

similar to the Anglo-American parlor songs of Foster (Chapter 34) and other nineteenth-century songwriters.

Gershwin, a talented pianist, became familiar with a variety of techniques developed by African American jazz performers, and gained renown for his ability to play songs in a particularly effective and jazzy way—and this afforded opportunities to him as a white musician that black musicians could not enjoy in the 1920s. As Gershwin began writing his own Broadway / Tin Pan Alley songs, he incorporated syncopations and harmonic variations that closely resembled improvised jazz. As a result, his songs became among the most commercially and artistically successful in the entire Tin Pan Alley repertory.

Not content with his commercial success, and also inspired by the goals of the Harlem Renaissance (p. 276), Gershwin joined those who sought to expand jazz into the cultivated sphere. A number of his instrumental works were both groundbreaking and much loved from their premiere—most notably the *Rhapsody in Blue*, which Gershwin performed at a concert entitled "An Experiment in Modern Music," held at New York City's Aeolian Hall on Lincoln's birthday, February 12, in 1924.

The concert was the brainchild of bandleader Paul Whiteman (1890–1967), whose jazz-band orchestra had become extremely popular in the early 1920s for its carefully planned and coordinated ensemble sound. Whiteman was among

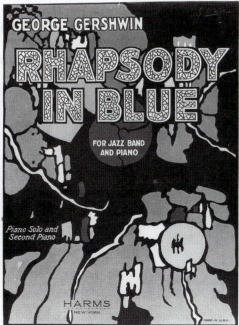

Cover for the jazz-band version of *Rhapsody in Blue*.

the leading advocates for the status of jazz as a uniquely American art music, and he enlisted Gershwin to write a new work to provide the finale of a concert that would demonstrate the cultivated status of jazz. The resulting *Rhapsody* was immediately hailed as the highlight.

RHAPSODY IN BLUE: TUNES COLLABORATIVELY DEVELOPED

Gershwin's accounts of how he created the *Rhapsody* became legendary: he told of having envisioned the work "on the train, with its steely rhythms, its rattlety-bang. . . . I suddenly heard, even saw on paper, the complete construction of the *Rhapsody*, from beginning to end." This image of inspired creativity is firmly in keeping with the ideals of individual genius we have seen associated with nineteenth-century heroic composers.

But the *Rhapsody* was a collaborative endeavor from the start: not only was it tailor-created for the Whiteman Orchestra (see below), it was also strongly influenced by the person responsible for the unique Whiteman sound: Ferde Grofé (1892–1972), principal arranger for the ensemble. There is still extensive debate about how much Grofé added to Gershwin's ideas—did he just assign Gershwin's notes to specific instruments, or did he tweak the music to tailor-fit the ensemble he knew so well, as had been his custom?

The *Rhapsody* is based on six musical ideas—five themes and a short motive (LG 37)—elaborated using different jazz performing conventions of the time, with the piano having the lion's share of the elaboration: like Mozart with his own concertos, Gershwin gave himself the platform to demonstrate his creativity in a semi-composed, semi-improvised framework. In some ways the work is very like a piano concerto—dialogue between the soloist and the larger ensemble, recurring stable and recognizable themes alternating with more fanciful and unpredictable virtuosity. In terms of overall form, however, it also evokes the kind of dance-hall medley that Gershwin would have associated with jazz performances of his Tin Pan Alley hits.

Paul Whiteman and his jazz-band orchestra, which premiered *Rhapsody in Blue* in 1924.

In order to make the *Rhapsody* more marketable through the sale of sheet music, Grofé subsequently arranged it for theater orchestra and eventually for full symphony orchestra, which is the version most commonly performed today. As Grofé moved further away from the original Whiteman scoring, the *Rhapsody* became more polished in sound quality; Gershwin's melodic and harmonic ideas remained, but the scrappy dance-band timbre was left behind.

The question of whether the *Rhapsody in Blue* truly is jazz has been debated from the day it was premiered. Since there have been many different arrangements and reinterpretations beyond the official Grofé scores, we might better ask whether a given performance (or arrangement) is in keeping with one of the several strands of music-making that have been described as jazz over the last century.

LISTENING GUIDE 37

 16:12

Gershwin: *Rhapsody in Blue*

DATE: Premiered 1924; reorchestrated by Ferde Grofé 1926, 1942

GENRE: Concerto-like, a one-movement "rhapsody"

PERFORMED BY: Philippe Entremont, piano; Philadelphia Orchestra; Eugene Ormandy, conductor

What to Listen For

Melody Bluesy, stepwise tunes alternate with more jagged and forceful disjunct ideas.

Harmony Consonant and tonal overall, incorporating the blues scale.

Form Recurring themes and motives, with some similarities to Baroque ritornello form.

Expression Draws on ragtime, blues, and jazz conventions to create a lively dialogue between piano and orchestra.

0:00   The opening clarinet solo, characterized by a unique glissando into the high range, leads into the *ritornello* theme:

0:07   *Ritornello* theme: bluesy, syncopated melody; clarinet answered by low brass.

0:35   *Stride* theme: chromatic, repeated notes heard first in the brass:

0:47   *Ritornello* theme featuring a solo "wah-wah" muted trumpet (with a rubber plunger), answered by the piano's *tag* motive:

1:01   *Ritornello* theme in full orchestra.
1:09   Piano solo builds on themes/motives introduced to this point, free and cadenza-like.
1:52   *Ritornello* theme in piano alternates with low woodwinds.
2:16   Piano solo builds again on themes/motives, with free tempo shifts.
3:09   *Ritornello* theme in full orchestra.
3:44   New: the broad *train* theme, led by trumpets in octaves and featuring flutter-tonguing (player's tongue is fluttered while blowing into the instrument):

continued on next page

4:29   *Stride* theme returns in full orchestra.

4:55   Tempo slows, solo clarinet is answered by a wah-wah muted trumpet.

5:18   New: the *shuffle* theme in full orchestra, played *marcato*:

6:17   Piano solo builds on the *stride* theme, horns join with a countermelody.

7:58   *Ritornello* theme in piano is followed by the *tag* motive.

8:10   *Ritornello* theme heard quietly in oboes and bassoons, piano and strings support it with clear downbeats.

8:35   Extended piano solo focusing on the *shuffle* theme.

10:50   New: expansive *love* theme in strings and winds, with a chromatic countertheme first in brass, then piano:

12:33   Extended piano solo elaborates on the *love* theme, with virtuoso passagework.

14:21   Brass join piano in varying the *love* theme, building to . . .

15:15   *Stride* theme in full orchestra.

15:46   *Ritornello* theme in full orchestra, piano answers with the *tag* motive.

▶|◀ Reflect

How do you think *Rhapsody in Blue* relates to jazz and the blues? What about its characteristics might lead you to connect it to an orchestral genre like a concerto?

YOUR TURN TO EXPLORE

Find a recording of a Tin Pan Alley song by Gershwin (*I Got Rhythm, 'S Wonderful, But Not for Me, The Man I Love,* or another) and compare it with the recording of *Billie's Blues.* What musical similiarities do you hear (in blue notes, syncopation, other melodic or rhythmic elements), and what differences? Do you think it's legitimate to think of Gershwin's compositions as jazz? Why or why not? Why might it matter whether this is jazz, and to whom?

Sounds American: Copland and Musical Nationalism in the United States

▶‖ **First, listen ...**

to section 7 from Copland's *Appalachian Spring,* and focus on the form (the phrase structure) of the tune. How is the form treated throughout?

> 66 I no longer feel the need of seeking out conscious Americanism. Because we live here and work here, we can be certain that when our music is mature it will also be American in quality."
>
> —Aaron Copland

Patriotism has been an essential part of national identity since democracies began to replace authoritarian states in the late 1700s. As a nation founded explicitly on ideals of democracy, the United States has rightly fostered pride in the principles that distinguish it from other countries. But as a nation of immigrants with diverse cultural heritages, part of a large continent that can equally legitimately claim the label "America," we have also struggled to define the shifting nature of American identity (understood as a quality that all U.S. citizens have in common). Music has always played a part in that definition, and some of the most compelling American sounds have emerged from attempts to integrate vernacular musical traditions with music that aims at a higher quality of the spirit.

Nonconcert traditions such as parlor songs (Chapter 34), brass band marches, and worship songs played vital roles in North American musical life of the late 1800s. Rural folk traditions were thought to be closely linked to the American spirit, and the composer who most successfully transformed these traditions into a national sound was Aaron Copland.

COPLAND AND THE AMERICAN ORCHESTRAL SOUNDSCAPE

Copland is one of America's greatest twentieth-century composers. Few have been able to capture the spirit of this country so successfully—his well-crafted and classically proportioned works have an immediate appeal. His ballet suites

KEY POINTS

- Several modernist composers in the United States attempted to craft a musical style that would reflect a truly "American" sound.

- Aaron Copland used the early American song *Simple Gifts* in his famous ballet *Appalachian Spring,* commissioned by the great choreographer/dancer Martha Graham.

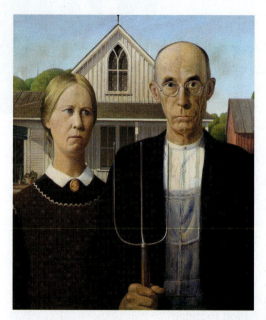

American Gothic, by **Grant Wood** (1891–1942), is an example of regionalism, celebrating rural life in the United States.

are quintessentially American in their portrayal of rural life (*Appalachian Spring)* and the Far West (*Rodeo* and *Billy the Kid)*.

Copland came self-consciously to an American sound: born in New York of Jewish immigrant parents, he trained in Europe with proponents of early twentieth-century modernism, then returned to the United States during the Great Depression of the 1930s and espoused the ideal that art should "serve the American people" during times of economic and social struggle. His new "American modernist" style was designed to have wide appeal and be "useful" in a variety of contexts (radio, film, theater). In keeping with this ideal, Copland wrote incidental music for plays and scores for significant films that spoke to the American condition during the Depression, such as *Of Mice and Men* (1939) and *Our Town* (1940).

While Copland admired jazz and incorporated it in his early works, his American style was rooted primarily in Appalachian and other Anglo-American folk melodies (as well as Mexican folk melodies). He also cited Stravinsky's startling approach to rhythm and orchestration as a basic influence. Like Stravinsky's early ballets, some of Copland's most successful compositions involved a collaboration with prominent dancers and choreographers, who were also seeking to establish a genuinely American tradition of modern dance.

Aaron Copland (1900–1990)

Copland was born in Brooklyn, New York, and during his early twenties studied in Paris with the famous teacher Nadia Boulanger. After his return from Paris, he wrote works in jazz and neo-Classical styles, but at the same time realized that a new public for contemporary music was being created by the radio and phonograph and film scores: "It made no sense to ignore them and to continue writing as if they did not exist."

The 1930s and 40s saw the creation of works that established Copland's popularity. *El Salón México* (1936) is an orchestral piece based on Mexican melodies and rhythms. His three ballets—*Billy the Kid, Rodeo,* and *Appalachian Spring*—continue to delight international audiences. Among his film scores are two on novels by John Steinbeck and William Wyler's *The Heiress,* which brought him an Academy Award. He wrote two important works during wartime: *A Lincoln Portrait,* for speaker and orchestra,

with texts drawn from Lincoln's speeches, and the Third Symphony. Despite his evident nationalism, Copland was investigated in the 1950s as a supporter of the Communist Party, and in 1953 he was removed from the inaugural ceremonies for President Eisenhower as a result of his leftist politics. In the 1960s, Copland demonstrated that he could also handle twelve-tone techniques when he wrote his powerful *Connotations for Orchestra.*

MAJOR WORKS: Orchestral music, including three symphonies, a piano concerto, *El Salón México* (1936), *A Lincoln Portrait* (1942), *Fanfare for the Common Man* (1942) • Ballets, including *Billy the Kid* (1938), *Rodeo* (1942), and *Appalachian Spring* (1944) • Operas, including *The Tender Land* (1954) • Film scores, including *Of Mice and Men* (1939), *Our Town* (1940), *The Red Pony* (1948), and *The Heiress* (1948) • Piano music • Chamber music • Choral music • Songs.

Appalachian Spring

Among Copland's ballets, *Appalachian Spring* is perhaps his best known, written in collaboration with the celebrated choreographer Martha Graham (1894–1991), who also danced the lead. Copland noted that when he wrote the music, he took into account Graham's unique choreographic style: "She's unquestionably very American: there's something prim and restrained, simple yet strong, about her, which one tends to think of as American." The ballet portrays "a pioneer celebration in spring around a newly built farmhouse in the Pennsylvania hills in the early part of the nineteenth century. The bride-to-be and the young farmer-husband enact the emotions, joyful and apprehensive, their new partnership invites." The ballet, which premiered in 1944 in Washington, D.C., was given new life in Copland's popular 1945 orchestral suite, set in seven sections.

The opening section of the suite introduces the characters in the ballet with a serene, ascending motive that evokes the first hint of daybreak over the vast horizon (LG 38). In the famous seventh part of the work, we hear the well-known early American song *Simple Gifts* ("'Tis the gift to be simple"), a tune associated with the Shaker religious sect, known for rituals that included spinning around and dancing (see below). This simple, folklike tune is designed to provide a quintessential American sound; Copland sets it in a clear-cut theme and variations, with a colorful orchestration tinged with gentle dissonance. The flowing tune takes on several guises, shaded by changing timbres, keys, and tempos.

Copland's music was quickly embraced as a truly American orchestral sound. It continues to be widely heard at events (or even in commercials!) that aim to emphasize national pride, as well as incorporated (and imitated) in movie scenes that illustrate the grandeur of the West. The America that his music envisions is a rural one, connected to the land and its traditions; it is also mostly an Anglo America, since the Appalachian tunes he employs have their roots in English folk music. Copland's goal was to create an inclusive soundscape for the United States; and his music is still a powerful presence in the cultural life of the nation.

Martha Graham dancing in the ballet *Appalachian Spring*.

Simple Gifts

Members of the Protestant Shaker sect in a dance. Lithograph by **Nathaniel Currier** (1813–1888).

▶|◀ Reflect

How many times did you hear the main melody played in this theme and variations? What techniques does Copland employ to maintain your interest as a listener? What kind of dancing can you imagine in this part of the ballet?

YOUR TURN TO EXPLORE

Identify two musical works (songs or any other genre) that you consider to be self-consciously American: not only the text, but the music as well. What elements of each work project its American identity? What kind of America does each work suggest—what kinds of individuals or attitudes or backgrounds does it include, and what kinds does it leave out? What parallels and contradictions can you find between the two different versions of "musical American-ness"?

LISTENING GUIDE 38   5:45

Copland: *Appalachian Spring*, excerpts

DATE: 1944; orchestral suite, 1945

GENRE: Ballet suite in seven sections

PERFORMED BY: New York Philharmonic; Leonard Bernstein, conductor

What to Listen For

Section 1

Melody A rising motive quietly unfolds, outlining a triad.

Rhythm/meter Very slow and tranquil; the changing meter is imperceptible.

Harmony Overlapping of chords (polychordal) produces a gentle dissonance.

Section 7

Melody Theme with four phrases (**a-a′-b-a″**); later variations use only parts of the theme.

Form Theme and five variations, based on a traditional Shaker song.

Timbre Each variation changes tone colors; individual instruments are featured.

Section I: Very slowly   2:42

0:00   Low strings on a sustained pitch; solo clarinet, then flute with a rising motive:

0:16   Violins and flutes alternate the rising figure; harp punctuates; other instruments enter, creating dissonance.
0:52   Violins in high range, with more movement; the rising figure is heard in various instruments.

1:25   Solos in various woodwinds and trumpet.

1:54   Solo oboe, then bassoon; descending motive.

2:31   Clarinet with a closing triad, over sustained harmony.

Section 7: Theme (*Simple Gifts*) and five variations   3:03

Theme

0:00   Solo clarinet with tune in four phrases (**a-a′-b-a″**), accompanied by harp (playing harmonics) and flute:

0:28   Brief transition.

Variation 1

0:34   Oboe and bassoon present the tune; grows dissonant, with *sforzando* on third phrase played by all woodwinds.

0:56   Short, rhythmic transition.

Variation 2

0:59   Tune in violas in augmentation (steady rhythmic accompaniment continues); violins (in octaves) enter in second phrase, in canon with the violas (dissonance on the last note is marked with arrow):

1:35   Transition.

Variation 3

1:45   Trumpets and trombones, with swirling strings; loud brass section; then quieter in woodwinds.

Variation 4

2:10   Woodwinds with a slower version of the tune.

Variation 5

2:30   Full orchestra with majestic, homophonic statement; somewhat dissonant; *fortissimo,* then dies out.

CHAPTER 50

Also American: Revueltas and Mexican Musical Modernism

▶‖ First, listen . . .

to the movement "Noche de jaranas" from Revueltas's *La noche de los Mayas*, focusing on the rhythmic movement. By now, you know how to listen for meter. How would you describe the metric treatment in this work? What traits make it sound dancelike?

Latin American musical repertories have long been important to Anglo-American audiences and musicians, especially in the areas close to the southern U.S. border: the culture and history of the United States and Mexico have been intertwined since well before the two countries came into their modern borders. Like their counterparts in the United States, other American musicians have worked to reconcile their connection to European traditions with crafting a uniquely American sound. And like Copland and Still, they have realized their nationalist approach largely through reference to vernacular traditions.

MUSICAL TRADITIONS OF MEXICO

The modern musical traditions of Mexico are rich and varied, embracing the indigenous Amerindian cultures as well as Hispanic culture. Mexico's ties to Spain began in 1519, when Spanish soldiers colonized the territory, and continued until 1821, when the country achieved its independence.

By the late nineteenth century, the goal of creating a nationally distinctive style lured musicians and artists alike to Amerindian and mestizo cultures. (Mestizos

KEY POINTS

- The music of Mexican composer Silvestre Revueltas is expressively nationalistic, with folkloric rhythms and melodies set in a dissonant framework.

- Revueltas celebrated the heritage of the ancient Mayan empire in his film score for *La noche de las Mayas* (*The Night of the Mayas*).

- Revueltas and other American modernists were influenced by the **mariachi ensemble**, a vernacular Mexican tradition.

Silvestre Revueltas (1899–1940)

Born in the mountain state of Durango, Revueltas was a child prodigy on violin and later studied composition at the Conservatorio Nacional de Música in Mexico City. He continued his studies in the United States until 1929, when he was called home by his friend Carlos Chávez to serve as assistant conductor of the Orquesta Sinfónica de Mexico.

With the onset of the Spanish Civil War in the late 1930s, the intensely political Revueltas went to Spain, where he participated in the cultural activities of the Loyalist government. Upon his return home in late 1937, he produced a series of masterworks, including his best-known orchestral piece, *Sensemayá* (1938), inspired by the verses of Afro-Cuban poet Nicolás Guillén (another anti-Fascist), which imitate onomatopoetically the sounds and rhythm of Afro-Cuban music and speak against colonial imperialism. In 1939, Revueltas wrote the film score for *La noche de los Mayas* (*The Night of the Mayas*), which projects a modern

primitivism not unlike Stravinsky's *Rite of Spring*. The composer died at age forty of alcohol-induced pneumonia.

Revueltas's love for Mexican provincial music is immediately obvious, voiced through lyrical, direct melodies that are driven by such rhythmic techniques as polyrhythms and ostinatos. Despite a modern harmonic language rich in dissonance and chromaticism, Revueltas's music is deeply emotional and Romantic in its inspiration. His skillful handling of the orchestral palette evokes the picturesque traditional orchestras of Mexico.

MAJOR WORKS: Orchestral music, including *Sensemayá* (1938) • Seven film scores, including *La noche de los Mayas* (*The Night of the Mayas,* 1939) • Chamber music, including *Homenaje a Federico García Lorca* (*Homage to Federico García Lorca,* 1937) • Two ballets • Songs, including seven *Cancione*s (1938, on texts by García Lorca).

are people of mixed Spanish and Amerindian ancestry; today they are the majority in Latin American countries.) The Mexican Revolution of 1910 further changed the artistic life of the country, conjuring strong feelings of patriotism. In the post-revolutionary period, sometimes called the "Aztec Renaissance," composers tried to evoke or suggest, rather than recreate, the character of this native music for a modern age. The works of Carlos Chávez (1899–1978), including seven symphonies and two Aztec ballets, are rich in Amerindian flavor. Chávez and Silvestre Revueltas were two of the most decisive influences on Mexican musical culture.

Carlos Chávez

SILVESTRE REVUELTAS: "MESTIZO REALIST"

Revueltas is considered a representative of "mestizo realism," a nationalist modernist movement that drew on elements of Mexico's traditional culture. His music is highly flavored with folk elements, especially mariachi band traditions.

La noche de los Mayas

After composing several orchestral and chamber works, Revueltas contributed scores to Mexican films. Most prominent is the one for *La noche de los Mayas* (*The Night of the Mayas*), a 1939 film by prolific Mexican director Chano Urueta that was billed as a "Mexican tragedy." Set at the time when European colonizers first came to the Americas,

In His Own Words

❝ There is in me a particular interpretation of nature. Everything is rhythm. . . . Everybody understands or feels it. . . . My rhythms are dynamic, sensual, vital; I think in images that meet in melodic lines, always moving dynamically."

—Silvestre Revueltas

Platform for dancers in front of the ancient Maya pyramid of Kukulcan, Yucatán.

it celebrates the heritage of the native Maya empire. The arrival of a white explorer sets up a story of conflicting cultures and a tragic love triangle. As was often the case in his compositions, Revueltas mostly evoked the musical soundscape of his country's traditions rather than using actual folk melodies.

After Revueltas's death, composer and director José Yves Limantour arranged excerpts from the full soundtrack into a four-movement suite that was premiered in 1961. The expanded percussion section of this work is especially striking: various Latin American instruments derived from the intersection of native, African, and European cultures—bongos, congas, tom-toms, rattles, guiro (a notched or grooved gourd), caracol (conch shell), and tumkul (a kind of log drum)—are featured prominently alongside the established timpani, bass drum, snare drum, and xylophone from the European orchestral tradition.

The second movement, "Noche de jaranas" ("Night of Revelry," LG 39), is taken from the early part of the film, where the newcomers—the white men—are welcomed by the Mayas into their festivities. It is labeled "Tempo di *son*," suggesting a popular Latin American dance genre based on a mixture of indigenous, African, and Spanish traditions. Unlike in a traditional *son*, which shifts between simple triple (3/4) and compound duple (6/8) meter, the meter of this work is irregular – alternating 6/8 meter with 5/8, in patterns that are not entirely predictable. Revueltas thus evokes the spirit of the *son* while experimenting with rhythmic energy and tension much the same way Stravinsky did in *The Rite of Spring*. Violins playing in parallel thirds, answered by the brass section, bring to mind the traditional style of the mariachi ensemble. The form of the movement resembles a

Musicians perform for an ancient Maya festival in this ninth-century fresco detail from Bonampak, Chiapas, Mexico.

classical rondo, featuring the return of distinctive melodic snippets and contrasts in melody, harmony, and timbre; at the end, Revueltas thins out the texture and fades the dynamics as if to depict revelers wandering away from their celebration but still dancing drunkenly. The mood of the movement is both playful and sarcastic.

By collaborating with film writers and producers, Revueltas was not only engaging in what was considered one of the most innovative multimedia traditions of the time, but also celebrating his national heritage through a distinctively modernist American soundscape.

▶|◀ Reflect

What effect do the shifting meters and syncopation in this movement have on you as a listener? Why do you think Revueltas chose this degree of rhythmic complexity to tell his story about the meeting of two cultures?

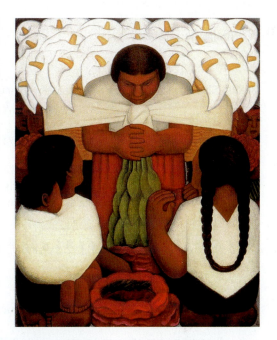

The murals of the Mexican painter **Diego Rivera** (1886–1957) glorify his native culture and people in an elegant social and historical narrative. *Flower Festival* (1925).

YOUR TURN TO EXPLORE

Find examples of music associated with Mexico (for example, mariachi ensembles), and compare it with music associated with South America (for example, Brazilian samba, Argentinian tango, or Chilean Andean traditions). What are the similarities and differences—in instrumentation, vocal quality, the use of solo voices versus ensembles, how featured voices or instruments are backed up by other voices/instruments, characteristic rhythmic patterns?

LISTENING GUIDE 39   5:30

Revueltas: "Noche de jaranas" ("Night of Revelry"), from *La noche de los Mayas* (*The Night of the Mayas*)

DATE: Film score, 1939; premiere of suite arrangement, 1961

GENRE: Suite from film score

PERFORMED BY: Los Angeles Philharmonic; Esa-Pekka Salonen, conductor

MOVEMENTS: I. "Noche de los Mayas"
II. "Noche de jaranas"
III. "Noche de Yucatán"
IV. "Noche de encantamiento" ("Night of Enchantment")

continued on next page

II: "Noche de jaranas"

What to Listen For

Melody Short snippets of the tune are passed around the ensemble; a contrasting flowing melody is heard in the central section.

Rhythm/meter Highly syncopated; alternation between compound (6/8) and irregular (5/8, 10/8) meters.

Expression Combines elements of a symphonic scherzo with Latin American *son* dance music.

Performing forces Full orchestra with piano and Latin American percussion instruments.

0:00 **A section**—strings play the main rondo theme in thirds (evoking a mariachi band sound), accompanied by Latin American percussion, alternating irregularly between 5/8 and 6/8 meter:

0:28 Piccolos join the ensemble.

0:45 Full orchestra, different timbres in dialogue with short melodic snippets; harmony is more unstable and unpredictable.

2:28 **B section**—a new metric pattern, 3+3+2 (8/8 meter), in trumpet and xylophone:

A slower, rising melodic idea in the French horns, then trumpets:

2:59 Quiet variant of the rhythmic idea in flutes and strings.

3:15 **A′**—modified return of the rondo theme, *forte*.

3:49 **B′**—Suddenly *pianissimo*, 8/8 meter returns in horns, with expanded orchestral reinforcement.

4:20 **C section**—dynamic builds to *fff* in the most regular meter up to this point, 6/8; powerful melody in the brass and strings, with a cross-rhythm in the accompaniment:

4:36 **A″**—a short transition in the low brass and percussion leads to the return of the opening rondo (5/8–6/8) theme; dynamics fade as if the ensemble were disappearing into the distance.

REPRESENTATIVE COMPOSERS

Igor Stravinsky

Aaron Copland

Silvestre Revueltas

George Gershwin

William Grant Still

Billie Holiday

IMPORTANT GENRES

neo-Classical:
  ballet, suite,
  symphony,
  concerto

film music

blues

big-band jazz

Modernist-Era Music

Listening Essentials

Melody: Melodies conceived instrumentally, with disjunct and wide-ranging lines; elements incorporated from folk music and jazz.

Rhythm/meter: Rhythmic diversity, including changing meters, polyrhythms, and frequent syncopation.

Harmony: Extremes of dissonance, expanded tonality; use of atonality, polychords and polyharmony, tone rows.

Texture: Contrapuntal, featuring linear movement and complex combinations of lines.

Form: Succinct, tight forms; older forms revived.

Timbre: Bright, lean sound, featuring winds and percussion with quickly shifting instrumental colors; piano becomes part of the orchestra.

Expression: Dramatic and emotional, often with high energy; extreme dynamic contrasts; in some cases, restrained and precise.

Performing forces: Unusual combinations and ranges of instruments; diverse percussion and non-Western instruments.

Listening Challenge

Now take the online Listening Challenge, where you'll listen to a mystery selection from the modernist era and answer questions about its elements: the nature of the different melodic lines; complexities in the rhythm and meter; changes in texture; the varied instruments (including percussion) and combinations of timbres; instances of dissonance and consonance; and how different moods are expressed throughout the work.

POSTMODERNISM

COMPOSERS AND WORKS

	1890	1900	1910	1920	1930	1940	1950	1960	1970	1980	1990	2000	2010	2020

John Cage **(1912–1992)**
Sonatas and Interludes

Leonard Bernstein **(1918–1990)**
West Side Story

George Crumb **(b. 1929)**
Caballito negro

John Williams **(b. 1932)**
Imperial March

Philip Glass **(b. 1937)**
Symphony No. 4 (*Heroes*)

Tania León **(b. 1943)**
Inura

David Bowie **(1947–2016)**
Heroes

John Adams **(b. 1947)**
Doctor Atomic

Jennifer Higdon **(b. 1962)**
blue cathedral

	1890	1900	1910	1920	1930	1940	1950	1960	1970	1980	1990	2000	2010	2020

EVENTS

1958 First mass-produced stereo recordings released.

1963 President John F. Kennedy assassinated.

1968 Martin Luther King Jr. assassinated.

1974 First home computers produced.

1975 Vietnam War ends.

1991 Soviet Union is dissolved.

2001 Terrorists attack the World Trade Center and Pentagon.
iTunes introduced.

2008 Barack Obama elected first African American president.

2018 NASA finds water on the moon's surface.

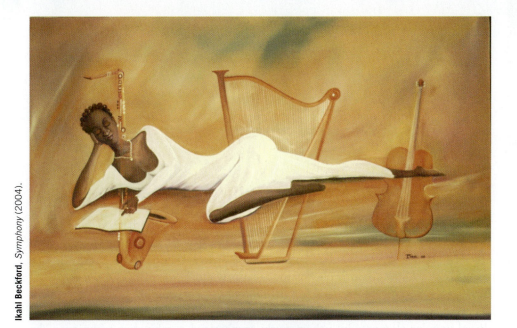

Postmodernism: Twentieth Century and Beyond

▶‖ First, listen...

to the song *The Night in Silence Under Many a Star*, by George Crumb, and see how many musical traits described in Part 1 you can identify: for example, the nature of the melodic line, the vocal technique, and the interaction between the voice and piano; the character of the rhythm and meter; and how technology is incorporated into the song. Listen several times to try to pick up multiple elements, but don't worry about "getting it right"—this is your first chance to apply these basic principles to an example of postmodern-era music.

LISTENING OBJECTIVES

By the end of Part 7, you will be able to

- hear the mixture of consonant and dissonant harmonies, as well as repetitive melodic fragments reaching toward longer gestures.

- perceive the era's eclectic and idiosyncratic approaches to expression and style.

- follow experimental techniques that expand the timbral capabilities of instruments and voices.

- identify formal procedures that unfold gradually, often building to longer structural shapes.

- recognize the influence of electronic technology and popular music styles.

- define some of the main vocal and instrumental genres in the postmodern era.

Beyond Modernism?

THE POSTMODERN TURN

No one agrees on how to define **postmodernism**, and perhaps, as with modernism, it makes more sense to talk about several different departures from tradition, as mid-twentieth-century artists strove to find new means of expression beyond the principles of modernism. With the increasing social turmoil that followed the Second World War, the arts passed through a period of violent experimentation with new media, new materials, and new techniques. Artists introduced popular elements into their work; emphasized combinative techniques like collage, pastiche, or quotation; and revived traditional and classical elements. Their ideas continue to open broad possibilities for artistic expression: all art—highbrow or lowbrow—is considered to have equal potential for greatness.

Art, Film, Literature

In architecture, for example, the trend is away from sleek glass skyscrapers and toward a more neo-eclectic look. While modernist designer Mies van der Rohe believed that "less is more," Robert Venturi, a leader in the postmodern movement in architecture, countered with "less is a bore," suggesting that buildings were more interesting if they had some decorative elements. One stunning example is Frank Gehry's design for the Walt Disney Concert Hall in Los Angeles, the interpretation of which has ranged from a blossoming flower to a sailing ship (see illustration at left).

A trend away from objective painting led to **abstract expressionism** in the United States during the 1950s and 60s. In the canvases of painters such as Robert Motherwell (see illustration opposite) and Jackson Pollock, space, mass, and color were freed from the need to imitate objects in the real world. The urge toward abstraction was felt equally in sculpture, as is evident in the work of such artists as Henry Moore (opposite) and Barbara Hepworth. At the same time, however, a new kind of realism appeared in the art of Jasper Johns, Robert Rauschenberg, and others, who owed some of their inspiration to the Dadaists of four decades earlier. Rauschenberg's aim, as he put it, was to work the "gap between life and art." This trend culminated in **pop art**, which drew its themes from modern urban life: machines, advertisements, comic strips, movies, commercial photography, and familiar objects connected

> 66 From Schoenberg I learned that tradition is a home we must love and forgo."
>
> —Lukas Foss

The Walt Disney Concert Hall in Los Angeles, designed by **Frank Gehry** (b. 1929) and completed in 2003, is considered a masterpiece of postmodern architecture.

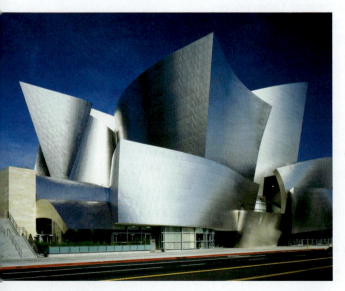

LEFT: In *The Red and Black #51*, by **Robert Motherwell** (1915–1991), abstract blocks of color adorn a musical score.

RIGHT: *Two Reclining Figures,* an abstract sculpture by English artist **Henry Moore** (1898–1986).

with everyday living. A similar aim motivated Andy Warhol's pop art paintings (p. 27) and the comic-strip art of Roy Lichtenstein.

Postmodernist art embraces a pluralistic attitude toward gender, sexual orientation, and ethnicity. One creative artist whose expression is distinctively feminist is Judy Chicago, best known for her *Holocaust Series* (below) and *The Dinner Table* (1979), a triangular table with thirty-nine place settings that pay tribute to important women throughout history. African American artist Faith Ringgold creates "storybook" quilts, narrative paintings with quilted borders; some of these make up a *Jazz Series*, depicting black musicians in the context of life in the 1920s and 30s. Artists have also featured recognizable images in their work, sometimes employing the technique of collage or quotation from a literary, musical, or visual source. Jasper Johns's work depicted common symbols—flags, numbers, letters (p. 300).

Postmodern ideas were easily extended to the medium of film, beginning with the "new wave" movement of the 1950s and 60s, epitomized in the films of Jean-Luc Godard (*Breathless,* 1960), Federico Fellini (*La Strada,* 1954; 8½, 1963), and Michelangelo Antonioni (*Blowup,* 1966; *The Passenger,* 1975). More recent directors who explore postmodernism include Jane Campion (*Two Friends,* 1986; a saga of two schoolgirls that is arranged in reverse order) and Quentin Tarantino, in the *Kill Bill* films (2003–04)—which pay homage to the Italian spaghetti western, Kung Fu movies, and other familiar stereotypes—and the genre-bending *Inglourious Basterds* (2009). Visual collage is used in Godfrey Reggio's non-narrative *Koyaanisqatsi* (1982; see p. 300) and *Powaqqatsi* (1988), both of which set soundtracks by minimalist composer Philip Glass (Chapter 55).

Feminist artist **Judy Chicago**'s (b. 1939) *Holocaust Project Logo* (stained glass, 1992). In this exhibit, the Holocaust provides a point from which to explore issues relating to the human condition.

Jasper Johns's (b. 1930) collage *Three Flags* (1958) overlays three canvases to skew how the viewer perceives a familiar image.

Postmodern literature takes many forms and approaches. Among the writers you might know are Kurt Vonnegut (*Slaughterhouse Five,* 1969), Maya Angelou (*I Know Why the Caged Bird Sings,* 1969), Margaret Atwood (*The Handmaid's Tale,* 1985; the basis for a Hulu series), Toni Morrison (*Beloved,* 1987), and Amy Tan (*The Joy Luck Club,* 1989). Even the epic fantasy novels of J. K. Rowling (*Harry Potter,* 1997–2007) and George R. R. Martin (*A Song of Fire and Ice,* 1996–2011; adapted for the TV series *Game of Thrones,* opposite) spin out postmodern themes.

Postmodernism in Music

Although a few composers continued the path set out by modernists toward ever stricter organization in music, others looked toward freer forms and procedures. The antirational element in art—stressing intuition, change, and improvisation—was favored by composers such as John Cage, who wrote **chance**, or **aleatoric**, music that left decisions determining the overall shape to the performer or to chance. Just as in the visual arts, the distinctions between elite and popular music are shrinking. We will hear, for example, how Philip Glass borrowed ideas from David Bowie's album *Heroes* as the starting point for his own symphony; and we will see how the film scores of John Williams have entered the realm of art music.

The globalization of society has hugely impacted musical composition, opening up a world of expression that draws on non-Western music and on the rich heritage of African American and Latin American styles, as noted already in the works of Still, Copland, Revueltas, and Gershwin, among others. American composer George Crumb (Chapter 52) experiments with radical uses of form and sound, while at the same time looking back to earlier influences. Others, like Philip Glass (Chapter 55), have reverted to a minimalist musical style built on small, repetitive ideas—a concept shared by hip-hop and rock.

A hyperkinetic scene of urban life, from **Godfrey Reggio**'s film *Koyaanisqatsi* (1982), for which Philip Glass wrote the minimalist musical score.

Multimedia and performance art pull together visual, aural, spoken, and dramatic modes of expression to challenge our notions of any one genre. The term "happening" was coined in the 1960s to describe a semi-improvised multimedia event that often depended on audience participation.

New Technologies

Probably the most important development that affected music during the mid-twentieth century was the refinement of recording and playback technologies, which heralded the advent of electronic music. Two trends emerged simultaneously in the late 1940s and early 50s. *Musique concrète,* based in Paris, relied on sounds made by any natural source, including musical instruments, that were recorded onto magnetic tape and then manipulated by various means.

Elektronische Musik, originating in Cologne, Germany, and explored by Karlheinz Stockhausen among others, used only electronically produced sounds. By the 1960s, compact and affordable synthesizers suited for mass production were being developed by Robert Moog and Donald Buchla, but it was a recording called *Switched-On Bach,* made in 1968 by Wendy Carlos (born Walter Carlos), that catapulted the synthesizer and the genre of electronic music to instant fame. Carlos composed with the Moog synthesizer for a variety of commercial purposes, including film scores for Stanley Kubrick's *A Clockwork Orange* (1971) and *The Shining* (1980).

German musicians Tassilo Ippenberger (right) and Thomas Benedix, of the techno group Pan-Pot, in their Berlin studio (2015).

In 1983, the Yamaha DX7, one of the best-selling synthesizers of all time, was unveiled. That same year saw the official adoption of a standardized protocol known as the Musical Instrument Digital Interface (MIDI), which allowed composers to record data such as pitch, duration, and volume on the computer for playback on one or more synthesizers. By the mid-1980s, digital-sampling synthesizers, capable of recreating a realistic-sounding grand piano, trumpet, violin, bird call, car crash, or any other sound that can be sampled, was accessible to the average musician. With the affordability of digital synthesizers and personal computers, and their ability to communicate with one another, the digital revolution took the world of electronic music by storm.

Much of the music we hear today as movie and TV soundtracks is electronically generated, although some effects resemble the sounds of conventional instruments so closely that we are not always aware of the new technology. Popular-music groups have been "electrified" for years, but now most of them regularly feature synthesizers and samplers that both simulate conventional rock band instruments and produce altogether new sounds; electronic resources like Autotune help them manipulate vocal and instrumental pitch either in the studio or in performance.

Tyrion Lannister, portrayed by Peter Dinklage, in the postmodern TV series *Game of Thrones*.

Collage, a major genre of art (see Johns's *Three Flags,* p. 300), has also found a place in music: composer Lukas Foss (1922–2009) juxtaposed or overlapped fragments of Bach, Handel, and Scarlatti in his *Baroque Variations,* just as John Lennon created a sound collage of special effects and vocals in *Revolution 9* (*The Beatles,* 1968). And the device of quotation has proved its significance to popular as well as art music, since the entire tradition of hip-hop hinges on the creative sampling and layering of musical excerpts in ways the composer feels are artistically striking and/or culturally significant. All these techniques and many more make up the palette of the modern composer. We will listen for the individuality of each musical voice as we try to comprehend the expressive and eclectic language of today's music.

New Sound Palettes: A Mid-Twentieth-Century American Experimentalist

> 66 I thought I could never compose socially important music. Only if I could invent something new, then would I be useful to society."
>
> —John Cage

▶‖ First, listen...

to the movement from Cage's *Sonatas and Interludes*. How might you describe the timbre of the piano? What do you notice is different from the works for solo piano we have studied so far?

Since the beginning of recorded history, musicians have been expanding their sound-production resources—by inventing new scales and harmonies, developing increasingly complex and versatile instruments, and training their bodies to sing and play in experimental ways. In order to do so, they have reached out to other cultures for inspiration, but also taken advantage of the inventiveness of their fellow musicians. The mid-twentieth century was an especially fertile time for musical expansion in North America, and we will consider one example by a composer who shaped such expansion: John Cage.

EARLY EXPERIMENTS

Henry Cowell

Tone clusters

Two earlier composers in particular helped shape Cage's pioneering genius. One, Henry Cowell (1897–1965), was drawn toward a variety of non-Western sources. His studies of the musics of Japan, India, and Iran led him to combine Asian instruments with traditional Western ensembles. Cowell also experimented with foreign scales, which he harmonized with Western chords. Several of his innovations involved the piano; these include **tone clusters** (groups of adjacent notes played with the fist, palm, or forearm) and the plucking of the piano strings directly with the fingers. This novel approach to the piano helped to inspire Cage's idea of the "prepared piano," which we will encounter below.

KEY POINTS

- Contemporary music often calls for innovative and highly virtuosic effects that challenge performers to new technical levels.

- Composer John Cage used a specially modified **"prepared" piano** to simulate the sound of the **Javanese gamelan**, an ensemble of metallic percussion instruments played in Indonesia (on the islands of Java and Bali, in particular).

John Cage (1912–1992)

Born in Los Angeles, Cage exhibited an early interest in non-Western scales, which he learned from his mentor, Henry Cowell. He soon realized that the traditional division between consonance and dissonance had given way to a new opposition between music and noise, as a result of which the boundaries of the one were extended to include more of the other.

In 1938, Cage invented what he called the "prepared piano," in which various foreign substances were inserted at crucial points in the strings of a grand piano. From this instrument came a myriad of sounds whose overall effect resembled that of a Javanese gamelan. Cage wrote a number of works for the prepared piano, notably the set of *Sonatas and Interludes*. His interest in indeterminacy, or chance, led him to compose works in which performers make choices by throwing dice.

Cage maintained an intense interest in exploring the role of silence, which led to a composition entitled *4'33"*, without any musical content at all, consisting of four minutes and thirty-three seconds of "silence." The piece was first "performed" by the pianist David Tudor in 1952. He came onstage, placed a score on the piano rack, sat quietly for the duration of the piece, then closed the piano lid and walked off the stage. Cage viewed *4'33"* as one of the most radical statements he had made against the traditions of Western music, one that raised profound questions. What is music, and what is noise? And what does silence contribute to music? In any case, *4'33"*, which can be performed by anyone on any instrument, always makes us more aware of our surroundings.

MAJOR WORKS: Orchestral music • Piano music, including *Music of Changes* (1951) • Prepared piano works, including *Bacchanale* (1940) and *Sonatas and Interludes* (1946–48) • Percussion works, including *First, Second, Third Construction* (1938, 1940, 1941) • Vocal works, including *Aria* (1958) • Electronic music, including *Fontana Mix* (1958), *Cartridge Music* (1960), and *HPSCHD* (for harpsichord and tapes, 1969) • Indeterminate works, including *4'33"* (for any instrument, 1952) • Writings, including *Silence* (1961), *Notations* (1969), *Themes and Variations* (1982), and *I–VI* (1990).

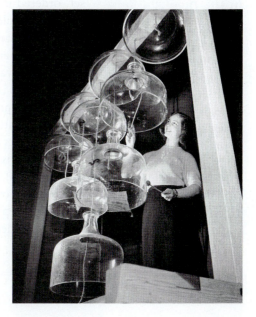

Marjorie Sweazey plays Harry Partch's cloud-chamber bowls, made from the tops and bottoms of large Pyrex bowls.

The most serious proponent of microtonal technique was Harry Partch (1901–1974), who developed a scale of forty-three **microtones** (intervals smaller than a semitone) to the octave in the 1920s and adapted Indian and African instruments to fit this tuning. Among his original instruments are cloud-chamber bowls (made of glass; right), cone gongs (made of metal), and gourd trees. Such instruments make melody and timbre, rather than harmony, the focus of his music.

THE MUSIC OF JOHN CAGE

Cage represents the type of eternally questing artist who no sooner solves one problem than presses forward to another. His works explored new sounds and concepts that challenged the very notion of what makes up music. Probably his most important contribution, and one that shaped many strands of music in the second

John Cage's prepared piano works call for screws, nails, and other materials to be inserted between the strings.

Chance music   half of the twentieth century, was the idea of **chance**, or **aleatoric**, music, where performance choices are left to the musicians. His experimental compositions and writings defined him as a leader in the postwar avant-garde scene.

Sonatas and Interludes

Sonatas and Interludes represents Cage's crowning achievement for the prepared piano, approximating the subtle sounds of the Javanese gamelan (p. 306) and preserving the effect of music floating above time. There are sixteen sonatas in this set, ordered in four groups of four, and separated by interludes (LG 40). Cage provides detailed instructions at the beginning of the score, indicating that forty-five of the piano's eighty-eight keys should be prepared by inserting nails, bolts, nuts, screws, and bits of rubber, wood, or leather at carefully specified distances. The effect is varied, depending on the material inserted, its position, and whether the soft pedal is depressed. Some strings produce a nonpitched, percussive thump, while others produce tones whose pitch and timbre are altered. This music is not concerned with the simultaneous sounding of pitches (harmony) but rather with timbral effects and the rhythmic grouping of sounds.

Sonata V is short but highly structured; its overall shape is binary (a prevalent form in the Baroque and Classical eras), with each section repeated (**A-A-B-B**). The sonority of the prepared piano is almost ethereal. Here and elsewhere, Cage's music for prepared piano is made of wholly original sounds that delight the ears and, as intended by the composer, "set the soul in operation."

In His Own Words

66 Once in Amsterdam, a Dutch musician said to me, 'It must be very difficult for you in America to write music, for you are so far away from the centers of tradition.' I had to say, 'It must be very difficult for you in Europe to write music, for you are so close to the centers of tradition.'"

—John Cage

LISTENING GUIDE 40   🎧 1:23

Cage: Sonata V, from *Sonatas and Interludes*

DATE: 1946–48 (first performed 1949)

OVERALL STRUCTURE: 16 sonatas, in four groups of 4, each group separated by an interlude

PERFORMED BY: Joshua Pierce, piano

What to Listen For

Melody Irregular, small-range phrases, in an undulating chromatic line; the second section is more disjunct.

Rhythm/meter Regular movement at the beginning, then a changing rhythmic flow, seemingly without a clear meter.

Form Two-part, or binary, form (**A-A-B-B**).

Timbre The piano produces percussive effects (both pitched and nonpitched), otherworldly sounds, and varied tone qualities.

0:00   **A section**—18 measures, grouped in irregular phrases (4 + 5 + 4 + 5 = 18).

Opening of sonata, with regular rhythmic movement and two-voice texture:

(una corda pedal)

An irregular sense of meter develops.

0:12   Upper line is sustained over a moving lower line (in the last 9 measures).

0:20   **A section** repeated.

0:38   **B section**—22½ measures, in irregular phrases (4 + 5 + 4 + 5 + 4½ = 22½).

Rests break the music into sections.

0:46   Quicker tempo, lines are more disjunct and accented.

Second half of **B section**, with more disjunct lines and accents:

0:55   Sustained dissonance at the closing.

1:00   **B section** repeated.

Cage's fascination with the Javanese gamelan orchestra, made up of metallic percussion, influenced his compositions for prepared piano.

▶|◀ Reflect

What do you think of the expressive results of Cage's "prepared" piano in performances of *Sonatas and Interludes?* How convincing do you find the prepared-piano timbre?

YOUR TURN TO EXPLORE

Find an example of music you think is experimental. What techniques and sounds make it seem new? In your opinion, what are the artistic goals of the composer and/or performer(s)?

Extended Techniques: Crumb and the New Virtuosity in America

▶‖ **First, listen...**

to Crumb's song *Caballito negro*, and focus on the timbre of the voice and instruments. How are the sounds you hear different from the conventional orchestral and vocal timbres we have been exploring?

> ❝ I think composers are everything they've ever experienced, everything they've ever read, all the music they've heard . . . I think there's a lot of music that has a darker side and maybe some of this music influenced me."
>
> —George Crumb

AVANT-GARDE VIRTUOSITY

Avant-garde musical styles call for a new breed of instrumentalists and vocalists, and a new arsenal of unusual techniques, to cope with the music's performance demands. The music of George Crumb, for example, borrows from art music traditions, folk themes, and non-Western sounds. Crumb displays a real talent for turning ordinary instruments, including the voice, into the extraordinary. His imaginative music resounds with extramusical and symbolic content that infuses it with a deep meaning waiting to be unlocked.

Crumb's *Caballito negro* (*Little Black Horse*)

Caballito negro (LG 41) is the last of three songs in Crumb's second book of madrigals. All three are set to poetry by the Spanish poet Federico García Lorca, and are scored for soprano with metallic percussion instruments and a flute or piccolo. The piccolo player uses a technique called **flutter-tonguing**: quickly moving the tongue as though "rolling an R" while blowing into the instrument. In *Caballito negro*, a hair-raising image of death, Crumb extracts only the two refrains from the poem, alternating between them: "Little black horse, where are you taking your dead rider? Little cold horse. What a scent of knife-blossom!" Most phrases end with a downward melodic line, on ominous words. The rhythmic treatment might remind you of the galloping horse in Schubert's equally chilling *Elfking* (Chapter 33), and the vocalist is even asked to whinny like a horse.

Flutter-tonguing

KEY POINTS

- American composer George Crumb pushes the limits of the human voice, calling for unusual effects (extended techniques) from many traditions, including non-Western music.

- In his four books of madrigals, which treat the voice as a virtuosic instrument, Crumb set texts by the Spanish poet Federico García Lorca.

George Crumb (b. 1929)

Crumb studied at Mason College of Fine Arts in Charleston, West Virginia, and earned graduate degrees at the University of Illinois and University of Michigan. He taught composition in Colorado and New York before he was appointed to the University of Pennsylvania, where he remained until he retired in 1999. Crumb has shown a special affinity for the poetry of Federico García Lorca, the great poet killed by the Fascists during the Spanish Civil War. Among his works based on García Lorca's poetry is the song cycle *Ancient Voices of Children*, which abounds in a number of unusual effects. He also set García Lorca's poetry in his four books of madrigals, in which he explores *Sprechstimme* (spoken melody), quarter tones, and a "white" tone (without vibrato) for the voice.

Crumb's music is focused on creating new sonorities as well as exploring theatrical concepts. In *Echoes of Time and the River*, for which he won a Pulitzer Prize in 1968, performers whisper and shout as they move around the stage. His music is charged with emotion, which derives from a highly developed sense of the dramatic. His use of contemporary techniques for expressive ends is extremely effective with audiences.

MAJOR WORKS: Orchestral music, including *Echoes of Time and the River* (1967) • Vocal music set to García Lorca poetry, including four books of madrigals (1965–69) and *Ancient Voices of Children* (1970) • Chamber music, including *Black Angel* (for electrified string quartet, 1970), *Lux aeterna* (*Eternal Light*, for voice and chamber ensemble with sitar, 1971), *Vox balaenae* (*The Voice of the Whale*, for amplified instruments, 1971) • Music for amplified piano, including two volumes of *Makrokosmos* (1972–73), *Music for a Summer Evening* (1974), *Zeitgeist* (1988), and *Otherworldly Resonances* (two pianos, 2003) • Other piano music.

In His Own Words

66 The artist, and particularly the poet . . . must heed only the call that arises within him from three strong voices: the voice of death, with all its foreboding; the voice of love; and the voice of art."

—Federico García Lorca

Both Cage and Crumb rely on the extraordinary creativity of others for their works to be successful, whether through modeling or through virtuosic performance. And this necessity of collaboration between composer and performer is one of the characteristic (and most wonderful) aspects of music, especially in an age of specialization and experimentation.

▶|◀ Reflect

Why do you think Crumb chose extended timbral techniques for his setting of García Lorca's *Caballito negro*? Which of the techniques do you find especially effective in conveying the mood of the poem? Are there any techniques that you think detract from the expressive effect of the song?

YOUR TURN TO EXPLORE

Choose an instrument that you find interesting (the human voice can count!), and try to find examples of musicians pushing the technical possibilities of that instrument. What kinds of extended techniques can you discover? Do they have a significant expressive potential, and if so, how? Do you think those techniques could find a place in your favorite repertories? Can you envision other techniques that might be musically expressive?

Crumb: *Caballito negro (Little Black Horse)*

DATE: 1965

GENRE: Song, from *Madrigals*, Book II

PERFORMED BY: Tony Arnold, soprano; Rachel Rudich, piccolo; David Colson, percussion

What to Listen For

Melody Highly disjunct, with extended techniques (flutter-tonguing, glissandos, whispering).

Rhythm/meter Regular pulsations but no firm sense of meter.

Expression Grimly playful and very animated, with a bright, hard sound.

Performing forces Soprano voice, with piccolo and metallic percussion (marimba, glockenspiel, antique cymbals).

0:00	Caballito negro.	**A**	Little black horse.
	¿Dónde llevas tu jenete muerto?		Where are you taking your dead rider?
0:30	Caballito frío.	**B**	Little cold horse.
	¡Qué perfume de flor de cuchillo!		What a scent of knife-blossom!
0:55	Caballito negro . . .	**A′**	Little black horse . . .
	Caballito frío . . .		Little cold horse . . .
	Caballito negro . . .		Little black horse . . .

Opening of song (tempo marking means "As fast as possible"), with pounding rhythm in piccolo and percussion, disjunct vocal line, and flutter-tonguing in piccolo:

Return of opening line, with the vocalist neighing like a horse:

53

Staged Sentiment: Bernstein and American Musical Theater

" Any composer's writing is the sum of himself, of all his roots and influences."

—Leonard Bernstein

▶‖ **First, listen...**

to the ensemble song *Tonight,* from Bernstein's *West Side Story,* focusing on the distinctive melody of each character or group. How does that melody convey the mood of the character or group? What happens in the last minute of the song, starting at about 2:41?

American musical theater is, like jazz, a tradition that is both rooted in the United States and tremendously influential and popular throughout the world. From the beginning, composers and lyricists of the **musical** (as it's most commonly known) have sought to make their themes current and vital, relevant to the concerns of their society. One such theme is urban life and especially urban violence. A powerful and pathbreaking treatment of that theme, which continues to influence theatrical multimedia today, is *West Side Story*, a collaboration between composer Leonard Bernstein, lyricist Stephen Sondheim, and choreographer Jerome Robbins—three of the most talented artists of the mid-twentieth century.

MUSICAL THEATER IN NORTH AMERICA

Although theatrical productions were banned in most of the earliest North American colonies on religious and moral grounds, by the early nineteenth century immigrant musicians were helping to build a tradition of musical theater in North America. In the mid-1800s, New York became the cultural center of the country. In midtown Manhattan, the heart of the theater district, theaters lined the wide street called Broadway. Here and throughout the country, minstrel shows were giving way to vaudeville; these productions still featured some blackface, but

KEY POINTS

- The roots of American musical theater lie both in vaudeville shows and in European operetta.

- **Musicals** feature romantic plots (some taken from novels), sometimes serious subject matter, comic moments, appealing melodies, and large ensembles and dance numbers; the dialogue is mostly spoken.

- The "golden age" of the American musical, the early to mid-1900s, was characterized by composer-lyricist teams (George and Ira Gershwin, Lerner and Loewe, Rodgers and Hammerstein).

- Leonard Bernstein, a versatile conductor and composer, wrote the music for *West Side Story,* which transports the Romeo and Juliet story into New York City and its gang warfare.

more and more the characters were taken from new immigrant populations from Italy, Eastern Europe, and Asia. While some musical routines were parodies of the "funny way" the immigrants talked and behaved, often the actors themselves were immigrants, and the music could be sentimental and nostalgic as well as humorous—continuing a tradition established by Stephen Foster in an earlier generation (see Chapter 34). The vaudeville tradition expanded in New York into the variety show, which continued to offer musical and theatrical sketches, now often strung together by a loose topical theme.

The American musical theater of today developed both from the variety show and from the operetta tradition of late nineteenth-century European composers such as Johann Strauss Jr. and the team of W. S. Gilbert and Arthur Sullivan (*The Pirates of Penzance,* 1879; *The Mikado,* 1885). The genre was revamped to suit American tastes, both by immigrant composers like Victor Herbert (*Babes in Toyland,* 1903) and by "locals" like Will Marion Cook, an African American composer whose *Clorindy, or The Origin of the Cakewalk* (1898) was both the first black production to play a major Broadway theater and the first musical to incorporate ragtime melodies and rhythms. By the 1920s, talented creative teams such as George and Ira Gershwin (*Lady, Be Good,* 1924) and Oscar Hammerstein and Jerome Kern (*Show Boat,* 1927) had ushered in what many consider the golden age of the American musical. In the ensuing decades, the musical established itself as America's unique contribution to world theater.

Plots for early musicals were often sentimental and contrived, but this changed when composers looked to sophisticated literary sources (*Show Boat,* for example, is based on the Edna Ferber novel). In the 1940s, interest grew in adding more serious dramatic elements (for example, in the Richard Rodgers and Oscar Hammerstein productions *Oklahoma!* 1943; *South Pacific,* 1949; *The King and I,* 1951; *The Sound of Music,* 1959). Noted composers of musicals in more recent decades include Stephen Sondheim (*Sweeney Todd,* 1979; *Into the Woods,* 1988), who lifted the genre to new levels of sophistication; and Andrew Lloyd Webber (*Cats,* 1981; *Phantom of the Opera,* 1986), who combined song and dance with dazzling scenic effects. Claude-Michel Schonberg (*Les Misérables,* 1987; based on the Victor Hugo novel) and Lin-Manuel Miranda (*Hamilton, 2015;* based on Ron Chernow's 2004 biography; p. 317) have brought history alive with memorable hit shows. Jonathan Larson's popular *Rent* (1996) is a modern rock opera based on Puccini's opera *La bohème,* and the Broadway hit *Wicked* (2003) derives from the classic book *The Wonderful Wizard of Oz* (1900, made into a movie with Judy Garland in 1939).

In recent years, musicals based on films—like the Disney studio's *Beauty and the Beast* (1994), *The Lion King* (1997), and *Aladdin* (2014)—have swept the Broadway stage, reversing the standard order of a hit musical generating a film. Seemingly unlikely subject matter has inspired other musicals, such as the coming-of-age show *Avenue Q* (2003), notable for its borrowings from *Sesame Street* and featuring "full puppet nudity"; *Spring Awakening* (2006), a rock musical based on a controversial play that deals with issues of abortion, rape, child abuse, and homosexuality; and the irreverent satire *Book of Mormon* (2014), about two young missionaries sent to Uganda, written by the team of the equally irreverent TV show *South Park.* Dance takes precedence over story line in musicals like *Billy Elliot* (2005, with music by Elton John), and plays a striking role in *West Side Story,* our focus here.

In His Own Words

❝ This will be our reply to violence: to make music more intensely, more beautifully, more devotedly than ever before."

—Leonard Bernstein

Plot sources

LEONARD BERNSTEIN AND *WEST SIDE STORY*

Maria (Elena Sancho Pereg) and Tony (Liam Tobin) in a 2012 Berlin performance of *West Side Story*.

Mambo

Composer/conductor Leonard Bernstein dedicated his life to promoting concert music to the general public, through his accessible compositions and his far-reaching educational efforts. Bernstein was deeply influenced both by Gershwin's successes in expanding the jazz idiom and by Copland's ability to create soundscapes that could quickly be recognized as reflecting American ideals. His most enduring project was a collaboration with several outstanding creative minds of the mid-1900s, which brought the culturally profound story of Shakespeare's *Romeo and Juliet* into the violent gang world of New York.

Bernstein, along with lyricist Stephen Sondheim and playwright Arthur Laurents, had first intended to replace Shakespeare's warring families with Jewish and Catholic families living in the tenements of Manhattan's Lower East Side. As the project developed, choreographer Jerome Robbins joined the team and suggested shifting the location to the West Side, turning the families into juvenile gangs, a topic that was saturating the news in the mid 1950s: the result was two gangs called the Jets and the Sharks (the latter a Puerto Rican group). Robbins was especially eager to depict the setting's "gritty realism," and encouraged Bernstein to incorporate not only elements of jazz and early rock-and-roll, but also Latino music like the **mambo**, an Afro-Cuban dance with a fast, syncopated beat that was extremely popular at the time.

This story of star-crossed lovers is presented in scenes of great tenderness, with memorable songs such as *Maria, Tonight,* and *Somewhere* alternating with electrifying dance sequences choreographed by Robbins. We will first hear *Mambo* (LG 42), part of the dance scene where Tony (former member of the Jets) meets Maria (related to the Sharks). To a lively Latin beat, the bongos and cowbells keep up a frenetic pulse under the shouts of the gang members and the jazzy riffs of the woodwinds and brass.

The *Tonight* Ensemble is set later the same day, after a fire-escape version of Shakespeare's famous balcony scene, where Tony and Maria first sing their love duet. As darkness falls, the two gangs anxiously await the expected fight, each vowing to cut the other down to size. Underneath the gang music, an ominous three-note ostinato is heard throughout. Tony sings the lyrical ballad *Tonight* over an animated Latin rhythmic accompaniment. The gang music returns briefly, after which Maria and later Tony repeat their love song, their voices soaring above the complex dialogue in an exciting climax to the first act.

West Side Story was an instant audience success, and more than fifty years later remains a powerful work of musical theater, which has claimed its place in North American culture not only through the remarkable 1961 film adaptation, but also as a favorite of school and college theatrical groups. Yet it also caused controversy, both because of the focus on violence and gangs (and essentially sympathetic

Rival gangs (the Sharks and the Jets) dance in a 2007 production of *West Side Story,* performed in Paris.

treatment of the gang members) and for what some considered a stereotypical portrayal of Latino characters. Certainly, however, it was a groundbreaking multi-media work, as well as a landmark in our society's continuing struggle with artistic depictions of violence.

Leonard Bernstein (1918–1990)

As a composer, conductor, educator, pianist, and television personality, Bernstein enjoyed a spectacular career. He was born in Lawrence, Massachusetts, entered Harvard at seventeen, attended the prestigious Curtis Institute of Music in Philadelphia, and then became a disciple of conductor Serge Koussevitzky. At twenty-five, he was appointed assistant conductor of the New York Philharmonic. When a guest conductor was suddenly taken ill, Bernstein took over a Sunday afternoon concert that was broadcast coast to coast, and led a stunning performance. Overnight he became famous. Fifteen years later, he was himself named director of the New York Philharmonic, the first American-born conductor to occupy the post.

As a composer, Bernstein straddled the worlds of serious and popular music. He explored his Jewish background in his Third Symphony (*Kaddish*) and also tried his hand at serial composition. But he was rooted in tonality, as he demonstrated in the choral masterwork *Chichester Psalms*. Bernstein's feeling for the urban scene, specifically that of New York City, is vividly projected in his theater music. In *On the Town, Wonderful Town,* and *West Side Story*, he created a sophisticated kind of musical theater that explodes with movement, energy, and sentiment. His harmonies are spicily dissonant, his jazzy rhythms have great vitality, and his melodies soar.

MAJOR WORKS: Orchestral music, including three symphonies (*Kaddish,* 1963) • Choral works, including *Chichester Psalms* (1965) • Operas, including *A Quiet Place* (1983) • Musicals, including *On the Town* (1944), *Wonderful Town* (1953), *Candide* (1956), and *West Side Story* (1957) • Other dramatic stage works, including the ballet *Fancy Free* (1944), the film score *On the Waterfront* (1954), and a staged *Mass* (1971) • Chamber and instrumental music • Solo vocal music.

LISTENING GUIDE 42   🎧 5:26

Bernstein: *West Side Story*, excerpts

DATE: 1957

GENRE: Musical theater

PERFORMED BY: Carol Lawrence (Maria), Chita Rivera (Anita), Larry Kert (Tony), Mickey Calin (Riff), Ken LeRoy (Bernardo); Max Goberman, music director

CHARACTERS: Maria, Puerto Rican sister of Bernardo   Riff, leader of the Jets
Tony, former member of the Jets   Bernardo, leader of the Sharks
Anita, Puerto Rican girlfriend of Bernardo

Act I: The Dance at the Gym, *Mambo*   1:48

What to Listen For

Melody Disjunct, with syncopated riffs (short ideas).

Rhythm/meter Fast-paced, duple-meter Afro-Cuban dance; highly rhythmic, with much syncopation.

Expression Frenetic Latin-American dance, with excited voices and hand-clapping.

0:00   Percussion introduction, eight bars, with bongos and cowbells; very fast and syncopated.

0:07   Brass, with accented chords; Sharks shout "Mambo!," followed by a quieter string line, accompanied by snare-drum rolls; accented brass chords return; Sharks shout "Mambo!" again.

0:28   High dissonant woodwinds in dialogue with rhythmic brass.

0:33   Trumpets play a riff over *fff* chords:

Woodwinds and brass alternate in a highly polyphonic texture.

1:00   Rocking two-note woodwind line above syncopated low brass:

1:13   Solo trumpet enters in a high range above a complex rhythmic accompaniment:

Complex *fortissimo* polyphony until the climax; rhythm slows as music dies away at the close.

Act I: *Tonight* Ensemble   3:38

What to Listen For

Melody Speech-like exchanges; soaring lines in the love duet.

Rhythm/meter Fast, accented, and rhythmic dialogue; ominous three-note ostinato; love song in duple meter with regular phrases and a gentle, offbeat accompaniment.

Texture Complex and polyphonic, with simultaneous lines.

Form 32-bar popular song form (8-measure sections, A-A'-B-A", starting at 1:26).

Setting: The neighborhood, 6:00-9:00 p.m. Riff and the Jets, Bernardo and the Sharks, Anita, Maria, and Tony all wait expectantly for the coming of night.

0:00   Short, rhythmic orchestral introduction featuring brass and percussion, based on a three-note ostinato [bracketed]:

Gangs sing in alternation.

0:07 **Riff and the Jets** The Jets are gonna have their day tonight.	**Bernardo and the Sharks** The Sharks are gonna have their way tonight.
Riff and the Jets The Puerto Ricans grumble: "Fair fight." But if they start a rumble, We'll rumble 'em right.	**Bernardo and the Sharks** We're gonna hand 'em a surprise tonight.
0:29 **Riff and the Jets** We're gonna cut them down to size tonight.	**Bernardo and the Sharks** We said, "O.K., no rumpus, No tricks." But just in case they jump us, We're ready to mix. Tonight.
All 0:43 We're gonna rock it tonight, We're gonna jazz it up and have us a ball! They're gonna get it tonight; The more they turn it on, the harder they'll fall!	**Unison chorus,** more emphatic and accented; with accented brass interjections.
Riff and the Jets Well, they began it!	**Bernardo and the Sharks** Well, they began it!

All

And we're the ones to stop 'em once and for all,
Tonight!

Anita

1:09   Anita's gonna get her kicks tonight.
We'll have our private little mix tonight.
He'll walk in hot and tired, so what?
Don't matter if he's tired,
As long as he's hot. Tonight!

Opening melody now in uneven triplet rhythm, sung sexily:

Tony

1:26   Tonight, tonight,
Won't be just any night,
Tonight there will be no morning star.

A section (8 bars):

Tonight, tonight,
I'll see my love tonight,
And for us, stars will stop where they are.

A' section (8 bars); higher range, more emotional.

continued on next page

1:52	Today the minutes seem like hours, The hours go so slowly, And still the sky is light . . . Oh moon, grow bright, And make this endless day endless night!	**B section** (8 bars); strings in canon with voice. **A" section** (8 bars); reaches climax, then cuts off.
2:15		**Instrumental interlude.**
	Riff (*to Tony*) I'm counting on you to be there tonight. When Diesel wins it fair and square tonight. That Puerto Rican punk'll go down, And when he's hollered "Uncle," We'll tear up the town!	**Return to opening idea,** sung more vehemently.

Ensemble finale

Maria sings *Tonight* in a high range, against simultaneous dialogue and interjections over the same syncopated dance rhythm that accompanied Tony's solo; dramatic climax on last ensemble statement of "Tonight!"

Maria (*warmly*) 2:41 [**A**] Tonight, tonight Won't be just any night, Tonight there will be no morning star,	**Riff:** So I can count on you, boy? **Tony** (*abstractedly*): All right. **Riff:** We're gonna have us a ball. **Tony:** All right. **Riff:** Womb to tomb! **Tony:** Sperm to worm! **Riff:** I'll see you there about eight. **Tony:** Tonight . . .
[**A′**] Tonight, tonight, I'll see my love tonight,	**Jets:** We're gonna jazz it tonight! **Sharks:** We're gonna rock it tonight!
And for us, stars will stop Where they are.	**Anita** Tonight, tonight, late tonight, We're gonna mix it tonight.
	Sharks They're gonna get it tonight! They began it, they began it,

Tony and Maria 3:07 [**B**] Today the minutes seem like hours,	**Anita**	⎡ Anita's gonna have her day, Anita's gonna have her day, Bernardo's gonna have his way tonight, tonight, Tonight, this very night, We're gonna rock it tonight.
The hours go so slowly,	**Sharks**	⎣ They began it . . .
And still the sky is light.	**Jets**	⎡ Tonight! They began it, And we're the ones to stop 'em once and for all! The Jets are gonna have their way, The Jets are gonna have their day, ⎣ We're gonna rock it tonight. Tonight!

[**A″**] Oh moon, grow bright,

And make this endless day endless night,
Tonight!

Sharks ⌈ They began it,
│ We'll stop 'em once and for all.
│ The Sharks are gonna have their way,
│ The Sharks are gonna have their day,
⌊ We're gonna rock it tonight, tonight!

▶|◀ Reflect

How does Bernstein distinguish the individual characters' melodies in the *Tonight* number even as he makes them into a unified ensemble? Are there particular characters/melodies that you find more compelling than others in this quintet?

YOUR TURN TO EXPLORE

Choose a musical or multimedia work that addresses violence explicitly. What attitude do the performers project toward that violence, and what do you think they want listeners to understand about it? How does sound—rather than just the meaning of words—contribute to the performers' message about violence? Do you think that message is legitimate? What problems do you see with either its style or its substance?

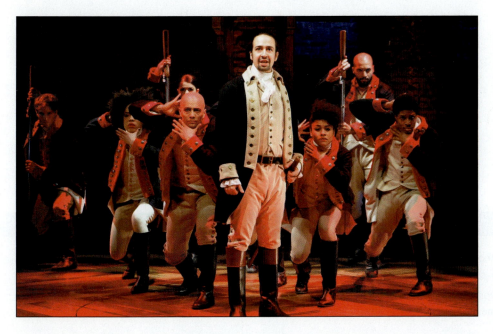

Composer Lin-Manuel Miranda in the title role of his 2015 blockbuster musical *Hamilton*.

Underscoring Meaning: Williams and Music for Film

66 So much of what we do is ephemeral and quickly forgotten . . . so it's gratifying to have something you have done linger in people's memories."

—John Williams

▶ǁ First, listen. . .

to John Williams's *Imperial March,* focusing on the instruments Williams uses to present and then modify the main theme through several variations. What are some of the most distinctive timbre combinations you hear?

Multimedia has often been a powerful way to express emotion, as we have seen with opera and ballet: several creative individuals collaborating on a total effect can produce extraordinary results. We can see this perhaps most clearly in contemporary multimedia: dramatic musical resources pioneered onstage have been transformed for the screen—film, television, and video games—so successfully that their emotional effects can stay with us for years. We will consider the work of perhaps the most prominent film composer of our day: John Williams, who has shaped decades of blockbuster movies with his imaginative soundtracks.

SOUND AND FILM

Music has played an indispensable role in creating some of the most memorable moments in film history. The opening of *2001: A Space Odyssey* (1968), the Paris montage from *Casablanca* (1942), and the shower scene in *Psycho* (1960) are all accompanied by music that has become an integral part of American culture. A composer's choices of style, instrumentation, and emotional quality are critical in fulfilling the director's vision. Even the absence of music in a scene or an entire movie (as in Alfred Hitchcock's *Lifeboat,* 1944) can contribute to the overall tone of the film.

KEY POINTS

- A film's music sets the mood and helps establish the characters and a sense of place and time.

- There are two principal types of music in a film: **underscoring** and **source music.**

- The film music of John Williams uses full orchestral resources and **leitmotifs** (recurring themes) associated with characters or situations.

Most Hollywood films use music to reflect the emotions of a given scene. John Williams, for example, guides us at the end of *E.T.: The Extra-Terrestrial* (1982) from sorrow at the apparent death of E.T. through joy at his recovery, excitement at the chase scene, and sadness at his final farewell. Howard Shore's scores to *The Lord of the Rings* trilogy help establish the dark, brooding mood surrounding Frodo's quest, but also bring out the contrasting moments of humor and tenderness.

Composers can create irony by supplying music that contradicts what is being shown, a technique called "running counter to the action." Perhaps the best-known musical/visual contradiction is the chilling climactic scene of *The Godfather* (1972). While filmgoers hear Bach organ music played during a baptism, they watch the systematic murders of Michael Corleone's enemies being brutally carried out. A number of action films since the 1990s, including Quentin Tarantino's *Pulp Fiction* (1994) and *Kill Bill, Vol. 1* and *Vol. 2* (2003–04), contain scenes of graphic violence accompanied by lighthearted rock music. This jarring contrast produces a sense of black comedy and raises questions about the superficial treatment of violence in today's media.

Music can help create a sense of place and time, as do the bagpipes in *Braveheart* (1995) and the guitar in *Brokeback Mountain* (2005). The instruments do not have to be authentic but can merely suggest a time period. In *Avatar* (2009), a small choir sings in "Na'vi"—a language developed exclusively for the movie—in keeping with the film's setting in a future utopia.

There are two main types of music in a film. **Underscoring**, which is what most people think of as film music, occurs when music comes from an unseen source, often an invisible orchestra. Music that functions as part of the drama itself is referred to as **source music**. For example, someone may turn on a radio, or a character may be inspired to sing. In *Rear Window* (1954), director Alfred Hitchcock employs only source music, which emanates from the various apartments on the main character's block. In *Boyz n the Hood* (1991), source music of classical, jazz, Motown, and rap helps define the figures of the story.

John Williams composed the score for Steven Spielberg's 1982 film *E.T.: The Extra-Terrestrial*.

Underscoring

Source music

JOHN WILLIAMS: *STAR WARS* AND BEYOND

It is difficult to overestimate Williams's importance to film music. His mastery of the techniques of **leitmotif** (a theme associated with a particular character) has defined the concept for our century; in *Jaws* (1975), for example, a scary two-note oscillating motive warns the audience of the shark's presence when the characters onscreen are oblivious to the danger, greatly intensifying the dramatic effect. Williams is often credited with the revival of the grand symphonic film score, writing unforgettable themes set in an accessible, neo-Romantic idiom. In keeping with postmodernist trends, he looked back to the familiar clichés and emotional appeal of older films. He also contributed to the 1980s hunger for sequels in movies like *Star Wars, Superman, Raiders of the Lost Ark,* and *Jurassic Park*.

The soundtrack to George Lucas's *Star Wars* has been called the greatest multi film score ever written. Several factors support this claim, including the unity Williams (perhaps inspired by Wagner's *Ring* cycle; see Chapter 41) achieves through multiple leitmotifs that return in the sequels and prequels. Each motive in the *Star*

Leitmotif

John Williams (b. 1932)

A native of Long Island, New York, Williams moved to Los Angeles as a youth, where he studied at UCLA. He then attended New York's Juilliard School, after which he worked as a jazz pianist. He began composing for television in the 1950s, and shifted to the big screen in the 1960s, when he wrote a series of scores for disaster films like *Jaws.* By the end of the 1970s, Williams had established himself as Hollywood's foremost composer, with three blockbusters to his name: *Star Wars, Close Encounters of the Third Kind,* and *Superman.* During the 1980s, he scored such box-office hits as the two *Star Wars* sequels, the *Indiana Jones* trilogy, and *E.T.,* and in the 1990s *Home Alone, Jurassic Park,* and *Schindler's List,* among many others. More recent scores include those to the first three *Harry Potter* films. In addition to this amazing lineup, Williams has also written classical works, including fanfares for the Olympics and inauguration music for President Barack Obama (*Air and Simple Gifts*). He served as the director of the Boston Pops Orchestra from 1980 to 1993.

Williams's film music explores the Wagnerian ideas of extended chromatic harmony and the use of leitmotifs—themes that represent a person, object, or idea—throughout a work. His writing is highly lyrical, providing eminently memorable themes that capture our imagination.

MAJOR WORKS: Orchestral works, including *Winter Games Fanfare* (1989), *Summon the Heroes* (1996), and concertos for various solo instruments • Chamber music, including *Air and Simple Gifts* (2009) • More than 90 film scores, including *Jaws* (1975), *Close Encounters of the Third Kind* (1977), *Star Wars* (1977–2019), *Superman* (1978), *Raiders of the Lost Ark* (1981), *E.T.: The Extra-Terrestrial* (1982), *Jurassic Park* (1993), *Schindler's List* (1993), *Harry Potter and the Sorcerer's Stone* (2001), *War Horse* (2011), *Lincoln* (2012) • Television series and themes, including *Gilligan's Island* (1964–65).

Luke Skywalker and Darth Vader duel with light sabers in *The Empire Strikes Back.*

Wars series—the opening fanfare (which becomes Luke Skywalker's theme), the "force" theme associated with the Jedi and Obi-Wan Kenobi, Yoda's gentle melody, Princess Leia's Romantic tune—supports the general nature of that character. Yet these motives can also be transformed to reflect totally different events. The theme for Luke Skywalker can sound sad or distorted when he is in trouble, triumphant when he is victorious. One of the finest musical moments occurs in *The Return of the Jedi* (1983). At the death of Darth Vader, his once terrifying theme is transformed into a gentle tune played by the woodwinds and harp.

Vader, the character whose rise and fall spans the first six *Star Wars* movies (and whose legacy continues in later films), does not have distinguishable music until *The Empire Strikes Back* (1980). His ominous-sounding theme, the *Imperial March* (LG 43), is first heard when he makes his appearance there, and its various motives are associated with this character throughout the rest of the films (in the prequels, they foreshadow who will become Darth Vader).

The march begins with an incessant stuttering rhythmic accompaniment that sets the mood for the powerful brass melody, which recurs in various guises. The minor tonality contributes to the dark character of the march, as do the occasional chromaticism and low-instrument timbres. A middle section introduces a lighter, more disjunct ostinato that accompanies an unpredictable French horn statement of the theme in which some phrase endings are elongated. This uncertainty gives way to the commanding opening music and theme statement, and the march finishes with a *fortissimo* pounding of the ostinato. The *Imperial March* has made its determined way into the public consciousness, heard often at sporting events between rival teams, in covers by rock bands, and as a favorite ringtone. Be sure to listen carefully for its occurrence in the sequels and prequels.

The Jedi master Yoda, who trains Luke Skywalker to fight against the Galactic Empire in *The Empire Strikes Back.*

The history of film music is now over a century old. During this time, the medium has attracted many of the world's best-known composers, including several we have met or will meet: Copland, Gershwin, Bernstein, Revueltas, and Philip Glass (Chapter 55). The Hollywood industry also supported a number of soundtrack specialists, who in addition to John Williams include Max Steiner (*Gone with the Wind*, 1939), Miklós Rózsa (*Ben-Hur*, 1959), Bernard Herrmann (*Vertigo*, 1958; *Psycho*, 1960), and Elmer Bernstein (*To Kill a Mockingbird*, 1962; *Ghostbusters*, 1984). While each composer brought an individual sound to his art, three general tendencies can be observed: the incorporation of the principles established by Wagner's music dramas; the assimilation of ever-changing trends in popular music; and the constant search for fresh, new sounds, including resources from across the globe. After one hundred years, film music remains a strong, vibrant medium and an integral part of the art of filmmaking.

▶|◀ Reflect

How does Williams use countermelodies and other polyphonic devices to change the expressive effect of the main march theme through the variations? If you know the movies in which the *Imperial March* is featured, how does the music help shape the dramatic effect of the scenes in which it appears?

YOUR TURN TO EXPLORE

Choose a favorite film and watch it a couple of times, paying attention to the use of sound. Which types of music discussed in this chapter are employed? Are there particular moments when you think sound and music are used most effectively? Conversely, can you identify moments where you feel the music is not effective for the dramatic purpose? How might a different choice at that point improve the effect?

LISTENING GUIDE 43 3:02

Williams: *Imperial March*, from *The Empire Strikes Back*

DATE: 1980

GENRE: Film score

PERFORMED BY: Skywalker Symphony; John Williams, conductor

What to Listen For

Melody Accented, disjunct melody, in two-measure phrases.

Rhythm/meter Marchlike, duple meter, with rhythmic ostinatos.

Harmony G minor theme, with some chromaticism.

Form Theme and variations.

| 0:00 | Introduction—rhythmic ostinato accompaniment sets the ominous mood; stuttering pattern, with repeated notes in horns, strings, and timpani. |
| 0:09 | Main theme is introduced by trumpets and other brass, in G minor, with stuttering accompaniment underneath: |

12-measure statement (4+4, then the last 4 repeated).

0:37	Accompaniment pattern; then other brass instruments join; fanfare builds in a *crescendo*.
0:46	New ostinato pattern; each downbeat is answered by a busy three-note motive in flutes, then strings.
1:04	Theme is varied in horns, played softly with an elongated note at the end of each two-measure phrase; new busy accompaniment is heard underneath.
1:37	Returns to the opening stuttering accompaniment, then rises a whole step.
1:47	Theme in trumpets, returns to G minor, with full orchestra playing ostinato accompaniment.
2:14	Theme in horns, with full orchestra playing *fortissimo*.
2:33	Stuttering accompaniment passage, leads to a coda.
2:42	**Coda**—varied brass statement of the theme grows dissonant; whirling strings lead to a final full orchestral statement of the ostinato.

Returning with Interest: Bowie, Glass, and Postmodern Elaboration

▶‖ **First, listen...**

to the first movement of Philip Glass's Symphony No. 4 (subtitled *Heroes*), and focus on the melodic ideas. Listen for any short or longer motives that are repeated. How are contrasting melodies differentiated?

> 66 You never knew with David [Bowie]. He was a master unto himself."
>
> —Philip Glass

T he ability to control creative content is both artistically and finan-cially crucial to an artist's success. Laws concerning copyright and the unauthorized use of other artists' materials have become increasingly strict in the last century. It was not always so: in earlier times, using material by another musician in one's work was considered a tribute to a skilled predecessor. This was true especially if, in the words of a contemporary of J. S. Bach, you "returned with interest": that is, if the material was integrated so that it presented a new creative perspective. Contemporary musicians often borrow each other's ideas, and the boundaries between art and commercial music have repeatedly been crossed in search of inspiration. We will hear one remarkable example that links two of the most successful musician-composers of the last few decades, David Bowie and Philip Glass.

David Bowie singing at a Toronto nightclub, March 1987.

DAVID BOWIE, CREATIVE CHAMELEON

From his start as a folk-rocker in the late 1960s to his astounding jazz-rock-hip-hop fusion album *Blackstar* released shortly before his death in January 2016, Bowie reinvented his artistic persona and musical style multiple times. One of the most

KEY POINTS

- Musicians often pay homage to earlier composers or elaborate on their ideas.
- David Bowie was one of the most inventive singer-composers of the late twentieth and early twenty-first centuries, working in a variety of rock and pop styles

and experimenting with collaborators from several traditions.

- Philip Glass, a prominent contemporary composer, borrowed from one of Bowie's most influential albums in crafting his Fourth Symphony, subtitled *Heroes*.

In His Own Words

❝ Soon after its composition [Bowie] began using the *Heroes* symphony for his walk-in music for some of his concerts. . . . there's a version [in his archive] in which he superimposed his voice singing *Heroes* on to the symphonic recording. . . . It would be amazing to find it."

—Philip Glass

significant shifts resulted from contact in the mid-1970s with minimalist musicians in New York City—part of a broader phenomenon often described as "Downtown music," which experimented with commercial styles as well as music from around the world.

Bowie collaborated with renowned sound producer Brian Eno on a series of groundbreaking albums (*Low* and *Heroes,* 1977; *Lodger,* 1979). The second of these albums, *Heroes,* reveals that Bowie was influenced not only by Eno's ideas of electronic "ambient" music (with a static soundscape rather than clear melodies or form) but also by the works of such minimalist composers as Steve Reich and John Adams (Chapter 57). *Heroes* was a great success both critically and financially; and the title song, one of Bowie's signature tunes, was taken up by many other artists over the years (including Prince, who sang it as a tribute to Bowie in one of his own last concerts).

HEROES: FROM ALBUM TO "SYMPHONIC BALLET"

One of the musicians who found the Bowie/Eno experiments particularly expressive was Philip Glass, a leader of the "Downtown NYC" creative group and leading exponent of **minimalist** composition. Building on the phase experiments of Steve Reich and others, Glass developed a consonant style based on repetitions of short motives that appealed to a wide audience in the 1980s and 90s and made him perhaps the most commercially successful composer of art music in the United States today.

Glass and Bowie had become good friends in the 1970s, and when it came to writing his first symphony, Glass turned to the music of Bowie and Eno for ideas. The resulting work (1992) subtly incorporated large sections of musical material from the entire *Low* album. In his fourth symphony, subtitled *Heroes,* Glass focused more on small borrowings from Bowie/Eno, and expanded the collaboration further to include modern dancer/choreographer Twyla Tharpe. In the composer's words, "I set *Heroes* as a six-movement work, each movement based on a theme from [the album] *Heroes,* with an overall dramatic structure that would be suitable for dance. The result is a symphonic ballet—a transformation of the original themes combined with new material of my own and presented in a new dramatic form."

While Glass's *Heroes* was indeed premiered to choreography by Tharpe, it has since been performed and recorded as a six-movement symphony. Each movement takes as a starting point one of the songs or instrumental tracks from the album: we will hear the first (LG 44), which is based on the title track. For those who have heard this song, there are a few clearly recognizable musical elements

The Philip Glass Ensemble performing in the Netherlands for the Lowlands Festival (2016).

Philip Glass (b. 1937)

Although Glass is often associated with the minimalist movement, he rejects that term, preferring to call himself a composer of "music with repetitive structures" and even a "classicist" because of his close study of composers such as Bach, Mozart, and Schubert. Glass studied flute as a young man, and then piano and composition at the Juilliard School of Music in New York in the early 1960s, where Steve Reich was a fellow student. Shortly after graduating, he studied with Nadia Boulanger in Paris (1964–66). There he was strongly influenced by new wave cinema and, through collaborating with Indian musicians Ravi Shankar (p. 38) and Alla Rakha on a film score, the additive nature of Indian rhythms. Returning to New York at the end of the 1960s, he encountered the phase music of Steve Reich and joined with that composer and others in creating an experimental tradition of "radical consonant" music in downtown New York City.

In 1971, the composer founded the Philip Glass Ensemble, with which he still performs on electronic keyboard instruments. The first of the three operas in his "Portrait Trilogy," *Einstein on the Beach*, premiered in both France and the United States in 1976, to enthusiastic response; the *Washington Post* called it "one of the seminal artworks of the century." Many commissions followed for both multimedia and instrumental works, making Glass one of the best-known composers of modern times. He has become renowned for his collaborations with artists in many media (from theater to film, visual art, and sound) and many traditions (non-Western, commercial-rock, jazz, concert music).

MAJOR WORKS: Operas, including *Einstein on the Beach* (1976), *Satyagraha* (1979), *Akhenaten* (1983) • A song cycle, *Songs from Liquid Days* (1986) on texts by songwriters such as David Byrne and Paul Simon • Film scores, including *Koyaanisqatsi, Powaqqatsi, Naqoyqatsi* • 12 symphonies, including *Heroes* • Much chamber music and several concertos.

in Glass's movement—for example, the alternation of two chords a third apart, a motive with two adjacent repeating notes, and a distinct rhythmic pattern from the song's refrain. The final effect, however, entirely reflects Glass's own musical voice: musical ideas are repeated in both short and longer units, with much interplay between contrasting orchestral timbres.

Bowie's response to Glass's symphony is revealing:

> Hearing this material is a bit like being introduced to a brother or sister that you've been told you had, and you weren't really aware of their existence. And when you do meet them, obviously the very familiarity of the family features registers, but there's a whole life and all these things have grown up without your knowledge. . . . It was as though Philip had fed into my voice . . . but somehow had arrived, I feel, a lot nearer to the gut feeling of what I was trying to do.

Though not all musical "returning with interest" may be as well received and amicable as the *Heroes* collaboration between Bowie and Glass (and Tharpe), there are abundant examples of successful crossover between traditions and media in contemporary music. Musical culture has been and continues to be dynamic as we move farther into the twenty-first century; no matter how traditions and genres evolve, there will always be musicians prepared to push their boundaries, joining forces to challenge and delight audiences around the world.

▶|◀ Reflect

How might the repetitive quality of Glass's style contribute to a meditative emotional state? Find and listen to a recording of Bowie's song. In what ways do you think Glass's movement is "in conversation" with Bowie's original?

YOUR TURN TO EXPLORE

Find a musical work that borrows significantly from earlier models, whether through digital sampling or re-use of melody, harmony, lyrics, and so on. Are there repertories/styles that rely more on borrowing than others? Why do you think the musicians have chosen to use specific ideas? What new elements are added to the borrowed material, and for what expressive goals? Do you think the result successfully "returns with interest"?

LISTENING GUIDE 44   5:55

Glass: Symphony No. 4 (*Heroes*), I

DATE: 1996

PERFORMED BY: American Composers Orchestra; Dennis Russell Davies, director

GENRE: "Symphonic ballet" in six movements

1. "Heroes"	4. "Sons of the Silent Age"
2. "Abdulmajid"	5. "Neukoln"
3. "Sense of Doubt"	6. "Schneider"

1: "Heroes"

What to Listen For

Melody Short motives are repeated and combined.

Rhythm/meter Moderate quadruple meter; regular use of syncopation, triplets, and four-note arpeggios.

Texture Increasingly layered polyphony, with homophony at the opening and close.

Expression Musical ideas develop slowly through extended repetition and layering; they reflect on motives of the song's melody.

0:00   Clarinets, bassoons, and horns softly introduce a two-note motive, punctuated by pizzicato strings and brass:

0:33   Change of timbre and mood as flutes and oboes enter; syncopated rhythms in horns and strings, glockenspiel on the second beat.

0:47   Winds in octaves present a descending-third motive from the opening of the song:

Motive is inverted, expanded, and repeated; a syncopated accompaniment continues with cross-rhythms between brass and strings:

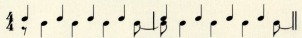

1:29   Flutes, oboes, and brass play triplets; strings continue with syncopation; the song motive shifts to the brass.

2:25   The brass now take on syncopation, triplets shift to the strings; a new scalewise melody in the winds, first descending stepwise then gradually rising in waves:

3:34   The song motive returns again in the brass as the descending/ascending melody continues in winds; strings now shift to repeated sixteenth-note arpeggios.

4:27   Repeat of previous section.

5:08   Modified return of the opening two-note motive and clarinet-bassoon-horn timbre, punctuated by arpeggios in flutes and harp.

Neo-Romantic Evocations: Higdon and Program Music into the Twenty-First Century

▶‖ **First, listen...**

to Jennifer Higdon's *blue cathedral*, paying special attention to the variety of timbres you hear. What instruments are featured, and how do they help establish different moods? What kind of story line or program might you associate with this work?

O ne trend in recent concert music, labeled **neo-Romanticism**, is represented by composers who embrace aspects of nineteenth-century orchestral sound. Among those aspects is program music, which as we saw earlier was very important to Romantic composers, from both a personal and a nationalist perspective. This importance has endured to the present, as musicians continue to draw on their biographical and cultural experiences as sources for expression. The example we will hear, by Jennifer Higdon, aims to "modernize" the nineteenth-century orchestral tradition. It also shows an influence of non-Western cultures that has lasted beyond John Cage, and that reflects the never-ending search for new ways to expand and renew the tradition of concert music for the twenty-first century.

A NEW ROMANTICISM?

We have traced several different approaches to making music new in the early twentieth century—and indeed, the multiple facets of modernism were very important to artists and their audiences. But the style that had developed in the 1800s never really went away; great works by renowned composers such as Beethoven, Brahms, Verdi, and Wagner were performed in concert halls and opera houses even as the modernists were proposing new alternatives. Some early

KEY POINTS

- Some recent compositional trends speak to audiences alienated by highly intellectual modernist music.
- **Neo-Romanticism** favors the lush harmonic language of the late Romantic era: the music is mostly tonal, chromatic, and highly virtuosic, with innovative timbre combinations.
- Neo-Romantic works often feature programmatic elements connected with a personal story, as in Jennifer Higdon's tone poem *blue cathedral*.

twentieth-century composers continued to update the Romantic style, building on the luxuriant orchestral tradition as well as the chamber genres that had been constantly evolving since the generation of Haydn and Mozart. One of the most prominent exponents of this continued commitment to Romantic ideals was American composer Samuel Barber (1910–1981), whose elegiac and well-loved *Adagio for Strings* (1936) is suffused with the feeling and grand gestures of the nineteenth century, and whose songs continue the multinational tradition of setting intense poetry to sweeping and beautiful melodies.

The music of Barber and others who upheld key elements of Romanticism was dismissed as regressive and antiquated by those who considered modernism the only legitimate artistic pathway into the twentieth century. The advent of postmodern styles, however, induced composers to look again to the past for inspiration—sometimes with an ironic or detached perspective, but sometimes with respect and perhaps even a touch of nostalgia for the expressive power of the Romantic style. In the last quarter of the twentieth century and into the twenty-first, orchestral repertories have been revitalized by this neo-Romantic reclaiming of nineteenth-century harmonic and melodic language in a new context—one that takes into account the complexities of a postmodern world.

Jennifer Higdon and *blue cathedral*

Hailed by one critic as a "savvy, sensitive composer . . . with a generous dash of spirit," Higdon is one of the most widely performed of living American composers.

In Her Own Words

❝ Can music reflect colors and can colors be reflected in music? . . . I often picture colors as if I were spreading them on a canvas, except I do so with melodies and harmonies, and through the peculiar sounds of the instruments themselves."

—Jennifer Higdon

Jennifer Higdon (b. 1962)

Born in Brooklyn, New York, Higdon pursued music studies at Bowling Green State University and then completed graduate degrees in composition at the University of Pennsylvania, where she studied with George Crumb (Chapter 52). She claims that "the sheer number of Beatles tunes I listened to helped me to realize the ability of music to communicate." Higdon has been recognized with prestigious awards: she received the Pulitzer Prize in 2010 for her Violin Concerto, written to show off Hilary Hahn's talents (p. 40). Since 1994, she has taught composition at the Curtis Institute of Music in Philadelphia.

Higdon's extensive output spans most genres, including orchestral music and compositions for her own instrument, the flute. Her "American" sound harks back to that of Aaron Copland, on which she imposes her own highly colorful timbral palette as well as dense textures and wide-ranging dynamics. Some works, like *blue cathedral*, exude a rich lyricism and shimmering beauty, while others, like *Fanfare Ritmico* and the Percussion Concerto, are more propulsive. Her rooting in tonality as well as the familiar quality in her music help mark her as a neo-Romantic.

MAJOR WORKS: Orchestral music, including *Fanfare Ritmico* (2000), *blue cathedral* (2000), *Concerto for Orchestra* (2002) • Concertos for oboe (2005), percussion (2007), violin (2008), and viola (2015) • Works for wind groups, including soprano saxophone concerto (with wind ensemble, 2009) • Chamber music, including *Amazing Grace* (for string quartet, 2002) • Choral works, including *Southern Grace* (1998) • Vocal works, including *Dooryard Bloom* (for baritone and orchestra, 2004) and the opera *Cold Mountain* (2015).

Higdon's *blue cathedral* evokes colorful Impressionist images like *Cathedral of Rouen: Full Sunlight, Blue Harmony and Gold* (1894), by **Claude Monet.**

Her music is richly neo-Romantic, displaying an innovative sound palette that has been described as "very American." Her orchestral work *blue cathedral* (LG 45) has already garnered status as a classic.

Written in 2000 to commemorate the anniversary of the Curtis Institute of Music in Philadelphia, *blue cathedral* is an orchestral tone poem with a subtext of personal grief over the untimely death from skin cancer of the composer's younger brother, Andrew Blue Higdon. Higdon explains that she was contemplating the remarkable journey of life. The title incorporates her brother's name, and she also provides evocative imagery to help us understand the broader goals of her composition:

> Blue . . . like the sky. Where all possibilities soar. Cathedrals . . . a place of thought, growth, spiritual expression . . . serving as a symbolic doorway into and out of this world. I found myself imagining a journey through a glass cathedral in the sky. . . . The listener would float down the aisle, moving slowly at first and then progressing at a quicker pace, rising towards an immense ceiling which would open to the sky. . . . I wanted to create the sensation of contemplation and quiet peace at the beginning, moving toward the feeling of celebration and ecstatic expansion of the soul, all the while singing along with that heavenly music.

The tone poem opens to shimmering, bell-like timbres (known as **tintinnabulation**) sounded over softly muted strings. An intimate dialogue ensues between an ethereal solo flute (Higdon's instrument) and solo clarinet (her brother's).

Throughout, there is a sense of continual expansion and ascent as the work builds toward several stirring climaxes. The open string sonority strongly evokes Copland's characteristic "American" sound, while plaintive solos are heard from darker instruments, like the English horn, viola, and cello (Higdon notes that she is "hyper-aware of color"). Near the end, more soothing colors appear, in the guise of pitched crystal glasses (a finger is run around the rims) and the chiming of some fifty Chinese reflex balls (left), played by most of the orchestra's musicians, a borrowing from Asian soundscapes.

Two Chinese reflex balls, like those played in *blue cathedral.*

In her use of characteristic tone colors and biographical elements, Higdon maintains the tradition of program music that spurred nineteenth-century composers to such imaginative heights. Her approach, popular with modern audiences, has helped keep the tradition of concert music vital and relevant to our day.

▶◀ Reflect

Now that you have read about Higdon's composition, how effective do you find her orchestration technique in telling her story? How does her use of orchestral timbres differ from other symphonic works you have heard?

LISTENING GUIDE 45   12:19

Higdon: *blue cathedral*

DATE: 2000

PERFORMED BY: Atlantic Symphony; Robert Spano, conductor

GENRE: Orchestral tone poem

What to Listen For

Rhythm/meter Mostly in 5/4 with a veiled sense of bar lines; some shifting meters.

Harmony Prominent use of major triads but with no strong sense of a key center.

Texture Homophonic, focusing on individual lines and duets.

Performing forces Large orchestra with many percussion instruments (crotales, celesta, marimba, vibraphone, bell tree, chimes, triangle, tuned glasses, Chinese reflex balls).

A section

0:00   Gentle, bell-like tintinnabulation, then muted lower strings, with a two-note descending motive.

0:47   Solo flute with a rising line, accompanied by muted string chords; no sense of pulse.

1:14   Solo clarinet answers, with harp and string accompaniment.

1:30   Duet between flute and clarinet in overlapping high-range lines:

2:18   Violin solo joins with ascending lines; builds to a large *crescendo* into the next section.

B section

3:07   Wavering horn chords alternate with open high strings; more rhythmic and syncopated:

Builds to a loud climax as strings ascend, punctuated by brass.

4:12   *Fortissimo* climax, then fades quickly.

4:23   **A section** returns briefly; a falling motive in strings.

C section

4:50   A sustained pitch and rhythmic percussion chords introduce solo instruments; plaintive English horn is accompanied by harmonics on harp and percussion in open fifths:

continued on next page

Other solo instruments enter one at a time (viola, piccolo, cello, oboe, bassoon) over now-syncopated accompaniment; crotales (antique cymbals) add a bell-like timbre.

6:13   Builds to a gentle climax, with syncopated chords continuing.

6:30   Violins and violas pass the theme between them in dialogue; the texture grows complex with imitation as the orchestration expands.

7:26   Quicker tempo, with focus on percussion and strings.

8:00   Shifting meters, with a lyrical melody floating across the bar lines; strings play in thirds, accompanied by swirling woodwinds; rhythmic excitement builds:

9:02   Broad, "flying" theme in full orchestra, in a slower tempo:

9:35   Return to the opening flute-clarinet duet (**A**), accompanied by quiet, wavering strings; English horn enters and "the clarinet continues on in the upward progressing journey."

10:26   String musicians play Chinese reflex balls, and brass musicians play tuned crystal glasses.

11:25   Prepared piano, with screws inserted in strings, sounds like chimes as the opening tintinnabulation returns.

YOUR TURN TO EXPLORE

Find a recent instrumental work that has an evocative title and/or a specific program. What musical elements does the composer use to convey that title or program? How does the availability of increasingly diverse musical styles in the twenty-first century give contemporary musicians more expressive options? What kinds of musical colors and devices might you choose to describe your emotional response to something that deeply concerns you today?

Reality Shows: Adams and Contemporary Opera

▶‖ **First, listen...**

to the chorus "At the sight of this" from John Adams's opera *Doctor Atomic*, focusing on the rhythm. What rhythmic techniques do you hear, and how do these help establish the mood?

66 Whenever serious art loses track of its roots in the vernacular, then it begins to atrophy."

—John Adams

Verdi once said that in musical theater, "it may be a good thing to copy reality; but to invent reality is much, much better." And operatic composers and librettists—like directors and their teams in film—have often sought deeper truths in stories based in fiction rather than fact. History, however, has also regularly been present in opera, since the actions of significant individuals have long fascinated us. In recent years, several composers have taken recent historical events as the basis for operatic treatment. Operas are not documentaries, however: much of the content of a "historical opera" is based on the creativity of librettist and composer, rather than on documented dialogue between real-life individuals. The goal of these works is to evoke the intensity and complexity of the time and the emotions felt by the historical actors, rather than to provide a factually accurate account. One noteworthy example is *Doctor Atomic*, a collaboration between composer John Adams and provocative playwright/director Peter Sellars.

In His Own Words

66 [I am] a very emotional composer, one who experiences music on a very physical level. My music is erotic and Dionysian, and I never try to obscure those feelings when I compose."

—John Adams

JOHN ADAMS AND POST-MINIMALISM

Minimalism has exerted a great influence on a variety of composers. Perhaps the most versatile of these "post-minimalists" is John Adams, whose works have gained wide appeal in large part because of their combination of accessible melodies and harmonies with intense, deeply expressive contemporary devices. Adams infuses the minimalist style with traits of neo-Romanticism, illustrated in his 2005 opera *Doctor Atomic*.

KEY POINTS

- Operatic composers sometimes choose historical topics, seeking to convey emotional truths through semi-fictional accounts of past events.

- American composer John Adams's eclectic approach combines elements of minimalism with traits of neo-Romanticism, forging a post-minimalist style in his opera *Doctor Atomic*.

333

Krishna displayed in his universal form as Vishnu, from the Sri Srinivasa Perumal Temple in Singapore.

Doctor Atomic

For his third opera, Adams chose as his subject the awe-inspiring creation of the atomic bomb by a team of scientists, headed by physicist J. Robert Oppenheimer, working at the Los Alamos Laboratory in New Mexico. Peter Sellars's fascinating libretto is based on the memoirs of the project's scientists and some declassified government documents, as well as the poetry of John Donne, Charles Baudelaire, and the sacred Hindu scripture *Bhagavad Gita (Song of God)*, the last three all literary texts well known to Oppenheimer. Adams's rich and dark score is complex texturally, as are his very human and well-developed characters.

The opera focuses on the last days and hours before the first atomic test on July 16, 1945. In Act I, chorus members sing of their hopes and fears about the invention—a twenty-one-kiloton atomic weapon. Oppenheimer, struggling with his conscience, sings a stunning aria that carries us to the depths of his soul as he looks with awe and trepidation at his creation.

In Act II, we learn that the test will go on while scientists worry about fallout: no one really knows what to expect, but one team member speculates that the atmosphere itself might catch on fire. Tension mounts as the chorus sings "At the

John Adams (b. 1947)

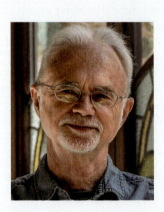

Adams was educated at Harvard University, where he was steeped in serialism. In his dorm room, though, he preferred to listen to rock: "I was much inspired by certain albums that appeared to me to have a fabulous unity to them, like . . . *Abbey Road* and *Dark Side of the Moon*." In 1972, he drove his VW Beetle cross-country to San Francisco, where he began teaching at the San Francisco Conservatory of Music, and quickly became an advocate for contemporary music in the Bay Area.

Adams first gained notice with two hypnotic minimalist works—*Phrygian Gates* (for piano, 1977) and *Shaker Loops* (for string septet, 1978)—then earned a national reputation with *Harmonium* (1980–81) and *Harmonielehre* (1984–85, which pays homage to Arnold Schoenberg), both written for the San Francisco Symphony. He attracted much attention with his opera *Nixon in China* (1987), on the historic visit of President Nixon in November 1972. The works that followed show an increasing awareness of the sumptuous orchestration and expressive harmonies of neo-Romanticism, including his next opera, *The Death of Klinghoffer* (1991), based on the 1985

hijacking of a cruise liner by Palestinian terrorists. The 2000 *El Niño*, a Nativity oratorio modeled on Handel's *Messiah*, has texts culled from English, Spanish, and Latin sources. Both these stage works were collaborations with stage director Peter Sellars.

Adams won a Pulitzer Prize for *On the Transmigration of Souls* (2002), commissioned to mark the first anniversary of September 11, 2001, setting texts based on victims' names. His 2005 opera *Doctor Atomic* may be his most dramatic work.

MAJOR WORKS: Stage works, including *Nixon in China* (1987), *The Death of Klinghoffer* (1991), *El Niño* (2000), *Doctor Atomic* (2005), and *The Gospel According to the Other Mary* (2011–13) • Orchestral works, including *Short Ride in a Fast Machine* (1986), *Tromba lontana* (1986), and *City Noir* (2009) • Chamber music, including *Phrygian Gates* (1977), *Shaker Loops* (1978), and *Chamber Symphony* (1992) • Vocal works, including *On the Transmigration of Souls* (In Memory of September 11, 2001—for chorus, children's chorus, and orchestra, 2002) • Tape and electronic works.

sight of this," a dramatic text from the *Bhagavad Gita* describing the moment when Krishna, an avatar (or incarnation) of Vishnu, reveals himself as the Supreme God, the all-powerful creator and destroyer of the world. Adams's spine-chilling chorus conveys the apprehension and terror of those about to witness the historic blast (LG 46). The fearsome text is declaimed on repeated notes in short phrases, punctuated with offbeat brass and percussion accents. An unsettling refrain ("O Master") recurs with even shorter, more dissonant tones. At the close, the crowd responds to the immense buildup of tension with mere utterances over distorted electronic sounds. The effect is thoroughly compelling.

The opera's last scene depicts the moments before the detonation, when a rocket sends out a two-minute warning and Oppenheimer sings, "Lord, these affairs are hard on the heart." The scientist recalls the Hindu text again to describe the explosion: "If the radiance of a thousand suns were to burst at once into the sky, that would be like the splendor of the mighty one."

In *Doctor Atomic*, Adams has taken a hugely complex subject that draws together science and art, and presented it in a multilayered, eclectic score that offers much to the imagination as well as to the ears. The topic of the opera also raises complex moral (and perhaps political) questions: What does it mean to make art about such a destructive and lethal technology? Do we run the risk of losing track of the horrors that followed these experiments (the bombing of Hiroshima and Nagasaki) by focusing on an individual's struggles through beautiful music?

Several of Adams's works have caused controversy, including his opera *The Death of Klinghoffer*, based on an episode in which Palestinian militants kidnapped a cruise ship and killed one of its Jewish passengers. Some saw it as a nuanced treatment of a complex global political problem, others were disturbed at what they felt was too sympathetic a portrayal of the terrorists and their cause. Adams is hailed as one of the most masterful contemporary composers in part because he constantly seeks to make his music relevant to the concerns of the twenty-first century.

Gerald Finley as physicist J. Robert Oppenheimer in the San Francisco Opera production of *Doctor Atomic*.

▶|◀ **Reflect**

How effective is Adams in conjuring up an image of the terrifying event described in the opera? How do the syncopation and offbeat accents contribute to the story?

YOUR TURN TO EXPLORE

Find an opera or other dramatic/multimedia work that takes a historical event as a starting point and provides an artistic interpretation of that event. How are different individuals characterized through music (high or low voice types, instrumental timbre for accompaniment, tuneful or dissonant melodies)? How do you think the composer wants us to interpret the event—is his or her artistic reading an appropriate interpretation given the historical facts? What recent event do you think might lend itself to operatic/dramatic treatment, and what kinds of musical choices would you make to convey the story?

LISTENING GUIDE 46

🎧 ▶️ 4:05

Adams: *Doctor Atomic*, "At the sight of this"

DATE: 2005

GENRE: Opera

SETTING: Los Alamos, New Mexico, 1945

LIBRETTIST: Peter Sellars

PERFORMED BY: Metropolitan Opera Orchestra and Chorus; Alan Gilbert, conductor

CHARACTERS: J. Robert Oppenheimer, a physicist (baritone)
Kitty Oppenheimer, his wife (mezzo-soprano)
General Leslie Groves, U.S. army engineer (bass)
Edward Teller, a physicist (baritone)
Robert R. Wilson, a physicist (tenor)
Jack Hubbard, chief meteorologist (baritone)
Captain James Nolan, an army officer (tenor)
Pasqualita, the Oppenheimers' maid (mezzo-soprano)

Act II, scene 3, chorus: "At the sight of this"

What to Listen For

Melody Short, choppy phrases with declaimed text; ideas are often repeated.

Rhythm/meter Syncopated, with many offbeat accents.

Harmony Sharply dissonant chords.

Form Verse/refrain structure with repeated sections and text.

A section

0:00   At the sight of this, your Shape stupendous,
Full of mouths and eyes, terrible with fangs.

Loud, fiery mood; offbeat horn accents.
Chorus with short phrases, recitative style.

Opening of chorus, with text delcaimed together:

Refrain

0:27   O O O O O.

Regular harsh chords on the main beats against a syncopated accompaniment.

A section, elongated

0:41   At the sight of this, your Shape stupendous,
Full of mouths and eyes, feet, thighs and bellies,
All the worlds are fear-struck, even just as I am.

A section repeated with harsh, offbeat, accented dissonances.

Refrain

1:06   O O O O Master.

Choral refrain, invoking Vishnu:

Single chords again on the main beats.

B section

1:19   When I see you, Vishnu, when I see you omnipresent,
Shouldering the sky, in hues of rainbow.

Connected chords, descending and chromatic,
against syncopated accompaniment.

Refrain

1:32   O O O O Master.

Single chord interjections again; active
accompaniment leads back to the **A section**.

A section

1:48   At the sight of this, your Shape stupendous,
With your mouth agape and flame-eyes staring—
All my peace is gone; O, my heart is troubled.

Repeated choral section; dissonant string chords.

Refrain

2:13   O O O O Master.

B section

2:26   When I see you, Vishnu, omnipresent, flame-eyes staring,
All my peace is gone, is troubled.

Connected chords as in the last **B section**.

B section, with sustained chords:

2:43   **Coda**

Disjunct high woodwinds, with agitated,
accented accompaniment.

3:00   Vocables: "Ee ee" (women)/"Do" (men).

Electronically generated sounds accompany
the vocables.

Syncretism and Universalism: León and the Intersection of Traditions

▶❚ First, listen...

to Tania León's "Understanding," from *Inura,* and focus on the interaction between percussion, strings, and voices. What recurring patterns do you hear, in both short and longer time spans? What is regular and what is unpredictable in this work?

Music that arises as the result of cultural encounters has long laid the foundation for dynamic new expressive possibilities, and these have only increased with modern globalization. Some twenty-first-century musicians have even made international collaboration a focus of their creative careers: for example, the well-known cellist Yo-Yo Ma (pictured on p. 40) has fostered a collective called the Silk Road Project, designed to bring together accomplished artists from Eurasian cultures to devise their distinctive messages. This intersectional approach can highlight the creative energy of communities that have historically been marginalized or considered less "artful." One of the most extraordinay musicians who have taken this path is Tania León, whose self-consciously syncretic (blended) style is at once progressive and representative of her remarkable heritage.

TANIA LEÓN'S *INURA*

One of the best examples of León's blended style is her ballet *Inura (In Motion),* written for DanceBrazil, an American company focused on Brazilian traditions. The text, a combination of Yoruba and Brazilian Portuguese, expresses an invocation to Exu, an important deity in the Afro-Brazilian tradition who is viewed as the

KEY POINTS

- International musical collaborations, sometimes with marginalized cultures, provide new possibilities for expression.

- Cuban-born composer Tania León has successfully blended musical traditions and styles representing

her diverse backgrounds; she views herself as a global citizen.

- León's ballet *Inura,* drawing on Afro-Brazilian traditions, is an excellent example of her syncretic, or blended, style.

messenger between the gods and people; Exu guards the energy that moves the universe and makes natural events occur. The movement called "Understanding" features, along with strings and SATB chorus of twelve voices, a five-person percussion ensemble, only one of whom reads pitch-notated music; the others play traditional Brazilian drums, idiophones, and a musical bow, following a rhythmic notation León has devised.

A steady rhythmic grid played by percussion instruments in complex intersecting patterns provides continuity within the movement, which otherwise alternates between voices and strings in both predictable and unpredictable ways. The opening appears to set up a recurring four-measure phrase, but then the music moves back and forth between four-measure and more irregular phrases. The first vocal episode returns twice as a sort of refrain, and string episodes are also repeated, as in rondo form—but the piece doesn't follow refrain structures we have encountered before. In a call-and-response practice with roots in Afro-diasporic cultures, two tenors periodically break from the singing group to give a speech-like call to which the group responds. The melodies use mostly pentatonic scales, echoing multiple folk traditions (see Chapter 39), but sometimes shift into minor tonality; repetitions of short motives are reminiscent of minimalist works, but also of Afro-diasporic dances.

Traditional Brazilian percussion instruments called for in *Inura* include djembe drums, bongo drums, and caxixi shakers.

Tania León (b. 1943)

Born in Havana, Cuba, to parents of mixed African, Asian, and European descent, León began studying piano at age four. In 1967, after formal studies in piano and composition at Havana's National Conservatory, she moved to New York, where two years later she became music director for the Dance Theatre of Harlem and began composing ballets for the troupe.

Shortly thereafter, León began serving as guest conductor for numerous U.S.-based and international ensembles, often promoting contemporary—and especially Latin American—music. In the late 1970s, she turned her energies again toward composition, and developed an individual style influenced by the diverse music of her youth in Cuba as well as modern classical music. As musical director for several Broadway shows (*The Wiz* and *Godspell*), she absorbed influences from jazz and gospel as well.

León has received many prestigious commissions and awards, and has taught at Harvard, Yale, the University of Michigan, and Brooklyn College, where she currently holds an endowed professorship. While some have called her style Afro-Cuban, she rejects such categorization, proclaiming that she is "totally anti-label." (See quote at the beginning of the chapter.) Still, Latin American and jazz rhythms are important to her compositional style, as is improvisation. Her music abounds with rhythmic energy, complex rhythms, dense textures, and colorful orchestration.

MAJOR WORKS: Stage works, including the opera *The Scourge of Hyacinths* (1994) and the ballets *Haiku* (1973) and *Inura* (2009) • Orchestral works, including *Latin Lights* (1979), *Batá* (1985), *Carabalí* (1991), and *Indígena* (1991) • Chamber works, including *Ethos* (2014) for piano quintet • *Four Pieces for Cello Solo* (1983) • *Rituál* (for solo piano, 1987) and other piano works • Vocal works.

The surdo, or large bass drum, is used in Brazilian traditional and samba music.

In "Understanding," as in many recent choral works, the virtuosic vocal writing requires an extraordinary level of rhythmic precision and tuning of dissonant intervals (especially major seconds and fourths). Though the percussion parts are inherently designed for instruments outside the Western tradition, their rhythms are much more intricate than what we might expect with simple dance-entertainment music.

Inura is a remarkable example of musical syncretism, combining instruments and languages and rhythms from ostensibly "low culture" Afro-diasporic religious practices with compositional approaches from Euro-American concert music. Here, León illustrates the potential of advancing traditions of multiple "ancestors" through mutual conversation, for the benefit (as she writes in the program notes) of "those who have yet to be born."

LISTENING GUIDE 47

 6:51

León: "Understanding," from *Inura* (*In Motion*)

DATE: 2009

GENRE: Ballet with mixed choir, strings, and percussion

PERFORMED BY: DanceBrazil and Son Sonora Ensemble

MOVEMENTS:	1. "The Power"	5. "Respect"
	2. "The Sharing"	6. "The Lust"
	3. "Teaching"	7. "Funny Battle"
	4. **"Understanding"**	8. "Manifest"

What to Listen For

Melody Modified pentatonic, arpeggiated (in both strings and voices); builds on short motives.

Harmony Pentatonic, with elements of minor; extensive use of the intervals second and fourth.

Texture Dense, layered; instruments and voices trade off.

Rhythm Regular dance patterns are overlaid with irregular syncopations.

0:00	First cycle (4 mm.): surdo, bongo, and tamborim (frame drum) in dialogue with mixed Brazilian percussion; regular duple along with syncopated triple meter.
0:09	Second cycle (4 mm.): Brazilian percussion establish a fast regular pattern.
0:16	Third cycle (4 mm.): other percussion play slightly off beat from Brazilian percussion's pattern.

Time	Description	Text
0:23	Fourth cycle (5 mm.): high strings in dialogue, playing an arpeggiated pentatonic scale.	[*Bracketed text below is shouted by the lead tenors.*]
0:32	Low voices enter, then high voices respond; most of the intervals are seconds and fourths.	Ìrunmalè e se ojú lè o,
0:48	String interlude, playing patterns similar to those in the fourth cycle, with cello added.	
1:07	Two tenors lead the full vocal ensemble in a call and response.	Òrò, Òrò, nlo o, Òrò, [Ìrunmalè se o] Igba ìmalè e se ojú lè o,
1:20	String interlude, playing similar patterns again, with double bass added; ends with a loud plucked chord.	
1:52	Full vocal ensemble in homorhythm; harmony is mostly pentatonic, moving toward minor.	Òrò, Òrò, nlo o, Òrò, Igba ìmalè e se ojú lè o
2:07	String interlude, with more imitation; pentatonic scale expands to six notes; builds to a high-range, sustained ending.	
2:28	Opening vocal melody, shortened, returns; low voices are answered by high.	Ìrunmalè e se ojú lè o, Òrò
2:47	Percussion instruments intensify their pattern.	
2:57	Two tenors (one at a time) lead a call and response with the full vocal ensemble.	[Ìrunmalè se o] Òrò [Ìrunmalè se o] Igba ìmalè e se ojú lè o, Òrò
3:15	String interlude, ends with a loud plucked chord.	
3:39	Full ensemble in homorhythm, with tenors interjecting.	Òrò Òrò, nlo o Osó ilé e se lè, Ìrunmalè e se ojú lè o Òrò Ò nlo Òrò Igba Òrò [Ìrunmalè e se ojú lè o] Igba ìmalè e se ojú lè o
4:15	String interlude, builds to a high range.	
4:36	Percussion pattern intensifies.	
4:45	Marimba added to percussion; low voices are followed by a marimba solo.	È ní s'ebo l'ore o,
5:07	Opening idea returns in low voices, then all voices sing in slow triplets, with two tenors interjecting.	Ìrunmalè e se ojú lè o, sebo l'ore Epo kété ní òro, [Ìrunmalè se o] Igba ìmalè e se o
5:31	String interlude, builds to a high range.	
5:56	Full homorythmic vocal ensemble, the two tenors interjecting.	Òrò, Òrò, nlo o, Omi ni sparó iná È Bàrá a dúró kò kikà [È Epo lero È sù] s'ebo l'ore Epo kété ní Odára kò je àdín È sù gbè ní
6:25	The two tenors lead the full homorhythmic ensemble; strings enter from low to high before the fade-out (text is interrupted mid-word).	[s' ù ní yióò gbà e / gbà e bo wa] Odára kò je àdín È sù gbè ní È ní s'ebo l'ore ní [s'ebo l'o...]

continued on next page

Translation

O spirits, keep your eyes over us, we pray, we pray, we pray here and now.

Keep your eyes over us, we pray, we pray.

Keep your eyes over our house, we pray, we pray.

Exu, you are the one who makes the good offerings.

Exu of the body, keep together with us, please accept our offerings.

Exu, palm oil is the color of all your power.

Exu, help. Exu, you are the one who makes the good offerings.

In Her Own Words

❝ For me, movement is music. When I hear music, movement materializes, and vice-versa. . . . There's dance in it. But to me, it's not dance—it's something indigenous and vital that had no connection to dance when I wrote it.❞

—Tania León

▶|◀ Reflect

How does León make "Understanding" sound like a spontaneous outpouring? How do you think each of the contrasting elements—voices, strings, percussion—helps express the meaning of the text?

YOUR TURN TO EXPLORE

Investigate the creative approach of another composer who has developed a culturally blended style (for example, Godwin Natoh, from Nigeria; Tan Dun, from China; John Tavener, from England) or the performance choices of cross-cultural ensembles like the International Silk Road Project, Vancouver Inter-Cultural Orchestra (Canada), or the National Arab Orchestra (U.S.). How do these musicians incorporate different traditions into a blended whole? What is the stated purpose of the composer or group (artistic or social), and how do they go about fulfilling it? In what ways do you find the music effective, and in what ways are you unconvinced?

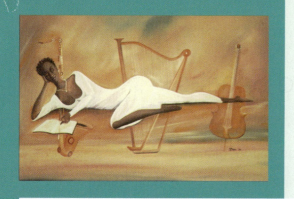

Postmodern Music

REPRESENTATIVE COMPOSERS

George Crumb   Jennifer Higdon

John Cage   John Williams

Leonard Bernstein   John Adams

Philip Glass   Tania León

IMPORTANT GENRES

song   tone poem

musical theater   opera

film music   ballet

sonata

Listening Essentials

Melody: Romantic "singing" melodies often built from smaller motives and with modernist unpredictability.

Rhythm/meter: Regular and repetitive rhythms, often borrowing ideas from non-Western and popular traditions.

Harmony: Triadic and consonant overall; tonality continues to expand, sometimes with non-Western harmonies.

Texture: Varied and specific to the particular composition, drawing on both Romantic and modernist styles; homophonic and polyphonic textures can be combined.

Form: Historical, chance- or process-based forms; structures borrowed from non-Western and popular traditions.

Timbre: Combination of Romantic orchestral resources and digital technology; non-Western instruments added.

Expression: Idiosyncratic and often reflecting a composer's biographical, spiritual, or social/political perspective; challenges the distinction between "high" and "low" art.

Performing forces: Unusual combinations and ranges of instruments, along with non-Western instruments.

Listening Challenge

Now take the online Listening Challenge, where you'll listen to a mystery selection from the postmodern era and answer questions about its elements: the role of melody vs. that of rhythm, and how the complexity of rhythm and meter is achieved; how harmony and texture are treated; how repetition contributes to the structure; and how technology influences the piece.

Music in Sacred Spaces

> **"** Praise Him with the sound of the trumpet: praise Him with the psaltery and harp. Praise Him with the timbrel and dance: praise Him with stringed instruments and organs. Praise Him upon the loud cymbals: praise Him upon the high sounding cymbals."
>
> —Psalm 150 (King James version)

From the time of ancient Greece, music was reputed to have divine origins, and celebrations for a particular god were marked by carefully chosen musical characteristics that were thought to be most "in tune" with that god's nature. The Mediterranean monotheistic faiths—Judaism, Christianity, Islam—similarly approached the reciting of scriptural text and prayer through song; Islamic calls to prayer are especially powerful in their sonic intensity. In the Western tradition, there have long been discussions about the role of music in Christian life: if it sets a religious text, does it enhance or distract from the words? If it has no text, can it soothe and exalt the spirit, or is it dangerously sensual and too closely connected to earthly concerns?

Simple prayer songs, or **plainchant**, were at the core of Christian religious practice from the time of the Apostles (Chapter 13: Gregorian chant, *Kyrie*; and Hildegard of Bingen, *Alleluia*). In fact, it was the impulse to document and standardize prayer throughout Christian lands that led to the development of musical notation around the year 800, during the reign of Charlemagne. Eventually, the wish to mark special celebrations brought the rise of polyphony, initially an elaboration of plainchant with a new simultaneous musical line. Cathedrals in vibrant cities, such as the church of Notre Dame in Paris, were especially active centers of elaborate polyphonic worship in the Middle Ages. To intensify special moments of musical prayer, musicians developed the **motet**, a musically complex and expressive spiritual song

A medieval chant manuscript, from the Seville Cathedral in Spain.

Angel Musicians, by **Hans Memling** (c. 1430–1494).

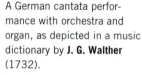

A German cantata performance with orchestra and organ, as depicted in a music dictionary by **J. G. Walther** (1732).

(Chapter 17: Josquin des Prez, *Ave Maria*), and a more elaborate celebration of the core Christian ritual, the **Mass** (Chapter 18: Giovanni Pierluigi da Palestrina, *Pope Marcellus* Mass). There were thus increasing opportunities for musicians to serve the church, and the majority of the music that has been preserved from earlier times was composed for sacred purposes.

With religious reforms in the 1500s came new approaches to the role of music in Christian worship that departed from Roman Catholic ideals. Congregationally focused music was essential to the vision of Martin Luther, and over the years the **cantata** (Chapter 20: Johann Sebastian Bach, *Wachet auf*), a musical parallel to the pastor's sermon, became a staple of the long, Sunday-morning Lutheran service. While the **oratorio** had developed in Catholic lands alongside opera as a resource to tell religious stories in dramatic form, it became most popular when transplanted to England and modified for Anglican-inspired taste, eventually far outshining other kinds of contemporary dramatic music (Chapter 21: George Frideric Handel, *Messiah*). The addition of instruments to what had been primarily vocal sacred traditions allowed musicians to incorporate the latest styles into their sacred compositions—a tendency praised by some music lovers but criticized by others who believed that popular trends disrupted the need to maintain continuity in worship. In the newly independent American colonies, evolving practices of congregational spiritual song provided a "homespun" alternative that Calvinists preferred over the more elaborate Catholic, Lutheran, and Anglican traditions.

As European culture underwent change in the 1700s with the Enlightenment and its emphasis on science and reason, religion began

A gospel group and its leader help to energize the congregation at a church in Paris.

playing a less prominent role in public life. Musicians were still working for their churches, but often on a one-time commission basis— this was the case with Wolfgang Amadeus Mozart and his *Requiem*. Some kinds of sacred music, especially the oratorio, began to be performed in concert, out of the context of their original worship function. This trend continued into the 1800s and beyond, with the texts and sentiments of the Requiem Mass especially continuing to appeal to many prominent composers. Giuseppe Verdi, Johannes Brahms (Chapter 42), and Gabriel Fauré exemplify in their *Requiem* settings the distinct approaches of the Italian, German, and French Romantic traditions.

Still, many musicians continued a strong commitment to religious music, often out of their own personal conviction. Especially in North America, various branches of Christian worship expanded on congregational hymns and expressive church choirs over the past century, leading to the flourishing African American spiritual and gospel traditions and other approaches to "praise" music. Reform Judaism was strongly influenced by the Lutheran musical tradition in its adoption of the organ and other instruments for religious celebrations, and a number of Jewish musicians have composed striking works that draw from their faith (Arnold Schoenberg, *A Survivor from Warsaw*; Leonard Bernstein, *Chichester Psalms*; Steve Reich, *Tehillim*).

Contemporary composers of both "art" and "popular" music still write in the sacred genres adopted by their predecessors (Andrew Lloyd Webber, *Requiem*; Paul McCartney, *Liverpool Oratorio*; Wynton Marsalis, *Blood on the Fields* oratorio). As international musical practices intersect and blend, spiritually syncretic traditions can also spur creative expression, as in the works of Cuban-born composer Tania León (Chapter 58: *Inura*). Ultimately, the potential for music to energize spiritual experience is a concept at the core of the Western tradition.

Music for Stage and Screen

> 66 I have always believed that opera is a planet where the muses work together, join hands and celebrate all the arts."
>
> —Franco Zeffirelli (1923–2019)

Like his royal father, King Louis XIV of France (r. 1643–1715) loved to dance in the court ballet. He's shown here in one of his first roles, as "the Sun," at age fourteen.

Music has been integrated into multimedia productions—involving speech, staging, and other visual or choreographed effects—since the earliest documented history of the West. The theatrical traditions of ancient Greece incorporated musical instruments, and actors intoned their lines in a style that was somewhere between speech and song. Dramatized scenes from biblical scripture were featured in Christian celebrations in the Middle Ages, building on the tradition of collective sung prayer.

As European traditions of stage performance developed in the Middle Ages and Renaissance, music often punctuated the action, as part of the plot (for example, a lover's serenade) or as sonic interludes between scenes. The plays of renowned authors such as Shakespeare are peppered with musical references, and there's evidence that characters would break into song in the

Female warriors, or Valkyries, from Wagner's opera of the same name.

middle of a line to liven up the performance (and provide "in-joke" references for the audience).

The idea of integrating music fully into the dramatic flow was an innovation of the Baroque era, first explored in the Italian courts and then adopted more widely for special celebrations. "Drama through music," as the tradition that later became **opera** was originally known, quickly became the favorite entertainment of the upper classes across Europe (Chapter 19: Henry Purcell, *Dido and Aeneas*). Musicians and playwrights alike were drawn to the enormous fortunes that could be made especially once opera became a public tradition in the mid-1600s as well as the opportunities for expressive intensity and constant innovation that were expected by enthusiastic audiences. Italian-style opera, the most widespread, spotlighted highly compensated superstar singers with extraordinary vocal skills. Also popular was the French operatic style, which relied less on vocal display and more on orchestral and ensemble effects and on dance. Other regional styles capitalized on the demands of the audience in that community: opera has always been a very adaptable medium.

As the operatic tradition expanded, it absorbed changing social concerns, and the interest in equality that characterized the eighteenth-century Enlightenment led to a new tradition of **comic opera** (*opera buffa*). In this tradition, music dramas used humor to provide gentle critiques of established conventions of class and gender (Chapter 32: Wolfgang Amadeus Mozart, *The Marriage of Figaro*). With the French Revolution came a reconfiguration of French musical theater: gone was the "old style" opera that had been associated with king and court, to be replaced by musical reflections of the changed political climate, with topics focusing on the evils of nobility and royalty. Musicians quickly tailored their multimedia for a changing world.

In the nineteenth century, expanding political unrest in Europe opened the door to even more pointed social critique, accompanied by more powerful and intense operatic soundscapes, though the Italian tradition continued to rely on "hit songs" by star singers (Chapter 40: Giuseppe Verdi, *Rigoletto*), and the French tradition explored exotic locales through grand scenarios. The German tradition, which up to now had been less active than its French and Italian counterparts, became more

Jelani Alladin as Kristoff and Sven the reindeer, in the 2017 Disney musical *Frozen*, based on the 2013 animated movie.

prominent at this time. Especially in the works of Richard Wagner, growing musical forces were marshalled to create multimedia productions designed to be epic in scale, both musically and dramatically (Chapter 41: *Die Walküre*). Mesmerized audiences streamed into Wagner's specially designed theater in Bayreuth, Germany, as they do today, with tickets selling out years in advance.

European opera sailed to North America with various immigrant populations, and by the mid-nineteenth century it was considered top-notch entertainment across economic lines. Troupes traveled throughout the United States, performing English translations and adaptations of European classics freely intermixed with popular songs of the time. Even the great multimedia entrepreneur P.T. Barnum, better known for his work with the Barnum and

Baley circus, made sure to sponsor musical theater as part of his entertainment empire. Another important presence on the American musical stage was the variety show, which intermingled comic skits with music and singing (and other acts such as magic and juggling), sometimes with a loosely strung plot (and often with excerpts from favorite operatic scenes). Only later in the nineteenth century did opera become "highbrow," separating entirely from the more "popular" variety-show tradition, as performers and audiences left behind translations and adaptations and strove for purity of the original musical text.

While some traditions exploit the power of entirely sung drama, other strands of musical theater combine spoken dialogue with musical "numbers." This was especially true of the strand that arose in North America in the early twentieth century, drawing on the variety show. As composers built this tradition of the **American Broadway musical**, they nonetheless often aimed at an intersection between the "low-art" Broadway commercial tradition and more "high-art" considerations, looking to achieve more lasting and profound dramatic effects (Chapter 53: Leonard Bernstein, *West Side Story*).

Meanwhile, choreographed dance arose in the Renaissance as a kind of spectacle much valued especially in France and in European centers influenced by French culture. **Ballet**, as it became known, was sometimes presented independently and sometimes integrated into sung or spoken drama, in order to create a more interesting and varied expressive effect. Partly because it had been so closely associated with royalty, ballet became less popular in France after the revolution. But it flourished at other European courts: in particular, Russian dancers, choreographers, and composers expanded the tradition in the nineteenth century (Chapter 43: Peter Ilyich Tchaikovsky, *The Nutcracker*), and brought innovation back to Paris in the early twentieth (Chapter 45: Igor Stravinsky, *The Rite of Spring*). Ballet became especially interesting to those seeking to explore modern approaches to multimedia in the last century, as well as to those looking for characteristic regional or national effects (Chapter 49: Aaron Copland, *Appalachian Spring*) or to blended traditions (Chapter 58: Tania León, *Inura*).

Dance of the Snowflakes, from Tchaikovsky's ballet *The Nutcracker*, performed by the English National Ballet.

In *Avatar* (2009), Oscar-winning composer James Horner drew on European folk traditions as well as synthesizer techniques to shape an ideal soundscape for a fantastic faraway world.

As the new medium of film emerged in the early twentieth century, it absorbed the multimedia resources of opera, ballet, and the Broadway musical. For silent films, musicians were hired to provide live soundtracks, responding to the changing dramatic effects on the screen similar to the way music had long enhanced staged drama and dance. With the arrival of synchronized sound, music was at the forefront: the "talking" scenes in the first commercial sound film, *The Jazz Singer* of 1927, in fact primarily involved singing. By the 1930s, Broadway musicals became all the more popular because of film versions, and even several films that were not originally shows (for example, *The Wizard of Oz* of 1939) followed the conventions of Broadway theater by featuring song-and-dance numbers.

Live instrumental music for silent films was replaced by an instrumental soundtrack, used to help underline dramatic interaction between characters. Several noteworthy composers of orchestral, theatrical, and dance music—including Bernstein, Copland, and Silvestre Revueltas (Chapter 50: *La noche de los Mayas*)—were asked to underscore sound films, while others made their mark primarily through film music (Bernard Herrmann, for example, provided the striking soundscapes for many of director Alfred Hitchcock's movies). The most prolific and sought-after contemporary film composer is probably John Williams (Chapter 54: *Imperial March*), who is responsible for the music for the *Star Wars* series as well as the first three Harry Potter films, *Jurassic Park*, and many others. The approach to film underscoring has been quite successfully extended to other modern multimedia like television and video games, where further innovations continue to develop.

Even as the field of musical multimedia has expanded in the last century, opera continues to provide some of the most remarkable theatrical experiences, and contemporary composers continue to draw on topics that address central cultural concerns of their audiences, as they have for centuries (Chapter 57: John Adams, *Doctor Atomic*). Crossover between contemporary traditions and styles has led to some innovative media experiments, as in the collaboration between David Bowie and Philip Glass (Chapter 55: *Heroes* Symphony). Now as in the past, music injects a crucial component of intensity into drama.

Music Among Friends

66 How sweet the moonlight sleeps upon this bank!/Here will we sit, and let the sounds of music/ Creep in our ears: soft stillness and the night/ Become the touches of sweet harmony."

—William Shakespeare,
The Merchant of Venice

anguage and music are closely connected in cultures across the globe, both helping to define the human tendency toward social interaction. Communal music-making, long associated with gatherings in the West, is described in the earliest recorded stories and legends, from the Greek tales of Homer to the mythology of Norse cultures.

In many world cultures, social music-making continues as an oral, unwritten tradition; examples range from the elaborate art music of India to Hopi Native

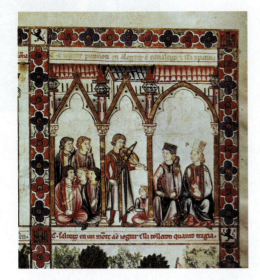

A troubadour performance, from the *Cantigas of Santa Maria* (thirteenth century).

American lullabies and folk traditions of West Africa. Europeans, however, began to document their "music among friends" almost as soon as they started writing down their worship music in the 800s, especially as it featured in the rich cultural activities that took place in medieval courts. In the late Middle Ages, songwriters known as **troubadours** and **trouvères** developed an elaborate tradition of sung love poetry, partly stemming from a long-standing practice of refined musical verse in the Mediterranean area, and designed to be performed by a skilled, self-accompanying singer and shared among members of the nobility (Chapter 14: Raimbaut de Vaqueiras, *Kalenda maya*). As the courtly love tradition expanded, some musicians created songs based on the complex and elegant interaction between simultaneous parts (Chapter 15: Guillaume de Machaut, *Ma fin est mon commencement*).

In the 1400s and 1500s, as disposable income grew within European society, more individuals became interested in having music for their own entertainment. And they could, now that printing presses were making music more widely available and more inexpensive to acquire. Composers began to focus on creating songs that would be both easy and fun for a group of friends to sing, and one approach to social song, known as the **madrigal**, became especially popular (Chapter 16: John Farmer, *Fair Phyllis*). It was largely through

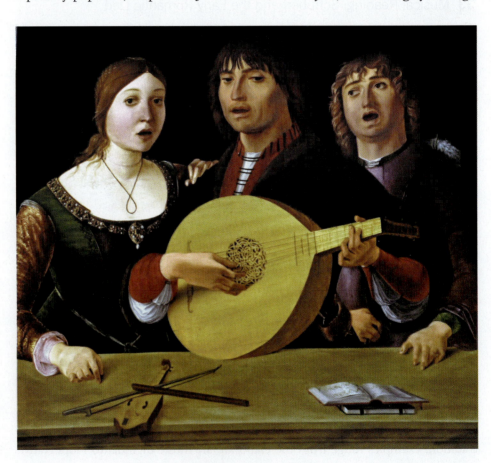

In *A Concert,* by **Lorenzo Costa** (1460–1535), friends sing an Italian secular song with lute and tiny violin.

the madrigal and related Renaissance song forms that musical literacy became established as an important social skill in the Western tradition.

The 1600s saw an increase in musical professionalism, and for a while there was a little decrease in amateur music-making. Professional musicians, however, became sensitive to listeners' musical experience and began creating works that would carry their audiences through expressive sonic "stories." Some of these stories included words, but others relied solely on the expressive power of instrumental sound. While musical narrative is not as explicit as spoken or written storytelling, it relies on clear patterns of repetition, contrast, and structural expectation. One of the most flexible musical "storytelling" resources of the Baroque era, the **fugue**, provides a wonderful example of sonic narrative from composer to listener (Chapter 24: Johann Sebastian Bach, "Little" Fugue in G Minor).

In his unfinished oil sketch of a "Schubertiad," Romantic artist **Moritz von Schwind** (1804–1871) shows Schubert at the piano performing with friends.

The eighteenth-century cultural interest in equality and democratic collaboration found musical expression in **chamber music**, built on interactions between a small group of musicians. Some chamber music was tailored for amateur entertainment, some for performance by professionals, but it all reflected an ideal of intimate "conversation" among equal participants (Chapter 25: Joseph Haydn, *Emperor* Quartet; Chapter 27: Wolfgang Amadeus Mozart, *Eine kleine Nachtmusik*). The later 1700s brought increasing attention to the expressive nuances that could be conveyed by the new "keyboard instrument with soft and loud" that we now call the piano, which became more and more the instrument of choice for chamber-music-making (Chapter 30: Ludwig van Beethoven, *Moonlight* Sonata).

Song made a strong comeback in the early 1800s. The new "Romantic" artistic sensibility was attracted to the intensity of poetic images, and musical settings of favorite poems became extremely popular for performance in the home and the semi-public salon (Chapter 33: Franz Schubert, *Elfking*). The growing presence of the piano as an elegant and desirable item of musical furniture was facilitated by the development of mass-manufacturing techniques that made the instru-

Joseph Joachim, premier violinist of the nineteenth century, and pianist Clara Schumann (1854). Pastel on paper by **Adolph von Menzel** (1815–1905).

ment more affordable. Pianos were used not only as the instrument of choice to accompany song but also on their own, in virtuosic performances (Chapter 35: Frédéric Chopin, *Revolutionary* Étude) as well as through music connected to social dancing and to a more reflective expression of emotion (Chapter 36: Fanny Mendelssohn Hensel, *The Year*).

Distinctions between high art and popular music had not been especially prominent before the 1800s, but they began to be made through the mass-marketing of sheet music to the rising middle classes. Especially in the United States there arose a tradition of songwriting for home entertainment and designed to sound "folksy"—specifically distinct from the cultivated complexity of European repertories. This could be

The interactive game Guitar Hero is only one example of how contemporary multimedia have opened up new ways for music to be shared among friends.

understood as the first self-consciously "popular" music tradition, though the definition of the term is very tricky (Chapter 34: Stephen Foster, *Jeanie with the Light Brown Hair*).

Certainly, alongside the printed sheet-music tradition, an oral tradition of music "by the people" continued—a truly *vernacular* approach, as opposed to the *cultivated* approach to music that requires training and musical literacy. Particularly influential on North American musical developments were the parallel streams of **ragtime/jazz** and **blues**, rooted in African American musical practices and expanded through multi-ethnic interactions in the later 1800s. Since blues and jazz were unwritten traditions, we can best study them through their appearance in early commercial recordings of the first decades of the 1900s (Chapter 46: Billie Holiday, *Billie's Blues*).

Blues and jazz influenced a variety of musicians, in North America and beyond. Some, in particular, were eager to blend the long-standing conventions of European art music with styles perceived as African American, in order to convey a particularly American artistic sensibility (Chapter 47: William Grant Still, Suite for Violin and Piano). Other North American musicians sought inspiration elsewhere as they crafted intimate music for the modern era. Looking westward from California, they considered Asian traditions and attempted to imitate these very non-European sensibilities (Chapter 51: John Cage, *Sonatas and Interludes*).

The nineteenth-century tradition of setting favorite poems has continued into the present, and has led some musicians to blend again the boundaries between art and popular, as well as Western and non-Western, traditions, an approach that some characterize as representative of our "postmodern" age. Blending genres from the distant past with cutting-edge experimental techniques, composers created songs that evoke the disruptive qualities of twentieth-century life (Chapter 52: George Crumb, *Caballito negro*). With the arrival of electric amplification in the 1920s, songs could be intimately whispered to a large auditorium, and indeed across the world through radio. This changed the nature of chamber music. We are now accustomed to feeling that a singer-songwriter with a guitar is conveying her message of love and friendship directly to us, even though we may be in a stadium audience of thousands, or one of millions watching YouTube. Still, there continue to be important distinctions between music understood as private or public, especially in the way we believe it affects us.

Music in Public Spaces

> **"** The introduction of a new kind of music be shunned as imperiling the whole state, since styles of music are never disturbed without affecting the most important political institutions."
>
> —Plato
> (c. 424–c. 348 BCE)

Music is often said to communicate directly to our emotions. From the earliest days of philosophical writing in the West, however, music has also been understood as serving essential social and political purposes. For example, the use of musical instruments (especially brass, woodwind, and percussion) to signal the arrival of an important personage or to encourage soldiers in battle is documented from the time of antiquity onward. This tradition was mostly improvised and orally transmitted rather than notated, which is why we don't have many specific examples of public music before the 1600s.

As European rulers developed a taste for elaborate music in all aspects of their lives, they commissioned many of the same musicians whom they had hired to compose sacred and theatrical works to write instrumental music to reflect the grandeur of their court. The most extraordinary patron of glorious sounds of

Music is a part of civic life, as shown in a detail of **Ambrogio Lorenzetti**'s (d. 1348) fresco *Good Government in the City*.

An intimate *Musical Evening*, painted by French artist **Miguel Angel Housasse** (1680–1730).

this sort was Louis XIV, king of France in the late 1600s. The tradition that he cultivated employed dozens of skilled musicians and was the envy of other royalty, who sought to build similar resources for their own celebrations. Grandeur in instrumental music quickly expanded beyond royal celebrations to include other occasions when it was possible to hear a large group of musicians display their astounding skill (Chapter 22: Bach, Orchestral Suite No. 3). Instrumentalists developed genres such as the **concerto** specifically to showcase their talents, as well as their ability to provide powerful sonic contrasts with the other members of their "bands" (Chapter 23: Antonio Vivaldi, *The Four Seasons*; Chapter 29: Joseph Haydn, Trumpet Concerto).

By the later 1700s, a rising fashion for instrumental music led to public-admission concerts that could give audiences a taste of the ultimate instrument, the multi-player orchestra (Chapter 26: Haydn, Symphony No. 100). Before this time, instrumental musicians almost invariably worked either for the church or for a wealthy patron. Opera was public in the sense that anyone with enough money could buy a ticket to the performance, but instrumental music was either entirely private or integrated into worship services. The rise of the **symphony** as a genre and the institution of public concerts opened up the grandeur of orchestral music to a larger audience; and the perceived messages of heroic struggle in the symphonies of Ludwig van Beethoven, in particular (Chapter 31: Symphony No. 5), fired up the imagination of the leaders of the growing Romantic movement (Chapter 28: Mozart, Symphony No. 40, the *Romantic*).

Indeed, the Romantics were especially enamored of instrumental music because they believed it had the power to express emotions beyond words—and the growing size of the orchestra offered more varied timbres and more stunning soundscapes. This can be seen most strikingly in the tradition of orchestral **program music** (Chapter 37: Hector Berlioz, *Symphonie fantastique*), which introduced a greater range of expressive nuance to the now-massive assembly of music professionals. Musicians of the 1700s had led their ensembles from the keyboard, or a soloist coordinated the cues: the nineteenth-century orchestra needed someone responsible for keeping tabs on dozens of musicians, each with a different part to play, and thus the role of the **conductor** was born.

As the century progressed and orchestral music became more and more important to European society, the debate intensified about its nature and purpose. Some musicians chose specific musical elements to spur regional or national pride (Chapter 38: Edvard Grieg, *Peer Gynt*). Others, like Johannes Brahms, insisted on the need to keep the meaning of music self-contained within sound, continuing to advocate the ideal of universal meaning beyond words. And some sought to push beyond the boundaries of orchestral convention by creating sound blends and melodies that could evoke exotic locales—from the far East or even from mythical antiquity (Chapter 44: Claude Debussy, *Prelude to "The Afternoon of a Faun"*).

In the early twentieth century, both African American and Euro-American composers sought to bring jazz into the realm of cultivated music. Paramount among these was George Gershwin, whose blending of styles demonstrated an exceptional mastery of classical and vernacular traditions alike (Chapter 48: *Rhapsody in Blue*).

The orchestral tradition is perhaps the most conservative of the streams of Western music. Symphony orchestras in the twenty-first century still play, and

An evening outdoor concert in 1744 by the Collegium Musicum of Jena, Germany, featuring an orchestra of strings, woodwinds, trumpets, and drums gathered around a harpsichord.

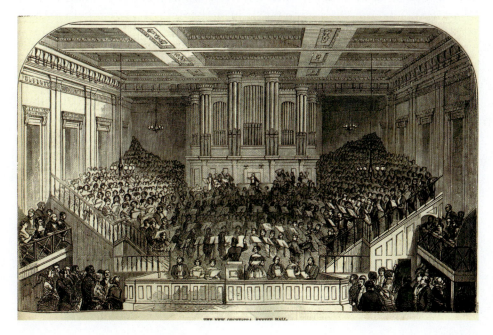

The New Orchestra in Exeter Hall, from the *Illustrated London News*, 1848.

The intimate atmosphere of Le Poisson Rouge, an avant-garde performance space in New York City, demonstrates the continuum between music in public spaces and music among friends.

audiences still thrill at, the repertory that defined the orchestra as a powerful expressive force more than two centuries ago. But composers on both sides of the Atlantic have continued to add to that tradition, in some cases collaborating in crossover traditions of "high" and "low" art (Chapter 55: Philip Glass, Symphony No. 4, *Heroes*). If anything, the last decades have seen a growing interest in new orchestral music, especially within the postmodern (and global) tradition called **neo-Romanticism** (Chapter 56: Jennifer Higdon, *blue cathedral*). In an increasingly sound-drenched and multimedia-saturated world, we encounter music in public all the time—in shops and restaurants, booming out of a passing car, beckoning to us from a TV or computer advertisement. Politicians choose music to reinforce their political messages; bands whip up college fans into a frenzy at football games. We would do well to listen to ancient philosophers' warnings about the power of sound to shape society, and the importance of a focused awareness of how that power operates.

The Notation of Pitch

Musical notation presents a kind of graph of each sound's duration and pitch. These are indicated by symbols called **notes**, which are written on the **staff**, a series of five parallel lines separated by four spaces:

Staff

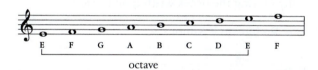

A symbol known as a **clef** is placed at the left end of the staff to determine the pitch names. The **treble clef** (𝄞) is generally used for pitches in a high range, and the **bass clef** (𝄢) for a lower group of pitches. These are the two most common clefs, though there are others associated with specific instruments.

Clef

Pitches are named after the first seven letters of the alphabet, from A to G. (From one note named A to the next is the interval of an **octave**.) The pitches on the treble staff are named as follows:

Pitch names

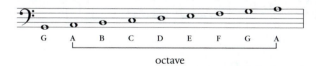

And those on the bass staff:

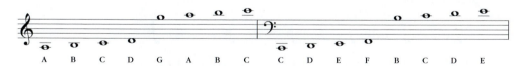

If you need to notate pitches above and below these staffs, short extra lines called **ledger lines** can be added:

Ledger lines

Middle C—the C that, on the piano, is situated approximately in the center of the keyboard—comes between the treble and bass staffs. It is represented by either the first ledger line above the bass staff or the first ledger line below the treble staff. This combination of the two staffs is called the **great staff** or **grand staff**:

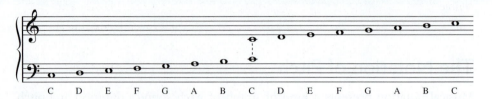

C   D   E   F   G   A   B   C   D   E   F   G   A   B   C

Accidentals   Signs known as **accidentals** are used to alter the pitch of a written note. A **sharp** (♯) before the note indicates the pitch a half step above; a **flat** (♭) indicates the pitch a half step below. A **natural** (♮) cancels a sharp or flat. Also used are the **double sharp** (×) and **double flat** (♭♭), which respectively raise and lower the pitch by two half steps—that is, a whole step.

In many pieces of music, where certain sharped or flatted notes are used consistently throughout, these sharps or flats are written at the beginning of each line **Key signature** of music, in the **key signature**, as seen in the following example of piano music. Here, the sharp symbol on the F line means that every F in the piece is played a half step higher, the black key F♯. Notice that piano music is written on the great staff, with the right hand usually playing the notes written on the upper staff and the left hand usually playing the notes written on the lower:

Chopin: Prelude in E Minor

The Notation of Rhythm

Note values   The duration of each pitch is indicated by the type of note placed on the staff. In the following table, each note represents a duration, or **value**, half as long as the preceding one:

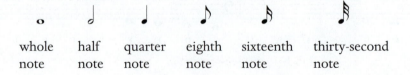

| whole note | half note | quarter note | eighth note | sixteenth note | thirty-second note |

In any particular piece of music, these note values are related to the beat of the music. If the quarter note represents one beat, then a half note lasts for two beats, a whole note for four; two eighth notes last one beat, as do four sixteenths.

Notes

Beats

(in quadruple, or 4/4, time)

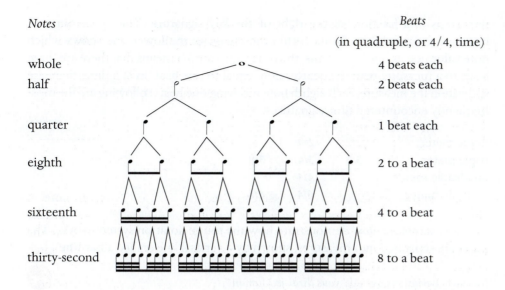

whole	4 beats each
half	2 beats each
quarter	1 beat each
eighth	2 to a beat
sixteenth	4 to a beat
thirty-second	8 to a beat

When a group of three notes is to be played in the time normally taken up by only two of the same kind, we have a **triplet**, indicated by a 3. **Triplet**

If we combine successive notes of the same pitch, using a curved line known as a **tie**, the second note is not played, and the note values are combined: **Tie**

beats: 4 + 4 = 8   2 + 4 = 6   1 + ½ = 1½

A **dot** after a note enlarges its value by half: **Dot**

beats: 2 + 1 = 3   1 + ½ = 1½   ½ + ¼ = ¾

Time never stops in music, even when there is no sound. Silence is indicated by symbols known as **rests**, which correspond in time value to the notes: **Rests**

whole rest	half rest	quarter rest	eighth rest	sixteenth rest	thirty-second rest

The metrical organization of a piece of music is indicated by the **time signature**, or **meter signature**, which specifies the meter: this appears as two numbers **Time signature** written as in a fraction, to the right of the key signature. The upper numeral indicates the number of beats within the measure; the lower one shows which note value equals one beat. Thus, the time signature 3/4 means that there are three beats to a measure, with the quarter note equal to one beat. In 6/8 time, there are six beats in the measure, each eighth note receiving one beat. Following are the most frequently encountered time signatures:

duple meter	2/2	2/4	
triple meter	3/2	3/4	3/8
quadruple meter		4/4	
sextuple meter		6/4	6/8

The examples below demonstrate how the music notation system works. The notes are separated into measures, shown by a vertical line (called a **bar line**).

Mozart: *Variations on "Ah! vous dirai-je Maman"*
(tune of *Twinkle, Twinkle, Little Star* and the *Alphabet Song*)

Clef: Treble
First pitch: C
Key signature: none = key of C major
Meter: Duple (2/4)
This is the original piano version of the tune that was composed by Mozart. Notice how turns decorate the familiar melody on the recording.

Brahms: *Lullaby (Wiegenlied)*

Clef: Treble
First pitch: A
Key signature: 1 flat (B♭) = key of F major
Meter: Triple (3/4)
Other features: Begins on an upbeat, after two rests.
This is the original vocal version by Brahms, sung in German on the recording. You may know the English lyrics.

Battle Hymn of the Republic (Civil War song)

Glo - ry, glo - ry hal - le - lu - jah! Glo - ry, glo - ry hal - le - lu - jah!

Glo - ry, glo - ry hal - le - lu - jah! His truth is march - ing on.

Clef: Treble

First pitch: G

Key signature: none = key of C major

Meter: Quadruple (4/4)

Other features: Many dotted rhythms.

This is a nineteenth-century brass band version of the tune from the Civil War era. The band plays only the familiar chorus on the recording.

Greensleeves (English traditional song)

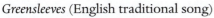

A - las, my love, — you do me wrong — to cast me off — dis - cour - teous - ly, Though

I have loved — you oh so long — de - light - ing in — your com - pa - ny.

Clef: Bass

First note: E

Key signature: 1 sharp (F♯) = key of E minor

Meter: Sextuple (6/8)

Other features: Begins on an upbeat, has dotted rhythms and added accidentals.

This Elizabethan-era song is played here on classical guitar.

absolute music Music that has no literary, dramatic, or pictorial program. Also called pure music.

a cappella Choral music performed without instrumental accompaniment.

accelerando Getting faster.

accent The emphasis on a *beat* resulting in its being louder or longer than another in a *measure*.

accompagnato Accompanied; also a *recitative* that is accompanied by orchestra.

accordion A musical instrument with a small keyboard and free-vibrating metal *reeds* that sound when air is generated by pleated *bellows*.

acoustic guitar A *guitar* designed for performance without electronic amplification.

acoustic music Music produced without electronics, especially amplifiers.

active chords In the *diatonic* system, chords that need to resolve to the *tonic chord*. These include the *dominant* and *subdominant* chords.

adagio Quite slow.

aerophone Instruments such as a *flute,* whistle, or *horn* that produce sound by using air as the primary vibrating means.

Afro-diasporic Connected to musical traditions of communities whose ancestors left Africa, often as slaves.

agitato Agitated or restless.

Agnus Dei The last musical section of the *Ordinary* of the *Mass*.

air Generally a tune, either vocal or instrumental; in the Baroque era, it designated a newly composed movement that did not fit any dance category.

aleatoric See *chance music*.

alla breve See *cut time*.

allegro Fast, cheerful.

Alleluia An item from the *Proper* of the *Mass* sung just before the reading of the Gospel; *neumatic* in style, with a long *melisma* on the last syllable of the word "Alleluia."

allemande German dance in moderate *duple meter,* popular during the Renaissance and Baroque periods; often the first *movement* of a Baroque *suite*.

alto Lowest of the female voices. Also contralto.

ambient music A type of music that emphasizes atmosphere rather than clear melodies or forms.

amplitude See *volume*.

andante Moderately slow or walking pace.

answer Second entry of the *subject* in a *fugue,* usually pitched a fourth below or a fifth above the subject.

anthem A religious choral composition in English; performed liturgically, the Protestant equivalent of the *motet*.

antiphonal Performance style in which an ensemble is divided into two or more groups, performing in alternation and then together.

antique cymbals Small disks of brass, held by the player (one instrument in each hand), that are struck together gently and allowed to vibrate. Also crotales.

aria Lyric song for solo voice with orchestral accompaniment, generally expressing intense emotion; found in *opera, cantata,* and *oratorio*.

arpeggio Broken chord in which the individual pitches are sounded one after another instead of simultaneously.

Ars antiqua The "old art" of twelfth- and thirteenth-century French polyphony, displaced by the *Ars nova*.

Ars nova "New art," the refined, complex style of *polyphony* in fourteenth-century France, as exemplified by Guillaume de Machaut.

art song A song set to a high-quality literary text, usually accompanied, and intended for concert performance. See also *Lied*.

a tempo Return to the previous tempo.

atonality Total abandonment of *tonality* (which is centered in a *key*). Atonal music moves from one level of *dissonance* to another, without areas of relaxation.

augmentation Statement of a *melody* in longer note values, often twice as slow as the original.

avant-garde French term that refers to new styles and techniques in the arts, especially in the early twentieth century.

bagpipe Wind instrument popular in Eastern and Western Europe that has several tubes, one of which plays the melody while the others sound the *drones,* or sustained notes; a windbag is filled by either a mouth pipe or a set of *bellows*.

ballad A form of English street song, popular from the sixteenth through the eighteenth centuries. Ballads are characterized by narrative content and *strophic form*.

ballad opera English comic opera, usually featuring spoken dialogue alternating with songs set to popular tunes; also dialogue opera.

ballade French poetic form and chanson type of the Middle Ages and Renaissance, with a courtly love text; also a Romantic genre, especially a lyric piano piece.

ballet A dance form featuring a staged presentation of group or solo dancing with music, costumes, and scenery.

ballet de cour An elaborately staged French courtly entertainment of the sixteenth and seventeenth centuries featuring dancing, singing, and acting.

banjo Plucked-string instrument with round body in the form of a single-headed drum and a long, fretted neck; brought to the Americas by African slaves.

bar form Three-part **A-A-B** form, frequently used in music and poetry, particularly in Germany.

bar (or **measure**) **lines** Vertical lines on a staff that separate measures; each measure gets a specific number of beats.

baritone Male voice of moderately low range.

bass Lowest of the male voices.

bass clarinet *Woodwind* instrument, with the lowest range, of the *clarinet* family.

bass drum *Percussion instrument* played with a large, soft-headed stick; the largest orchestral drum.

bass viol See *double bass.*

basso continuo Italian for "continuous bass." See *figured bass.* Also refers to a performance group with a chordal instrument (*harpsichord, organ*) and one bass melody instrument (*cello, bassoon*); also continuo.

bassoon *Double-reed woodwind* instrument with a low range.

baton A thin stick, usually painted white, used by a *conductor* to keep time.

beat Regular pulsation; a basic unit of length in musical time.

bebop Complex *jazz* style developed in the 1940s. Also bop.

bel canto "Beautiful singing"; elegant Italian vocal style characterized by florid melodic lines delivered by voices of great agility, smoothness, and purity of tone.

bell The wide or bulbed opening at the end of a wind instrument.

bell tree Long stick with bells suspended from it, adopted from *Janissary music.*

bellows An apparatus for producing air currents in certain wind instruments (*accordion, bagpipe*).

bent pitch See *blue note.*

big band Large *jazz* ensemble popular in the 1930s and 40s, featuring sections of *trumpets, trombones, saxophones* (and other *woodwinds*), and rhythm instruments (*piano, double bass, guitar,* drums).

big-band era See *Swing Era.*

binary form Two-part (**A-B**) form with each section normally repeated. Also two-part form.

blue note A slight drop of pitch on the third, fifth, or seventh note of the scale, common in *blues* and *jazz.* Also bent pitch.

blues African American form of secular *folk music,* related to *jazz,* that is based on a simple, repetitive poetic-musical structure.

bongo A pair of small drums of differing pitches, held between the legs and struck with both hands; of Afro-Cuban origins.

bop See *bebop.*

bourrée Lively French Baroque dance type in *duple meter.*

bow A slightly curved stick with hair or fibers attached at both ends, drawn over the strings of an instrument to set them in motion.

brass instrument Wind instrument with a cup-shaped mouthpiece, a tube that flares into a *bell,* and slides or valves to vary the pitch. Most often made of brass or silver.

brass quintet Standard chamber ensemble made up of two *trumpets, horn, trombone,* and *tuba.*

bridge Transitional passage connecting two sections of a composition; also transition. Also the part of a string instrument that holds the strings in place.

Broadway musical A work of *musical* theater that is performed in New York City's major theater district (Broadway).

buffo In *opera,* a male singer of comic roles, usually a *bass.*

bugle *Brass instrument* that evolved from the earlier military, or field, *trumpet.*

cadence Resting place in a musical *phrase;* musical punctuation.

cadenza Virtuosic solo passage in the manner of an improvisation, performed near the end of an *aria* or a *movement* of a *concerto.*

call and response Performance style with a singing leader who is imitated by a *chorus* of followers. Also *responsorial singing.*

camerata Italian for "salon"; a gathering for literary, artistic, musical, or philosophical discussions, notably the Florentine Camerata at the end of the sixteenth century.

camp meeting A musical gathering where *hymns, spirituals,* and folk songs were sung; popular in nineteenth-century America.

canon Type of *polyphonic* composition in which one musical line strictly imitates another at a fixed time interval throughout.

cantabile Songful, in a singing style.

cantata Vocal genre for solo singers, *chorus,* and instrumentalists based on a lyric or dramatic poetic narrative. It generally consists of several *movements,* including *recitatives, arias,* and ensemble numbers.

cantor Solo singer or singing leader in Jewish and Christian liturgical music.

cantus firmus "Fixed melody," usually of very long notes, often based on a fragment of *Gregorian chant,* that served as the structural basis for a *polyphonic* composition, particularly in the Renaissance.

caracol A wind instrument made from a conch shell.

castanets *Percussion instruments* consisting of small wooden clappers that are struck together; widely used to accompany Spanish dancing.

castrato Male singer who was castrated during boyhood to preserve his soprano or alto vocal register; prominent in seventeenth- and early eighteenth-century *opera.*

caxixi An ancient African percussion instrument popular in Brazil; a shaker consisting of basket with a gourd bottom filled with seeds.

celesta *Percussion instrument* resembling a miniature upright *piano,* with tuned metal plates struck by hammers that are operated by a keyboard.

cello (also violoncello) Bowed-string instrument with a middle-to-low range and dark, rich sonority; lower than a viola.

chaconne Baroque form in moderately slow *triple meter,* featuring *variations* that are based on a repeated *chord* progression.

chamber choir Small group of up to about twenty-four singers, who usually perform *a cappella* or with piano accompaniment.

chamber music Ensemble music for up to about ten players, with one player to a part.

chance music Music that makes a deliberate use of indeterminancy, or chance, in its performance; also aleatoric.

changing meter Shifting between *meters,* sometimes frequently, within a single composition or *movement;* also shifting meter.

chanson French *monophonic* or *polyphonic* song, especially of the Middle Ages and Renaissance, set to either courtly or popular poetry.

character piece A short, lyric piano work often with a descriptive title; popular in the nineteenth century.

chimes *Percussion instrument* of definite pitch consisting of a set of tuned metal tubes of various lengths suspended from a frame and struck with a hammer.

Chinese reflex balls Metal balls that are rolled in one hand, designed to improve motor skills; in music, they produce a jingling sound.

choir A group of singers who perform together, usually in parts, with several on each part; often associated with a church.

chorale Congregational *hymn* of the German Lutheran church.

chord Simultaneous combination of three or more *pitches* that constitute a single block of *harmony.*

chordal *Texture* comprised of *chords* in which the *pitches* sound simultaneously; similar to *homorhythmic.*

chordophone Instrument that produces sound from a vibrating string stretched between two points; the string may be set in motion by bowing, striking, or plucking.

chorus Fairly large group of singers who perform together, usually with several on each part. Also a choral *movement* of a large-scale work. In *jazz,* a single statement of the melodic-harmonic pattern.

chromatic *Melody* or *harmony* built from many if not all twelve pitches of the *octave.* A chromatic scale consists of an ascending or descending sequence of half steps.

church cantata A multimovement work for solo singers, chorus, and orchestra set to a religious text and structured around a Lutheran *chorale;* the Lutheran service equivalent of the Catholic *Mass.*

clarinet *Single-reed* woodwind instrument with a wide range of sizes.

clavichord Stringed *keyboard instrument* popular in the Renaissance and Baroque that is capable of unique expressive devices not possible on the *harpsichord.*

clavier Generic word for stringed *keyboard instruments,* including *harpsichord, clavichord,* and *piano.*

climax The high point in a melodic line or piece of music, usually representing the peak of intensity, *range,* and *dynamics.*

coda The last part of a piece, usually added to a standard form to bring it to a close.

codetta In *sonata-allegro form,* the concluding section of the *exposition;* more broadly, a brief *coda* concluding an inner section of a work.

col legno *String instrument* technique in which the strings are hit with the wood of the *bow.*

collage A technique drawn from the visual arts whereby musical fragments from other compositions are juxtaposed or overlapped within a new work.

collegium musicum An association of amateur musicians, popular in the Baroque era. Also a modern university ensemble dedicated to the performance of early music.

comic opera Comprising English *ballad opera,* Italian *opera buffa,* French *opéra comique,* and German *Singspiel.*

common time See *quadruple meter.*

compound meter *Meter* in which each main beat is divided into three rather than two.

computer music A type of electro-acoustic music in which computers assist in creating works through sound synthesis and manipulation.

concert band See *wind band.*

concert overture Single-movement concert piece for *orchestra,* typically from the Romantic period and often based on a literary program.

concertmaster The first-chair violinist of a symphony *orchestra.*

concerto Instrumental genre in several *movements* for solo instrument (or instrumental group) and *orchestra.*

concerto form Structure commonly used in first movements of concertos that combines elements of Baroque *ritornello* procedure with *sonata-allegro form.*

concerto grosso (also **ensemble concerto**) Baroque concerto type based on the opposition between a small group of solo instruments (the concertino) and *orchestra* (the ripieno).

conductor Person who, by means of gestures, leads performances of music ensembles, especially *orchestras, bands,* or *choruses.*

conga Afro-Cuban dance performed at Latin American Carnival celebrations. Also a single-headed drum of Afro-Cuban origin, played with bare hands.

congregational singing Simple worship music, often monophonic, in which the church congregation participates; often associated with Lutheranism and Calvinism. See also *chorale.*

conjunct Smooth, connected *melody* that moves principally by small *intervals.*

consonance Concordant or harmonious combination of *pitches* that provides a sense of relaxations and stability in music.

continuo See *basso continuo.*

contour The overall shape of a melodic line. It can move upward or downward or remain static.

contrabass See *double bass.*

contrabassoon *Double-reed* woodwind instrument with the lowest *range* in the woodwind family. Also double bassoon.

contralto See *alto.*

contrapuntal *Texture* employing *counterpoint,* or two or more simultaneous melodic lines.

contrary motion Motion in opposite directions between individual lines in a *polyphonic* work.

contrast The use of opposing musical elements to emphasize difference and variety.

cornet Valved *brass instrument* similar to the *trumpet* but more mellow in sound.

Council of Trent A council of the Roman Catholic Church that convened in Trent, Italy, from 1545 to 1563 and dealt with *Counter-Reformation* issues, including the reform of church music.

countermelody An accompanying *melody* sounded against the principal melody.

counterpoint The art of combining in a single *texture* two or more simultaneous melodic lines.

Counter-Reformation A Catholic reform movement, in reaction to the Protestant Reformation, that began with the 1545−63 *Council of Trent.*

countersubject In a *fugue,* a secondary theme heard against the *subject;* a countertheme.

courante French Baroque dance, a standard *movement* of the *suite,* in *triple meter* at a moderate tempo.

cover Recording that remakes an earlier, often successful recording with the goal of reaching a wider audience.

cowbell Rectangular metal bell struck with a drumstick; used widely in Latin American music.

Credo The third musical section of the *Ordinary* of the *Mass.*

crescendo Growing louder.

crossover Recording or artist that appeals primarily to one audience but becomes popular with another as well (e.g., a *rock* performer who makes *jazz* recordings).

crotales See *antique cymbals.*

Cubism Early twentieth-century art movement begun in Paris, characterized by the fragmentation of forms into abstract or geometric patterns.

cut time A type of *duple meter* interpreted as 2/2 and indicated as ¢; also *alla breve.*

cyclical form Structure in which musical material, such as a *theme,* presented in one *movement* returns in a later movement.

cymbals *Percussion instruments* consisting of two large circular brass plates of equal size that are struck sideways against each other.

da capo An indication to return to the beginning of a piece; Italian for "from the head," or "top."

da capo aria Lyric song in *ternary,* or **A-B-A**, form, commonly found in *operas, cantatas,* and *oratorios.*

decrescendo Growing softer.

development Structural reshaping of thematic material. The second section of *sonata-allegro form;* it moves through a series of foreign keys while *themes* from the *exposition* are developed.

dialogue opera See *ballad opera.*

diatonic *Melody* or *harmony* built from the seven pitches of a *major* or *minor scale.* A diatonic scale encompasses patterns of seven *whole steps* and *half steps.*

Dies irae Chant from the *Requiem Mass* whose text concerns Judgment Day.

diminuendo Growing softer.

diminution Statement of a *melody* in shorter note values, often twice as fast as the original.

disjunct Disjointed or disconnected *melody* with many leaps.

dissonance Combination of tones that sounds discordant and unstable, in need of resolution.

divertimento Classical-era instrumental genre for chamber ensemble or soloist, often performed as light entertainment. Related to *serenade.*

Divine Offices Cycle of daily services of the Roman Catholic Church, distinct from the *Mass.*

djembé A goblet-shaped drum originally from West Africa, with skin heads struck by the hands and ropes for tuning; also used in Brazilian traditional music.

dolce Sweetly.

dominant The fifth scale step, *sol.*

dominant chord *Chord* built on the fifth scale step, the V chord.

double To perform the same *notes* with more than one voice or instrument, either at the same pitch level or an *octave* higher or lower.

double bass Largest and lowest-pitched member of the bowed string family. Also contrabass or bass viol.

double bassoon See *contrabassoon.*

double exposition In the *concerto,* twofold statement of the *themes,* once by the *orchestra* and once by the soloist.

double reed A *reed* consisting of two pieces of cane that vibrate against each other.

double-stop Playing two notes simultaneously on a string instrument.

downbeat First *beat* of the *measure*, the strongest in any *meter*.

drone Sustained sounding of one or several pitches for harmonic support, a common feature of some folk musics.

duo An ensemble of two players.

duo sonata A chamber group comprised of a soloist with piano. Also, in the Baroque period, a *sonata* for a melody instrument and *basso continuo*.

duple meter Basic metrical pattern of two *beats* to a *measure*.

duration Length of time something lasts; e.g., the vibration of a musical sound.

dynamics Element of musical expression relating to the degree of loudness or softness, or *volume*, of a sound.

electric guitar A *guitar* designed for electronic amplification.

electronic music Generic term for any composition created by electronic means.

elektronische Musik Electronic music developed in Germany in the 1930s that uses an oscillator to generate and alter waveforms.

embellishment Melodic decoration, either improvised or indicated through *ornamentation* signs in the music.

embouchure The placement of the lips, lower facial muscles, and jaws in playing a wind instrument.

encore "Again"; an audience request that the performer(s) repeat a piece or perform another.

English horn *Double-reed* woodwind instrument, larger and lower in *range* than the *oboe*.

English madrigal English secular *polyphonic* song (for two to six voices) developed from the Italian *madrigal*; often lighter and less serious, featuring *refrain* syllables (fa-la-la); largely cultivated by amateurs.

ensemble concerto See *concerto grosso*.

episode Interlude or intermediate section in the Baroque *fugue* that serves as an area of relaxation between statements of the *subject*. In a Baroque *concerto*, the free and inventive material that alternates with returns of the *ritornello*, or instrumental refrain.

equal temperament Tuning system (used today) based on the division of the *octave* into twelve equal *half steps*.

espressivo Expressively.

estampie A dance form prevalent in medieval France, either sung or performed instrumentally.

ethnomusicology Comparative study of musics of the world, with a focus on the cultural context of music.

étude Study piece that focuses on a particular technical problem.

euphonium Tenor-range brass instrument resembling the *tuba*.

exoticism Musical style in which *rhythms*, *melodies*, or instruments evoke the color and atmosphere of far-off lands.

exposition Opening section. In a *fugue*, the first section in which the voices enter in turn with the *subject*. In *sonata-allegro form*, the first section in which the major thematic material is stated. Also statement.

Expressionism A style of visual art and literature in Germany and Austria in the early twentieth century. The term is sometimes also applied to music, especially composers of the Second Viennese School (Schoenberg, Berg, Webern).

extended technique An unusual effect created by the voice or by an instrument, sometimes drawn from non-Western music.

falsetto Vocal technique whereby men can sing above their normal *range*, producing a lighter sound.

fantasia Free instrumental piece of fairly large dimensions, in an improvisational style; in the Baroque era, it often served as an introductory piece to a *fugue*.

figured bass Baroque practice consisting of an independent bass line that often includes numerals indicating the harmony to be supplied by the *basso continuo* keyboard player. Also thorough-bass.

film music Music that serves as either background or foreground for a film.

flamenco A musical dance style from Andalusia (in southern Spain), often associated with Gypsy performers, featuring improvisational singing, finger snapping, foot stomping, and guitar strumming.

flat sign Musical symbol (♭) that indicates lowering a pitch by a *half step*.

fluegelhorn Valved brass instrument resembling a *bugle* with a wide bell, used in *jazz* and commercial music.

flute Soprano-range *woodwind* instrument, usually made of metal and held horizontally.

flutter-tonguing Wind instrument technique in which the player's tongue is fluttered as though "rolling an R" while he or she blows into the instrument.

folk music See *traditional music*.

form Structure and design in music, based on repetition, contrast, and variation; the organizing principle of music.

formalism Tendency to elevate formal above expressive value in music, as in twentieth-century *neo-Classical* music.

forte (f) Loud.

fortepiano Forerunner of the modern *piano* (also *pianoforte*).

fortissimo (ff) Very loud.

four-hand piano music Chamber music genre for two performers playing at one or occasionally two pianos, allowing for home or *salon* performances of orchestral arrangements.

French horn See *horn*.

French overture Baroque instrumental introduction to an *opera*, *ballet*, or *suite*, in two sections: a slow opening followed by an *Allegro*, often with a brief reprise of the opening.

frequency Rate of vibration of a string or column of air, which determines *pitch.*

fugato A fugal passage in a nonfugal piece, such as in the *development* section of a *sonata-allegro form.*

fugue *Polyphonic* form popular in the Baroque era, in which one or more themes (especially the *subject*) are developed by imitative *counterpoint.*

futurism An early twentieth-century anti-establishment artistic movement that emphasized the machine age and the dynamism of the era.

galliard Lively, *triple-meter* French court dance.

galop A fast-paced, duple-meter dance popular in the mid-nineteenth century, with a galloping kind of step.

gamelan Musical ensemble of Java or Bali, made up of *gongs, chimes, metallophones,* and drums, among other instruments.

gapped scale A scale that lacks some pitches of the seven-note *diatonic* scale; for example, a five-note (*pentatonic*) scale has two gaps.

gavotte *Duple-meter* French Baroque dance type with a moderate to quick *tempo.*

genre General term describing the standard category and overall character of a work.

gigue Popular English Baroque dance type, a standard *movement* of the Baroque *suite,* in a lively *compound meter.*

glee club Specialized vocal ensemble that performs popular music, college songs, and more serious works.

glissando A rapid slide through pitches of a *scale.*

glockenspiel *Percussion instrument* with horizontal, tuned steel bars of various sizes that are struck with mallets and produce a bright metallic sound.

Gloria The second musical section of the *Ordinary* of the *Mass.*

gong Percussion instrument consisting of a broad, circular metal disk suspended on a frame and struck with a heavy mallet; produces a definite pitch. See also *tam-tam.*

gospel music Twentieth-century sacred music style associated with Protestant African Americans.

grace note Ornamental note, often printed in small type and not performed rhythmically.

Gradual Fourth item of the *Proper* of the *Mass,* sung in a *melismatic* style, and performed in a *responsorial* manner in which soloists alternate with a choir.

grand opera Style of Romantic *opera* developed in Paris, focusing on serious, historical plots with huge choruses, crowd scenes, elaborate dance episodes, ornate costumes, and spectacular scenery.

grave Solemn; very, very slow.

Gregorian chant *Monophonic* melody with a freely flowing, unmeasured vocal line; liturgical chant of the Roman Catholic Church. Also plainchant or plainsong.

ground bass A repeating *melody,* usually in the bass, throughout a vocal or instrumental composition.

guiro A Latin American scraper made from a gourd that is notched or grooved.

guitar Plucked-string instrument originally made of wood with a hollow, resonating body and a fretted fingerboard; types include *acoustic* and *electric.*

guitarra moresca A strummed string instrument introduced to Spain by the Moors; an early version of the guitar.

half step Smallest *interval* used in the Western system; the *octave* divides into twelve such intervals. On the piano, the distance between any two adjacent keys, whether black or white. Also *semitone.*

Harlem Renaissance An early twentieth-century artistic and cultural movement centered in New York's Harlem and focused on a rebirth of African American arts.

harmonic variation The procedure in which the *chords* accompanying a *melody* are replaced by others. Often used in *theme and variations* form.

harmonics Individual, pure sounds that are part of any musical tone; in string instruments, crystalline pitches in the very high *register,* produced by lightly touching a vibrating string at a certain point.

harmony The simultaneous combination of notes and the ensuing relationships of *intervals* and *chords.*

harp Plucked-string instrument, triangular in shape with strings perpendicular to the soundboard.

harpsichord Early Baroque *keyboard instrument* in which the strings are plucked by quills instead of being struck with hammers like the *piano.*

heterophonic *Texture* in which two or more voices (or parts) elaborate the same melody simultaneously, often the result of *improvisation.*

hip hop Black urban art forms that emerged in New York City in the 1970s, encompassing *rap* music, break dancing, and graffiti art as well as the fashions adopted by the artists. The term comes from the *vocables,* or non-lexical syllables, used by rap artists.

homophonic *Texture* with a principal *melody* and accompanying *harmony,* as distinct from *polyphony.*

homorhythmic *Texture* in which all voices, or lines, move together in the same *rhythm.*

horn Medium-range valved *brass instrument* that can be played "stopped" with the hand as well as open. Also *French horn.*

hornpipe Country dance of the British Isles, often in a lively *triple meter;* optional dance movement of solo and orchestral Baroque *suites.* A type of *duple-meter* hornpipe is still popular in Irish traditional dance music.

humanism A new way of thinking in the sixteenth century that focused on human issues and the individual.

hymn Song in praise of God, often sung by a whole congregation.

idée fixe "Fixed idea"; term coined by Berlioz for a programmatic musical idea that links different *movements* of a work.

idiophone Instrument that produces sound from the substance of the instrument itself by being struck, blown, shaken, scraped, or rubbed. Examples include bells, rattles, *xylophones*, and *cymbals*.

imitation Melodic idea presented in one *voice* or part and then restated in another, each part continuing as others enter.

Impressionism A French movement developed by visual artists who favored vague, blurring images intended to capture an "impression" of the subject. Impressionism in music is characterized by exotic *scales*, unresolved *dissonances*, parallel *chords*, rich orchestral tone colors, and free *rhythm*.

improvisation The creation of music while it is being performed, as in Baroque *embellishment, cadenzas* of *concertos, jazz,* and some non-Western musics.

incidental music Music written to accompany dramatic works.

inflection Small alteration of the pitch by a *microtonal interval.* See also *blue note.*

instrument Mechanism that generates musical vibrations and transmits them into the air.

interactive performance Computer-supported, collaborative music-making that includes live performers interacting with computers, interconnected performance networks, and online improvisation.

interlude Music played between sections of a musical or dramatic work.

intermedio In the Italian Renaissance, a work performed between the acts of a play.

intermezzo Short, lyric piece or *movement,* often for piano. Also a comic *interlude* performed between acts of an eighteenth-century *opera seria.*

interval The distance and relationship between two *pitches.*

inversion Mirror or upside-down image of a *melody* or pattern, found in *fugues* and *twelve-tone* compositions.

irregular meter An atypical metric scheme, often based on an odd number of *beats* per *measure* (e.g., 5/4, 7/8, 11/4).

Italian overture Baroque *overture* consisting of three sections: fast-slow-fast.

Janissary music Music of the military corps of the Turkish sultan, characterized by *percussion instruments* like the *triangle, cymbals, bell tree,* and *bass drum* as well as *trumpets* and *double-reed* instruments.

jarabe Traditional Mexican dance form with multiple sections in contrasting *meters* and *tempos,* often performed by *mariachi* ensembles.

jazz A musical style created mainly by African Americans in the early twentieth century that blended elements drawn from African musics with the popular and art traditions of the West.

jazz band Instrumental ensemble made up of reed (*saxophones* and *clarinets*), brass (*trumpets* and *trombones*), and rhythm sections (*percussion, piano, double bass,* and sometimes *guitar*).

jig A vigorous dance developed in the British Isles, usually in *compound meter;* became fashionable on the Continent as the *gigue;* still popular as an Irish traditional dance genre.

Kapellmeister A German term referring to the leader of a musical chapel, either at court or at a church.

kettledrums See *timpani.*

key Defines the relationship of *pitches* with a common center, or *tonic.* Also a lever on a *keyboard* or *woodwind* instrument.

key signature Sharps or flats placed at the beginning of a piece to show the *key* of a work (there are no sharps or flats if the key is C major or A minor).

keyboard instrument Instrument sounded by means of a keyboard (a series of keys played with the fingers). See also individual types.

koto Japanese plucked-string instrument with a long rectangular body, thirteen strings, and movable bridges or frets.

Kyrie The first musical section of the *Ordinary* of the *Mass.* Its construction is threefold, involving three repetitions of "Kyrie eleison" (Lord, have mercy), three of "Christe eleison" (Christ, have mercy), and again three of "Kyrie eleison."

largo Broad; very slow.

Latin jazz A *jazz* style influenced by Latin American music, which includes various dance rhythms and traditional *percussion instruments.*

Latin rock Subgenre of *rock* featuring Latin and African *percussion instruments* (*maracas, conga drums, timbales*).

legato Smooth and connected; opposite of *staccato.*

leitmotif "Leading motive," or basic recurring *theme,* representing a person, object, or idea; widely used in Wagner's *music dramas.*

librettist The author of a *libretto.*

libretto Text or script of an *opera, oratorio, cantata,* or *musical* (also called the "book" in a musical).

Lied German for "song"; most commonly associated with the solo *art song* of the nineteenth century, usually accompanied by *piano.*

Lieder Plural of *Lied.*

lining-out A *call-and-response* practice prevalent in early America and England; a singer leader alternates with the congregation, whose members may sing slight variants of the melody when they respond.

liturgy The set order of religious services and the structure of each service, within a particular denomination (e.g., Roman Catholic).

lute Plucked-string instrument of Middle Eastern origin, popular in western Europe from the late Middle Ages to the eighteenth century.

lyre Ancient plucked-string instrument of the *harp* family, used to accompany singing and poetry.

lyric opera Hybrid form combining elements of *grand opera* and *comic opera* and featuring appealing melodies and romantic drama.

madrigal Renaissance secular work originating in Italy for voices, with or without instruments, set to a short, lyric love poem; also popular in England.

madrigal choir Small vocal ensemble that specializes in *a cappella* secular works.

madrigalism A striking effect designed to depict the meaning of the text in vocal music; found in many *madrigals* and other genres of the sixteenth through eighteenth centuries. See also *word-painting.*

maestoso Majestic.

major-minor tonality A harmonic system based on the use of *major* and *minor scales,* widely practiced from the seventeenth to the late nineteenth century. See also *tonality.*

major scale Scale consisting of seven different pitches that comprise a specific pattern of *whole* and *half steps* (W-W-H-W-W-W-H). Differs from the *minor scale* primarily in that its third degree is raised half a step.

mambo Dance of Afro-Cuban origin with a highly syncopated *quadruple-meter* rhythmic pattern.

maracas Latin American rattles (*idiophones*) made from gourds or other materials.

march A style incorporating characteristics of military music, including strongly accented *duple meter* in short, repetitive sections (*strains*).

marching band Instrumental ensemble for entertainment at sports events and parades, consisting of wind and *percussion instruments,* drum majors/majorettes, flag bearers, and baton twirlers.

mariachi Traditional Mexican ensemble popular throughout the country, consisting of *trumpets, violins, guitar,* and bass guitar.

marimba *Percussion instrument,* a mellower version of the *xylophone;* of African origin.

masque English genre of aristocratic entertainment that combined vocal and instrumental music with poetry and dance, developed during the sixteenth and seventeenth centuries.

Mass Central service of the Roman Catholic Church.

mazurka Type of Polish folk dance in *triple meter.*

measure, or **bar** Metric grouping of *beats,* notated on the musical staff and separated by vertical *bar lines.*

medium Performing forces employed in a certain musical work.

medley A composition built on a series of well-known tunes that may be loosely connected or from different sources.

Meistersinger A German "master singer," belonging to a professional guild. Meistersingers flourished from the fourteenth through the sixteenth centuries.

melismatic Melodic style characterized by many notes sung to a single text syllable.

melodic variation The procedure in which a melody is altered while certain features are maintained; often used in *theme and variations* form.

melodrama A dramatic genre featuring spoken dialogue or recitation, in alternation with orchestral music.

melody Succession of single *pitches* perceived by the ear as a unity.

membranophone Any instrument that produces sound from tightly stretched membranes that can be struck.

metallophone *Percussion instrument* consisting of tuned metal bars, usually struck with a mallet.

meter Organization of *rhythm* in time; the grouping of *beats* into larger, regular patterns, notated as *measures.*

metronome Device used to indicate the *tempo* by sounding regular *beats* at adjustable speeds.

mezzo forte (mf) Moderately loud.

mezzo piano (mp) Moderately soft.

mezzo-soprano Female voice of middle range.

microtone Musical interval smaller than a *semitone* (*half step*), prevalent in some non-Western musics and some modern music.

MIDI Acronym for Musical Instrument Digital Interface; technology standard that allows networking of computers with electronic musical instruments.

minimalism Contemporary musical style featuring the repetition of short melodic, rhythmic, and harmonic patterns with little variation. See also *post-minimalism, spiritual minimalism,* and *process music.*

Minnesingers Late medieval German poet-musicians.

minor scale Scale consisting of seven different pitches that comprise a specific pattern of *whole* and *half steps* (W-H-W-W-H-W-W). Differs from the *major scale* primarily in that its third degree is lowered half a step.

minstrel show A late nineteenth-century American entertainment featuring white performers in blackface acting out stereotypes of African American slaves.

minuet An elegant *triple-meter* dance type popular in the seventeenth and eighteenth centuries; usually in *binary form.* See also *minuet and trio.*

minuet and trio An **A-B-A** form (A = minuet; B = trio) in a moderate *triple meter;* often the third movement of the Classical *multimovement cycle.*

modal Characterizes music based on *modes* other than major and minor, especially the early church modes.

mode *Scale* or sequence of notes used as the basis for a composition; major and minor are modes.

moderato Moderate.

modernism Early twentieth-century movement in the arts and literature that explored innovative, nontraditional forms of expression. See also *postmodernism.*

modified strophic form Song structure that combines elements of *strophic* and *through-composed* forms; a

variation of strophic form in which a section might have a new *key*, new *rhythm*, or varied melody.

modulation The process of changing from one *key* to another.

molto Very.

monody Vocal style established in the Baroque era, with solo singer(s) and instrumental accompaniment.

monophonic Single-line *texture*, or melody without accompaniment.

motet *Polyphonic* sacred or devotional genre of choral music.

motive Short melodic or rhythmic idea; the smallest fragment of a *theme* that forms a melodic-harmonic-rhythmic unit.

movement Complete, self-contained part within a larger musical work.

muezzin A male crier who sounds the Muslim call to prayer from the top of a mosque.

multimovement cycle A three- or four-movement structure used in Classical-era instrumental music—especially the *symphony, sonata, concerto,* and in *chamber music*; each movement is in a prescribed *tempo* and *form*; sometimes called sonata cycle.

music drama Wagner's term for his operas.

musical Genre of twentieth-century musical theater, especially popular in the United States and Great Britain; features spoken dialogue and a dramatic plot interspersed with songs, ensemble numbers, and dancing.

musical bow An instrument with a string held taut by a flexible curved stick, played by plucking or striking the string.

musique concrète Music made up of natural sounds and sound effects that are recorded and then manipulated electronically.

mute Mechanical device used to muffle the sound of an instrument.

nakers Medieval percussion instruments of Middle Eastern origin, resembling small kettledrums and played with the hands.

neo-Classicism A twentieth-century style that combined elements of Classical and Baroque music with modernist trends.

neo-Romanticism A contemporary style of music that employs the rich harmonic language and other elements of Romantic and post-Romantic composers.

neumatic Melodic style with three to five notes set to each syllable.

New Orleans jazz Early *jazz* style characterized by multiple improvisations in an ensemble of *cornet* (or *trumpet*), *clarinet* (or *saxophone*), *trombone, piano, double bass* (or *tuba*), *banjo* (or *guitar*), and *drums*; repertory included *blues, ragtime,* and popular songs.

ninth chord Five-note *chord* spanning a ninth between its lowest and highest *pitches*.

nocturne "Night piece"; introspective work common in the nineteenth century, often for piano.

Noh **drama** A major form of Japanese theater since the late fourteenth century; based on philosophical concepts from Zen Buddhism.

non troppo Not too much.

nonlexical syllable Syllable that does not carry specific meaning; a nonsense syllable, often sung in madrigals.

nonmetric Music lacking a strong sense of *beat* or *meter,* common in certain non-Western cultures.

notation The practice of writing down music, as opposed to *oral tradition.*

note A musical symbol denoting *pitch* and *duration.*

oboe Soprano-range, *double-reed* woodwind instrument.

octave *Interval* between two notes eight *diatonic* pitches apart; the lower note vibrates half as fast as the upper and sounds an octave lower.

octet *Chamber music* for eight instruments or voices.

offbeat A weak *beat* or weak portion of a beat.

opera Music drama that is generally sung throughout, combining the resources of vocal and instrumental music with poetry and drama, acting and dancing, scenery and costumes. See also *aria, recitative.*

opera buffa Italian comic opera, sung throughout.

opéra comique French comic opera, with some spoken dialogue.

opera seria Tragic Italian opera.

operetta Small-scale operatic work, generally light in tone, with spoken dialogue, song, and dance.

Opus number (Op.) A number, often part of the title of a piece, designating the work in chronological relationship to other works by the same composer.

oral tradition Music that is transmitted by example or imitation and performed from memory.

oratorio Large-scale dramatic genre originating in the Baroque, based on a text of religious or serious character, performed by solo voices, *chorus,* and *orchestra*; similar to *opera* but without scenery, costumes, or action.

oratory A prayer chapel within a church; the origin of the genre term *oratorio.*

orchestra Performing group of diverse instruments in various cultures; in Western art music, an ensemble of multiple strings with various *woodwind, brass,* and *percussion instruments.*

orchestration The technique of setting music for instruments in various combinations.

Ordinary Sections of the Roman Catholic *Mass* that remain the same from day to day throughout the church year, as distinct from the *Proper,* which changes daily according to the liturgical occasion.

organ Wind instrument in which air is fed to the pipes by mechanical means; the pipes are controlled by two or more keyboards and a set of pedals.

organum Earliest kind of *polyphonic* music, which developed from the custom of adding voices above a *plainchant*; they first ran parallel to the chant at the interval of a fifth or fourth and later moved more freely.

ornamentation See *embellishment*.

ostinato A short melodic, rhythmic, or harmonic pattern that is repeated throughout a work or a section.

overture An introductory *movement*, as in an *opera* or *oratorio*, often presenting melodies from *arias* to come. Also an orchestral work for concert performance.

parlor song A song, usually accompanied by piano, intended for home entertainment; the term is particular to nineteenth-century America.

part book A bound music book—either print or manuscript—with music for a single vocalist or instrumentalist.

part song Secular vocal composition, unaccompanied, in three, four, or more parts.

partita See *suite*.

pas de deux A dance for two that is an established feature of classical ballet.

passepied French Baroque court dance type; a faster version of the *minuet*.

patron (patroness) A person who supports music or musicians; a benefactor of the arts. See also *patronage*.

patronage Sponsorship of an artist or a musician, historically by a member of the wealthy or ruling classes.

pavane Stately Renaissance court dance in *duple meter*.

pedal point Sustained *pitch* over which the *harmonies* change.

pentatonic scale Five-note pattern used in some African, Far Eastern, Central European, and Native American musics; can also be found in Western music as an example of exoticism. See also *gapped scale*.

percussion instrument Instrument made of metal, wood, stretched skin, or other material that is made to sound by striking, shaking, scraping, or plucking.

period-instrument ensemble Group that performs on historical instruments or modern replicas built after historical models.

phrase A musical unit; often a component of a *melody*.

pianissimo (*pp*) Very soft.

piano (*p*) Soft.

piano Keyboard instrument whose strings are struck with hammers controlled by a keyboard mechanism; pedals control dampers in the strings that stop the sound when the finger releases the key.

piano quartet Standard chamber ensemble of *piano* with *violin*, *viola*, and *cello*.

piano quintet Standard chamber ensemble of *piano* with *string quartet* (two *violins*, *viola*, and *cello*).

piano trio Standard chamber ensemble of *piano* with *violin* and *cello*.

pianoforte Original name for the *piano*.

piccolo Smallest *woodwind* instrument, similar to the *flute* but sounding an *octave* higher.

pipe A medieval three-holed, end-blown flute.

pitch Highness or lowness of a note, depending on the *frequency*.

pizzicato Performance direction to pluck a string of a bowed instrument with the finger.

plainchant, or **plainsong** See *Gregorian chant*.

plectrum An implement made of wood, ivory, or another material used to pluck a *chordophone*.

pluck To sound the strings of an instrument using fingers or a *plectrum* or pick.

poco A little.

polonaise Stately Polish processional dance in *triple meter*.

polychord A single *chord* comprised of several chords, common in twentieth-century music.

polyharmony Two or more streams of *harmony* played against each other, common in twentieth-century music.

polymeter The simultaneous use of several *meters*, common in twentieth-century music and certain African musics.

polyphonic Two or more melodic lines combined into a multivoiced *texture*, as distinct from *monophonic*.

polyrhythm The simultaneous use of several rhythmic patterns or *meters*, common in twentieth-century music and certain African musics.

polytonality The simultaneous use of two or more *keys*, common in twentieth-century music.

post-minimalism Contemporary style combining lush harmonies of neo-Romanticism with high-energy rhythms of minimalism; John Adams is a major exponent.

postmodernism A movement in the arts and literature that reacts against early modernist principles through the use of classical and traditional elements. See *modernism*.

post-Romanticism A trend at the turn of the twentieth century in which nineteenth-century musical characteristics like *chromatic* harmony and expansive melodies are carried to the extreme.

prelude Instrumental work preceding a larger work.

prelude and fugue Paired *movements*, the *prelude* in a free form, the *fugue* in a strict, imitative form.

prepared piano Piano whose sound is altered by the insertion of various materials (metal, rubber, leather, and paper) between the strings; invented by John Cage.

presto Very fast.

process music A compositional style in which a composer selects a simple musical idea and repeats it over and over, as it's gradually changed or elaborated upon. See also *minimalism*.

program music Instrumental music endowed with literary or pictorial associations, especially popular in the nineteenth century.

Proper Sections of the Roman Catholic *Mass* that vary from day to day throughout the church year according

to the liturgical occasion, as distinct from the *Ordinary,* in which they remain the same.

Psalms Book from the Old Testament of the Bible; the 150 Psalm texts, used in Jewish and Christian worship, are often set to music.

psaltery Medieval plucked-string instrument consisting of a sound box over which strings were stretched.

pure music See *absolute music.*

quadruple meter Basic metrical pattern of four beats to a measure. Also *common time.*

quarter tone An *interval* halfway between two notes a *half step* apart.

quintet *Chamber music* for five instruments or voices. See also *brass quintet, piano quintet, string quintet,* and *woodwind quintet.*

quotation music Music that cites another work or works, presenting them in a new style or guise.

ragtime Late nineteenth-century piano style created by African Americans, characterized by highly syncopated melodies; also played in ensemble arrangements. Contributed to early *jazz* styles.

range Distance between the lowest and highest *pitches* of a melody, an instrument, or a voice.

rebec Medieval bowed-string instrument, often with a pear-shaped body.

recapitulation Third section of *sonata-allegro form,* in which the thematic material of the *exposition* is restated, generally in the *tonic.* Also *restatement.*

recitative Solo vocal declamation that follows the inflections of the text, often resulting in a disjunct vocal style; found in *opera, cantata,* and *oratorio.* Can be *secco* or *accompagnato.*

reed Flexible strip of cane or metal set into a mouthpiece or the body of an instrument; set in vibration by a stream of air. See also *single reed* and *double reed.*

Reformation Religious movement of the sixteenth century, led by Martin Luther and John Calvin among others, that resulted in the establishment of Protestant churches.

refrain Text or music that is repeated within a larger form.

register Specific area in the range of an instrument or voice.

relative key The major and minor key that share the same *key signature;* for example, D minor is the relative minor of F major, both having one flat.

repeat sign Musical symbol (||: :||) that indicates the repetition of a passage.

Requiem Mass Roman Catholic *Mass* for the Dead.

resolution Conclusion of a musical idea, as in the progression from an *active chord* to a *rest chord.*

response Short choral answer to a solo *verse;* an element of liturgical dialogue.

responsorial singing Singing, especially in *Gregorian chant,* in which a soloist or a group of soloists alternates with the choir. See also *call and response.*

rest chord A chord that achieves a sense of *resolution* or completion, normally the *tonic.*

restatement See *recapitulation.*

retrograde Backward statement of a *melody.*

retrograde inversion Mirror image of the backward statement of a *melody.*

rhyme scheme The arrangement of rhyming words or corresponding sounds at the end of poetic lines.

rhythm The controlled movement of music in time.

rhythmic variation The procedure in which note lengths, *meter,* or *tempo* is altered. Often used in *theme and variations* form.

riff In *jazz,* a short melodic *ostinato* over changing harmonies.

ring shout Religious dance of African American slaves, performed with hand clapping and a shuffle step to *spirituals.*

ritardando Holding back, getting slower.

ritornello Short, recurring instrumental passage found in both the *aria* and the Baroque *concerto.*

rock A style of popular music with roots in rock and roll but differing in lyric content, recording technique, song length and form, and range of sounds. The term was first used in the 1960s to distinguish groups like the Beatles and the Rolling Stones from earlier artists.

rocket theme Quickly ascending rhythmic melody used in Classical-era instrumental music; the technique is credited to composers in Mannheim, Germany.

rondeau Medieval and Renaissance fixed poetic form and French chanson type with a courtly love text.

rondo Musical form in which the first section recurs several times, usually in the *tonic.* In the Classical *multimovement cycle,* it often appears as the last *movement* in various forms, such as **A-B-A-B-A, A-B-A-C-A,** and **A-B-A-C-A-B-A.**

round Perpetual *canon* at the *unison* in which each voice enters in succession with the same melody (for example, *Row, Row, Row Your Boat*).

rounded binary Composition form with two sections, in which the second ends with a return to material from the first; each section is usually repeated.

rubato "Borrowed time," common in Romantic music, in which the performer hesitates here or hurries forward there, imparting flexibility to the written note values.

sacred music Religious or spiritual music, for church or devotional use. See also individual types.

salon A gathering of musicians, artists, and intellectuals who shared similar interests and tastes, hosted by a wealthy aristocrat.

Sanctus The fourth musical section of the *Ordinary* of the *Mass.*

sarabande Stately Spanish Baroque dance type in *triple meter,* a standard *movement* of the Baroque *suite.*

SATB Abbreviation for the standard voices in a *chorus* or *choir*: soprano, alto, tenor, bass; may also refer to instrumental ranges.

saxophone Family of *single-reed* woodwind instruments commonly used in *wind* and *jazz bands*.

scale Series of pitches in ascending or descending order, comprising the notes of a *key*.

scat-singing A *jazz* style that sets syllables without meaning (*vocables*) to an improvised vocal line.

scherzo Composition (scherzo and trio) in **A-B-A** form, usually in *triple meter*; replaced the *minuet and trio* in the nineteenth century.

score The written form of a musical composition.

secco *Recitative* singing style that features a sparse accompaniment and moves with great freedom.

Second Viennese School Early twentieth-century group of composers, including Arnold Schoenberg and his pupils Anton Webern and Alban Berg, who wrote in the style known as *serialism* (*twelve-tone music*).

secular music Nonreligious music; when there is text, it is usually in the *vernacular*.

semitone Also known as a *half step*, the smallest *interval* commonly used in the Western musical system.

septet *Chamber music* for seven instruments or voices.

sequence Restatement of an idea or *motive* at a different pitch level.

serenade Classical instrumental genre that combines elements of *chamber music* and *symphony*, often performed in the evening or at social functions. Related to *divertimento*.

serialism Method of composition in which various musical elements (*pitch, rhythm, dynamics, timbre*) may be ordered in a fixed series; also called *twelve-tone music*.

seventh chord Four-note combination of notes consisting of a *triad* with another third added on top; spans a seventh between its lowest and highest notes.

sextet *Chamber music* for six instruments or voices.

sextuple meter *Compound* metrical pattern of six *beats* to a *measure*.

sforzando (sf) Sudden stress or accent on a single note or chord.

sharp sign Musical symbol (♯) that indicates raising a pitch by a *half step*.

shifting meter See *changing meter*.

side drum See *snare drum*.

simple meter *Meter* in which the *beat* is divided into two, as opposed to *compound meter*.

sinfonia Short instrumental work, found in Baroque *opera*, to facilitate scene changes.

single reed A *reed* consisting of one piece of cane vibrating against another part of the instrument, often a mouthpiece.

Singspiel Comic German drama with spoken dialogue; the immediate predecessor of Romantic German *opera*.

sitar Long-necked *chordophone* of northern India, with movable frets and a rounded gourd body; used as a solo instrument and with *tabla*.

slide In bowed string instruments, moving from one pitch to another by sliding the finger on the string while bowing. Also the mechanism by which a trombone changes pitch.

snare drum Small cylindrical drum with two heads.

son A genre of traditional Mexican dances that combine compound duple with triple meters.

sonata Instrumental genre in several *movements* for soloist or small ensemble.

sonata-allegro form The opening *movement* of the *multi-movement cycle*, consisting of themes that are stated in the first section (*exposition*), developed in the second section (*development*), and restated in the third section (*recapitulation*). Also called sonata form.

sonata rondo A structure that combines elements of *sonata-allegro form* with the *refrain* idea of a *rondo*.

song cycle Group of songs that are unified musically or through their texts.

song plugger A person who demonstrated and sold sheet music on New York's Tin Pan Alley.

song without words An early Romantic-era genre of piano music featuring song-like textures and forms.

soprano Highest-ranged voice, normally possessed by women and boys.

source music A film technique in which music comes from a logical source within the film and functions as part of the story.

sousaphone *Brass instrument* adapted from the *tuba* with a forward bell that is coiled to rest over the player's shoulder for ease of carrying while marching.

spiritual Folklike devotional genre of the United States, sung by African Americans and whites.

spiritual minimalism Contemporary musical style related to *minimalism*, characterized by a weak pulse and long chains of lush progressions—either *tonal* or *modal*.

Sprechstimme A vocal style in which the melody is spoken at approximate pitches rather than sung on exact pitches; developed by Arnold Schoenberg.

staccato Short, detached notes, marked with a dot above them.

staff The five parallel lines on which *notes* are written.

stanza A unit or verse of poetry; also a *strophe*.

statement See *exposition*.

steamroller effect A drawn-out *crescendo* that builds to a climax; an orchestral device used in early symphonic writing, often credited to German composers.

steel drum A *percussion instrument* made from an oil drum, developed in Trinidad during the 1930s and 40s.

stopping On a *string instrument*, altering the string length by pressing it on the fingerboard. On a *horn*, playing with the bell closed by the hand or a *mute*.

strain One of a series of contrasting sections found in *ragtime* and *marches*; in *duple meter* with eight- or sixteen-measure themes.

stretto In a *fugue*, when entries of the *subject* occur at faster intervals of time so that they overlap, forming dense, imitative *counterpoint*. Stretto usually occurs at the climactic moment near the end.

stride A jazz piano style featuring swing rhythms.

string instruments Bowed and plucked instruments whose sound is produced by the vibration of one or more strings. Also *chordophone*.

string quartet *Chamber music* ensemble consisting of two *violins*, *viola*, and *cello*. Also a multimovement composition for this ensemble.

string quintet Standard chamber ensemble made up of either two *violins*, two *violas*, and *cello* or two violins, viola, and two cellos.

string trio Standard chamber ensemble of two *violins* and *cello* or violin, *viola*, and cello.

strophe A unit or verse of poetry; also a *stanza*.

strophic form Song structure in which the same music is repeated with every *stanza* (*strophe*) of the poem.

Sturm und Drang "Storm and stress"; late eighteenth-century movement in Germany toward more emotional expression in the arts.

style Characteristic manner of the presentation of musical elements (*melody, rhythm, harmony, dynamics, form, texture, tempo*).

subdominant Fourth scale step, *fa*.

subdominant chord Chord built on the fourth scale step, the IV chord.

subject The main idea or *theme* of a work, as in a *fugue*.

suite Multimovement work made up of a series of contrasting dance movements, generally all in the same *key*. Also *partita*.

surdo A large bass drum used in Latin American traditional music.

swing *Jazz* term coined to describe Louis Armstrong's style; more commonly refers to *big band* jazz.

Swing Era The mid-1930s to the mid-1940s, when *swing* was the most popular music in the United States. Important musicians of the era were Louis Armstrong, Duke Ellington, and Benny Goodman.

syllabic Melodic style of one note set to each text syllable.

Symbolism Literary movement that paralleled *Impressionism*, in which poetic images were invoked through suggestion or symbol rather than literal description.

symphonic poem One-movement orchestral form that develops a poetic idea, suggests a scene, or creates a mood, usually associated with the Romantic era. Also *tone poem*.

symphony Large work for *orchestra*, generally in four *movements*.

symphony orchestra See *orchestra*.

syncopation Deliberate upsetting of the *meter* or pulse through a temporary shifting of the accent to a weak *beat* or an *offbeat*.

syncretic style A blended style achieved by a merger of discrete musical practices and traditions.

synthesizer Electronic instrument that produces a wide variety of sounds by combining sound generators and sound modifiers in one package with a unified control system.

tabla Pair of single-headed, tuned drums used in north Indian classical music.

tamborim A small Brazilian frame drum originally of African origin.

tambourine *Percussion instrument* consisting of a small round drum with metal plates inserted in its rim; played by striking or shaking.

tam-tam A flat gong of indefinite pitch. See also *gong*.

tape music Type of *electronic music* in which sounds are recorded on tape and then manipulated and mixed in various ways. See also *musique concrète*.

tempo The rate of speed or pace of music.

tenor drum *Percussion instrument*, larger than the *snare drum*, with a wooden shell.

tenor Male voice of high range. Also a part, often structural, in *polyphony*.

ternary form Three-part (A-B-A) form based on a statement (**A**), contrast (**B**), and repetition (**A**). Also three-part form.

tertian harmony *Harmony* based on the *interval* of the third, particularly predominant from the Baroque through the nineteenth century.

texture The interweaving of melodic (horizontal) and harmonic (vertical) elements in the musical fabric.

thematic development Musical expansion of a *theme* by varying its melodic outline, *harmony*, or *rhythm*. See also *thematic transformation*.

thematic transformation The changing of a *theme's* character through varied tempos, instrumentation, harmony, rhythm, or instrumental color.

theme Melodic idea used as a basic building block in the construction of a piece. Also *subject*.

theme and variations Compositional procedure in which a theme is stated and then altered in successive statements; occurs as an independent piece or as a *movement* of a *multimovement cycle*.

theme group Several *themes* in the same *key* that function as a unit within a section of a form, particularly in *sonata-allegro form*.

third *Interval* between two notes that are three *diatonic* scale steps apart.

thirty-two-bar song form Popular song structure that divides into four sections (A-A-B-A) of eight measures each.

thorough bass See *figured bass*.

three-part form See *ternary form.*

through-composed Song structure that is composed from beginning to end, without repetitions of large sections.

timbales Shallow, single-headed drums of Cuban origin, played in pairs; used in much Latin American popular music.

timbre The quality of a sound that distinguishes one voice or instrument from another. Also tone color.

timpani *Percussion instrument* consisting of a hemispheric copper shell with a head of plastic or calfskin, held in place by a metal ring and played with soft or hard padded sticks. A pedal mechanism changes the tension of the head, and with it the *pitch.* Also kettledrums.

Tin Pan Alley Nickname for the popular music industry centered in New York City from the nineteenth century through the 1950s. Also the style of popular song in the United States during that period.

tintinnabulation A bell-like style developed by Estonian composer Arvo Pärt, achieved by weaving *conjunct* lines that hover around a central pitch; from the Latin word for bell.

toccata Virtuoso composition, generally for *organ* or *harpsichord,* in a free and rhapsodic style; in the Baroque era, it often served as the introduction to a *fugue.*

tom-tom Cylindrical drum without snares.

tonal Based on principles of major-minor *tonality,* as distinct from *modal.*

tonality Principle of organization around a *tonic,* or home, pitch, based on a *major* or *minor scale.*

tone cluster Highly dissonant combination of *pitches* sounded simultaneously.

tone color See *timbre.*

tone poem See *symphonic poem.*

tone row An arrangement of the twelve *chromatic* pitches that serves as the basis of a *twelve-tone* piece.

tonic The first note of the *scale,* or key; *do.*

tonic chord *Triad* built on the first scale note, the I chord.

traditional music Music learned by *oral transmission* and easily sung or played by most people; may exist in variant forms. Also folk music.

transition See *bridge.*

transposition The shifting of a piece of music to a different pitch level.

tremolo Rapid repetition of a note; can be achieved instrumentally or vocally.

triad Common *chord* type, consisting of three *pitches* built on alternate notes of the *scale* (e.g., steps 1-3-5, or *do-mi-sol*).

triangle *Percussion instrument* consisting of a slender rod of steel bent in the shape of a triangle, struck with a steel beater.

trill Ornament consisting of the rapid alternation between one note and the next.

trio A second, or contrasting, section of a *minuet and trio* or *scherzo and trio;* also a contrasting *strain* in a *march;* also an ensemble of three players.

triple meter Basic metrical pattern of three *beats* to a *measure.*

triplet Group of three equal-valued notes played in the time of two; indicated by a bracket and the number 3.

trombone Tenor-range *brass instrument* that changes pitch by means of valves.

troubadours Medieval poet-musicians in southern France.

trouser role A young male dramatic role performed by a woman in male clothing.

trouvères Medieval poet-musicians in northern France.

trumpet Highest-pitched *brass instrument* that changes pitch by means of valves.

tuba Bass-range *brass instrument* that changes pitch by means of valves.

tumkul A type of log drum used in traditional music of Mexico.

tutti "All"; the opposite of solo.

twelve-bar blues Musical structure based on a repeated harmonic-rhythmic pattern, twelve measures long: I–I–I–I / IV–IV–I–I / V–V–I–I.

twelve-tone music Compositional procedure of the twentieth century based on an ordering of all twelve chromatic pitches (in a *tone row*), without a central pitch, or *tonic,* according to prescribed rules.

two-part form See *binary form.*

underscoring A technique used in films in which the music comes from an unseen source.

unison "Interval" between two notes of the same pitch (for example, two voices on the same E); the simultaneous playing of the same note.

upbeat Last *beat* of a *measure,* a weak beat that anticipates the *downbeat.*

variation The compositional procedure of altering a preexisting musical idea. See also *theme and variations.*

vaudeville A light comedic variety show with music featuring popular song, dance, comedy, and acrobatics; flourished in the late nineteenth and early twentieth centuries.

venue Place where a performance happens; a concert space.

vernacular The common language spoken by the people as distinguished from the literary language, or language of the educated elite.

verse In poetry, a group of lines constituting a unit. In liturgical music for the Catholic Church, a phrase from the Scriptures that alternates with the *response.*

vibraphone A *percussion instrument* with metal bars and electrically driven rotating propellers under each bar that produces a *vibrato* sound, much used in *jazz.*

vibrato Small fluctuation of pitch used as an expressive device to intensify a sound.

Viennese School The main composers of the Classical era (Haydn, Mozart, and Beethoven), active in Vienna.

vihuela A type of Mexican *guitar* with a rounded back, common in *mariachi* ensembles.

viola Bowed-string instrument of middle range; the second-highest member of the *violin* family.

violin Soprano, or highest-ranged, member of the bowed-string instrument family.

violoncello See *cello.*

virelai Medieval and Renaissance fixed poetic form and French chanson type with a courtly love text.

virtuosic Demanding remarkable technical ability.

virtuoso Performer of extraordinary technical ability.

vivace Lively.

vocables Nonsense, or *nonlexical,* syllables, lacking literal meaning.

vocalise A textless vocal melody, as in an exercise or concert piece.

voice In a *fugue,* a melodic line. Keyboard fugues of the late Baroque period, such as those by J. S. Bach, commonly have four distinct voices even though they are played by a single musician.

volume Degree of loudness or softness of a sound; also amplitude. See also *dynamics.*

Wagner tuba A *tuba* developed specifically for Wagner's opera cycle *The Ring of the Nibelung;* the instrument was adopted by other late nineteenth-century composers.

wah-wah mute A trumpet mute that produces an onomatopoetic sound like a voice saying "wah-wah."

waltz Ballroom dance type in *triple meter;* in the Romantic era, a short, stylized piano piece.

whole step Interval consisting of two *half steps.*

whole-tone scale Scale pattern that's built entirely of *whole-step* intervals, common in music of the French Impressionists.

wind band Instrumental ensemble ranging from forty to eighty members or more, consisting of wind and *percussion instruments.* Also concert band.

woodwind Instrumental family made of wood or metal whose tone is produced by a column of air vibrating within a pipe that has holes along its length.

woodwind quintet Standard chamber ensemble consisting of *flute, oboe, clarinet, bassoon,* and *horn* (not a woodwind instrument).

word-painting Musical pictorialization of words as an expressive device; a prominent feature of the Renaissance madrigal.

work song Communal song that synchronized group tasks.

xylophone *Percussion instrument* with tuned blocks of wood suspended on a frame, laid out in the shape of a keyboard and struck with hard mallets.

CREDITS

Photos

Page 3: Scala / Art Resource, NY. © 2019 Artists Rights Society (ARS), New York / ADAGP, Paris; **p. 4**: Mike Forster / Alamy Stock Photo; **p. 5**: Joseph Sohm / Shutterstock; **p. 6**: AP Photo / Gina Gayle; **p. 7**: Fort Worth Star-Telegram / MCT via Getty Images; **p. 8**: Stig Alenäs / Alamy Stock Photo; **p. 12** (top): Clearview / Alamy Stock Photo; (bottom): Marie Stone / Getty Images; **p. 15**: Fernand Ivaldi / Getty Images; **p. 16**: FRANÇOIS LENOIR / Reuters; **p. 20**: Digital Image © The Museum of Modern Art / Licensed by SCALA / Art Resource, NY. © 2019 Stiftung Arp e.V., Berlin/Rolandswerth / Artists Rights Society (ARS), New York; **p. 24**: Newark Museum /Art Resource, NY; **p. 27**: FORRAY Didier / SAGAPHOTO.COM / Alamy Stock Photo. © 2019 The Andy Warhol Foundation for the Visual Arts, Inc. / Licensed by Artists Rights Society (ARS), New York; **p. 29**: Gregory Davies / Alamy Stock Photo; **p. 31**: Owen Franken / Getty Images; **p. 32**: Pete Leonard / Getty Images; **p. 34**: Bridgeman Images; **p. 37** (top left): David Corio / Getty Images; (top right): Photo of EJ Jones courtesy of Kim Hill; (bottom): Sean Drakes /LatinContent / Getty Images; (top): Bruno De Hogues / Getty Images; (bottom): DESHAKALYAN CHOWDHURY / AFP / Getty Images; **p. 40** (top left): epa european pressphoto agency b.v. /Alamy Stock Photo; (top right): Reuters; (bottom): Hill Street Studios / Getty Images; **p. 41** (right): Joey Foley / Getty Images; (left): Heritage Image Partnership Ltd / Alamy Stock Photo; **p. 42** (top): Dave Benett / Getty Images; (bottom, both): Photo © Chris Stock / Bridgeman Images; **p. 43** (top): Cultura Creative (RF) / Alamy Stock Photo; (bottom): OnTheRoad / Alamy Stock Photo; **p. 44** (top left): Jack Vartoogian / Getty Images; (top middle): Royalty-Free / Corbis; (top right): © chrisstockphoto / Alamy Stock Photo; (bottom): Jim Forney; **p. 45**: Dave Schlabowske / The LIFE Images Collection via Getty Images; **p. 46**: Xinhua / Alamy Stock Photo; **p. 47**: Washington Post / Getty Images; **p. 48**: Hiroyuki Ito / Getty Images; **p. 49**: Matthew Simmons / Getty Images; **p. 50**: age fotostock / Alamy Stock Photo; **p. 53**: AP Photo / Henny Ray Abrams; **p. 55** (top): Junko Kimura / Getty Images; (bottom left): Ian Dagnall / Alamy Stock Photo; (bottom right): Art Library / Alamy Stock Photo. © 2019 Estate of Pablo Picasso / Artists Rights Society (ARS), New York; **p. 56**: Erich Auerbach / Hulton Archive / Getty Images; **p. 57**: ©Elliott Franks / ArenaPal / The Image Works.

Page 61: Alfredo Dagli Orti / Art Resource, NY; **p. 62**: Scala / Art Resource, NY; **p. 63**: Photo 12 / Alamy Stock Photo; **p. 64** (top): INTERFOTO / Alamy Stock Photo; (bottom): Album / Alamy Stock Photo; **p. 65**: The Picture Art Collection / Alamy Stock Photo; **p. 67**: Tallandier / Bridgeman Images; **p. 68** (left): Album / Alamy Stock Photo; (right): Public Domain; **p. 69**: FLHC 1A / Alamy Stock Photo; **p. 72**: Album / Alamy Stock Photo; **p. 73**: The Print Collector / Alamy Stock Photo; **p. 74** (top): Photo © Odile Nöel / Bridgeman Images; (bottom): De Agostini Picture Library / Bridgeman Images; **p. 78** (top): Album / Alamy Stock Photo; (bottom): Photo 12 / Alamy Stock Photo; **p. 80**: Anthony Scibilia / Art Resource, NY; **p. 82** (top): Album / Alamy Stock Photo; (bottom): classicpaintings / Alamy Stock Photo; **p. 83**: INTERFOTO / Alamy Stock Photo; **p. 85**: Ian Dagnall / Alamy Stock Photo; **p. 86** (left): Bridgeman Images; (right): IanDagnall Computing / Alamy Stock Photo; **p. 87**: Lebrecht Music & Arts / Alamy Stock Photo; **p. 89**: Bibliothèque Nationale, Paris / Bridgeman Images; **p. 92** (top): PRISMA ARCHIVO / Alamy Stock Photo; (bottom): ART Collection / Alamy Stock Photo; **p. 94**: IanDagnall Computing / Alamy Stock Photo.

Page 95: Art Resource, NY; **p. 97**: Art Heritage / Alamy Stock Photo; **p. 98**: PRISMA ARCHIVO / Alamy Stock Photo; **p. 99**: (top): Classic Image / Alamy Stock Photo; (bottom): Adam Eastland Art + Architecture / Alamy Stock Photo; **p. 100**: Album / Alamy Stock Photo; **p. 101**: Peter Willi / Bridgeman Images; **p. 102** (top): Erich Lessing / Art Resource, NY; (bottom): HIP / Art Resource, NY; **p. 104**: © DeA Picture Library / Art Resource, NY; **p. 105**: Lebrecht Music & Arts / Alamy Stock Photo; **p. 106**: Art Collection 2 / Alamy Stock Photo; **p. 108**: De Agostini Picture Library / Bridgeman Images; **p. 110** (top): © Chronicle / Alamy Stock Photo; (bottom): De Agostini Picture Library / Bridgeman Images; **p. 114**: Cameraphoto Arte, Venice / Art Resource, NY; **p. 115**: Gerald Coke Handel Collection, Foundling Museum, London / Bridgeman Images; **p. 116**: Album / Alamy Stock Photo; **p. 117**: Lebrecht Music & Arts / Bridgeman Images; **p. 120**: Photo © Graham Salter / Bridgeman Images; **p. 121** (top): Lebrecht Music & Arts / Bridgeman Images; (bottom): HIP / Art Resource, NY; **p. 125** (top): Galleria Querini-Stampalia, Venice / Bridgeman Images; (bottom): Lebrecht Music & Arts / Alamy Stock Photo; **p. 126**: DEA / G. CIGOLINI / Getty Images; **p. 130**: imageBROKER / Alamy Stock Photo; **p. 132**: G. Dagli Orti / De Agostini Picture Library / Bridgeman Images. © The Josef and Anni Albers Foundation / Artists Rights Society (ARS), New York, 2019; **p. 135**: Art Heritage / Alamy Stock Photo.

Page 137: Heritage Image Partnership Ltd / Alamy Stock Photo; **p. 138**: Roland Nagy / Alamy Stock Photo; **p. 139**: Joseph Sohm / Visions of America / Getty Images; **p. 140** (top): Mondadori Portfolio / Art Resource, NY; (bottom): Scala / Art Resource, NY; **p. 142**: bpk Bildagentur / Historisches Museum der Stadt Wien / Art Resource, NY; **p. 144**: Lebrecht Music & Arts / Bridgeman Images; **p. 145**: Lebrecht Music & Arts / Bridgeman Images; **p. 146**: Historisches Museum der Stadt Wien, Vienna / Bridgeman Images; **p. 148**: bpk Bildagentur / Schoenbrunn Palace / Art Resource, NY; **p. 150**: Casa Goldoni, Venice / Bridgeman Images; **p. 152**: Erich

Music

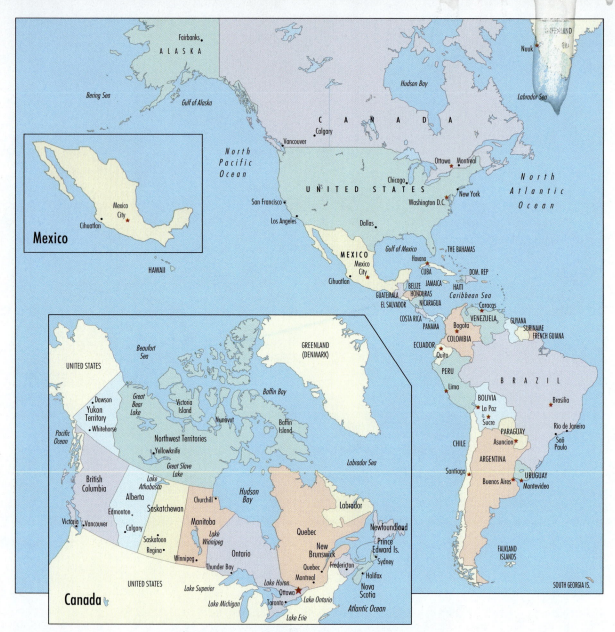
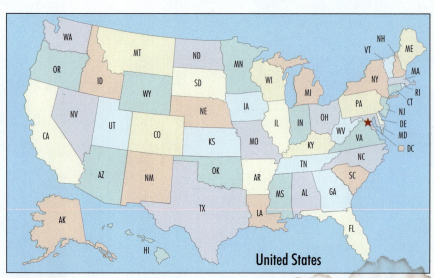

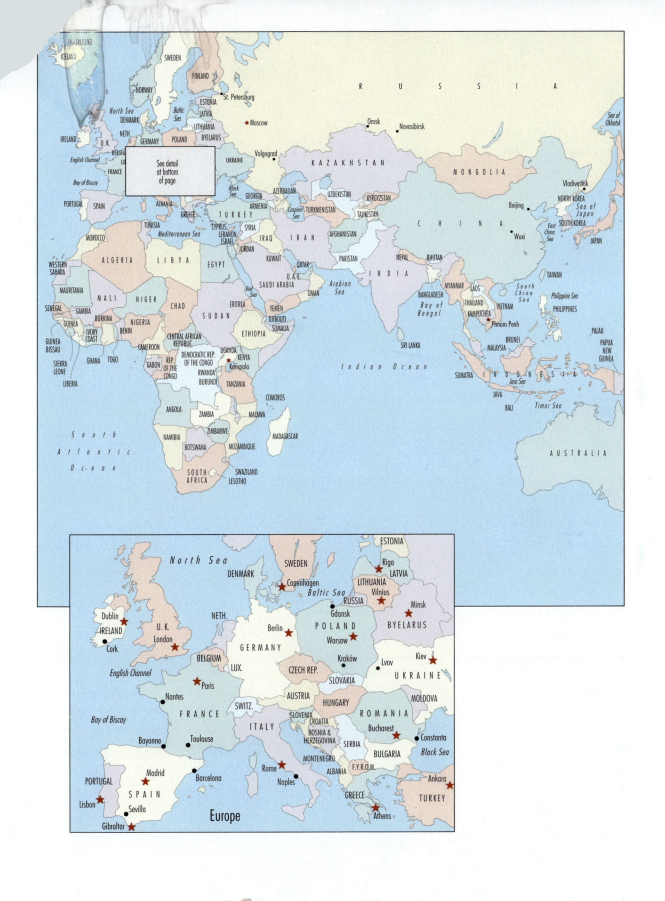

Europe